Key Issues in Organizational Communication

It is often said that the practice of management is in crisis. Managers are finding it harder than ever to develop strategies which withstand the shocks of the marketplace. Often, they reach for prescriptions for success that turn out to be no more than passing fads.

Key Issues in Organizational Communication cuts through these conflicting issues to show how organizational communication plays a vital role in helping organizations confront a world in which uncertainty rules. Arguing that many managers fail to adequately consider the communication consequences of the decision-making process and its impact on organizational effectiveness, it shows how insights gleaned from organizational communication offer a route through these dilemmas.

Based on cutting-edge research undertaken by the authors, this book takes key organizational issues and links them to the core theme of communication. The result is a comprehensive guide to organizational communication useful for managers, academics and students.

Featuring contributions from the UK, USA, Canada, New Zealand, Australia and Norway, this is a uniquely international text bringing multiple perspectives to bear on an increasingly important aspect of management practice.

Dennis Tourish is Professor of Communication at Aberdeen Business School in the Robert Gordon University.
Owen Hargie is Professor of Communication at the University of Ulster, and Adjunct Professor at the Norwegian University of Science and Technology.

Key Issues in Organizational Communication

Edited by
Dennis Tourish and Owen Hargie

Routledge
Taylor & Francis Group

LONDON AND NEW YORK

First published 2004
by Routledge
11 New Fetter Lane, London EC4P 4EE

Simultaneously published in the USA and Canada
by Routledge
29 West 35th Street, New York, NY 10001

Routledge is an imprint of the Taylor & Francis Group

Typeset in Goudy by Wearset Ltd, Boldon, Tyne and Wear
Printed and bound in Great Britain by TJ International Ltd, Padstow, Cornwall

British Library Cataloguing in Publication Data
A catalogue record for this book is available from the British Library

Library of Congress Cataloging in Publication Data
Key issues in organizational communication/edited by Dennis Tourish,
Owen Hargie.
     p. cm.
Includes bibliographical references and index.
     1. Communication in organizations. I. Tourish, Dennis. II. Hargie,
Owen.
HD30.3.K485 2004
658.4'5–dc21   2003008609

ISBN 0–415–26094–9 (hbk)
ISBN 0–415–26093–0 (pbk)

For Naheed and Patricia, in appreciation of all their love, encouragement and understanding.

Contents

Illustrations

Figures

Tables

Boxes

Reflective exercises

Contributors

Oluremi Ayoko is a lecturer in Business Communication at the University of Queensland, Australia (r.ayoko@business.uq.edu.au).

Devon Brown is a researcher at the University of Colorado at Boulder, USA (devonbrn@yahoo.com).

Phillip G. Clampitt is Professor of Information Sciences at the University of Wisconsin-Green Bay, USA, and a Senior Partner with Metacomm, a communications consulting firm (clampitt@itol.com).

Patrick Dawson holds the Salvessen Chair of Management at the University of Aberdeen, Scotland, where he is also Director of Graduate Programmes (p.dawson@abdn.ac.uk).

Stanley Deetz, is Professor of Communication at the University of Colorado at Boulder, USA (sdeetz@prodigy.net).

Greg Fisher is a lecturer in management at the Australian National University, Australia (greg.fisher@anu.edu.au).

Yuka Fujimoto is a lecturer in management at Deakin University, Australia (fujimoto@deakin.edu.au).

Owen Hargie is Professor of Communication at the University of Ulster, Newtownabbey, Northern Ireland (odw.hargie@ulst.ac.uk).

Charmine Härtel is Associate Professor of Management at Monash University, Australia (charmine.hartel@buseco.monash.edu.au).

Leigh Kibby is a researcher in management at Monash University, Australia, and also works as a management consultant (kinematic@bigpond.com).

Paula O'Kane is a researcher in the School of Communication, University of Ulster, Jordanstown, Northern Ireland (pm.okane@ulst.ac.uk).

Ashly Pinnington is a senior lecturer in Management at the University of Queensland, Australia (a.pinnington@business.uq.edu.au).

Michelle Pizer is a researcher in management at Monash University, Australia, and is a practising counselling psychologist (mpizer@netspace.net.auu).

Monica Rolfsen is Associate Professor of Organizational Development, Norwegian University of Science and Technology, Trondheim, Norway (monica.rolfsen@sintef.no).

Matthew W. Seeger is Associate Professor in the Department of Communication, Wayne State University, Detroit, USA (matthew.seeger@wayne.edu).

Olav Sletta is Professor Emeritus in the Department of Education, Norwegian University of Science and Technology, Trondheim, Norway (olav.sletta@svt.ntnu.no).

James R. Taylor is Emeritus Professor of Communication, University of Montreal, Quebec, Canada (jr.taylor@umontreal.ca).

Dennis Tourish is Professor of Communication at Aberdeen Business School in the Robert Gordon University, Aberdeen, Scotland (d.j.tourish@rgu.ac.uk).

Harald Valås is Professor in the Department of Education, Norwegian University of Science and Technology, Trondheim, Norway (harald.valaas@svt.ntnu.no).

M. Lee Williams is Professor of Communication at Southwest Texas State University, USA (mw02@swt.edu).

Theodore E. Zorn is Professor of Management Communication at Waikato University, New Zealand (tzorn@mngt.waikato.ac.nz).

Preface

Organizations around the world are in crisis. They are increasingly expected to deliver products and services better, faster and cheaper than their rivals – a far from easy task. These pressures arise in a world that is more interdependent than ever, and in which it is increasingly difficult to predict from where the next shock to the global economy will come. How do organizations, managers and employees cope with such a climate? How can they hope to sustain any sense of common purpose in the face of so many overwhelming challenges? This book has been inspired by these questions, and by the conviction that communication is central to any attempt to answer them.

Organizational communication is one of the fastest growing of academic disciplines. The importance of communications for corporate life is now widely recognized, and research publications in this field have mushroomed in the past few years. There is considerable evidence to show that companies with effective communication strategies are successful, while those with poor internal communications tend to flounder. However, a gap still remains between the triangular strands of the day-to-day practice of organizations, management theory, and communications research. For example, most managers intuitively know that a motivated workforce is important if they are to achieve their goals. Yet many organizations enthusiastically embrace practices that reduce the loyalty, commitment and motivation of their staff. From our experience of teaching, researching and consulting, we felt that more could be done to address these problems, and bring together the strands of management theory, communications research and management practice.

It was with this sense of purpose that we embarked upon the mission of putting together this book. Our main concern was to critically examine the true impact of key current themes in management for the practice of communications. As part of this we wished to examine these issues at both an operational and a theoretical level. The first step was to identify the key issues themselves. We did this by examining the current literature, by careful consideration of our own first hand experience of carrying out consultancy work in numerous organizations, and by listening to the concerns of the practitioners that we dealt with on our management courses. We then invited distinguished academics to consider and summarize how useful, valid or relevant the issues actually were in the light of the available evidence. In particular, we gave individual contributors the task of considering the interrelationships between each issue and perspectives derived from organizational communication.

The book itself has fifteen chapters. In the first chapter we set the scene for what follows by examining the wider context of management and the crises faced by organizations. In particular, we provide a backdrop that shows a mural of both organizational science and organizational communication. We also illustrate how the issues covered in this book are essential to effective management practice. Then, in Chapter 2 we discuss the consequences for organizations of the current corporate pandemic of downsizing, and demonstrate how the quick financial fix of firing staff has blinded managers to the true costs of this false economy. As any construction worker will testify, it is always easier to knock down than to build up, and we demonstrate why companies should remember this maxim in relation to the mad syndrome of organizational downsizing.

One of the topics that has attracted enormous interest in recent years has been the omnipresent phenomenon of uncertainty and the individual human instinct to reduce it. Linked to this theme is that of change – a rapidly changing world is a more uncertain place. There is much wisdom in the famous words of the American politician and inventor Benjamin Franklin, written in 1789: 'In this world nothing can be said to be certain, except death and taxes.' However, while we all know that the times are always a-changin' and that the only certainty is uncertainty, there is a definite need for more guidance about how the realities of uncertainty and change can best be handled by managers in the chameleon-like world of the average organization. In Chapters 3 and 4 these issues are addressed. In Chapter 3 Phillip Clampitt and M. Lee Williams present a wider analysis of the impact and effects of uncertainty for the organizational world, and offer suggestions about how these can be dealt with. Yet change, like the poor, will always be with us, and so, in Chapter 4, implications for the management of change are explored by Patrick Dawson.

One of the most significant changes in recent years has been the adoption of technologies to facilitate message delivery and flow. The organizational landscape has been clearly marked by the Internet explosion that has affected almost every aspect of corporate life. Information zooms along the web at speeds hitherto undreamed of. Technology has been linked closely to the notion of knowledge transfer and sharing. Accordingly, Chapters 5 and 6 examine the fields of technology and information. In Chapter 5 the positive and negative impacts of the virtual corporate world are assessed by our co-worker Paula O'Kane and ourselves. Knowledge, like water, is everywhere and yet can often be hard to harness. It is essential for corporations to divine where the rich sources of knowledge lie and tap this for maximum use. Thus, in Chapter 6 Theodore E. Zorn and James Taylor examine this key issue of knowledge management.

One perennial problem in companies is the herd instinct of managers. The childlike desire to be up to speed with the gizmos and games we see our peers playing with never leaves us. We want to be up-to-date and in fashion. Being left out or left behind is not an option. And so, once a new managerial band-wagon rolls by, everyone tries to jump on it, lest they be left behind, and become a source of merriment for various onlookers. In Chapter 7 Monica Rolfsen explains the psychological principles behind this phenomenon and explicates the importance for managers of understanding the dangers of blindly copying what we see others doing, rather than what is right for our own circum-stances. A large part of this response is, of course, emotional. No account of human nature can ignore the affective domain. Indeed, emotions are now recognized as central to the human condition and a core determinant of behavi-our. As such, in Chapter 8 Charmine Härtel, Leigh Kibby and Michelle Pizer present an in-depth analysis of the features, functions and outcomes of emotion-ality in organizations.

One area that is often linked to emotions is that of attitude. Similarly, the field of motivation draws on both of these concepts. But how do these all hang together and what shapes do they make as they blow in the organizational breezes? Harald Valås and Olav Sletta attempt to answer such questions in Chapter 9. They examine the contributions of both attitudes and motivation to organizational life, and investigate how and in what ways these two areas can be integrated into a single model. A particular context where attitudes are very important is in intercultural communication. As the world increasingly begins to resemble the oft-touted 'global village', differences in culture come into sharper focus. In this milieu, an awareness of the nuances of cultural codes is increasingly important. So, in Chapter 10 Oluremi Ayoko, Charmine Härtel, Greg Fisher and Yuka Fujimoto examine how companies can best equip their staff with communication competencies for multicultural environments.

A common problem for all firms is the decision about to what extent employees and other stakeholders should participate in the overall corporate thrust. These issues are focused upon in Chapters 11 and 12. The notion of the organization as a participatory democracy is debated by Stanley Deetz and Devon Brown in Chapter 11. They present a detailed analysis of this issue from the often-ignored perspective of communication theory, illustrating how *voice* is an important aspect of effective corporate functioning. In most walks of life we like to think that we can make our point and that we will be listened to. Unfor-tunately, many organizations still operate a top-down voice system, where the communication channel is seen as equivalent to a broadcast station with no equivalent of even a phone-in for feedback from those at the receiving end. The dangers of such an approach are documented by us in Chapter 12, where we examine the role of upwards communication. We review research to show the positive benefits of encouraging open and honest feedback from staff at all levels. Likewise we also flag the dangers. Basically, if employees are discouraged from expressing their views on organizational performance, managerial emperors are very likely to end up with the corporate equivalent of no clothes.

Organizational culture can either encourage or discourage employee voice, and so in Chapter 13 Ashly Pinnington presents an analysis of this area. Culture, like fast-food restaurants, seems to be ubiquitous. It is a term that is both widely used and often abused. It can mean all things to all people. Ashly Pinnington delineates the defining features of this concept. He also highlights the pitfalls of a unitary approach to organizational culture, showing how it can lead to institutional intolerance of diversity. Instead he argues convincingly for culture as a plurivocal phenomenon. This resonates with Matthew Seeger's stance in Chapter 14, on the ethical side of organizational life. Given that the new millennium witnessed a plethora of scandals in which dubious ethical practices led to financial ruin for a range of companies, this topic has received a great deal of recent attention. Matthew Seeger offers a theoretical template with accompanying practical road map to enable organizations to follow the right moral path. Finally, we conclude the book by addressing the issue of assessing communicative performance. Without benchmarking and target-setting it is very difficult, if not impossible, to measure change. We therefore recommend the communication audit approach as a way of measuring and monitoring the key issues presented throughout the book.

Taken as a whole, this book presents the reader with a depth analysis of the current state of key issues in the field. One of its key features is that contributors have been drawn from a wide variety of countries, including the UK, the US, Canada, Australia, New Zealand and Norway. In this way, we hope that the text is more free of ethnocentric biases and monocultural assumptions than can often be found in this kind of endeavour. Given its reach, the book also contains perspectives on organizational communication from a range of disciplines, including communication, psychology, organization studies, management and education. While we make no claims that the resulting book is a complete and comprehensive analysis of the entire domain (no book ever could be), the material covered herein represents a rich, technicolor picture of organizational communication. As such, it will be of direct relevance to practising managers, to students of management and communication, and to academics and researchers.

Dennis Tourish and Owen Hargie
September 2003

1 The crisis of management and the role of organizational communication

Dennis Tourish and Owen Hargie

Introduction

What does the future hold for the theory and practice of management? What role, if any, is there for organizational communication in these deliberations? Exactly which aspects of communication contribute centrally to the core of corporate practice? This book addresses itself to these and other key issues. In this chapter our objective is to contextualize the book by examining a number of areas central to this overall ambition.

- *We look at the business context in which most organizations now work.* Many if not all are under enormous external pressure. The agenda faced by managers is crowded to breaking point. These pressures sometimes see organizations fragment rather than cohere. A primary focus on the bottom line has often elbowed other considerations, including communication, to the sidelines. In the process, the theory and practice of management has entered into crisis. Many aspects of this crisis are explored in this book, and we showcase some of the main themes in the present chapter.
- *We explore whether organizational communication makes any difference to how organizations function and how their internal relationships are managed.* Recent years have seen a voluminous research literature into the human dimensions of organizational functioning. Communication has contributed to this, directly and indirectly. Our discussion of these issues does not presume that all members of organizations share a common set of interests and a readily agreed set of priorities or goals – what some researchers would describe as a 'unitarist' or 'functionalist' bias. Rather, it is to emphasize that while many management theorists have been developing inclusive agendas of involvement, participation and empowerment, most management practice has been marching to the beat of a different drum, and in the opposite direction.
- *We discuss precisely what we mean by the terms 'communication' in general, and organizational communication in particular.* Our intention is to alert readers at the outset to the themes that they will find in the chapters to follow. Contributors to this volume repeatedly discuss the communications

implications of issues that have been deemed vital to the theory and practice of management. It is essential that readers appreciate the full range of
issues implied by any discussion of communication, the better to grasp their
full implications.

- *We summarize some key debates in the field concerning the parameters of organization science and organizational communication.* Thus, we acknowledge that
  there is no one agreed agenda guiding communication research, or a single
  theoretical paradigm that is employed when communication processes are
  analysed. For example, some researchers adopt a critical management
  perspective, in which a principal concern is to explore relationships of
  power and domination. Others pursue a more positivistic agenda, characterized by a search for causal explanations of observable phenomenon.
  Readers will find a variety of approaches in the text, and are alerted here to
  some of the main issues involved.

Clearly, therefore, this book is not intended as an introductory text on organizational communication or management. While we outline some basic principles of communication in this chapter, the main thrust of the book is to
explore the brutal dilemmas that now confront organizations daily, and illuminate many of the debates engulfing the field from the often neglected perspective of communication studies.

The business context of organizational communication

Humans are easily tempted to interpret the world as more volatile, fast changing,
tempestuous, uncertain and unpredictable than it actually is, and to assert that
each of these conditions prevails more than during any other period of history.
This seems to be an endemic part of the human condition. As the Bavarian
comic Karl Valentin once put it, 'In the past even the future was better'. We
make no such claims. However, this book has been prompted by the realization
that society faces many challenges, none more so than in the field of work. Our
economy is certainly more globalized than ever before, and therefore prone to
sudden shocks inspired by unanticipated events beyond the control of even the
most far-seeing manager. To take the most obvious example, the terrorist attacks
in New York on 11 September 2001 sent political, social and economic shock-
waves around the globe, and helped usher in a period of instability characterized
by war with Iraq, sudden stock market fluctuations and a heightened mood of
fear that is clearly not conducive to the orderly functioning of business.

The fate of individual companies illustrates the strains most are now exposed
to. In 1989 Mitsubishi was a key global player. It even acquired a 51 per cent
stake in New York's Rockefeller Center. This corporate giant, seemingly so
infallible, proceeded to lose $330m. in 1999 (Hitt, 2000). Even more famously,
IBM was ranked as the number 1 corporation in the US by *Fortune* magazine in
the early 1980s. It featured as one of the 'excellent' companies profiled in the
best-selling management book of all time – *In Search of Excellence* (Peters and

Waterman, 1982). By 1995 it had tumbled to a position of 281 in the *Fortune* 500 – a shadow of its former pre-eminent self. As we write this chapter, sections of the business press have begin to float another previously unthinkable possibility – that the Ford Motor Company may be heading for disaster, and even bankruptcy (Wachman, 2003).

But it is more than just the fate of a few individual companies in the US and Japan that is at stake. The technology index peaked in March 2000, but in the following three years £778bn. was wiped from the value of British company shares (Connon, 2003). A period of what had been dubbed 'irrational exuberance' (Shiller, 2001) shuddered to a halt. Micklewhaite and Wooldridge (2000: 120), two stalwart defenders of globalization, conceded that there existed 'a universal feeling that every manager now faces a world in which the old certainties have been replaced by a string of unpleasant surprises and in which strategy has devolved from long-term planning to simple panicking.'

These developments, not to mention other famous and notorious debacles such as the Enron scandal, have created what can only be described as a crisis of legitimacy for the profession of management. More evidence has accumulated that many of the most prized organizational interventions spawned by the management theory and guru industry have a limited to non-existent effect on performance. Jackson (2001), in surveying much of the evidence, cited the following dismal data:

- Of 500 companies studied, only one-third felt that programmes such as Total Quality Management had a significant impact on their profitability.
- Only 20 out of 100 British firms thought that their adoption of organizational improvement plans improved their financial performance.
- An analysis of managers in 100 companies looking at 21 different programmes found 75 per cent of managers unhappy with the results.
- A review of 787 companies around the world found that 70 per cent of managers thought the management tools they were exhorted to use generally promised more than they delivered.

In addition, much attention has been focused on the behaviours of senior executives. There can be no more apposite illustration than Jack Welch, formerly CEO of General Electric (GE), and lauded in some circles (though not by us) as the best corporate leader of the twentieth century. Welch started his retirement in a novel fashion by commencing an extramarital affair with an editor of the *Harvard Business Review*, who had been sent to interview him. His subsequent divorce brought to light a number of intriguing facts such as that he had amassed a personal fortune of over $900m., while firing tens of thousands of workers, that his retirement package included a $9m. a year pension, plus use of GE's Boeing 737 and a Central Park apartment, free wine, food, laundry, toiletries, limo services, security, country club memberships, and Wimbledon, Red Sox and Yankee tickets (Helmore and Morgan, 2002). In many senses this epitomized the excesses of the era.

The problems that have arisen from unbridled greed at the top have been widely acknowledged, and not just among 'the usual suspects' in the anti-globalization movement. Noted management guru Charles Handy commented gloomily: 'The danger is that the flaws in the capitalist system may be its undoing, leaving us with something much worse ... My hope is that we can do something about the flaws in capitalism ... although I am not optimistic' (Handy, 2001: 119).

The language used has on occasion been vitriolic. Leading management thinker Henry Mintzberg offered the following opinion: 'We live in a crazy world. It's totally scandalous. In the US business has literally bought its way into government ... We've gone completely out of balance ... At the moment everything is totally imbalanced towards business: it completely dominates the social and government sectors too' (Caulkin, 2003: 10).

The data is compelling. Eighty-six per cent of the stock market gains of the 1990s went to only 10 per cent of the population, cementing the power of business and making the US the most unequal society in the world apart from Nigeria (Handy, 2001). Social cohesion has been seriously wounded. One of the most interesting books dealing with this (the evocatively entitled *Bowling Alone*), argued forcefully that Americans had seen a drastic collapse of honesty and trust, because of the rise of crude individualism and the consequent erosion of vital social networks (Putnam, 2001).

Perhaps inevitably, the theoretical basis of management has also been called into question. Traditionally, management was viewed as a process involving planning, organizing, commanding, controlling and co-ordinating (Fayol, 1949). These and other certainties (for example unity of direction, unity of command and a clear chain of authority) may well have been appropriate in a stable environment, but seem less applicable in the context of virtual, e-commerce and service oriented companies, all competing in a globalized economy (Harvey and Buckley, 2002). More recent management thinkers have advocated a culture of empowerment (or liberation), on the basis that the new knowledge economy requires the active, willing and creative contribution of a workforce to an organization's bottom line (see Collins, 2000, for an account and critique). The stimulus for such ideas has been provided by changes in the economy.

More than half of the total GDP in rich economics is now derived from what is defined as knowledge-based work, while knowledge workers account for eight out of ten new jobs (Dess and Picken, 2000). These authors conclude that 'to compete in the information age, firms must increasingly rely on the knowledge, skills, experience, and judgment of *all* their people. The entire organization, collectively, must create and assimilate new knowledge, encourage innovation, and learn to compete in new ways in an ever-changing competitive environment' (Dess and Picken, 2000: 18).

Ideas of empowerment naturally follow – people's willing involvement in job tasks, necessary for the innovation required by knowledge-oriented firms, presumes some measure of autonomy and discretion over what they do. Moreover, when at work, people generally prize the ability to realize their full potential as individuals (Mitroff and Denton, 1999), to do work that has some social meaning or social value (Ashmos and Duchon, 2000), and to enjoy the feeling of being part of a larger community (Mirvis, 1997). They also aspire to live and work in an integrated fashion (Pfeffer, 2001). None of these needs is likely to be met in an authoritarian environment.

The problem, however, is clear. It is one thing to stress the need for empowerment. Whether it can thrive in an environment that Mintzberg describes as 'crazy', in which most business leaders still instinctively respond to problems with a strong need to command and control, in which corporations are widely regarded as having too much power, and in which senior executives are ridiculed for their pay and benefits is another matter.

Frequently, these paradoxes have been disregarded by management theorists. It is often assumed that management is 'the rational administration of unitary organizations. Organizations are assumed to be social technologies, or "tools", systematically designed in order to attain specific goals' (Thomas, 2003: 29). Moreover, where it is addressed at all, power is most often discussed simply as 'a matter of strategic resource control or illegitimate moves in the legitimate organization game' (Clegg, 2003: 537), rather than as the exercise of control over one person or group by others. It is thus implied that organizations are geared to the achievement of ends that are both socially useful and generally shared – assumptions that in truth are ever more widely contested. Within this framework, a variety of management gurus produce recipes for organizational success, with all the panache of a magician who performs miracles – aided by smoke, mirrors, and his audience's willing suspension of disbelief. Senior managers are urged to pursue the latest miracle cure through a process that is nine-tenths diktat to one-tenth persuasion. In reality, such has been the ferocity of life in the workplace over recent years that most employees greet such efforts with 'a healthy mixture of confusion, scepticism and even cynicism' (Miles, 2001: 317). It is not insignificant that one of the most widely read writers on organizations is Scott Adams, whose Dilbert cartoons depict a workforce constantly bombarded by brainless management initiatives devoid of any real sense. Nevertheless, many practising managers eagerly embrace each new development, however untested its assumptions might be (Harvey and Buckley, 2002).

Thus, we regularly see the appearance of management prescriptions fatally hobbled by their own internal contradictions. It is quite common to find gurus (and others) advocating such approaches as participation, and yet creating programmes 'whose successful implementation depends upon the use of hierarchy, unilateral control, and employee limited freedom' (Argyris, 2001: x). For example, Beer and Eisenstat (2000) identified a number of barriers to organizations effectively implementing their chosen strategies – what they dubbed 'the silent killers'. Among the killers listed is a top-down or laissez-faire senior management style, which stops those at the top receiving enough corrective input to the decision making process. Their recommended solution, however, 'starts with the top team of the business unit or corporation defining its strategy', (Beer and

Eisenstat, 2000: 30), and then proceeding to sell it down the line. A unitarist focus is simply assumed, and a top-down strategy recommended – as part of the attempt to move organizations beyond top-down strategies.

It is our belief, and a driving force behind this book, that such paradoxes could be addressed more effectively if communication theory – concerned as it is with how meaning is formed and then shared between people – was more often incorporated into the analysis. However, it seemed to us that a great deal of the general writing on management has neglected to fully incorporate a study of the communication processes involved. Where communication is acknowledged at all it is frequently addressed in passing, and more often with the assumption that it is a phenomenon that is self-explanatory and hence one that requires no deeper level of analysis. Likewise, in many organizations, communication is recognized as being important but little or nothing is done about it. The attitude seems to be that the formal recognition and endorsement of the need for better communication will somehow, by a process of osmosis, bring it to pass. This emu-like approach to strategic communication is of course doomed to failure. A major objective of this text is to showcase the importance of devoting time and resources to communication. It is also our intention to address this issue by building some much-needed bridges between two often disparate fields of study – management and organizational communication.

Communication and organizational effectiveness

Communication is central to any study of what managers do, and to the effectiveness or otherwise of organizations. Managers devote much of their time to interactions with staff. Manager-watching studies have revealed that they spend over 60 per cent of their working time in scheduled and unscheduled meetings with others, about 25 per cent doing desk-based work, some 7 per cent on the telephone, and 3 per cent 'walking the job' (Schermerhorn, 1996).

These activities are embedded in dense networks of relationships between managers and employees. Most such communication is face-to-face, and most of it is task-related rather than personal in content. Managers spend much of their day communicating with many people, in brief interactions which are nevertheless of enormous significance in determining the communication and cultural climate of their organizations (Tourish and Hargie, 2000a). Effective management depends on open communication, and requires an interpersonal style characterized by warmth, candour, supportiveness and a commitment to dialogue rather than monologue. Indeed, it has also been shown that 'communication, especially oral skills, is a key component of success in the business world … executives who hire college graduates believe that the importance of oral communication skills for career success is going to increase' (O'Hair *et al.*, 2002: 3). No wonder that Mintzberg (1989: 18), having surveyed a wide range of evidence, drew the following conclusion: 'The manager does not leave meetings or hang up the telephone in order to get back to work. In large part, communication *is* his or her work.'

Research findings have long suggested that the effective management of communication processes brings large-scale organizational benefits. In a review of the research, Clampitt and Downs (1993) concluded that the benefits obtained from quality internal communications include:

- improved productivity
- reduced absenteeism
- higher quality (of services and products)
- increased levels of innovation
- fewer strikes, and
- reduced costs.

Within the fields of human resources management (HRM) and organizational behaviour there has also been a huge growth of study into what are generally defined as high performing work organizations (HPWOs) – those that tend to outperform their rivals over a long period of time. Extensive summaries of this evidence can be found in Pfeffer (1994, 1998); Collins and Porras (2000); O'Reilly and Pfeffer (2000); J. Collins (2001) and Reichfield (2001). Much of this relates directly to communication processes, and is concerned with the impact of such practices on employee commitment.

A report summarizing the results of a human capital audit into the British Aerospace industry is typical of the data (Thompson, 2002). This explored the impact of high performance work organizations, generally characterized by good communication, semi-autonomous teams, employee participation, high levels of training and performance based rewards. The audit found that:

- 'Companies high in the HPWO index in 1999 recorded sales per employee in 2002 of £162k, compared to £62k for those low on the index – a difference of 161 per cent. In value-added per employee the corresponding figures were £68k and £42k – a difference of 62 per cent' (p.5).
- 'Use of profit sharing and of share ownership schemes in 1997 correlated with higher sales per employee and higher value-added per employee respectively in 2002. Greater provision of information to employees – through, for example, briefing groups – were associated with higher levels of profit per employee, and employee turnover was lower where firms gave employees more responsibility for the quality of their work' (p.5).
- 'Greater investment in management development was associated with high levels of value-added per employee. Companies investing heavily in management development recorded value-added per employee of £68k compared to £42k in companies that invested less – a difference of 62 per cent' (p.6).

Another example of the importance of communication was a survey in which 2,600 UK employees clearly expressed the view that what was most demotivating of all was lack of communication from managers, citing issues such as a complete absence of interaction, a general lack of feedback, or meetings taking place behind closed doors (Reed Employment Services, 2002).

In relation to employee satisfaction, the Gallup Poll organization produced a scale (Q12) comprising twelve questions, which are rated by staff on a one to five scale. These encompass issues such as the extent to which respondents feel they know what is expected of them at work, whether they are recognized for good performance, if their supervisor cares about them, and to what degree they believe that their opinions seem to matter. Thus, much of this Q12 scale relates to communication by managers. From its database of surveys of more than one million employees in the USA, Gallup found a significant link between scores on this scale and business performance (Caulkin, 1998). Organizations where staff scored highly outperformed their rivals on a range of measures of productivity, such as employee retention, profitability, and customer satisfaction. In like vein, companies in the UK which featured on the list of best 100 companies to work for have been shown to consistently outperform the FTSE normal share index (*Sunday Times*, 2003). This pattern is also reflected in data from the US. Companies on the list of *Fortune* best companies to work for found that their share values rose 37 per cent annualized over a three-year period up to 2000, compared with 25 per cent overall (Levering and Moskowitz, 2000).

The data on the importance of commitment, especially in the modern knowledge economy, is overwhelming. A longitudinal study of entrepreneurial companies in Silicon Valley discovered that those founded under a 'commitment' model had twelve times the likelihood of advancing to a successful initial public offering (Burton and O'Reilly, 2000). Interestingly, and in an industry where rapid ascent can just as easily be the prologue to a dramatic fall, no firm founded with a commitment approach to managing people failed during a five-year period (Hannan *et al.*, 2000). The story is repeated in the UK. A nationwide survey of 7,500 UK workers found that where employees were highly committed to their employers they delivered 112 per cent three-year returns to shareholders. Employees with low commitment returned only 76 per cent over the same period (Internal Communication, 2000).

The measures required to generate commitment are not necessarily complex, but they do involve a strong emphasis on communication. Take, for example, a study into 135 high-performing US companies (Towers-Perrin, 1993). In these, there was a definite tendency to seek suggestions from frontline employees, delegate, develop two-way communications and seek suggestions. Seventy-four per cent of employees in such organizations felt that their manager or supervisor asked them for ideas on improving efficiency. In another study of poorer performing organizations this figure was only 41 per cent. The evidence thus shows that commitment and enhanced performance is forthcoming when employees' participation is invited and welcomed, and is facilitated by the building of strong systems to promote effective internal communication.

However, most organizations do not pursue the practices that produce high commitment. We alluded above to impressive data on HPWOs, including a human capital audit in the British aerospace industry (Thompson, 2002). The latter report found that when all the work practices that characterize a HPWO were taken into account, only 11 per cent of establishments were using two-thirds or more. Forty-five per cent were using less than half. Moreover, although the only type of training that was clearly correlated with improved financial results was that related to people management, such training constituted the smallest amount of the already limited amount available – barely 18 per cent. Worse still, spending on management development appeared to be falling. Such data may have a bearing on the persistent finding, typified by a study of 216 international and global manufacturing businesses, to the effect that 'the strategic management of both international and global operations is still poorly executed in very many Europe-based manufacturing businesses' (Sweeney and Szwejczewski, 2002: 1).

Positive communication policies have also been eroded. Large-scale workplace industrial relations surveys in the UK showed that in 1980 about 34 per cent of workplaces had formal joint consultative committees between managers and workers. This was down to 29 per cent by 1998 (Millward *et al.*, 2000). Predictably, all this means that commitment is actually on the wane, at a time when most organizations would say that it has become more important than ever. A UK Gallup *Q12* survey found that only 17 per cent of workers felt engaged (i.e. loyal and productive) with their workplace, 63 per cent were not engaged (i.e. they were not psychologically bonded to the organization) and 20 per cent were actively disengaged (i.e. they felt psychologically absent, and were intent on running the organization down) (LaBarre, 2001). As one measure of the costs involved, those in the latter category had twice the level of absenteeism of those in the first.

Falling commitment is linked to an intensification of workplace pressure. In Chapter 2, we discuss downsizing, and its devastating impact on morale, cohesion and commitment. But the problem is wider than this. For example, data was gathered from a sample of more than 10,000 individuals in Britain each year between 1991 and 1999, focusing mostly on the public sector. It found deteriorating levels of job satisfaction throughout and sharply rising stress levels – the size of the deterioration measuring between one half-point and one full point on a standard General Health Questionnaire mental stress scale (Gardner and Oswald, 2001). In similar vein, Mirvis (1997: 198) summarized a wealth of available data in the US to conclude that the dominant climate in the workplace had become one of 'fear, pressure and impermanence'.

The reality of much workplace communication is well illustrated in the following e-mail, sent by Neal Patterson, CEO of Cerner Corporation (a major US health care software development company) to his line managers. The effects can be readily imagined:

> We are getting less than 40 hours of work from a large number of our ...
> EMPLOYEES ... The parking lot is sparsely used at 8a.m.; likewise at 5p.m.
> ... NEVER in my career have I allowed a team which worked for me to

think they had a 40-hour job … I STRONGLY recommend that you call some 7a.m., 6p.m. and Saturday a.m. team meetings … My measurement will be the parking lot … The pizza man should show up at 7.30p.m. to feed the starving teams working late.

(Cited by Wong, 2001: 1)

Driven by a variety of factors beyond the scope of this chapter, it is therefore clear that there is a large and seemingly growing gap between the best data and theories of management, and what is actually happening on the ground. It hardly overstates the case to describe this as a crisis. The question arises: what can organizational communication bring to the study of these issues?

Organizational communication and the crisis of management

We want here to indicate the breadth of the field, and so demonstrate how the core concerns of organizational communication intersect with the challenges of management at many critical points. The chapters that follow then showcase these intersections in action.

Organizational communication, as a discipline, is now many decades old, with the 'modern' study of the subject generally held to date from the late 1930s (Tompkins and Wanca-Thibault, 2001). Typically, it looks at how people ascribe meanings to messages, verbal and nonverbal communication, communication skills, the effectiveness of communication in organizations, and how meanings are distorted or changed while people exchange messages, in both formal and informal networks. More generally, seven main traditions in communication research have been identified by Craig (1999) as follows:

1   *rhetorical* (communication as the practical art of discourse)
2   *semiotic* (communication as the manipulation and study of signs)
3   *phenomenological* (communication as the study of the experience of others)
4   *cybernetic* (communication as information processing)
5   *sociopsychological* (the process of expression, interaction and influence)
6   *sociocultural* (symbolic processes that produce shared social and cultural understandings)
7   *critical* (a discursive reflection on moves towards understanding that can never be fully achieved, but the act of which is emancipatory).

Each of the above traditions is concerned with various elements of communication (Hargie *et al.*, 2004).

- *Communicators* refer to the people involved. Personal attributes such as the age, gender, dress, physique and disposition of those involved influence both our own actions and our reactions to the behaviour of others (Hargie and Tourish, 1999). An important attribute is what Goleman (1997) termed 'emotional intelligence'. After examining studies involving hundreds of large organizations, he concluded that this was the dimension that characterized star performers. Emotional intelligence includes the ability to persuade and motivate others, to empathise and build relationships, to handle one's own and other people's emotions, to give open and honest feedback sensitively, to form alliances, to monitor one's own behaviour, and to read organizational politics. It refers to the core skills of social awareness and communication.

- *Messages* are the signals and symbols we use to convey what we mean. Communication messages are usually delivered in a visual, auditory, tactile or olfactory format (Hargie and Dickson, 2004). We are more conscious of the first three. Visual messages include written communication, as well as all of the nonverbal modes (clothes, jewellery, facial expressions, gestures, and so on) prevalent in social encounters. Auditory communication may be face-to-face or mediated by telephone. Tactile communication refers to the use of touch and bodily contact (handshakes, hugs, kisses). Finally, olfactory messages include the use of perfumes, after-shaves, deodorants, and all the other types of scent, which in fact serve to disguise our natural body odours and project a certain image.

- *Channel* describes both the medium and the means used to deliver messages. The 'means' of communication would include face-to-face, telephone, pager, written (fax, e-mail, 'snail mail', newsletter), audio and video. In face-to-face contact, communication occurs through the medium of the visual, auditory and olfactory channels, while the tactile channel may or may not come into play. A skilled communicator will select, and maximize the use of, the channel most appropriate to the achievement of the goals being pursued, bearing in mind that employees tend to prefer face-to-face communication with managers (Tourish and Hargie, 1993).

- *Noise* is the term used to describe anything that distorts or interferes with meanings and messages. Dickson (1999) identified a number of barriers to communication, the main ones being:

  - *Environmental* This includes a whole range of factors. For example, the layout of furniture can facilitate or inhibit interaction, intrusive noise may be disruptive, and heating and lighting can be conducive or uncomfortable.
  - *Disability* Physical, neurological or psychiatric impairment can make normal channels or patterns of interaction difficult, or even impossible. Examples include sensory handicaps such as sight or hearing loss, and conditions such as Parkinson's disease or severe depression.
  - *Psychological* This refers to the 'baggage' we carry with us into social encounters. These include the personal biases or stereotypes that influence how we perceive and interpret what a particular person is saying.
  - *Semantic* This occurs when the actual meaning of what is being communicated becomes distorted due to language or cultural differences between the communicators.

- *Demographic.* In particular, differences in age and gender have been shown to have the potential to cause problems during social encounters. To take but one example, when a male listener nods his head he is likely to be communicating to the speaker 'I agree', but when a female nods her head she may just be indicating 'I am listening' (but not necessarily agreeing) (Stewart and Logan, 1998).
- *Organizational* Barriers to communication can be constructed by the organization itself. For example, we worked in one corporation where the CEO sent an edict to all employees that no one was in future permitted to send any e-mails directly to him. Rather, they all had to go through the line management hierarchy. This was a very disabling and disempowering message and a definite obstacle to upwards feedback. Other examples of organizational barriers include the disparate physical location of staff who should be working closely together, a lack of a coherent strategy for team briefing, or overburdened, stressed and under-resourced supervisors who simply do not have sufficient time to devote to communication.

- *Feedback* allows us to evaluate our performance. We receive feedback both from the verbal and nonverbal reactions of others, and from our own responses. This latter process, which is known as 'self-monitoring', involves being aware of what we say and do in social encounters, and of its effect upon others. Skilled communicators are high self-monitors who continuously analyse and regulate their own behaviour in relation to the responses of others.
- *Context* Communication does not occur in a vacuum. It is embedded within a particular context, which in turn has a major impact upon behaviour. A manager will behave totally differently when disciplining a member of staff in the office, as opposed to when calling at the home of the same person following the death of a child. In each case, the situation plays a key part in shaping the response.

It is evident from this that communication dynamics are thoroughly insinuated into the fabric of organizational life. We would argue that organizations cannot be thoroughly understood without bringing a communication perspective to bear. Indeed, attempts to even define what organizations are would founder without a clear acknowledgement of communication processes. Ocasio (2002: 42) conceptualized organizations as 'social systems of collective action that structure and regulate the actions and cognitions of organizational participants through its rules, resources, and social relations'. In like vein, Huczynski and Buchanan (2001: 5) iterated that: 'An organization is a social arrangement for achieving controlled performance in pursuit of collective goals'. Organizations involve:

- *Social arrangements,* where people come together to interact and organize themselves in a certain way. There are systems set in place whereby members interact with one another, both formally and informally.

- *Controlled performance*, which entails the setting of standards for outputs, measurement of performance against these standards, and the implementation of corrective action as required. Rules are laid down and employees have to accept and abide by these. This is facilitated by a managerial structure, and the pooling of shared resources.
- *Collective goals*, wherein members work together to achieve shared aims and common objectives. Organizational members are expected to hold certain values and to think in particular ways. It is the accepted norm that employees should contribute to the corporate 'mission'.

In this book, we and our fellow contributors are particularly concerned with how the main elements of communication described here interact with the processes of management, to produce positive or negative outcomes. We now explore various theoretical paradigms that guide research within the field, and which also must be taken into account.

Theoretical paradigms in organizational communication research

Organizational communication has been variously conceived as what people who are academic students of communication do, it can be viewed simply as the study of communication in organizations, or the term has been taken to mean the use of communication to describe and explain organizations (Deetz, 2001). Given the breadth of its core concerns, it qualifies to be regarded as a subset of the wider study of organizations. If organizational theory can be conceptualized as generalizations about organizations, then most contributions to the field in its entirety can be dated from the last half of the twentieth century (Starbuck, 2003). In a highly influential paper, reproduced in a text specifically devoted to debate about the role of organization science, Burrell and Morgan (2000) proposed that four theoretical paradigms could be observed in this work. These were functionalist, interpretive, radical humanist, and radical structuralist.

- *Functionalism* is 'characterised by a concern for providing explanations of *the status quo, social order, consensus, social integration, solidarity, need satisfaction* and *actuality*. It approaches these general sociological concerns from a standpoint which tends to be *realist, positivist, determinist* and *nomothetic*' (Burrell and Morgan, 2000: 112). The aim is 'to create general theories about organizations and their members, which are reminiscent of the powerful universal laws found in the natural sciences' (Donaldson, 2003: 41). From the perspective of communication, studies in this tradition would be concerned with issues such as the causal relationship between communication satisfaction and organizational productivity, and be characterized by questionnaire-based data collection and rigorous quantitative analysis.
- The *interpretivist* perspective is 'informed by a concern to understand the world as it is, to understand the fundamental nature of the social world at

the level of subjective experience. It seeks explanation within the realm of individual consciousness and subjectivity, within the frame of reference of the participant to the observer of action' (Burrell and Morgan, 2000: 114). Fundamentally, the argument is that 'the social world cannot be understood in the same way as the natural and physical worlds' (Hatch and Yanow, 2003: 65). Interpretivist communication scholars are involved in exploring questions like what sense individual members of organizations make of communication processes, and how they understand or misunderstand messages received from management. It is likely that data will be obtained by qualitative methods such as depth interviews, from which major themes in understanding can be extracted.

• The *radical humanist* paradigm has much in common with interpretivism, but in addition is concerned 'to develop a *sociology of radical change* from a *subjectivist* standpoint … its frame of reference is committed to a view of society which emphasises the importance of overthrowing the limitations of existing social arrangements' (Burrell and Morgan, 2000: 117, emphasis in original). This approach has led to a burgeoning growth in what has more widely been termed critical management studies (CMS) (Adler, 2002). One of its central preoccupations has been a critique of existing ideologies (Willmott, 2003) – in particular, the assumption that they are value-free, self-evident, morally superior or bereft of power-based implications. Communication scholars so inclined would, for example, tend to ask how communication processes in organizations reinforce systems of domination and exploitation. Data will also be likely to be obtained by qualitative methods.

• The *radical structuralist* paradigm is 'a *sociology of radical change* from an *objectivist* standpoint … Radical structuralism is committed to *radical change, emancipation,* and *potentiality,* in an analysis which emphasises *structural conflict, modes of domination, contradiction* and *deprivation.* It approaches these general concerns from a standpoint which tends to be *realist, positivist, determinist* and *nomothetic*' (Burrell and Morgan, 2000: 119, emphasis in original). Communication researchers influenced by this paradigm will also be concerned with issues of power and domination, but be more likely to utilize quantitative methods in their data collection and look for explicitly causal relationships between variables.

Each paradigm has been robustly defended and critiqued (see Corman and Poole, 2000) – the paradigm wars are well and truly alive in communication science. All this has been deplored by some as representing an unhelpful fragmentation of the field (Pfeffer, 2000), and welcomed by others as providing the means of bringing multiple perspectives to bear on an inherently messy reality (Van Maanen, 2000). Despite a tendency towards polarized debate, it has also been recognized that 'scholars cross paradigms because the world of organizations is far too complex for any single theoretical approach to fully grasp' (Fairhurst, 2000: 121). It is therefore increasingly usual to find studies that straddle the typology laid out by Burrell and Morgan – to the occasional howls of anguish from outraged purists.

This book has been partly inspired by the belief that the study of organizational communication has opened up a vast range of methodological approaches and theoretical insights that must be regarded as central to the future of management in the twenty-first century. We outlined the challenges facing the study and practice of management above. It is little wonder that texts have now been published with such titles as *The Organization in Crisis* (Cooper and Burke, 2000) – a proposition with which few would dissent. If the academic exploration of organizations and organizational communication has become fissured, it has done little more than mimic the external world it studies. The challenge is to make the best sense we can of this crisis, to understand its causes in more detail, to identify the role of communication in the various issues involved and, we would argue, to clarify the contribution that communication can make to building better organizations and better societies.

Conclusion

Many management interventions can be likened to the Native American rain dance, and indeed are often inspired by a similar desperation for results. Fantastic interventions are enacted and often enjoyed by the central characters. The spectacle can also be fascinating for the uninvolved observer. But for all the drama and passion expended in their performance, they exert no appreciable impact on actual outcomes. Downsizing, in particular, has been a central part of the managerial rain dance in recent years and, as our own chapter in this text will illustrate, is almost wholly associated with negative organizational outcomes. A main concern of this book, therefore, is to critically examine the true impact of key current themes in organizational communication for management practice.

This is no easy task. As this chapter has demonstrated, the study of organizations is a discipline characterized by multiple theoretical paradigms and methodological perspectives – as it should be. Reality is multifaceted, never more so than in the context of work. There is little agreement among scholars on the precise nature of the problems afflicting organizations, how they should be studied, or indeed what measures of organizational effectiveness are most appropriate. We have not attempted to foist any one theory on our contributors. Some remain within one preferred orientation, while others (ourselves included) adopt a more eclectic approach, surfing across theories and paradigms as demanded by and relevant to the context of the discussion. Readers will therefore find a variety of approaches at play in the ensuing text, and are invited to engage critically with the analyses on display.

Our hope is that, by the end of the journey, students of management will have a better appreciation of the role communication occupies in their field, and that students of communication will more clearly understand how the world of management frames so much of human behaviour. Too often, managers grow frustrated by the intangibility of communication dynamics, and put their attention instead on whatever appears to be more easily measured. But, as Einstein once commented, 'Not everything that can be counted, counts – and not everything that counts, can be counted.' We believe that those who neglect communication will develop a very partial insight into the fascinating, contradictory, contested, interactive, infuriating, iterative and above all vital world of organizations. This volume is an attempt to broaden our vision to encompass much more of the territory around and within us.

2 The communication consequences of downsizing trust, loyalty and commitment[1]

Dennis Tourish and Owen Hargie

Introduction

Researchers have increasingly argued that much of mainstream management practice is characterized by the enthusiastic adoption of fads (for example, Shapiro, 1995; Jackson, 2001). Managers embark on radical programmes of restructuring that throw their organizations into turmoil, but which are often based on little or no evidence that they work (Newell *et al.*, 2001). Indeed, research often discovers that far from having a benign or even neutral impact, many such initiatives inflict severe damage (see Chapter 7, for a fuller discussion of fads). Re-engineering is one of the best examples of a self-proclaimed revolutionary practice that failed in the overwhelming majority of cases where it has been implemented (Knights and Willmott, 2000).

Much of the practitioner literature on these issues, as this chapter will show, seems to assume that destructive organizational initiatives can be salvaged by the skilled use of communication messages to engineer internal and external support for the mad, the bad or the cack-handed. The assumption is that there are no unpalatable messages, just poor communication strategies. The central focus of this chapter is on one such initiative, downsizing, which has been an integral part of the re-engineering movement. Downsizing has spread like a contagious disease through both the public and private sectors. It has been endemic in company takeovers (Hubbard, 2000), when 'merge and purge' seems to be the order of the day. This chapter looks at what it has meant, the rationale for its implementation, the evidence as to its effectiveness, and the communication consequences of its implementation. As will be shown, the issues raised go far beyond downsizing.

One conceptualization of communication is that it is largely a mediating device between management intentions (whatever the intention happens to be) on the one hand and their execution on the other. Within this instrumentalist perspective, the moral properties of downsizing, and its psychological consequences, are largely irrelevant. The emphasis is on how particular ends will be reached, while the ends themselves are unquestioned and assumed to be value free. An alternative perspective is that the dialogic properties of communication systems have a transformative impact on management intentions and fundamental notions of what it means to do business (Deetz, 1995a). Here, communication is regarded as an integral part of the entire organizational operation – it both reflects and shapes the way business is done. Downsizing is an excellent example of a popular management approach that helps to illuminate these issues.

The impact of downsizing

Reductions in workforces (RIFs) have been a major trend in both the public and private sectors over the past two decades. The general name given to this phenomenon is that of downsizing, defined as 'an intentional reduction in the number of people in an organization. It is accomplished via a set of managerial actions, which may include the use of hiring freezes, layoffs, and normal or induced attrition' (Freeman, 1999: 1507). The intentional aspect of workforce reduction strategies is what commonly distinguishes downsizing from organic decline in a given industry or sector (McKinley et al., 2000). The activity also appears in different guises using pseudonyms such as 'rightsizing', 'rationalization', 'de-layering', 'finding the right staffing level', 'achieving staffing equilibrium', or 'letting people go'. We know of one CEO who introduced a wave of redundancies by telling those affected that he was 'inviting you to fulfil your potential elsewhere'. Whatever the nomenclature, its aim has been to promote organizational efficiency, productivity, and/or competitiveness (Cameron, 1994).

Given this intention, and the implied benefit, its popularity is scarcely surprising. One survey found that one-third to one-half of all medium and large US firms had downsized annually since 1988 (Henkoff, 1994). The effects have been far-reaching. A study of fifty Fortune 500 firms with over 50,000 employees, covering the period between 1987 and 1997, found that workforces were reduced by an average of 20 per cent – more than 1.2 million people (Schultze, 2000). A Towers-Perrin consulting firm survey found that two-thirds of white-collar employees reported their company had downsized or experienced major restructuring in the previous two years (Conrad and Poole, 1998).

Public sector downsizing has also been rampant. This has often been interpreted as part of a worldwide movement to reinvent government (Lynch and Cruise, 1999). For example, a survey of downsizing in Australia found that only one in six of the public sector organizations that responded had *not* downsized or delayered between 1993 and 1995 (Dunford et al., 1998). But as this craze swept organizations worldwide, what were its effects? In answering this question, we look at two types of effect, economic and psychological.

The economic impact of downsizing

In general, the research literature has disclosed a gap between the avowed goals of downsizing and what has been achieved. A review of 3,628 companies over a fifteen-year period looked at Return on Assets (ROA) – a useful measure of profitability. It found that ROA in companies that downsized 'declined in the downsizing year and the first year subsequent to the downsizing. There was a slight improvement in year two, but it was not sufficient to restore the ROA to its pre-downsizing level' (Morris *et al.*, 1999: 82). Other critical accounts of the results obtained from downsizing have been reported. In particular, Kabanoff *et al.* (2000) looked at 300 downsizing events in US companies over a period of eight years. They found that

> downsizing, on average, produces no improvement in firms' performance relative to their industry or their own prior performance, except for a short-lived gain in productivity; downsizing organizations that show no sustained improvement in financial performance are those in which there is a managerial focus only on cost-cutting, while those that show improvement have a managerial focus on increasing productivity, or reorganizing and restructuring.
>
> (Kabanoff *et al.*, 2000: 24–5)

Burke and Greenglass (2000) found that two-thirds of firms that downsized during the 1980s were behind industry averages on a variety of financial and productivity measures for the 1990s.

A study has also been conducted into the effects of downsizing on patient care, in 281 acute care hospitals. It found that morbidity and mortality rates were 200–400 per cent higher in those that downsized their traditional head count in an across the board way (Murphy, 1994). Cost savings had also dissipated within eighteen months, with costs rising to pre-downsizing levels in a relatively short period of time.

The economic case against downsizing is clear. In essence, it is like the brilliant wheeze of a man who chops off his fingers one by one, in order to remove any unnecessary appendages. Organizations that embrace it in the pursuit of economic gain overwhelmingly find their profits in decline. Initially, this is surprising. On reflection it becomes less so. An Olympic team that shrinks its numbers below that of the competition is unlikely to win gold medals. However, the impact of downsizing is much wider than this.

The psychological impact of downsizing

From the perspective of this book, research into the effects of downsizing on psychological constructs of organizational life (such as trust and loyalty), and its direct impact upon the quality of communication, is particularly important. A plethora of problems have been identified (Cameron *et al.*, 1991; Cole, 1993) as emanating from downsizing, including:

- reduced cross-unit and cross-level knowledge from interpersonal interactions
- loss of personal relationships between employees and customers, and the disruption of predictable relationships

- increased interpersonal conflict
- greater resistance to change
- more centralization in decision making
- decreased employee morale, commitment and loyalty.

Symptoms among survivors include:

> denial, job insecurity, feelings of unfairness, depression, stress and fatigue, reduced risk taking and motivation, distrust and betrayal, lack of reciprocal commitment, wanting it to be over, dissatisfaction with planning and communication, anger at the layoff process, lack of strategic direction, lack of management credibility, short-term profit focus, and a sense of permanent change ... some optimism, lots of blaming others, and a thirst for information.
>
> (Burke and Cooper, 2000: 8–9)

We will examine these issues in more depth.

1 Reduced loyalty

It has been widely argued that loyal employees make extra efforts in their work, can be positive public relations representatives in the external world, and are more likely to go beyond the norm in doing small things that improve organizational effectiveness (see Organ, 1988). Some researchers (most noticeably Pfeffer, 1994; 1998) have argued that 'the human equation' is a fundamental attribute of organizational success, and a central feature of strategies likely to secure ongoing competitive advantage. However, research into the effects of downsizing has shown that:

> the loyalty factor was suffering a slow burial in many companies. Survivors expected that there would be further restructurings, and that the organizational changes would be pushed through in the same way – with a lack of communication, lack of consultation, lack of resources and training.
>
> (Littler et al., 1997: 75)

The view of many managers involved in downsizing seems to be that if you want loyalty you get a dog. Myopic managers such as this will tend to find that employees, like dogs, often bite back when attacked. Exchange theory shows that what we give out to others we tend to get back from them in spades. The norm of reciprocity means that an organization that shows no loyalty to staff receives none in return (Tourish and Hargie, 2000a). One effect of downsizing is that job insecurity has grown, with attendant feelings of bitterness, anxiety, disenfranchisement and concern for the future (Feldheim and Liou, 1999). Such insecurity has been found to be associated with deterioration in general psychological health and both job and organizational withdrawal (Dekker and

Schaufeli, 1995). The effects on loyalty and trust, and hence on organizational performance, can be readily imagined.

The decline in loyalty has not been confined to the shop floor. Worrall *et al.* (2000) reported on the results of a survey of Institute of Management members in the UK. Sixty per cent of middle managers reported a decline in their loyalty during the preceding period, over 70 per cent a decrease in morale and 60 per cent a decrease in their motivation. Those respondents who had been involved in restructuring involving redundancy reported even higher levels of disaffection. Clearly, downsizing increases work pressures on the managers who remain, now faced with a more alienated workforce. The expectation is that the managers concerned will show a greater flexibility and adaptability, have an improved ability to manage people and show a greater strategic orientation (Dunford *et al.*, 1998). However, the reality is that morale and loyalty suffer, as managers struggle with job descriptions that in many cases have moved from the demanding to the impossible.

One of the core sets of needs identified by Ibrahim Maslow was those related to belongingness (Maslow, 1970). We have a strong need to be part of groups or organizations, to feel wanted by the people in them, and sense that we belong with them. In turn, we give our loyalty to them. But we also expect this to be a two-way process. If these groups respond by rejecting us, then the bonds begin to fracture and eventually break. A possible response to the breaking of organizational loyalty chains is to feel the desire for a new beginning. One way to cope with trauma is to move on by moving away. A clean break and a new start can help to heal the hurt. Thus, following the traumatic event of downsizing, some employees who remain will begin to look for possible moves elsewhere. Such motivation is heightened by nagging doubts and questions such as: 'Am I next for the chop?' and 'Will this company survive?' Fear and failure are sad Siamese twins. No one wants to be the last rat on board as the ship goes down. Where viable alternative employment options exist for staff they are likely to feel a psychological pull towards them and a push away from their present organization.

2 Decreased satisfaction

A study of Canadian hospitals found that those that had downsized were significantly more likely to report lower employee satisfaction and greater internal conflict (Wagar and Rondeau, 2000). A further case study looked at a 2,509-bed medical rehabilitation hospital employing 500 people on a full-time basis (Mullaney, 1989). In a significant downsizing, 8 per cent of the total workforce was eliminated. Commitment and satisfaction declined for workers and management staff. Such declines were also noted in departments spared the full effects of downsizing – i.e. staff unaffected by the process still vicariously felt its effects.

Another cause of dissatisfaction is the feeling of helplessness. Staff who believe they have been doing a good job inevitably feel let down when the axe begins to swing. People can then come to believe that they have been unfairly penalized, and so it does not really matter what they do – their fate will be decided by others in any event. When what we do seems to have no influence upon the negative outcomes that accrue, we tend to become apathetic, passive and dejected. This is part of the well-researched psychological phenomenon known as *learned helplessness* (Seligman, 1975). Employees who survive the downsizing cull may believe they have no real say in their future. Creativity and innovation decrease. People do what they are told to do, leave decision making to others, and expect the worst. This is an unpropitious context for organizational success.

3 Increased uncertainty

One study has looked at the communication consequences of downsizing in an Australian health care organization (HCO), where the number of staff employed was being reduced from 660 to 250 (Tourish *et al.*, unpublished manuscript). An interesting feature of this study is that both those going and the survivors were working alongside each other for a period of months after the layoffs were announced. This enabled the attitudes of both groups to be probed in a more in-depth fashion than is normally found in the literature. Overall, the research pointed to the following main trends:

- Uncertainty rises for both survivors and those terminated. Uncertainty does not ease with the announcement of who has lost their jobs, but endures for some considerable time, as people transfer their anxiety from the immediate issue of termination to that of reorganization, and their place within new structures. Role uncertainty in the face of environmental ambiguity takes the place of job anxiety.
- Staff within downsized organizations perceive large gaps between the amount of information they receive and the amount of information they need, irrespective of whether they are among those laid off or not.

In this HCO, downsizing was a largely unavoidable response to international shifts in health care delivery for mental patients. Large-scale mental health hospitals are increasingly a thing of the past. Yet even when downsizing is the rational response to such imperatives the experience is traumatic, destructive of interpersonal relationships and harmful to attempts to ensure that all employees feel they are receiving an adequate amount of information on key business issues. Faced with uncertainty, people articulate a need for more information. The problem may also be that because downsizing produces enormous levels of uncertainty, no amount of information provision will feel enough for employees. This suggests that managers' attempts to improve the communication climate are less likely to find a receptive context. In consequence, the general management task becomes all the harder.

4 The loss of social capital

Social capital refers to the ability of people to work together for common purposes in groups and organizations (Coleman, 1988). It has two main components: associability and trust (Leana and Van Buren, 2000). Associability describes the extent to which group objectives are given priority over individual desires. Trust refers to the willingness of people to engage in affiliative behaviours even when one does not know other parties well, but we have some direct contact with them and/or some positive attitude towards their reputation. Clearly, the constructive management of social capital is central to organizational success. Implicitly or otherwise, trust is the glue that holds the human enterprises known as organizations together. The evidence reviewed here would suggest that 'The workforce reduction downsizing strategy is the strategy most noted to erode trust within organizations' (Feldheim and Liou, 1999: 58).

This disassociation and reduction in trust can also be destructive of the culture of the organization, where companies associate themselves with a model attaching a high value to employee contributions. Trust is replaced by cynicism and a feeling of betrayal. The evidence increasingly suggests that durability in relationships is an important predictor of the adoption of high-performance work practices, because of the need for cooperation and trust (for example, O'Reilly and Pfeffer, 2000). It has been suggested that the employment practices that promote organizational social capital include job security, or at least the provision that if downsizing occurs it is a last rather than first resort (Pil and MacDuffie, 1996).

One potential problem following downsizing is that of survivor guilt. Following any major trauma, those who survive are often left with a myriad of mixed feelings. A common one is that of guilt at having been left relatively unscathed while others have suffered. While such guilt may initially be sublimated by feelings of 'Thank goodness it was them and not me', it can later emerge as a form of delayed reaction. This, of course, depends upon the individual. Some will take the view that it is 'the luck of the draw' or the organizational jungle perspective of 'survival of the fittest' (i.e. it was the weak who inevitability suffered). Much depends upon the attribution process. If the employee attributes the decision to layoff certain people to internal causes ('they were not good enough, whereas I am a top employee'), then there is likely to be less guilt. However, if an external attribution is made ('We were all good and management just picked on some of us'), then guilt and indeed anger are more likely. Following downsizing, employees will have watched close colleagues suffer. The ensuing guilt for at least some of those who remain (especially those who by nature are person-centred and affiliative) may well be dysfunctional.

The human costs described here arise partly from the obvious breaking of the traditional psychological contract implicit to the downsizing process. Employees tend to feel that employer promises to them have been broken. Ironically, a purely instrumental view of organizational relationships driven by an accountancy paradigm is least likely to deliver sustainable competitive advantage in today's knowledge economy. Managers who develop such a modus operandi become like Oscar Wilde's definition of a cynic: they know the cost of everything but the value of nothing. The notion of organizational 'history' has been shown to be important (Deal and Kennedy, 1999). Just as families have roots, and these are important for its members so too, it is argued, a sense of a valued corporate history is vital for the workforce. But a history dominated by accounts of how former family members have been eliminated is scarcely one on which people will reflect with pride.

A further problem with downsizing is that when people go they take their knowledge with them. The organization loses the non-transferable 'tacit knowledge' that is in their heads and not on files that can be read by others (Herson, 2000). This may be knowledge of technologies, best practices, processes, markets or indeed customers. The cost of losing such knowledge can be very great. Furthermore, it may take some time before this impacts upon the bottom line.

There will also be a loss of the informal 'fast track' procedures within the organization. In any company, even those with a high level of codification of knowledge and processes, there is always an element of 'who you know not what you know'. Human beings will always find a way of circumventing process and once the social structure of an organization is disrupted, the personal favours and informal processes that allow things to happen quickly in exceptional circumstances will disappear through the loss of personnel and changes in the structure of an organization.

In addition, the impact of the loss of 'tacit knowledge' to an organization should not be underestimated. Knowledge management experts have long acknowledged the importance of the informal communication network in the dissemination of knowledge within the organization (see Chapter 6, in this volume). Knowledge networks grow organically and are dependent upon social interaction. The disruption of teams, company structure and the reduction in trust in the organization damages these knowledge networks. Not only is 'tacit knowledge' lost to the organization as individuals leave but those remaining within the organization can lose access to their knowledge network through the reorganization. 'Early adopters' of new processes, skills, knowledge and cultural ideologies, who are important in the championing of change within the organization, lose confidence and possibly their status in new teams, slowing the dissemination process through the organization.

Although it is also difficult to compute the value of trust, it is clearly a social construct which is hard to build and yet easy to destroy. The loss of trust can have very serious consequences, since this dimension is at the very heart of relationships (Hargie and Dickson, 2004). In the downsizing game, trust and relationships may be particularly damaged because, counter-intuitively, most firms that engage in this activity are not in a straightforward profits crisis. One study found that, in any given year, 81 per cent of companies downsizing were profitable (Burke and Cooper, 2000). Employees may therefore assume that their employers had the time to pursue other profit improvement strategies, but disregarded them without sufficient thought for the human consequences.

Furthermore, this transparent loss of trust is at odds with the organizational imperative to achieve quality, since it undermines the basis for employee involvement in work practices that underlie quality systems. (As Feldheim and Liou (1999: 63) put it, when 'cost considerations replace quality considerations, the principles of employee empowerment, responsibility and loyalty are sacrificed for a reduction in overhead. This tradeoff results in a loss of employee trust in the organization and betrayal of the concept of work.'

The impact of the psychological costs of downsizing may be hard to place on a balance sheet. Nevertheless, it is severe. Given that so much of an organization's ability to achieve its bottom line financial objectives depends on intangible factors such as trust, loyalty and associability, the damage inflicted by downsizing on its social capital is one of the most obvious reasons why the practice fails to live up to expectations. This begs the question of why it remains so popular.

Reasons for downsizing

Many companies faced with problems still immediately embark on workforce reduction strategies. An outstanding example in the UK is that of Corus, the steel manufacturing company. In early 2001, it announced that 6,050 jobs were to be eliminated (Morgan, 2001b). The company's chairman, an accountant, also said that further capital investment was not on his agenda, spending was to be kept to a minimum and more job cuts were not ruled out. It will be recalled that such a finance-driven agenda has been found to be the least successful basis for downsizing (Kabanoff *et al.*, 2000).

In essence, Corus serves as a good example of irrational management behaviour. The research evidence indicates that the company's actions will deliver the opposite of what is intended. It is as though a steady stream of volunteers keep jumping from a cliff, convinced that this time they will achieve unassisted flight. The corpses below suggest otherwise. But people keep on jumping. How can this be? There are several possible factors, many rooted in communication processes, which we believe can help to explain this conundrum.

1 What gets rewarded, gets done

The evidence is that managers who downsize are rewarded, even though the practice does not genuinely improve profitability and effectiveness. This is the equivalent of paying managers for each person who jumps off the cliff. Revealingly, Corus's announcement of redundancies saw the company's shares rise in value by 10 per cent (Morgan, 2001a) – an immediate reward for those senior managers with stock options in the company. Nor is this atypical. One study of popular management techniques found that they did not lead to improved economic performance (Staw and Epstein, 2000). However, the companies that used them were more admired, perceived to be more innovative and rated higher in management quality. Accordingly, their chief executives were paid more than those that did not utilize the techniques – a level of remuneration inspired by the achievement of greater internal and external legitimacy, through association with management actions deemed popular. Moreover, it is increasingly the case that top managers who fail to raise the value of shares in their company will actually lose legitimacy, and with it, their jobs. In the ten years up to 2000, such a fate befell top managers in AT&T, Sears, General Motors, Xerox, Coca-Cola, Aetna and other well-known corporations (Reich, 2001). Downsizing may therefore be conceived as a short cut to legitimacy, and hence to heightened prestige, remuneration and, paradoxically, job security for the managers who embrace it. Its actual impact on their organizations is neither here nor there.

2 Illusions in leadership

Illusions in the transformative potential of leadership within organizations are widespread (Tourish and Pinnington, 2002). The business press routinely depicts leaders as all-powerful, all-knowing and the controller of the organization's destiny in a complex environment (Meindl *et al.*, 1985). The corollary is the expectation that leaders, on assuming office, will rapidly diagnose strengths and weaknesses, articulate compelling new strategies, propose plans for restructuring and generally show they are in control (Dobrzynski, 1993). As has also been pointed out, the brutal truth is that even the process of developing an understanding of an organization, never mind devising a convincing strategy to address its problems, is in reality rather complex (Denis *et al.*, 2000). The task of building and maintaining relationships is onerous and requires mastery of a large repertoire of complex communication skills (Hargie and Tourish, 1997). However, the pressure of expectations may compel top managers to seek a short cut to success. Looking for rapid cost reductions through RIFs has the apparent advantage of simplicity and immediacy. Building strong partnerships with a workforce may take years. A programme of redundancies can be announced almost at once. Thus, if people will not jump voluntarily over the cliff, they may need to be pushed.

3 Downsizing as a system of self-persuasive narratives

Fundamentally, organizations depend on metaphors and stories to rationalize their actions (Morgan, 1997). These assist all organizational members with the vital process of sense-making (Weick, 1995). Such narratives are used to sell what is happening internally, and achieve legitimacy. They also have an external role, convincing the business press, the stock market and industry partners that a well thought through and integrated strategy underpins the workforce reduction programme. In the process of developing such narratives, managers may become intoxicated by their own rhetoric. They can then assume that the metaphors they construct are a more faithful depiction of reality than they are. Constant repetition also helps people to inoculate themselves against doubt.

The process can be defined as one of self-persuasion – i.e. by focusing our communication efforts on the positive reasons for something, aimed at others, we nevertheless wind up reconvincing ourselves (Pratkanis and Aronson, 1991). According to Downs (1995), the main narratives of this kind attached to downsizing include the following:

- *The Lean and Mean Story* Downsizing is portrayed as part of a cost cutting programme. Metaphors to do with weight loss and athletics are common – 'we are fighting the flab', 'we must beat the competition', and 'we must win the battles ahead'.
- *The Strategic Flexibility Story* Here, technological change bears the opprobrium for what is deemed necessary. The narrative proclaims that a particular product or technology is no longer required. Opponents of downsizing are likened to the Luddites, who fought against new machinery introduced by the Industrial Revolution in the eighteenth century. Irrelevant historical analogies or misplaced international comparisons displace critical thinking.
- *The Learning Organization Story* This is a more modernist narrative, hinging on the need for continued learning and continuous improvement. People are told that their job has changed and that they no longer have the skills required for the new jobs that are emerging. Superfluous to requirements, they have become 'the weakest link'. Their departure is essential for the prosperity of the rest of 'the team'.
- *The Mystical Management Story* We have, above, noted an excessive reliance on superhuman leaders. Hence, the narrative frequently emerges that organizations desperately need leader managers capable of inspiring people to do more with less. Such narratives are especially common during delayering processes, described by Mintzberg as 'the process by which people who barely know what's going on get rid of those who do' (Mintzberg, 1996: 62). Downsizing enables organizations to dispose of those who lack 'the right stuff' to become transformational leaders, and whose existence is deemed to be necessary for survival.
- *The We're Out of Money Story* The organization proposes that it does not have enough funds to keep everyone on board, due to market conditions. Some employees must be culled so that the rest of the herd can be fed. If insufficient numbers volunteer, they will be conscripted.
- *The Eye on the Prize Story* This is a variation of the previous narrative. Vital and life-affirming goals are proposed, but are linked to the need to reduce expenses. A greater prize lies ahead, and there is no gain without pain. It is assumed, usually wrongly, that this prize will be sufficient to energize survivors and minimize the negative psychological consequences of the downsizing process.

Sense-making is often driven by plausibility rather than accuracy. In terms of the cliff-jumping metaphor, there are many well-documented instances where cult leaders have persuaded scores of seemingly intelligent people to commit suicide. Each of the narratives sketched above may have an internal logic that renders them more persuasive than would be justified by a scrutiny of objective data. This becomes especially potent if an organization's internal communication systems are afflicted by the problem we describe below.

4 The absence of critical feedback

There is now considerable evidence indicating that top managers tend to overestimate the gains from downsizing while underestimating its negative consequences. A particular problem here, from a communication perspective, is the difficulty for senior managers in obtaining critical feedback about decisions made.

One study of Institute of Management members in the UK obtained responses from 1,313 people, ranging across the entire spectrum of managers from company chairman to junior managers (Worrall et al., 2000). Eight hundred and eighteen respondents had experienced organizational restructuring, most of which involved some sort of downsizing. The study revealed a stunning gap in perceptions of its effects. For example, the net agreed score (i.e. the percentage of respondents agreeing with a proposition minus the percentage disagreeing) for chairs, CEOs and MDs saying participation in decision making had increased in the aftermath of downsizing was 60; directors, 34; senior managers, 6; middle managers, 4 and junior managers, –3. In terms of whether productivity had increased the figures were 70, 47, 16, 12 and –1; for whether the speed of decision making had increased they were 48, 24, –5, –7, –25. Thus, senior managers were much more likely to view downsizing as effective than their most junior colleagues. The further apart the management levels surveyed, the greater the gulf in perceptions. It is therefore hardly surprising that when those at the top view downsizing as having benefited their organizations they are keen to implement it again, whatever the feelings of everyone else.

A likely reason for the perceptual gap noted here can be found in ingratiation theory (Jones, 1990), an issue we discuss further in Chapter 12. Essentially, this proposes that those with a lower level of status habitually exaggerate the extent to which they agree with the opinions and actions of higher status people, as a means of acquiring influence with them. It should also be remembered that self-efficacy biases suggest that most of us imagine we are better on various crucial dimensions of behaviour than we actually are (Myers, 1996). For example, one survey found that 95 per cent of drivers rated themselves as better at driving than the average driver (Hargie et al., 1999). Researchers have thus generally found that managers view the defective and uncritical feedback they receive from subordinates as accurate, sincere, and well meant (Rosenfeld et al., 1995) – it is in line with their self-efficacy biases.[2] In this context, it would appear that downsizing has a negative effective on organizational performance. However, few people are willing to tell senior managers this. A vicious cycle is set in motion, in which a destructive initiative is enacted, senior managers receive mostly positive feedback on its effects – and resolve to do it all over again. Those who have jumped over the cliff never return to say how awful the experience was. Those who implement the jump schedule tell the boss what a wonderful success it all has been. The boss then resolves to organize another session of cliff jumping, for those unable to make it the first time.

5 The priority of short-term relationships

As has been widely discussed, downsizing as a fad originated in the US – a country that does not have a regulatory tradition of job property rights (Fukuyama, 1995). Moreover, the 'new psychological contract' stresses personal responsibility for career development, commitment to certain kinds of work rather than a given organization, constant change, acceptance of job insecurity, and the abandonment of the notion that a career can be built within one organization (Cavanaugh and Noe, 1999). As Pfeffer (1994) has wryly noted, this new contract looks surprisingly like the old contracts found in the eighteenth and nineteenth centuries. Thus employment practices that emphasize short-term relationships have a long historical pedigree. Downsizing is consistent with such short-term relationships. Yet this runs contrary to what systematic research studies continue to find. In a major survey of 15,945 employees in the UK, Moskowitz and Levering (2001) identified the top fifty companies. They found that 'The winners are providing an environment in which the workers are treated as important contributors rather than as hired hands' (p.3). In the top companies, employees felt that the company *cared*. Managers who hardly know their staff, and who maintain a purely fiscal relationship with them, will be less worried about their fate when they jump over the cliff.

Downsizing is also consistent with external short-term relationships. The focus on purely fiscal objectives rather than long-term strategies is concurrent with short-term relationships with suppliers based on costs and pricing issues rather than a long-term shared destiny, shared benefits relationship. Both internal and external relationships like this are destructive in the longer term (Reichfield, 2001).

6 Irrationality and the principle of social proof

Puzzlement in the face of the popularity of downsizing suggests a belief that human decision making is inherently rational. We have frequently found that students tend to just assume that major management decisions *must* have been the result of intense reflection, research and debate, and therefore have some logic behind them. In reality, a great deal of evidence suggests that much human thought is irrational (for example, Dawes, 2001). Irrationality derives from a number of reflexive responses. As discussed above, downsizing originally acquired enormous popularity within the US. It was then always likely that what has been defined as the principle of social proof would come into play. Fundamentally, this means that we are inclined to decide whether something is rational and desirable on the extent to which we see other people either doing it or wanting it (Cialdini, 2001). It is for this reason that political advertise-ments invariably show candidates for high office surrounded by hordes of cheer-ing admirers. The implication is that since the leader is so highly esteemed by others, he or she should also be esteemed by you. In this case, organizations throughout the world observed the trend towards downsizing in the US, assumed that it was the outcome of a rational process of decision making, and rushed to emulate it at home – in the interests of remaining competitive. The psychology is similar to that of a mob, each member of the crowd convinced that the presence of others bestows legitimacy on their actions. Precisely this dynamic would appear to lie behind the adoption of management fads in general. These fads are not really surprising. We all define problems in terms of the solutions that are available to us. If people offer managers what appear to be highly successful solutions, then organizational problems are recast in this light. Thus, if other organizations are singing the praises of cliff jumping, it becomes a must-do for us too. We cannot be left out or left behind.

The role of communication

A vast amount of practitioner-oriented literature has been published, advising managers on how best to approach downsizing (for example, Cameron et al., 1991; Heenan, 1991; Cameron, 1994; Feldman and Leana, 1994). Underpinning much discussion is the assumption that most organizations have failed to ade-quately address the people factor in their dealings with survivors (Appelbaum et al., 1999). An obvious issue is therefore whether management communication strategies may be able to eliminate or at least reduce the destructive con-sequences discussed above. This issue surfaces in many empirical investigations.

We would argue that such questions raise ethical issues, though they rarely feature in the literature. Rosenblatt and Schaeffer (2000) are a notable excep-tion. The implication of some writing seems to be that whatever the destructive impact of downsizing on people and businesses, communication may be enlisted in some attempt to enable managers to implement it, while evading the psycho-logical levies described in this chapter. Ethically, it is questionable whether communications practitioners should see their primary role as that of corporate spin doctors helping to reconcile people to whatever management initiatives happen to come along. Rather, we would argue that communication can be most usefully conceptualized as a dialogic facilitator of long-term relationships in which downsizing is noticeable by its absence. This becomes clearer if we consider the research findings on the role of communication during downsizing processes.

What communication accomplishes, and what it doesn't

Various studies have investigated, sometimes incidentally, whether communica-tion can mitigate some of the negative impacts of downsizing. At best, the evid-ence is equivocal. In a study of the perceptions of 1,363 nurses involved in a downsizing process in Ontario hospitals, Murphy (1994) found that much depended on how the process was managed and communicated. In particular, *perceived fairness* had a significant impact on levels of absenteeism and professional efficacy. Greater communication efforts and improved staff participation in downsizing activities (for example, in helping determine the criteria for layoffs) also had significant impacts on these variables. On the other hand, the mere presence of an organizational vision was unrelated to more positive outcomes. Thus, active communication seemed to be a key factor. Other research has found that when criteria or procedures applied in layoffs are seen as fair, employee commitment and performance are less likely to decrease (for example Brockner *et al.*, 1995). Providing clear explanations of why downsizing is necessary (and assuming that it is!), treating all employees with dignity and using fair procedures all seem to be vital for maintaining any chance of survivor trust (see Mishra and Spreitzer, 1998).

Such findings are consistent with the view that organizational members are likely to feel deprived when they think they do not know what is going on (Miller *et al.*, 1994). They lend empirical support to the proposition that keeping surviving workers informed of changes by explaining the rationale behind them can reduce some of the more negative consequences of downsizing (Feldman, 1989). It should be noted that none of this work suggests the negative effects can be entirely eliminated. At best, it seems that communication reduces some of the worst trauma, much as does a pressure dressing on a wound.

It seems inescapable that job instability erodes social capital within firms (Leana and Van Buren, 2000). Such erosion may be endemic to downsizing, whatever the organizational context. As Pfeffer (1998: 174) put it, 'the evidence indicates that downsizing is guaranteed to accomplish only one thing – it makes organizations smaller'.

Thus, managers cannot assume that the good intentions that may underlie particular episodes of downsizing will be enough to ensure widespread understanding, support or compliance. Moreover, suspicion, misunderstanding and hostility may be inevitable, whatever the context of downsizing. Where downsizing is an unavoidable part of a process designed to deliver a wider social benefit, an enormous attention to communication processes is still required, in order to minimize the harmful psychological consequences discussed in this chapter. It may be doubted whether downsizing conducted by profitable organizations, and intended to strengthen profits further, can ever be communicated in such a way that the negative psychological effects can be avoided.

In general, the literature suggests that organizational members feel deprived when they think they do not know what is going on (Miller *et al.*, 1994). This is likely to impact on organizational performance. Increased information flow may ease some of the sense of deprivation. For example, Schweiger and DeNisi (1991) looked at the impact of a realistic merger preview in an organization announcing a merger with consequent job losses. One plant received the realistic merger preview, while another received limited information, in line with normal company policy. News of the merger generated additional stress globally, with perceived uncertainty and absenteeism rising, and job satisfaction, commitment, and perceptions of the firm's trustworthiness deteriorating. However, the experimental plant scored significantly lower on perceived uncertainty and significantly higher on job satisfaction, commitment and perceptions of the company's trustworthiness, honesty and caring than the plant that received limited information. Again, this research does not suggest that a more open flow of information eliminates such problems as reduced commitment. At best, the problem is eased.

It has therefore been argued that keeping surviving workers informed of changes by explaining the rationale behind them is central to success, and that this involves reassuring them about their future status within the organization (Feldman, 1989). However, there are two problems with this sort of counsel.

The first is that around 67 per cent of firms that downsize in a given year also do so the following year (Mishra *et al.*, 1998). Employees are well aware of this. Moreover, the psychological contract has been broken once. Why should people believe it will not be broken again? Communication researchers have long established that when there is a gap between our nonverbal behaviour (or what we do) and our verbal behaviour (i.e. what we say), most people put more credence on the former (Hargie and Dickson, 2004). The propensity to engage in further downsizing makes it hard to reassure people about their future. Even if genuine reassurances can be offered, it will be quite a challenge to get anyone to believe them. For staff it is a case of 'Fool me once, shame on you. Fool me twice, shame on me.' This suggests that downsizing may lock management communication strategies into a spiral of crisis for some considerable time.

The second problem is that managers are likely to have a different perception from their staff of what constitutes adequate information for the purpose of reducing uncertainty. For example, Shaughnessy (1986) found that 15 per cent of employees in a federal government RIF said they got adequate information about the cutback. At the same time, 50 per cent of personnel managers involved said employees got as much information as they needed. Thus, it appears that the general guideline stressing the need to improve information flow during RIFs will be difficult to implement in practice. Managers tend to underestimate how much information their employees need, while overestimating the amount of information they are transmitting – in line with their self-efficacy biases. Meanwhile, ingratiation theory suggests that few employees will draw this to their attention. The result is likely to be a disabling mismatch of perceptions.

Another study found that employees affected by downsizing in the context of asset divestiture, but who perceived greater procedural justice in selection criteria, had higher levels of trust in a new ownership and a greater degree of post-divestiture commitment to the organization (Gopinath and Becker, 2000). Interestingly, this research also found that

> communications from management (from a variety of sources, including e-mail, staff meetings, and personal interactions) … helped employees

understand the events relating to the divestiture [and] increased employees' perceptions of the procedural justice of the divestiture and layoffs. Further, the extent to which communications were seen by employees as helpful was predictive of future levels of trust and commitment.

(Gopinath and Becker, 2000: 74–5)

Nevertheless, decision makers frequently assume that confidentiality during RIFs is important, fearing that announcements of imminent downsizing can cause people to be discouraged, disobedient or render them more likely to leave (Greenhalgh, 1993). However, the evidence in general supports the view that 'depriving continuing employees of information during RIFs does not appear to alleviate their job fears; rather, in the absence of official communication, survivors frequently rely on rumours that depict a more hopeless picture than is justifiable and result in greater uncertainty' (Johnson *et al.*, 1996: 144). Of course, this does not mean either that maintaining a strong flow of information will be sufficient to eliminate uncertainty or keep it at pre-downsizing levels.

Thus the focus of some writing on communication during downsizing has been to find a means of reducing rumours and avoiding prolonged uncertainty. For example, Kilpatrick (1999) stressed the importance of using formal and regular channels of communication, and argued that 'Employees should be provided all information that it is possible to share without jeopardizing the organization's survival ... Communication – frequent, consistent and open – is one of the most important variables in the implementation of a downsizing plan' (Kilpatrick, 1999: 215–16).

One of the few accounts of successful downsizing in the literature also highlights the role of communication. The study looks at a firm that downsized and relocated (Starkweather and Steinbacher, 1998). The firm reported a 30 per cent increase in product volume, the achievement of a 98 per cent quality acceptance rate, and a 6.5 per cent increase in productivity per employee. Information overload was a key part of management's strategy. First, the decision to downsize and relocate was instantly announced, minimizing the scope for rumours. A new company newsletter was created. So was a forum whereby employee questions could be submitted anonymously. The management team continued to share information about profits, business plans, performance and other company issues. They also involved the local media, who publicized the availability of a highly trained workforce. However, some distinctive features of this situation should be noted. The company employed only 300 people and downsized at the height of an economic boom. Its small size and the relative availability of alternative employment are likely to have reduced people's anxiety, far beyond what would be possible with large organizations or during economic downturns.

Clearly, downsizing is sometimes unavoidable. We have given the example here of mental health hospitals, where changed patterns of care have reduced the need for large institutions with many staff. Sometimes, organizations may find themselves in situations where an unavoidable commercial imperative requires this type of action. However, the evidence suggests that such circumstances arise more rarely than many managers think. They are insufficient to explain the popularity of downsizing. We have also explored the psychological and communication consequences of the process. Added to the economic costs, they are compelling arguments in favour of using downsizing as a last resort rather than a first.

Thus, communication has a certain ameliorative effect, but to a lesser extent than may be commonly supposed. The main findings from this research in terms of implications for practice are summarized in Box 2.1.

Conclusion

The term managerialism generally refers to the increased power of managers within modern organizations (Tourish, 2000). It has been pointed out that managers often 'actually function as an independent group actualizing particular interests of their own' (Deetz, 1992: 212). Thus, untrammelled power held by any one group increases the prospects of that group using that power to its own advantage, whatever the wider social consequences. Ultimately, we would argue that this provides a useful context in which to appraise downsizing and other management fads.

Some top executives with share options in their companies have indeed gained, prioritizing their personal well-being above that of the organizations in their charge. However, managers would do well to heed Boyle's (2000) many warnings about the pitfalls of over-reliance upon numbers. As we have shown, downsizing has failed to deliver wider economic benefits and has also exacted an enormous psychic toll on the millions of people it has affected. It is indeed often the case that the process would be more aptly termed dumbsizing. Its continued popularity calls to mind a well-known definition of insanity – repeating the same course of action, while expecting different results. In this context, it is debatable whether communication can or should serve the instrumental role of merely transmitting information about the inherently unpalatable. From an applied perspective, the research literature suggests that communication can indeed ameliorate some of the worst psychological consequences of downsizing – but only partially, and then only if a number of conditions have been met, including that the downsizing itself is a last resort rather than a first.

A primary role of communication is to ensure consistency between different management messages, and between management rhetoric and behaviour. A fundamental problem with downsizing is that many companies pursue it as a cost reduction strategy, while simultaneously advocating high-involvement work programmes and total quality management systems. Yet 'employee trust and empowerment, often shattered in the process of downsizing, are the engines that make these initiatives work' (Mishra *et al.*, 1998: 84). Communication has a fundamental role in maintaining relationships. It cannot accomplish this while being deployed by managers intent on disregarding the most elementary needs of their employees.

Box 2.1   The communication consequences of downsizing

The search for alternatives
- Communicate extensively at all times, and about your organization's problems as well as its achievements. Cultivate a reputation for openness.
- Avoid downsizing or other management initiatives appearing as a bolt from the blue.
- Consider other options (for example, attrition, hiring freezes, voluntary retirements).
- Develop a communication strategy that extends participation in decision making and transforms internal organizational relationships.
- Ensure that your behaviour is consistent with your communication messages. For example, do not issue statements saying people are your most important assest one week, and announce layoffs the next.
- Make downsizing a last resort rather than a first. Be seen to make an enormous effort to avoid this.

Implementation: when downsizing is unavoidable
- Get the downsizing over and done with in one go. Avoid one round of layoffs leading to another.
- Communicate obsessively and at length. In particular, over-communicate about why downsizing is unavoidable. Use all available channels and media (dedicated intranet site, special news sheets, meetings, video, etc.). Have a rumour 'hotline' that employees can ring to check out the truth of what the grapevine is telling them.
- Involve employees in all aspects of the implementation effort. For example, include staff in deciding criteria for layoffs.
- Be honest. If you don't know something, say so.
- Seek upward and especially critical feedback on what you are doing.
- Provide support to managers, survivors and victims. In particular: avoid layoffs by memo or e-mail – give news face-to-face; allow for anger, disbelief, grief and goodbyes; treat all parties with respect.
- Expect a decline in morale, loyalty, and trust whatever you do.

Moving forward
- Reduce role anxiety as quickly as possible. Clarify where people fit in the new structure and what is expected of them.
- If further redundancies are not planned, say so loudly, insistently and often.
- Focus on other challenges, and explain how the new structure will help.
- Evaluate the effectiveness of what has happened.

More fundamentally, the dialogic properties inherent to communication suggest that the development, utilization and institutionalization of effective communication systems into organizations must also transform how they function (Deetz, 1995b). In particular, they are likely to promote a more participatory and democratic ethos in business (see Chapter 11, in this volume). Where this occurs, the enthusiastic adoption of unproven but highly dangerous fads is less likely to occur. Communication is a transformative ingredient in organizational life. This means that its effective utilization transforms how the goals of managers are formulated, as well as the goals themselves. There is an urgent need for fewer fads in management practice. A longer term perspective would prioritize the importance of social capital and hence human relationships. Organizational communication, divested of its instrumentalist interpretations, can make a significant contribution to this process.

Notes

1 We would like to thank Debbie Daly of Unipart, for her invaluable comments on an earlier draft of this chapter.
2 We would point out, here, that we have frequently presented this research to senior management teams. All immediately perceive the relevance of the research, and agree that it accurately describes much of what occurs. However, in line with self-efficacy biases, the majority also assume that it does not apply to them and that they are in that elusive upper quartile with an accurate feel for communication processes within their own organizations. Our subsequent work with communication audits has rarely found this assumption to be warranted.

3 Communicating about organizational uncertainty

Phillip G. Clampitt and M. Lee Williams

The presumption of certainty fades as the pace of organizational change increases. In today's business climate, conventional management practices such as making detailed plans, clearly defining job responsibilities, and meeting carefully established objectives often produce artificial certainty that can be debilitating (Clampitt and DeKoch, 2001). Consequently, effectively managing uncertainty assumes greater importance than ever before. Unfortunately, few tools exist for thinking about and acting on uncertainty (Kotter and Schelesinger, 1979; Conner, 1993).

Translating the uncertainties of organizational life into a viable communication strategy presents a formidable challenge to communication scholars and practitioners. Scholars must grapple with how to explain and predict the role of uncertainty in organizational communication practices. For instance, they might investigate how organizational leaders discuss (or avoid) the uncertainty inherent to the business environment. Practitioners are concerned with instituting specific strategies and techniques that enable organizations to effectively manage the uncertainty. In this chapter, we address both challenges. In the first part, we focus on the relevant research by briefly reviewing the literature, introducing the Uncertainty Management Matrix, and sharing our research findings. In the second part, we adopt a practitioner's perspective by providing an assessment model, discussing communication strategies, and reviewing several case studies.

Research perspective

Insights from past research

Physicists, mathematicians, philosophers, psychologists, communication researchers, and organizational theorists have all studied uncertainty. Integrating the efforts of scholars from such a wide range of disciplines is a formidable task. Nevertheless, we can identify seven general insights gleaned from the literature that provided the basis for this chapter.

First, uncertainty is the inherent state of nature. The second law of thermodynamics states that the 'entropy of a system increases as the system undergoes a spontaneous change' (Rossini, 1950: 68). Physicists explain the essentially chaotic and random behavior of gasses with this law (Atkins, 1984). This does not mean that there is a complete lack of order but that the patterns appear on a higher level. Werner Hiesenberg's famous uncertainty principle echoes a similar theme: 'The more precisely we determine the position [of an electron], the more imprecise is the determination of velocity in this instance, and vice versa' (Cassidy, 1992: 228). In a similar vein, Gödel's celebrated incompleteness theorem asserts that 'some statements about natural numbers are true but unproveable' which means they are formally considered 'undecideable' (Dawson, 1999). In short, the spirit of uncertainty pervades the scientific literature and culture.

Transforming the sentiments of the hard to the soft sciences is as natural as it is challenging. It is natural because most social scientists and organizational theorists accept the fact that the world is chaotic, contradictory, and incompletely apprehended. For example, Kahneman *et al.*'s (1982) noteworthy research regarding decision making begins with the premise that 'Uncertainty is a fact with which all forms of life must be prepared to contend' (p.508). It is challenging because understanding how people learn how to operate in such a world is difficult. Initially some social psychologists hypothesized that 'tolerance for uncertainty' was a personality trait. Today the consensus seems to be that 'tolerance for uncertainty' is more of a cognitive and/or emotional orientation (Furnham, 1995).

Second, 'tolerance for uncertainty' is a robust construct that has been conceptualized and measured in a number of different ways. In one sense, uncertainty can be defined by its opposite. Certainty means that something is fixed or settled. Those who are certain are free of doubt; they are sure of what they know. To embrace uncertainty is to embrace doubt. It is to question what is fixed and settled. However, the distinction between certainty and uncertainty is not an either/or proposition. There are degrees of uncertainty. Thus, a continuum may be the best way to conceptualize uncertainty. The degree to which individuals embrace uncertainty describes their tolerance level.

A variety of concepts are related to uncertainty including chaos, vagueness, provisionalism, complexity, randomness, and ambiguity. Psychologists have been particularly intrigued by the notion of ambiguity, which is a somewhat less encompassing idea than uncertainty. Ambiguity implies that the alternatives are known, while uncertainty implies that the alternatives are potentially unknown and even unknowable. Psychologists' interest in uncertainty and ambiguity grew out of their research on authoritarianism, no doubt, driven by the horrors of World War II. Adolf Hitler was not one to tolerate ambiguity or uncertainty (Adorno *et al.*, 1950). Indeed, Frenkel-Brunswik (1949) defined intolerance of ambiguity as a personality variable possessed by individuals who have a 'tendency to resort to black-white solutions, to arrive at premature closure as to valuative aspects, often at the neglect of reality, and to seek for unqualified and unambiguous overall acceptance and rejection of other people' (p.115). Her notion highlights the conceptual link between the inability to think in terms of probabilities and the intolerance of ambiguity.

Transforming this concept into a measurable construct proved somewhat elusive. Numerous self-report measures were developed based on slightly different conceptualizations (Budner, 1962; Ehrlich, 1965; MacDonald, 1970; Furnham, 1994). For instance, Budner (1962) developed a scale that has been widely used and considered psychometrically sound. He defined tolerance for ambiguity as 'the tendency [to interpret] ambiguous situations as desirable' (p. 29). He argued that ambiguous situations are 'characterized by novelty, complexity, or insolubility' (p.30). However, in a rigorous study involving twelve different measures, Kreitler *et al.* (1975) argued that ambiguous situations occur for one of three basic reasons: (1) the situation can be interpreted in a variety of ways, (2) the situation is difficult to categorize, and (3) the situation involves contradictions and conflict.

Over the years the dynamic interplay between the conceptual definition and its related measurement tools have resulted in a healthy debate. Perhaps it should not be surprising that there is some ambiguity regarding the definition of 'ambiguity'. Indeed, Bochner (1965) discovered nine primary and nine secondary characteristics of the tolerance for ambiguity concept. Norton (1975) content-analyzed references to ambiguity in *Psychological Abstracts* from 1933 to 1970 and found that eight categories emerged. But he also noted 'the essence of each category interpenetrates the essences of all other categories' (p.609). In short, uncertainty like ambiguity is associated with a number of closely related concepts, but at the core there are a few fundamental notions that pervade the various definitions.

Third, people have different tolerance levels for uncertainty that are associated with a number of factors. We can draw reasonable conclusions from the various measures used to assess tolerance for uncertainty (or ambiguity). For instance, we are confident that different people experience different levels of tolerance for uncertainty. The reason for those differences remains an important research issue. As seen in Table 3.1, scholars have found that those who are less tolerant of uncertainty (or ambiguity) tend to be more dogmatic, conservative,

Table 3.1   Issues linked to tolerance of uncertainty

People with high tolerance for uncertainty tend to:	People with low tolerance for uncertainty tend to:
• be less dogmatic • be less ethnocentric • be less 'generally' conservative • perceive ambiguous stimuli as desirable and challenging • rely less on authorities for opinions • be more self-actualized • be more flexible • prefer objective information.	• be more dogmatic • be more ethnocentric • be more 'generally' conservative • avoid ambiguous stimuli • rely more on authorities for opinions • be less self-actualized • be more rigid • prefer information supportive of their views.

Note
This table is based on reviews by Kirton (1981) and McPherson (1983).

ethnocentric and are inclined to prefer more supportive and less objective information than those who are more tolerant (Kirton, 1981; McPherson, 1983). Some researchers speculate that the underlying desire of those who are less tolerant of uncertainty is to avoid conflict and anxiety (Hamilton, 1957). On the flip side, researchers typically have not reported that tolerance for uncertainty varies on the basis of gender, age, or education level (Furnham, 1995). Many different approaches and methods were used in these largely unreplicated studies, which make it difficult to draw any firm conclusions. Moreover, it is difficult to ascertain causality because the tolerance for uncertainty has been used as both an independent and dependent variable. Does dogmatism cause intolerance for uncertainty? Or, does intolerance for uncertainty cause dogmatism?

Hofstede (1980) is not afraid to speculate on the direction of the influence. He believes that some cultures foster greater uncertainty avoidance than others. Societal rules, rituals, educational standards, religious orientations, and technologies are cultural forces that shape an individual's responses to uncertainty. Hofstede's 'Uncertainty Avoidance Index' is based on three survey questions and has been administered in forty countries. The data were used to rank-order all forty countries on the Index. Countries such as Greece, Portugal and Japan were highly ranked on the UAI, indicating a desire to avoid uncertainty. Other countries like Singapore, Denmark and Great Britain received much lower rankings. Hofstede links the rankings to a wide array of issues ranging from propensity for traffic accidents to preferences in managerial style.

Fourth, people are usually, though not always, motivated to reduce uncertainty. Communication scholars have been particularly interested in the impact of uncertainty on interpersonal relationships. In fact, Berger and Calabrese (1975) proposed the 'Uncertainty Reduction Theory' which basically argues that during initial encounters people naturally experience uncertainty and they seek to reduce the uncertainty by gathering more information. The higher the uncertainty, the greater the motivation. This proposition resembles Festinger's (1962) notion that people are motivated to reduce high levels of 'cognitive dissonance'. The proposition may sound intuitively correct, but the research is unsupportive (Sunnafrank, 1990). In fact, an individual's level of uncertainty is not really that important; it is 'wanting knowledge rather than lacking knowledge [that] promotes information seeking in initial encounters with others' (Kellerman and Reynolds, 1990: 71). The motivation to reduce uncertainty is greater in the workplace than in many social situations. Therefore, it is not surprising that researchers have found considerable evidence indicating that newly hired employees use a variety of overt and covert techniques to reduce certain types of organizational uncertainty (Teboul, 1994). Likewise, in times of major change, many employees seek information, even rumours, to decrease their uncertainty levels (Eisenberg and Riley, 1988; Clampitt and Berk, 1996).

Fifth, people reduce uncertainty through heuristics or rules of thumb that are often useful but sometimes detrimental. A classic group of studies by Kahneman et al. (1982) demonstrated that 'in making predictions and judgments under uncertainty, people do not appear to follow the calculus of chance or statistical theory of prediction. Instead, they rely on a limited number of heuristics which sometimes yield reasonable judgments and sometimes lead to severe and systematic error' (p.48). Other scholars make a similar point by arguing that individuals and organizations simplify the world in order to achieve satisfactory, if not optimal, outcomes (Simon, 1957; March and Simon, 1958; Cyert and March, 1963). Thus, rationality is bounded by the heuristics people employ.

Stereotypes, for example, are heuristics that work from time to time. But they can also be misleading. Consider these two questions: Is a woman more likely to work as an actress or a postal employee? Is a young attractive woman living in Los Angeles more likely to work as an actress or postal employee? Since there are far more female postal employees than actresses, the answer to the first question is obvious. But if one plays the probabilities, the answer is the same for the second question. Most people don't play the odds and answer the second question based on their stereotype of young, attractive women living in Los Angeles. Kahneman *et al.* (1982) label this phenomenon the 'representativeness' heuristic in which people make judgments based on the degree to which X is representative of Y. People use two other common heuristics: availability and anchoring. Availability involves the bias introduced into decision making because of the availability of certain information as opposed to that which is not readily accessible. Anchoring involves bias introduced by the initial starting point of an analysis of problems. Thus, most people use rules of thumb like representativeness, availability, and anchoring as ways to make decisions when faced with uncertainty.

MacCrimmon and Wehrung (1986) offer a parallel approach, arguing that risk (or uncertainty) management involves five phases: recognizing risks, evaluating the risks, adjusting the risks, choosing among risky actions, and tracking the outcomes. They use their REACT model to research the actual decision making practices of executives. They developed a survey based on a number of hypothetical risky situations such as how to deal with an impending lawsuit and how to invest corporate earnings. The survey asked the executives to make decisions based on the facts presented. The researchers evaluated the 'riskiness' of the decisions based on the actual outcome probabilities and drew some intriguing conclusions. For example, they found that risk-taking varies by situation, particularly whether it is a personal or organizational decision. Generally, those executives who were most successful took the most risks. Finally, like Kahneman *et al.* (1982), they found that executives often focus on one or two attributes of a risky situation. In other words, they use rules of thumb to strip away much of the uncertainty during the recognition and evaluation phases. Sometimes this is wise, but at other times, they inadvertently dismiss vital information.

Sixth, acknowledging uncertainty allows communicators to achieve a variety of conversational and persuasive objectives. The exemplary research of Beach and Metzger (1997) on 'claiming insufficient knowledge' examined how uncertainty is used as a tool to achieve certain interpersonal objectives. They conducted an in-depth analysis of typical conversations occurring in the legal, medical, and other settings. Usually people mark their uncertainty in conversations by saying, I don't know or I'm not sure. These scholars concluded that:

> 'I don't know' can function as a resource for qualifying responses to prior inquiries, avoiding or neutralizing others' projects and trajectories. In some cases, 'I don't know' was shown to be employed as a craftily devised method for disattending, neutralizing and implementing topic transition. In other environments, 'I don't know' functioned to delay and possibly reject invitations and/or requests.
>
> (Beach and Metzger, 1997: 579)

Persuaders use uncertainty in a similar way. Politicians, for instance, routinely deliver vague messages in order to avoid premature disclosure of positions on controversial issues (Alston, 1964; Thayer, 1967). In fact, stating issues with which an audience disagrees in an ambiguous way can positively affect the speaker's character ratings (Williams and Goss, 1975). Thus, equivocating is an effective stalling strategy, allowing speakers to circumvent audiences' premature negative evaluations. In essence, uncertainty becomes a tool for managing difficult issues. These scholars differ from the mainstream because they essentially ignore any controversies about an individual's internal state and instead focus on the rhetorical use of uncertainty in various situations.

Seventh, organizations typically try to reduce the amount of environmental uncertainty. Scholars investigating uncertainty in the organizational arena usually take either an internal or external tact. Those who take the internal tact are concerned with the impact of uncertainty on employees. For example, some researchers have claimed that newly hired employees who experience high levels of uncertainty tend to be less satisfied with their jobs, less productive, and more likely to voluntarily leave their organizations (Hecht, 1978; Wanous 1980; Spiker and Daniels, 1981). Any number of factors, including role ambiguity or information overload, can produce employee uncertainty. Employees who have been recently hired, work in matrix organizations or are involved in major change efforts are prone to be exposed to these factors. Therefore, practitioners have usually been motivated to find ways to either reduce the perceived uncertainty or mitigate the deleterious outcomes.

Obviously another major source of uncertainty comes from the external environment. One concern is how uncertainty in the environment impacts employee behaviour, but the vast amount of organizational literature addresses a more macro-level challenge: how should an organization conceptualize and manage an essentially chaotic array of environmental issues, such as changing government regulations, consumer demands and competitive pressures? Theorists, scholars, and consultants have offered a variety of answers to this fundamental question. System theorists use the 'law of requisite variety' to argue that the organizational complexity should match environmental complexity (Ashby, 1952; Lawrence and Lorsch, 1967). In fact, Burns and Stalker's (1961) classic study of twenty English and Scottish organizations indicated that more 'mechanistic' organizational structures worked best in stable environments, while more 'organic' structures worked best in dynamic environments. Nevertheless, most organizations seek out tools that reduce the perceived uncertainty. Indeed much of the literature discusses powerful analytical techniques, including strategic planning, cost-benefit analysis and the like, which are designed to categorize, quantify, and reify the future (Clampitt and DeKoch, 2001).

In recent years, less static and more fluid approaches have emerged that seek to effectively adapt to uncertainty rather than eliminate it. For example, Courtney *et al.* (1997) identify four levels of uncertainty that organizations can face when forecasting about the future: a clear-enough future, alternate futures, a range of futures, and true ambiguity. They suggest that the organization's strategic posture should be directly related to the type of uncertainty faced. Scenario planning, for instance, would be appropriate for an organization facing a discrete set of 'alternative futures' such as whether a new competitor enters the market or not. In contrast to more scholarly approaches, these consultants are concerned with how to effectively manage uncertainty. Clearly, new approaches focusing on the benefits of uncertainty are starting to emerge.

The Uncertainty Management Matrix

Past research has provided many useful insights about the management of uncertainty. Individuals as well as organizations are often uncomfortable with uncertainty due to the inherent lack of predictability, complexity, and unsurity. Uncertainty tends to be cognitively and emotionally challenging. It creates a feeling of vulnerability or anxiety that can lead to actively distorting perceptions and information. This can produce premature closure, false dichotomies, rejection of relevant information, rigid categories, and regression to old rule-of-thumb models of thinking. In addition, the randomness associated with uncertainty makes it difficult to develop strategies that appropriately adapt to present and future circumstances.

As past research has clearly indicated, people have a tendency to either avoid or embrace uncertainty. The Uncertainty Management Matrix juxtaposes the individual employee's tolerance for uncertainty and the organization's desire to embrace uncertainty (see Figure 3.1). Those who embrace it see uncertainty as challenging, desirable, invigorating, and useful. They do not try to artificially drive the ambiguities and contradictions out of the situation. Those who avoid uncertainty tend to shun complexities and novelty, and prematurely structure ambiguous situations. Organizations, like employees, tend to either avoid or embrace uncertainty. Organizations can drive out uncertainty by overly relying on 'success recipes', the overuse of consultants, and rigid control procedures. They can embrace it by encouraging meaningful dialogue, fostering innovation, and de-emphasizing rigid planning processes.

The conceptual relationship between the way employees and organizations

Embrace

	Stifling climate 3	Dynamic climate 4
Employee's approach to uncertainty	Status quo climate 1	Unsettling climate 2

Avoid

Avoid   Embrace

Figure 3.1 The Uncertainty Management Matrix

manage uncertainty is fairly straightforward. As suggested in Figure 3.1, there are four basic possibilities:

- *Status Quo Climate*   Employees and the organization both avoid uncertainty. Employees want few surprises and they rarely get them.
- *Unsettling Climate*   Employees desire certainty while they perceive the organization as embracing uncertainty. Thus employees become unsettled and perhaps overwhelmed by the chaotic work environment.
- *Stifling Climate*   Employees embrace uncertainty but they perceive that the organization avoids it. The result: employees feel stifled.
- *Dynamic Climate*   Both employees and the organization embrace uncertainty. Employees want change and progress and the organization promotes it.

Each quadrant represents a different kind of organizational climate, with varying beliefs, values, assumptions, and ways of communicating.

Measuring the management of uncertainty

We developed the Working Climate Survey (see Appendices 3.1 and 3.2, pages 58–9) to quickly determine which quadrant of the Uncertainty Management Matrix best describes employee experiences. Several data sets, scale development procedures, and factor analyses were employed to refine the instrument (Clampitt *et al.*, 2000). The first twelve items on the scale measure the degree to which an individual avoids or embraces uncertainty. Three factors underlie this Personal Uncertainty Score: (1) perceptual uncertainty, which addresses the individual's willingness to actively look at different perspectives, new ideas, or signs that the situation is changing, (2) process uncertainty, which addresses the employee's comfort in making a decision on an intuition or a hunch, and (3) outcome uncertainty, which addresses the individual's need to have detailed plans or know the specific outcome of a task or project. The items on this scale are summed so that a high score indicated a greater tendency for the person to embrace uncertainty.

Items 13 to 24 on the Working Climate Survey measure employees' perceptions of how their organization manages uncertainty. The three underlying factors for the Work Environment Uncertainty Score are: (1) perceptual uncertainty, which assesses the degree to which the organization is willing to actively look for new ideas to address problems or signs that the situation is changing, (2) expressed uncertainty, which assesses the degree to which the organization encourages employees to express doubts or misgivings, and (3) outcome uncertainty, which assesses the degree to which the organization needs detailed plans or a specific outcome before starting a project. The items on this scale are summed so that a high score indicated a greater tendency for the organization to embrace uncertainty.

The Uncertainty Management Matrix displayed in Figure 3.2 joins the individual employee's tolerance for uncertainty (as measured by the Personal Uncertainty Score) and the organization's desire to embrace uncertainty (as measured by the Work Environment Uncertainty Score). A median split procedure was used to divide each measure into levels of high or low (i.e. embrace or avoid uncertainty).

Research findings

To date, over 1,000 employees have taken the Working Climate Survey. The database includes employees from a wide variety of organizations as well as a mix of managerial and non-managerial employees. The normative data includes 36 per cent males and 64 per cent females. Job positions are identified as: 9 per cent top management, 40 per cent management, 27 per cent non-management professional, 19 per cent non-management, and 5 per cent other. The average age is 39.4 years, with employees ranging from 16 to 74 years old. The average

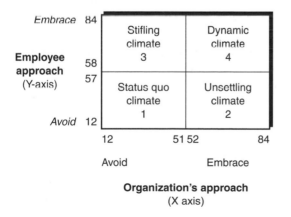

Figure 3.2 Plotting scores on the Uncertainty Management Matrix

tenure at their current job is 7.0 years, with time on the job ranging from 1 month to 40 years.

The database reveals some interesting trends about the various climates:

- In the Status Quo Climate, there are proportionately more non-profit organizations than financial, industrial, and information/technology organizations.
- In the Unsettling Climate, there are proportionately more financial organizations; however, other types of organizations are relatively equally distributed.
- In the Stifling Climate, the types of organizations are relatively equally distributed.
- In the Dynamic Climate there are proportionately more financial, information/technology, and industrial organizations than non-profit organizations.
- A larger proportion of top managers and managers are in the Dynamic Climate and Stifling Climate. These are climates where employees embrace uncertainty.
- Proportionately more women are in the Unsettling and Status Quo Climates (both of which are climates where employees avoid uncertainty) than in the Dynamic and Stifling Climates.
- Employees in the Dynamic and Unsettling Climates (both of which are climates where employees see their organization embracing uncertainty) express more satisfaction with their job, more commitment to their organization, greater identification with their organization, more satisfaction with organizational communication, more satisfaction with communication with their supervisor, and less cynicism about organizational life.
- Employees in the Status Quo and Stifling Climates (both of which are climates where employees see their organization avoiding uncertainty) express less satisfaction with their job, less commitment to their organization, less identification with their organization, less satisfaction with organizational communication, less satisfaction with communication with their supervisor, and more cynicism about organizational life.

Overall, these results suggest the following order of desirability of organizational climates (from most to least desirable climates): Dynamic Climate, Unsettling Climate, Stifling Climate, Status Quo Climate.

Practitioner perspective

Assessing the management of uncertainty

The glorification of change is widespread in many organizations today (Zorn *et al.*, 1999). Restructuring, reengineering, transformation, and renewal are seen as marks of progress. Employees are expected to add 'flexibility' to their repertoire of contemporary work skills. But the current romance with change masks a variety of problems. Change often creates high uncertainty, and many are being forced to change beyond their psychological, or perhaps even physical limits. Often organizational change is not sequential (i.e., one change followed by another) but simultaneous (Conner, 1993). The mental demands of work, family, and citizenship in a diverse society create enormous challenges for twenty-first century workers (Kegan, 1994). The volume and pace of change reduces feelings of constancy and stability while greatly increasing feelings of randomness and uncertainty.

To maximize effectiveness, organizations must conceive a change model which takes into consideration not only the environmental factors calling for change but also their employees' ability to embrace uncertainty and readiness for change. The Working Climate Survey and Uncertainty Management Matrix can be used to develop a framework for assessing perceptions about uncertainty as well as implementing change strategies (see Box 3.1).

Step 1

The first step in this process is to select the unit of change. Often organizations make the mistake of designing a change process for the organization as a whole where 'one message fits all'. Unfortunately, this approach fails to consider the complexities of sub-systems as well as diverse populations in the organization. Failure to consider the sub-audiences can lead to inappropriate strategy selection and unenlightened communications. To truly understand and analyse the organization before implementing change, it is our belief that all change efforts must initially focus on work units under the span of control of a manager. For most organizations, the lowest level work units are under the direction of a first-level supervisor.

Step 2

After determining the work units in an organization, the next step is to use the Working Climate Survey to measure how employees embrace or avoid uncertainty as well as how they perceive their organization dealing with uncertainty. As discussed earlier, this instrument (see Appendices 3.1 and 3.2, pages 58–9) produces two scores. The Personal Uncertainty Score (items 1–12) ranges from 12 to 84, with a high score indicating the employee embraces uncertainty.

Box 3.1   Assessment steps

Step 1	• Select proper unit of analysis.
Step 2	• Administer Working Climate Survey to unit.
Step 3	• Determine predominant working climate.
Step 4	• Develop action plans.
Step 5	• Implement action plans.

The Work Environment Uncertainty Score (items 13–24) also ranges from 12 to 84, with a high score indicating the employee perceives the organization embracing uncertainty.

After all employees in a work unit have completed the two scales, each individual can then be placed in one of the four climates in the Uncertainty Management Matrix (see Figure 3.2). Normative data (n = 789) indicate the median score for personal uncertainty is 57, the mean is 57.31, and the standard deviation is 8.11 (Clampitt and DeKoch, 2001). Normative data for work environment uncertainty indicate the median score for work environment uncertainty is 51, the mean is 51.75, and the standard deviation is 9.66. Using these norms, each employee's Personal Uncertainty Score can be plotted on the Y axis and Work Environment Uncertainty Score plotted on the X axis. The intersection of these scores places the employee in the Status Quo Climate, Unsettling Climate, Stifling Climate, or Dynamic Climate.

Step 3

Next, the climate configuration for the individuals in each work unit is assessed to determine the predominant climate for the unit. For example, if a work unit contains ten employees, comprised of seven in the Unsettling Climate and three in the Status Quo Climate, the predominant climate for this work unit is Unsettling. Since social units tend create a common reality (Weick, 1995), most work units should converge around a predominant climate. We suggest that if 60 per cent or more of the employees are identified in the same climate, the work unit should be classified as having a predominant climate. Two other configurations are also possible. Work units can be bifurcated, where approximately one-half are grouped in one climate and approximately one-half are in another climate. Units can also be mixed, where there is no clear pattern for one climate to prevail over others.

Step 4

Once work units in an organization have been classified, the next step is to create an action plan that best fits the climate of each work unit. Across the organization, it is possible that one climate predominates, but typically all four climates will be represented. For ultimate effectiveness, action plans for each climate should be developed instead of focusing exclusively on the most frequently occurring climate.

An important question that must be addressed is whether a work unit climate is acceptable or if changes need to be made. The practitioner should first ask whether the climate needs to be changed. It is entirely possible, for instance, that a Status Quo Climate best fits the environmental or organizational situation. While a shift to a Dynamic Climate might improve employee satisfaction and commitment, it may not be possible or even appropriate. For example, workers at a fast-food restaurant may not particularly enjoy the routine but such a shift might involve such expenditures of scarce resources that the organization chooses not to make the investment.

Developing action plans is easiest when work units can be classified as having a predominant climate. When work units are bifurcated (i.e. divided into two relatively equal climates) or mixed, planning is more difficult. If units are bifurcated, managers can develop plans for the two separate subgroups and design semi-autonomous strategies. While this procedure is not as efficient, it adapts to the uncertainty orientations of the employees and should produce greater change. In work units that have mixed climates, managers are forced to deal more with individuals than groups. Here change strategies are directed more towards the specific needs of individual employees, and managers must work on more of a one-to-one basis. In addition, managers must understand each of the cultures represented in their work unit as well as develop a larger repertoire of skills.

Step 5

The final step in this process is implementing the action plans. The determination of necessary resources, time required, specific tactics to follow, and management training are all dependent on the climate of each work unit. Judicious implementation across the various climates will adapt to the distinctive needs of employees in the various work units, thereby effectively managing uncertainty and increasing the probability of organizational effectiveness.

Communication strategies

Our assessment process does not imply that one climate is necessarily more appropriate than another. Each presents a special challenge. Assuming that altering the climate suits the situation, then the practitioner needs to develop the appropriate transformation approach. Based on our research, we can suggest ways to achieve meaningful change in each quadrant (see Table 3.2).

Status Quo Climate

Employees in the Status Quo Climate lack confidence in their own abilities to embrace uncertainty and they share the same view about their organization. Our research suggests that positive benefits can occur by cultivating an organizational climate perceived as embracing uncertainty. In other words, the initial objective should be to shift the climate from the Status Quo to Unsettling. This implies an emphasis on the organizational level rather than the individual employee level. Educating individual employees about the competencies associated with embracing uncertainty usually proves more difficult than shifting perceptions of the organization. Strategically this means gradually introducing changes in organizational procedures and practices that foster greater awareness and discussion of uncertainty. Employees may not readily accept these changes,

Table 3.2 Approaches for transforming uncertainty management climates

	Status Quo	Unsettling	Stifling	Dynamic
Focus	Cultivate an organizational climate that embraces uncertainty.	Encourage employee development in order to sustain the organization's ability to embrace uncertainty.	Utilize the unit to encourage the organization to embrace uncertainty.	Provide parameters and focus for embracing uncertainty.
Strategy	• Gradually introduce the need for organizational change. • Properly balance the need for change with the unit's comfort level.	• Personalize the implications of organizational uncertainty. • Legitimize concerns about personal implications. • Develop necessary competencies.	• Establish relationships with key organizational 'change agents'. • Seek positions to gain influence in the power structure. • Create mechanisms to foster awareness and discussion of uncertainty.	• Make value-driven choices and tradeoffs. • Listen and respond to feedback about strategic choices. • Drive towards action.
Tactics	• Focus on issues external to the unit. • Frame the challenge in terms of 'what if' situations. • Constantly reassure employees. • Use opinion leaders to create acceptance. • Publicize small successes. • Symbolically acknowledge uncertainty.	• Provide training in managing emotions, expectations, and problem solving. • Translate abstractions into concrete examples. • Create 'spaces' to jointly explore the implications of uncertainty. • Encourage dialogue that elicits emotional responses.	• Network. • Exercise patience. • Develop leadership skills (e.g. organizing, meeting management). • Provide training on listening, framing, and relational sensitivity. • Develop programmes, procedures, and processes to harvest and respond to dissent.	• Track and rigorously assess responses to ongoing initiatives. • Develop symbolic ways to energize but limit employees. • Develop employees' conceptualizing skills. • Use strategic ambiguity. • Frame issues in terms of values, goals, and responses to initiatives.

continued

Table 3.2 continued

	Status Quo	Unsettling	Stifling	Dynamic
What to avoid	• Assuming that employees will readily acknowledge and understand the uncertainty. • Discounting the organization's vulnerability. • Setting unrealistic expectations of organizational leaders. • Underestimating the momentum of avoidance.	• Assuming that employees will know what to do after they acknowledge uncertainty. • Assuming that employees will react 'logically' to uncertainty. • Expecting that everyone can acquire the appropriate skills.	• Assuming that the organization desires to embrace uncertainty (e.g. dissent). • Focusing on winning every argument at the expense of relationship development. • Allowing the expression of opinion to become more important than problem solving (e.g. 'I bitch, you fix').	• Assuming that the organization can embrace all uncertainties. • Blindly focusing on procedures and processes. • Becoming overconfident of success because the organization is on the 'cutting edge'. • Avoiding evaluation of initiatives.

so change agents need to balance their initiatives with employees' comfort level.

Any number of different tactics might be employed to implement this strategy. For example, a change agent might initially focus on issues external to the unit, thereby creating the right balance between comfort and discomfort. Likewise, posing hypothetical scenarios can encourage employees to think about the inherent uncertainties in the organizational environment. Using opinion leaders to create acceptance of new thinking routines and publicizing small successes can also ease employees into the Unsettling Climate.

Unsettling Climate

Employees who dwell in the Unsettling Climate believe that their organization embraces uncertainty, but feel ill-equipped to personally do so. These employees tend to be almost as satisfied and committed as those living in the Dynamic Climate. Some may never be able or motivated to acquire all the uncertainty management competencies. Yet, the organization has a vested interest in encouraging as many employees as possible to develop these abilities. Without that kind of leadership, the organization cannot sustain these highly motivating climates. Strategically this means that change agents need to start personalizing the implications of the organizational uncertainty. In the Unsettling Climate, uncertainty is present but impersonal, while in the Dynamic Climate it is both present and personal. Of course, that shift may induce anxieties driven by emotions and skill deficiencies. So wise strategists attack those issues as well.

Tactically, change agents might start with providing training in managing emotions, expectations, and problem solving. At a more fundamental level, employees who have traditionally been buffered from organizational uncertainty need to confront concrete examples, not mere abstractions. This means change agents need to create 'spaces' to explore and discuss uncertainty. These 'spaces' could range from a face-to-face meeting focused on discussing new industry trends to electronic bulletin boards designed to create an on-going dialogue about an issue impacting the organization. The right kind of virtual or physical space can serve to cultivate an employee comfort level with organizational uncertainty. However, change agents should avoid assuming that employees will know what to do after acknowledging the uncertainty or that they will always react logically (as opposed to emotionally) to their heightened sensitivities.

Stifling Climate

Employees in the Stifling Climate are frustrated because they feel well equipped to manage uncertainty but believe their organizations do not respond in kind. Sometimes units like this get labeled as troublemakers or malcontents because they may verbalize their frustration. The challenge for a unit in this situation is to use their expertise and insight to transform the organization in positive ways. Strategically they can do so by establishing relationships with influential organizational leaders, seeking positions of influence, and creating mechanisms designed to better manage uncertainty in the organizational environment.

Translating this strategy into action requires patience above all. Employees will need to develop networks of influence as well as the necessary leadership and communication skills. In particular, employees need to focus on sensitivity to relational dynamics because of their tendency to think, 'I see the big picture, you don't'. (Clearly, such attitudes tend to *build* rather than *tear down* barriers.) Assuming that these employees have acquired the appropriate skills and started to exert some influence, they still will need to establish organizational routines, such as creating the appropriate procedures, policies and practices to transform the organization. For instance, at one manufacturing plant we developed a process designed to quickly harvest employee dissent by routinely e-mailing different groups of employees a short questionnaire asking them about their current concerns about the plant (Clampitt et al., 2000). This process encouraged executives to respond to the concerns, thereby communicating about a range of issues they would never have discussed using their former procedures. Some organizations are simply unwilling to tolerate 'dissent' of this type. Change agents need to be aware of this possibility.

Dynamic Climate

The Dynamic Climate might seem to be the ideal. After all, both the employees and organization embrace uncertainty. But employees and organizations can embrace too much uncertainty, thereby rendering both ineffectual. In short, they can chase too many different possibilities, always dreaming and exploring while not accomplishing much of anything. Therefore, units in this quadrant need parameters and focus. On a strategic level, this requires that they make value-driven choices and act on those decisions. It also requires that the unit listen and respond to feedback about those strategic choices.

On a tactical level a variety of approaches may be used to implement these strategies. Leaders can frame issues in terms of values and goals, while developing symbolic tools that both energize and limit the organization. For example, Appleton Papers has used the value of CFQ (Customer Focused Quality) to embrace all kinds of new initiatives designed to foster better relationships with existing customers while still providing the focus necessary for progress (Clampitt, 2000). In some cases executives chose not to pursue some opportunities because they lacked a deep understanding of customers in those markets. At the most fundamental level, these tactics are designed to develop employees' conceptualizing skills, allowing them to quickly link the 'big picture' (for example values, goals, etc.) to specific decisions. Of course, such mental acumen proves useless without putting systems in place to clearly track and evaluate responses to on-going initiatives.

Case studies

In the final section of this chapter we discuss several case studies illustrating the successful transformation of employee units from one climate to another.

Transforming a Status Quo Climate

While deregulation is a fact of life for utility companies in the US today, this is a relative recent change. Up until the 1970s, many of these companies had a virtual monopoly and operated in a Status Quo Climate. Such was the case of a large utility company in the southwestern region of the United States. This organization supplied electricity for almost a million customers as well as providing water and flood management for state residents. The organization owned the dams that generated the electricity as well as the power lines and distribution centres. Since, by law, there was no competition, they were free to set utility rates as they pleased. Even when customers complained and circumstances called for improved services, the organization often was slow to respond. Due to their exclusive control, management was able to avoid uncertainty and ignore growing discontent from the external environment. By following long-established policies and procedures, they could deliver a quality product (at least in the eyes of management!) and minimize the need for disruption and change. Employees were well paid and enjoyed working in an organization that provided long-term security, a community spirit, and freedom to pursue individual, non work related activities such as hunting and fishing.

Status Quo climates include employees that avoid uncertainty as well as an organization that resists change. This mentality was evidenced in an analogy often repeated by the general manager of the utility company. Since many of the employees were males from a rural, agricultural background, he would metaphorically refer to the organization as a produce company. He asserted that they not only owned the fields (i.e., generation plants) but also the farm-to-market roads (i.e., power lines), and the market place (i.e., delivery to customers). The company could decide what crops to grow, how many, and when they would be shipped. Delivery was dependent on their choosing, supply and demand was under their control, and profits were inevitable. Even though they avoided uncertainty, the organization prospered, and employees grew accustomed to a work pace that was predictable, routine, and non-innovative.

With the introduction of deregulation in the utility industry, however, this Status Quo Climate was forever changed. In an effort to survive, the utility company was forced to attend to the external environment, embrace uncertainty, and change employee values within the organizational culture. The general manager helped transform the organization by adjusting his produce analogy. His new message was that even though they no longer owned all the fields (i.e., generation plants) and there were new players in the market place, they still controlled the roadway (i.e., power lines). He helped employees see how their forty years of experience gave them a significant advantage over the competition, and how their new business plan was a variation of the theme they had always followed. Their new direction would focus on establishing competitive rates for using their power lines as well as expanding their water resources business, which was less vulnerable to external competition. While the new environment would be more unsettling, employees were reassured to see they still maintained a degree of control and that changes could be negotiated at a manageable pace.

Transforming a Stifling Climate

Employees in a Stifling Climate embrace uncertainty but perceive the organization as avoiding uncertainty. Typically, they are employees in development areas who are on the informational cutting-edge, are cognizant of the latest technology, are well networked to sources external to the organization, and are eager to experiment with new ideas and procedures. These employees experience considerable discontent, however, when their organization resists change, follows established bureaucratic procedures, and is reluctant to take financial risks. Frustration mounts when their innovative proposals are met with either overt rejection by management or more subtle forms of disconfirmation such as indifference, delayed responses, and critical humour.

University campuses often unwittingly cultivate Stifling Climates. Many faculty members are interested in developing new courses or proposing innovative partnerships with other colleagues or universities only to find that their larger university system is not prepared to accommodate them. Such was the case of one professor who helped author a grant whereby universities in Italy, Austria, and the United States would cooperatively deliver a web-based virtual international classroom. The large state university where the professor taught readily endorsed his participation since it fell under the university's initiative on the use of innovative teaching technology and international involvement. However, the professor soon discovered that the infrastructure of his university created more obstacles than support. First he learned that since the course was not taught on-campus or at one of the off-campus facilities, there was no way he could be paid for teaching the course. The state had no established procedures for web-based, international ventures, and the university lacked the resources to influence state policy. Then it was discovered that the university had no provisions under which an international course could be taught as part of the professor's regular workload, and that it would have to be taught as an overload. Finally, the grants office created additional obstacles when it, under the university's operating policy, required a large percentage of the grant funding be directed to this office for processing the grant. In actuality, the professor did all the work without input from the grants office, but the university required that all projects be processed through this office and pay the appropriate fees. The response of the professor, after enduring all the hassles created by the university, was 'No good deed goes unpunished!' He had embraced the uncertainty of pursuing an innovative teaching partnership but was stifled by an organizational system driven by a rigid set of established procedures that were resistant to change. He, of course, was not alone. Many others had run into similar problems.

Assuming that the professors at this university want to transform the climate, they have various options available. One would be to persuade university officials to create a separate entity in the organization with the personnel and resources to pursue more innovative projects. Coordinators in this office of special projects could be assigned to less orthodox proposals that meet key university initiatives. They would serve as well-informed liaisons that could circumnavigate the complexities of bureaucratic structures and locate sources of funding separate from established institutions with their entangling policies and requirements. For example, they might arrange for professors to receive one-quarter to one-half release time from the university to participate in the web-based virtual international classroom. Funding for the release time could come from private donations or endowments designed to support innovative teaching or research projects. Such a process would bypass the restrictive organizational structure that is not prepared to manage pioneering projects as well as eliminate the excessive fees levied by the grants office.

Transforming an Unsettling Climate

The supervisors of a 150-employee dairy plant may have lacked confidence in their own abilities to embrace uncertainty but they knew all too well that the organization's executive team readily took on the challenges of an ever-changing competitive environment. Typically when there were new organizational initiatives, the supervisors would simply wait for new rules and regulations detailing how they should implement the initiatives. Even though the supervisors were given latitude to adjust the regulations to better 'fit' their unit, they avoided doing so because, after all, 'rules are rules'. It was clear that the flexible orientation of the dairy's executive team did not permeate the supervisory rank. (It is interesting to note that while the Unsettling Climate best characterized the atmosphere for this supervisory team, the Status Quo Climate best characterized most of the union members.)

To create a climate that was more in line with the executive team's culture, a consulting team was brought in to 'develop the leadership potential' of this group. In other words, the objective was to develop the competencies of the supervisors so that the Unsettling Climate was transformed into a Dynamic one.

The consultants' first task was formulate a set of plant value statements with the supervisors. The objective was for them to develop an approach or a thinking process for making decisions and managing conflicts that went beyond typical rules and regulations.

The consultants held frequent training sessions to ensure that the supervisors were consistently applying this management style. They role-played numerous situations in which a supervisor could use a value-driven verses a rule-driven approach to manage conflicts. This was difficult for some who routinely fell back on their rule-driven (and certainty-producing) mindset. However, a few of the supervisors were particularly adept at embracing the uncertainty inherent in the value-driven approach.

The consultants then held individual coaching sessions with these particularly skilled individuals. One supervisor emerged as the natural leader; he had the ability to both advocate and build the Dynamic Climate. He had much to do with transforming the climate and was eventually promoted to be the plant manager.

Was this process successful? We believe so. Executives started noticing that supervisors more readily promoted new initiatives and resolved conflicts in more productive ways. In fairness, we should point out that some of the supervisors never really acquired uncertainty-embracing skills but enough did to impact the atmosphere of the entire plant. In fact, the transformation of the supervisory team set in motion a change for many union employees from a Status Quo to Unsettling Climate.

Transforming a Dynamic Climate

While the Dynamic Climate fosters a great working environment, from time to time it may lead to some unique challenges. The Boldt Company, for example, has a leadership team that perfectly fits the Dynamic Climate profile. The team consists of veterans accustomed to an ever-changing marketplace who have both the skill and desire to adapt to the environment. Not surprisingly, the company shares those characteristics by regularly looking for new business opportunities, changing direction when necessary and innovatively responding to new challenges. But several years ago these very characteristics – which foster a highly motivating 'can do' working environment – turned out to be a double-edged sword. The company pursued growth for growth's sake, resulting in taking on some unprofitable projects that drove corporate profits below the industry average.

Addressing this issue required an adept touch because senior executives wanted to preserve the motivating climate. Two particular actions, one serendipitous and the other planned, provided just the nudge to move the company in the right direction.

The serendipitous action involved a discussion of financial issues at a strategic planning retreat. One executive started talking about the need for everyone to find themselves in the 'financial levers'. A dialogue ensued about the proper pronunciation of the word 'lever'. This became a running joke at meetings for the next year but it also drew everyone's attention to the critical issue.

The other action involved creating a communication strategy designed around the theme of 'seizing opportunities for profitable growth'. The notion of 'profitable growth' was critical because it put parameters on the type of growth the company would pursue. Executives weaved this theme into their communications on every possible occasion. For example, employees were invited on a rotating basis to ask questions of the executive team. Whenever someone asked about why the company chose to pursue or not pursue a particular project, the executives linked their answer back to the 'profitable growth' notion. As a result of these sustained actions, the company became more focused as they pursued their profit goals. In short, the company further focused the Dynamic Climate of the organization. In fact, survey data revealed that even with these subtle changes, employee job satisfaction, motivation and commitment remained high.

Conclusion

Traditionally, communication practitioners have devised clever ways to hide or suppress the inherent uncertainties associated with organizational life. Business writers, for example, routinely advised organizational leaders to 'avoid weasel words' and 'use definitive language' (Ober, 1998). Our research and consulting experiences suggest that such practices may create clarity at the expense of distorting the realities that organizations face. Leaders who suppress uncertainty do so at their organization's peril, since their employees tend to be less satisfied and more cynical than those who work in uncertainty-embracing organizations. The challenge for communication scholars and practitioners lies in developing theories, strategies, and practices that focus on embracing uncertainty. This chapter provides only an initial and tentative response to that challenge. Much work remains to be done; that *is* a certainty.

Appendix 3.1: Working Climate Survey

Objective: The purpose of this survey is to accurately describe your working climate. Please note: your responses are confidential, this is *not* a test, and there are no right or wrong answers.

Instructions: Below you will find 24 statements about your approach to various situations. Some items may sound similar, but they address slightly different issues. Please respond to all items. *Indicate your degree of agreement with each statement by placing the appropriate number in the box next to each item.* Please use the following scale:

[1] Strongly disagree	[2] Moderately disagree	[3] Slightly disagree	[4] No feeling	[5] Slightly agree	[6] Moderately agree	[7] Strongly agree

Section A: These questions concern your preferred individual style of working

1	I'm comfortable making a decision on my gut instincts.	
2	I actively look for signs that the situation is changing.	
3	When I start a project, I need to know exactly where I'll end up.	
4	I'm comfortable using my intuition to make a decision.	
5	I'm always on the lookout for new ideas to address problems.	
6	I need to know the specific outcome before starting a task.	
7	I'm quick to notice when circumstances change.	
8	I'm willing to make a decision based on a hunch.	
9	I easily spot changing trends.	
10	I don't need a detailed plan when working on a project.	
11	I need a definite sense of direction for a project.	
12	I'm comfortable deciding on the spur-of-the-moment.	

Section B: *The following questions concern your work environment*

13	My organization is always on the lookout for new ideas to address problems.	
14	In my organization, being unsure about something is a sign of weakness.	
15	My organization easily spots changing trends.	
16	My organization doesn't need a detailed plan when working on a project.	
17	Even after my organization makes a decision, it will re-evaluate the decision when the situation changes.	
18	My organization needs to know the specific outcome before starting a project.	
19	My organization doesn't encourage employees to discuss their doubts about a project.	
20	When my organization starts a project, it needs to know exactly where the project will end up.	
21	My organization actively looks for signs that the situation is changing.	
22	My organization doesn't want employees to admit that they are unsure about something.	
23	My organization wants precise plans before starting a job or project.	
24	My organization discourages employees from talking about their misgivings.	

Appendix 3.2

Scoring Instructions*

Step 1: Reverse score items 3, 6, 11, 14, 18, 19, 20, 22, 23, and 24 so that $1 = 7$, $2 = 6$, $3 = 5$, $4 = 4$, $5 = 3$, $6 = 2$, and $7 = 1$.

Step 2: Sum items 1–12 to get the Personal Uncertainty Score.

Step 3: Sum items 13–24 to get the Work Environment Uncertainty Score.

Step 4: Plot scores on Figure 3.2.

*Readers can also use the following website for automatic tabulation: www.iMetacomm.com. Select the 'tools' tab.

4 Managing change

Communication and political process

Patrick Dawson

Introduction

This chapter sets out to examine organizational change and communication. It provides a brief overview of the main competencies and guidelines offered in the prescriptive change management literature and a critique of the dominant Organizational Development (OD) approach. It is argued that the common claim that communication is fundamental to change is too readily linked with an assumption that communication is an apolitical neutral activity and that the OD perspective (which emphasizes planned participative change strategies) is an accurate reflection of how change unfolds in practice. However, this perspective is increasingly being called into question by the work of change writers who take a more critical perspective (for example Collins, 1998; Burnes, 2000; Knights and Willmott, 2000). These writers demonstrate how the process of change does not roll out in an uncomplicated way – as many stage models suggest (Collins, 1998), nor can it be viewed as an apolitical process (Buchanan and Badham, 1999). This chapter thereby sets out to counter-balance uncritical OD accounts on communication and change through incorporating an analysis of political processes.

The section that follows commences with a brief overview of the treatment of communication in the change management literature. A number of best practice guidelines are identified and the dominant planned approach to change is critically appraised. The need to address the influence of power and politics on communication and change is then taken up in a section on political process. Some of the more critical studies on organizational change are used to question a commonly held assumption (noticeable within the prescriptive literature) that communication is neutral and apolitical. The chapter concludes by calling for further critical discussion and research on how information is used and communicated in the purposeful objective of securing particular political ends during the process of organizational change.

Change management: The communication imperative

Within the popular management literature, John Kotter (1996) has put forward an eight-stage model on how to successfully manage change. This comprises:

1   Communicate a sense of urgency.
2   Create a vision.
3   Communicate the vision.
4   Form a powerful coalition.
5   Empower others to act.
6   Plan short-term wins.
7   Consolidate change.
8   Institutionalize new approaches.

Kotter (1996) noted how 50 per cent of companies fail during the earlier stages of change and this is often because of a failure by senior executives to effectively communicate and establish a sense of urgency. Communicating the vision is also viewed as a critical stage in leading change. He argues that change leaders should communicate their vision in many different forums over and over again if they wish to develop an effective implementation strategy. On the flip side, he claims that a major reason why change initiatives fail is because of ineffective communication. This takes three main forms:

1   Communication is limited to only a few memos.
2   The head of the company makes many speeches but everybody else remains silent.
3   There is effort in communicating the vision but the behaviour of some highly visible individuals conflicts with the message communicated, and employee cynicism results.

As Kotter pointed out:

> Communication comes in both words and deeds. The latter is generally the most powerful form. Nothing undermines change more than behavior by important individuals that is inconsistent with the verbal communication. And yet this happens all the time, even in some well-regarded companies.
>
> (Kotter, 1996: 10)

Conventional texts on managing change recognize communication as one of the most important aspects in an organization undergoing change (Jackson and Callan, 2001). For example, Hayes (2002) argued that the features of communication networks and the effects of interpersonal relations can have a major influence on the process and outcomes of organizational change. Particular attention is given to the notion of 'effective communication' that informs employees, enables feedback and promotes widescale consultation. Many writers in this area assume that such action will overcome resistance to change (resistance is often seen to stem from natural anxiety, ignorance and misunderstanding) by stimulating interest and commitment and thereby reducing opposition (for example Paton and McCalman, 2000).

Hersey and Blanchard (1988) argued that communication is a key process skill required of change agents to get others to understand and accept change.

Drawing on the work of Bennis (1984), Carnall (2003) viewed this as involving an ability to communicate clear objectives, to be consistent especially under conditions of change, and to ensure that others understand and are aware of the reasons and intentions of change. These three competencies he labels as: the management of attention, the management of trust, and the management of meaning (Carnall, 2003). Paton and McCalman (2000) also identified a number of competencies or guidelines on effective communication and change. These are as follows:

- to customize the message to ensure that it is set at an appropriate level to be understood by the intended audience
- to set the tone of the message so it does not offend or seem patronizing
- to recognize that communication is a two-way process and that feedback is essential
- to do as you say (to practise what you preach)
- to use the appropriate medium to ensure penetration, so that the message reaches those it is intended to reach in the time required.

Similarly, the dominant textbook OD approach to organizational change – which developed from the pioneering work of Kurt Lewin (1947) – also spotlighted the importance of communication and employee involvement (Huse, 1982). This approach is based on the human relations perspective that emphasizes the importance of participation and collaboration through a two-way process of communication (French and Bell, 1983). Typically (Beckhard, 1969), the OD approach:

- is planned
- attempts to consider and include all members of the organization
- involves the proposed change being supported by top management
- has the objectives of change as being to improve working conditions and organizational effectiveness
- involves an emphasis being placed on behavioural science techniques, which facilitates communication and problem solving among members.

As a planned approach to change management it prescribes a number of key steps. These were explained by Collins:

> While *n-step* guides to change may differ in terms of the number of steps they assume necessary for success in change management, they are similar along a few key dimensions ... the key features of under-socialized models of change include: a 'rational' analysis of organizational change; a sequential approach to the planning and management of change; [and] a generally up-beat and prescriptive tone.
>
> (Collins, 1998: 84)

The OD approach to change management: a reappraisal

The most common distinguishing characteristics of modern OD approaches are summarized in Box 4.1, based on the work of French (1969) and French and Bell (1983).

The OD approach involves a number of steps, commencing with the appointment of a change agent (usually an individual outside the organization) who intervenes to start the change process. Information is then gathered from the client system (data) in order to identify the major areas in need of change and following feedback to the client appropriate plans are formulated and action taken. Planning is generally viewed as a collaborative process based on valid information. Following implementation, changes are evaluated and action taken to ensure the 'institutionalization' of change occurs (Burke, 1994). In the action-research model of OD (that entails cycles of data gathering, diagnosis and feedback), the six major steps comprise: identifying a need for change; selecting an intervention technique; gaining top management support; planning the change process; overcoming resistance to change; and evaluating the change process (Aldag and Stearns, 1991). Taken as a whole, this approach downplays political process in searching for a common consensual view that is held by all employees and in so doing, adopts a normative framework that promotes a one best way to

Box 4.1 Modern OD approaches to change

- The focus of the change effort is on the whole system (whether an organization or a divisional department).
- The change programme involves planned interventions that are introduced systematically.
- Top-down strategies are applied: that is, change begins at the top of an organization and is gradually applied downward throughout the organization.
- Employees at all levels of an organization must engage with the proposed change (in other words, change must never be forced).
- Change is made slowly, allowing for the continual assessment of change strategies.
- Specialist change agents are typically used to guide OD programmes.
- The approach is interdisciplinary, drawing on behavioural science knowledge.
- OD programmes are based on data, so that choices are made on the basis of objective information rather than on the basis of assumptions about what the real issues are.
- The objective of change narratives are to achieve lasting rather than temporary change within an organization.
- The OD approach can be used with both healthy and unhealthy organizations.

manage change that will increase both organizational effectiveness and employee well-being. The professional consultants engaged in OD are not concerned with the development of theory or with the design of systematic programmes of research but, rather, with a set of normative prescriptions which guide their practice in managing change (Ledford *et al.*, 1990).

This leaves open the question of: what are the foundations of this approach and how useful is OD to understanding communication and change in the twenty-first century? To answer this question, we must return to the seminal work of Kurt Lewin who has been identified as the founding father of OD. As Burke has indicated:

> His thinking has had a more pervasive impact on organization development, both direct and indirect, than any other person's ... According to Lewin, behavior is a function of a person's personality, discussed primarily in terms of motivation or needs, and the situation or environment in which the person is acting. The environment is represented as a field of forces that affect the person. Thus, a person's behavior at any given moment can be predicted if we know that person's needs and if we can determine the *intensity* and *valence* (whether the force is positive or negative for the person) of the forces impinging on the person from the environment.
>
> (Burke, 1994: 41)

As a German Jew, Lewin was forced to leave Germany in 1933 and this early experience of anti-Semitism is shown in his concern for democracy and participation at the workplace (De Board, 1978). His work on inter-group dynamics and change has proven to be particularly influential on those practising within the field of Organizational Development (OD), and many theories of organizational change originate from his landmark work on planned change (Kreitner and Kinicki, 1992). Essentially, Lewin (1951) argued that in order for change to be successfully managed it is necessary to follow three general steps, comprising: unfreezing, changing, and refreezing. Unfreezing is the stage in which there is a recognized need for change and action is taken to unfreeze existing attitudes and behaviour. This initial phase is seen to be critical to gaining employee support. For example, in his pioneering research (some of which was published after his death in 1947), Lewin found that in order to minimize worker resistance, employees should be brought in to participate in the process of planning proposed change programmes (Clutterbuck and Crainer, 1990).

Managing change through reducing the forces that prevent change, rather than through increasing the forces which are pushing for change, is central to Lewin's approach and his technique of force-field analysis (1947). He maintained that within any social system there are driving and restraining forces which serve to maintain the status quo, and that organizations generally exist:

> In a state of equilibrium which is not itself conducive to change ... The opposing pressures of driving and restraining forces will combine to produce

a quasi-stationary equilibrium – a kind of temporary state of balance. In order to promote the right conditions for change, individuals have to identify driving and restraining forces. Then there has to be an unfreezing of the quasi-stationary equilibrium. This means creating an imbalance between the driving and restraining forces.

(Wilson, 1992: 29–30)

The example of drink-driving illustrates this where, although there may be strong driving forces to stop drinking and driving, such as public condemnation, fear of losing one's driving licence, cost, new laws, publicity campaigns, disapproval of spouse and the concern of harming others, the restraining forces of habit, camaraderie, relief of tension, friends drinking, social pressure and the dislike of coercive methods may act to maintain the status quo. If these two opposing forces are equal in strength, then a state of equilibrium is said to exist. Consequently, to bring about change you either need to increase the strength of the driving forces or decrease the strength of the resisting forces. For example, publicity campaigns and television advertisements that stress the antisocial and irresponsible behaviour of drink-drivers can have a major influence on public behaviour and attitudes. Communicating a message not only about the illegality of such behaviours but also about the dangers and dire effects on other people's lives can bring about significant changes in public values and beliefs. This illustrates the key role of communication in facilitating change.

In the management of organizational change, the focus of OD specialists has been on communicating information that will serve to unfreeze the system through reducing the restraining forces rather than increasing the driving forces (Gray and Starke, 1988; Weisbord, 1988). Once an imbalance has been created then the system can be altered and a new set of driving and restraining forces put into place. A planned change programme is implemented, and only when the desired state has been achieved will the change agent set about 'refreezing' the organization. The new state of balance is then appraised and, where appropriate, methods of positive reinforcement are used to ensure employees 'internalize' attitudes and behaviours consistent with new work regimes.

Lewin's planned model of change is an integral part of the conventional orthodoxy taught in business departments and management schools around the world. This is surprising in the 1990s and 2000s, given that the linearity of the model is not supported by the empirical evidence (McLoughlin and Clark, 1994; Allan, 1995). As Kanter and colleagues indicated, 'organizations are never frozen, much less refrozen, but are fluid entities' (Kanter *et al.*, 1992: 10). However, the persistence of this model may not only reflect its historical antecedents and a reluctance to change course outlines, but also be due to the symbolic and legitimating function it affords the change agent. As Buchanan and Boddy argued:

Before dismissing rational-linear models of change, it is necessary to consider the symbolic function of such processes in sustaining the 'myth of organizational rationality' and, by implication, sustaining the legitimacy of the change agent. Such linear models may have a poor relationship with the actual unfolding of organizational changes, while in practice playing a significant symbolic and legitimating function in scripting the ritual that the change agent is required and expected to follow to gain organizational acceptance.

(Buchanan and Boddy, 1992: 24)

The strength of the Lewinian model also lies in its simple representation (which makes it easy to use and understand); however, this is also its major weakness as it presents a unidirectional model of change. In other words, by creating an image of a need to design in stability (refreezing), the model has a tendency to solidify what is a dynamic and complex process. It may also result in the creation of cultures and structures not conducive to continuous change. On this point, Marvin Weisbord (1988) has argued that Lewin's concept begins to fall apart as the rate of market and technological change enters a state of perpetual transition, rather than the 'quasi-stationary equilibrium'. The OD camp has also been criticized for failing to account for the increasing incidence of revolutionary change which, according to Dunphy and Stace (1990), may more effectively be achieved by coercive top-down strategies of change. For example, they point out that OD practitioners have tended to focus on collaborative models, whereas corporate strategy consultants have tended to select dictatorial transformation as the appropriate strategy for managing large-scale discontinuous change. Dunphy and Stace argued that, whilst there is a place for each strategy, selection should be made on the basis of dominant contingencies rather than assuming that there is a one best way to fit all occasions.

These non-participatory routes to change draw attention to the exercise of power and the management of conflict. Simple guidelines to effective communication no longer align with actual strategies for bringing about company change nor do they reflect the way communication can act as a powerful tool in ensuring certain preferred outcomes over others. As Buchanan and Badham (1999), in their text on power, politics, and organizational change, iterated, much of the literature on effective change management has largely ignored this issue of political competence and how these skills and knowledge are central to managing in a 'high velocity' organizational context. Indeed as they put it: 'the main argument of this book is that the change agent who is not politically skilled will fail' (p.231). Similarly, Senior (1997), in her book on organizational change, devoted a chapter to the politics of change stressing how issues of power and political action are evident in change programmes where individuals and/or groups seek to influence the attitudes and behaviour of others. Consequently, although academics have generally been slow to criticize the relevance of this model and continue to spread the Lewinian view of change management among their students, there is now a growing recognition of the need for alternative strategies for change (Dunphy and Stace, 1990; Dawson, 1994) and of the political processes involved in the successful management of change (Dawson, 2003).

Beyond n-step models and towards a political process approach

Over the last two decades, the area of change management has been bombarded by books that seek to offer simple recipes for the successful management of change in the never-ending search for competitive advantage (Paton and McCalman, 2000; Hayes, 2002; Carnall, 2003). There are a number of popular accounts which have been produced by leading business figures such as Geneen (Geneen with Moscow, 1986) and Iacocca (Iacocca with Novak, 1985), as well as the more consultant 'guru' publications of writers such as Peters (1988; 1993; 1997), Waterman (Peters and Waterman, 1982) and Kanter (1990). As Huczynski (1993) pointed out in his book *Management Gurus: What Makes Them and How to Become One*, successful gurus tend to share a common set of ideas, which whilst dressed differently represent the reproduction of some fairly long-standing assumptions that support management. In other words, for these ideas to be acceptable they should not undermine the pervasive ideology of management (Grint and Woolgar, 1997). Similarly, academics have tended to be seduced by the attractiveness of memorable models and planned step guides to change, which enable lecturers to portray an ability to keep pace with the barrage of popular panaceas and offer students readily digestible practical benefits.

This reluctance to revisit existing intellectual frameworks is a common phenomenon and is highlighted by the broad range of conventional change models that have tended to dominate academic debate on the study of organizational change (Collins, 1998; Graetz *et al.*, 2002). The continued support for recipe models is surprising given that the linearity of such approaches is not supported by the empirical evidence (McLoughlin and Clark, 1994). As Jick and Peiperl indicated:

> There are no sure-fire instructions that, when scrupulously followed, make change succeed, much less eliminate or solve the problems accompanying any change process. Changing is inherently messy, confusing, and loaded with unpredictability, and no one escapes this fact.
>
> (Jick and Peiperl, 2003: xv)

An example of this was illustrated by Kimble and McLoughlin (1995) in their article on computer-based information systems and the work of managers. From an empirical study of workplace change they concluded that their findings demonstrated the importance of a processual approach:

> The authors believe that theories and methodologies that attempt to locate change in its social and historical context should be developed further ... Technological and organizational development needs to be viewed as a continual and ongoing process. We found in our research that managers were not always prepared for the long time scale over which change takes place, nor for the many twists and turns of the change process.
>
> (Kimble and McLoughlin, 1995: 66)

Another example of the political process of change was usefully demonstrated by Cameron Allan (1995), who provided an analysis of the introduction of Total Quality Management (TQM) into an Australian bank. He described how the process of change involved three distinct periods. In the first period (1986–89), Vicbank identified TQM as a potential means of ensuring business success in a highly competitive finance market. They employed a consultant to help manage the change process, but the uptake of TQM only proved successful in a number of discrete areas and was met with considerable middle managerial resistance. The TQM programme floundered and employee scepticism rose. In a second attempt to introduce change (1989–90), senior management revised their implementation strategy. They placed greater attention on the human resource issues of managing cultural change and yet assumed that they could get everyone to agree to a common set of values and beliefs; as such, this initiative was also destined to fail. In the third period (1990–91), Vicbank brought in communication consultants to help them re-establish TQM. As Allan concluded:

> As successive difficulties arose, the organization evaluated and reappraised the progress to date, assessed new options and implemented new strategies to overcome resistance and implement organizational change. This cycle of experimentation and revision demonstrates that the pathway to organizational change cannot be represented by a straight line or roman road but rather, is a complex, temporal and iterative process. The outcomes of and the barriers to change are never fully known at the outset. The change process will always involve the unanticipated.
>
> (Allan, 1995: 136)

In the UK, an article by Wilkinson and Marchington (1994) that examined TQM and the personnel function in fifteen UK companies also illustrated how change does not take place in a simple linear fashion. In practice, the route to TQM is often marked by a series of stops and starts, of doubt, quandary, scepticism and withdrawal as well as apparent progress (Dawson and Palmer, 1995). These studies highlight how managing communication and change is about managing an unfolding, non-linear, political process in which players are rarely clearly defined and often hold conflicting views and interests. There will be collaboration and conflict, coercion and consultation, in change initiatives, which seek to bring about a fundamental alteration in organizational tasks and activities. During this political process there are likely to be a number of unforeseen contingencies that may necessitate a modification of intended pathways and stated objectives of achieving future planned states. These participatory and non-participatory routes to change draw attention to the exercise of power and the management of conflict. Simple guidelines to effective communication no longer align with actual strategies for bringing about company change nor do they reflect the way communication can act as a powerful political tool in ensuring certain preferred outcomes over others. Drawing on Robbins (1996), Senior (1997: 148) explained that politics can best be understood as 'power in action' that: 'happens whenever people get together in groups and where an individual or group seeks to influence the thoughts, attitudes or behaviours of another individual or group'.

Given the importance of political process to communication, there is a surprising lack of reference to power and politics in the prescriptive literature on change management (Paton and McCalman, 2000). In much of this conventional work, the tendency has been to concentrate on the 'what, when, who and how' of communication rather than on the interpretation and purposeful use or withholding of information in order to achieve a preferred outcome that may not be in the interests of others (Nilakant and Ramnarayan, 1998; Hayes, 2002). Similarly, in the communication literature on change there is little concern with communication as part of an ongoing political process in 'the potential ability to influence behaviour, to change the course of events, to overcome resistance, and to get people to do things that they would otherwise not do' (the definition of power given by Pfeffer, 1993: 204–5). As Lewis and Seibold's (1998) useful review of this large body of literature has shown, there is a tendency for communication scholars to focus on planned organizational change and identify the need for a more integrative conceptual framework for understanding communication and change implementation. Lewis and Seibold (1998) concluded that a communication perspective can significantly improve our understanding of the 'introduction and enactment of planned change efforts', and yet they also provided a rather uncritical, apolitical and linear account of the change process.

In contrast, studies on gender and change, especially within public sector organizations, have demonstrated the importance of power and control in making sense of change (Itzin and Newman, 1995). This more critical work not only introduces the notion of patterns of power and authority in shaping the experience of change at work (French, 1995; Harlow *et al.*, 1995), it also illustrates how the need for well-developed communication and collaborative skills in managing change could provide opportunities for women to be more active agents in steering change (Newman, 1995). These studies also note how the realizations of such opportunities are often prevented by political process and the gendered relations of power in organizations (Williams and Macalpine, 1995). Buchanan and Badham (1999) extended this argument in their book *Power, Politics and Organizational Change*. They argued that the degree of political intensity varies between different change contexts and that this will in turn influence the effectiveness of a range of strategies for managing change. Whilst in one context a more open and communicative approach may be appropriate, under different conditions there may be less time and reason to engage employees in change strategies which may require power-coercive solutions. As they explained:

> Change which is more marginal to the success of the business and which can be implemented at a more relaxed pace allows for extensive participation ... Change proposals which are critical and challenged may have to be driven using power-coercive solutions.
>
> (Buchanan and Badham, 1999: 181)

Power-coercive solutions often involve the manipulation of information in order to communicate to influence decisions and perceptions rather than to provide some form of neutral account (that is, more Machiavellian-type strategies). In a study of TQM and Business Process Re-engineering (BPR), Kelemen *et al.* (2000) used empirical case study data to spotlight how a failure to engage internal stakeholders on the benefits of change resulted in a reconfiguration of change outcomes and a heightening of political game playing. Thus it would appear that not only is communication a central part of the political process of change, but a failure to engage key stakeholder groups through communication can in itself heighten political activity during processes of change. If this growing concern with political process within the change management literature is correct, then there is a need to reconsider the tendency to treat communication as an apolitical component in the change management process.

Politics, communication and the management of change

Following the work of Child (1972), major change can be seen to necessitate strategic choices which are modified and challenged collectively by the workforce, or by individuals and groups of managers who are responsible for the implementation of change. These political processes include elements of conflict and resistance, decision and non-decision making activities, processes of negotiation and consultation, and the multi-level and external individual and group influence on the substance, transition and outcomes of change. They draw attention to the ongoing power plays and political activity, as well as the management of meaning and communication in the construction and reconstruction of change accounts. For example, after-the-fact histories can provide powerful justifications for current courses of action, making the 'legitimate' reconstruction of past events an important political means to promoting future possible change outcomes. In short, political process is endemic to organizations and central to processes of workplace change and the management of information. As noted elsewhere:

> Communication is central to change, but it also needs to be understood in context. As supported by much of the literature, employee communication should be ongoing and consistent. However, change often involves competing narratives, which draws attention back to the political process of change. The choice of what, when and how to communicate as well as the releasing of disconfirming information are often political issues. Communication is an important vehicle both for those seeking to steer change in certain directions and to those wishing to resist the preferred change outcomes of others.
>
> (Dawson, 2003: 174)

As such, the process of communication should not be viewed as a neutral activity but, rather, as part of a political process in which certain individuals and groups typically seek to achieve certain preferred outcomes over others. For example, the political change agenda of management may be consciously serviced by a language that aims to be seen as 'firm' and 'fair' in articulating the need for change, or a 'survival crisis' may be promoted and supported by various forms of communication which seek to engage employees with the urgency of change. Communication is thereby a key political element in the 'successful' management of change, within a context in which there may be considerable disagreement over what constitutes a 'successful' outcome. Substantial time and effort may be spent on communicating management's rationale for change in order to create a climate which is not only conducive to change, but also strongly committed to the senior management's 'vision' of the future. In the case of trade unions, communication is often a significant factor that helps explain why certain change initiatives have been able to harness extensive trade union support (in terms of gaining acceptance for the programme from external full-time trade union officials and internal union representatives), whilst others have not (Dawson, 2003).

Both Pfeffer (1981; 1993) and Pettigrew (1973; 1985) have criticized the more rationalistic, deterministic and ahistorical views on organizational decision making in claiming that politics is at the core of organizational life and should be viewed as a key activity. For example, Pettigrew perceived the organization as a political system in which a central concern of management is how to create and sustain change agendas. This often requires change agents to spend time forming and nurturing coalitions (with other interest groups) in order to pursue their own goals for change. Instead of stressing the politics of work from a critical perspective – as suggested by industrial sociologists – Pfeffer identified his perspective explicitly with management and their political strategies, whilst Pettigrew analysed the prospects for strategic change from more of a top management perspective.

In contrast, the political process approaches that have emerged over the last decade stress both the explicit and covert strategies pursued by different players in the change or reproduction of management structures and organizational schemes, and point at the contextual, political, open ended and indeterminate nature of decisions and change processes (Dawson, 2003). Researchers from a critical processual perspective have stressed the embedded and inescapable nature of political processes and actor strategies (Knights and Murray, 1994). From a more cultural perspective, political processes are seen as being coloured by, as well as contributing to, the organizational systems of meaning (Alvessen, 2002). The more covert forms of political process may be evident in the legitimization of certain norms and values that, while often remaining implicit, nevertheless serve to influence individual and group responses to change. Kamp (2000: 77), drawing on the work of Hildebrandt and Seltz (1989), referred to the social principles that shape norms and provide the 'lens through which external conditions of possibility are interpreted'. She referred to this as a layer of 'stiffened politics' (stabilized patterns of politics) which she argued explains how continuity rather than change marks shop floor politicking where employees are 'often stuck in old marriages' unable to engage actively in the shaping and reshaping of change. As Kamp stated:

> Politics is actually about constructing what is considered rational and legitimate decision making ... [The issues] are in fact selective. Some issues are intended to change, others to remain unchanged; political processes are at stake when some conflicts are brought up, while others are hidden. Consequently, political processes cannot easily be delimited to certain social actions; rather, they should be treated as an aspect of social action. Focus on political processes means focus on the actors, who have different goals, values and preferences, and attempt to promote them by different means. And here the actors do not stand equal. Relations of power, on the one hand, constitute the conditions and possibilities for the actors' engagement in political processes; on the other hand, the relations of power are produced and reproduced by political processes.
>
> (Kamp, 2000: 76)

Accordingly, communication is a key element in the political process of change in drawing attention to certain positions and views and hiding others. This is particularly evident in the *post hoc* rationalizations of change that tend to smooth over the messy and rough political edges of change and yet, are also used to identify practical guidelines on the management of change. It is perhaps not surprising that around 70 per cent of all major change initiatives fail to meet their stated objectives when strategies are based on constructed rather than actual accounts of change processes.

Conclusion

This chapter has examined communication and change. At the outset, it was noted how the conventional change management literature has sought to identify ingredients of good practice in the 'successful' management of change. Emerging from the human relations movement the Organizational Development (OD) School has continued to promote the need for participatory change strategies with a two-way communication process that encourages and allows for employee involvement (French and Bell, 1983). Resistance and conflict is often seem to be the result of poor communication, the spreading of rumours and misinformation, and an inability to allay the natural fears and anxieties of employees awaiting the unknown (Paton and McCalman, 2000). In providing clear communication on change through appropriate mediums at a tone and pitch suitable to the audience and in practising what is preached, then a programme of effective communication in the 'successful' management of change can be put into place (Kotter, 1996; Carnall, 2003). By contrast, however, the more critical literature on change management questions this apolitical approach to change management and argues that change agents must use communication as another political tool in the tough contact sport of 'winning the turf game' (Buchanan and Badham, 1999). The politics of change is viewed as a part of organizational life (Dawson, 2003; Senior, 1997) in which power plays and the management of meaning is critical to the way others view and experience change (Itzin and Newman, 1995; Collins, 1998).

Under this more critical perspective, communication and change is part of a political process in steering an organization from one configuration to another. To paraphrase Pfeffer, the use of power is about changing the course of events by getting people to change in ways that they would otherwise not do (Pfeffer, 1993). Politics as 'power in action' (Robbins, 1996) is thereby evident within communication processes that seek to influence the views and behaviours of others, especially in change agent engagement in what Buchanan and Badham (1999) referred to as 'power-assisted steering'. As Dunphy and Stace (1990) have shown, in certain circumstances there may be little time for participative strategies and a more coercive approach may be appropriate. Similarly, the political intensity associated with managing a change that is viewed by many as important and necessary is going to be markedly different from a radical change initiative where the strategy is highly contested and questioned.

Whilst communication is central to both of these contrasting settings, there is no simple set of ingredients to guide effective communication strategies across these very different contextual landscapes. As such, managing communication is part of the political process of managing change and is rarely simply about openness, transparency and industrial democracy. Although effective communication strategies cannot simply be cast as the open, democratic, participative type of Lewinian approach, neither can they be cast as Machiavellian mushroom type strategies ('keep them in the dark, feed them shit and watch them grow') of coercion and deceit. It remains a complex process that, despite all our current research efforts, requires further debate and critical appraisal. In short, there is a need for further empirical research on communication and change as a political process within organizations.

5 Communication without frontiers

The impact of technology upon organizations

Paula O'Kane, Owen Hargie and
Dennis Tourish

I think there is a world market for maybe five computers
(Thomas Watson, Chairman of IBM, 1943)

Introduction

Communication has been shown to be at the centre of successful organizations (for example Clampitt and Downs, 1993; Hargie and Tourish, 2000) and so the challenge for businesses is to create a communication system that is both effective and efficient. In so doing they must address the needs of their customers, external stakeholders, such as suppliers or shareholders, and internal clients or employees. A key feature of the organizational landscape has been the surging river of technology that has become a torrent in recent years. Its impact has been evident in every aspect of organizational life. When harnessed effectively, this has proved to be a definite boon. As noted by Cohen (2000: 12), 'electronic media has come to the forefront of human resources to solve critical challenges in employee communication'.

At the same time, as we shall illustrate in this chapter, there are also dangers. Billions of dollars were lost in the great dot.com investment mania in the 1990s. Investors felt they simply *had* to join in the collective madness of the race for stocks in this virtual wonderland. It was as if the technology was a form of Midas touch that would turn shares to gold. But, of course, it all came to an abrupt and sorry end as companies folded and fortunes vanished (Cassidy, 2002). In the same way, the implementation of new technology must not be viewed as a panacea that will in and of itself solve problems. Rather, it must fit neatly into an already existing communication strategy. For many years, Audi motor cars were promoted with the advertising slogan 'Vorsprung durch Technik' (progress through technology). However, technology alone does not lead to progress. It merely offers new opportunities that need to be properly harnessed if benefits are to be reaped. As summarized by Gattiker (2001: 185), 'with every opportunity for positive outcomes, we also have a chance to have negative results instead. It is not so much the technology as the way we use the technology that will shape our information future'. This chapter therefore not only examines the functions and benefits of the main devices available for e-communication, but also evaluates their accompanying limitations. It further identifies key management considerations central to its effective operation, especially in relation to group working.

The use of technology in the communication process has been termed *electronic communication* or *e-communication*. E-communication tools have emerged from the bedrooms of geeks and the garden sheds of nerds to form a vital part of the communicative infrastructure of organizations. Traditional media, such as written messages, phone calls and face-to-face contact, are now often replaced by e-mail as the preferred channel in the business world, while glossy brochures and organization-wide memos find their importance diminishing with the increasing use of Internet and intranet applications. These changes have influenced organizational communication, both internally and externally. Foreman (1997) suggested three key elements in producing an integrated communication package: atmosphere, process and methods. To maximize the impact of technology as a communication method, organizations must be aware of the possible benefits and associated problems in order to create both the process and atmosphere necessary for effective communication.

The one certainty about technology is that it moves rapidly. In the techno-world the times are always a-changin'. For example, a few years ago WAP (Wireless Application Protocol) was the exciting new technology, allowing access to the Internet and intranet on mobiles, and then picture messaging was the next wave of enthusiasm. What the future will bring is in the imagination of professionals the world over. The software packages and related programmes and devices are also continually updated. The main focus of this chapter will be upon e-mail and the Internet (which encompasses the intranet and extranet), from which most other applications are derived. But first we want to say a little about adoption. The decision to adopt is of course a prerequisite to the implementation of any innovation.

Flanagin (2000) proposed three key areas that influence adoption:

1 *Organizational features* such as age, size and culture. Younger, larger, firms with higher levels of technology tend to implement innovations earlier. This does not restrict adoption to these corporations, rather it indicates that some may need to take into consideration other factors such as ensuring that employees are introduced gradually to the technology and are provided with sufficient support to master it.

2 *Perceived benefits* of increased communication and information flow, and organizational advantage (in the form of greater profits and enhanced reputation). The company needs to assess these possibilities before introducing technology in order to ensure that their expectations are met when it is introduced. At the individual level, the *media substitution hypothesis* purports that people who already carry out a particular job function, such as sending regular memos or carrying out research, will be more likely to start using new technologies if they facilitate these particular functions (Atkin *et al.*, 1998).

3 *Social pressures* such as self-image and the 'face' an organization presents to its customers, competitors and suppliers can encourage it to adopt e-communication. If the e-train is filling up fast, no company wants to be left in the waiting room when it departs. It is a case of wishing to present an up-to-date, modern image of the business. For instance, in 2002 the cooker group Aga announced that it had spent over £3m. over the past two years launching its website, but admitted that the site was failing to generate significant revenue in its own right. Despite this, the company also said it would continue with the site as part of its marketing strategy.

As Finnegan (1989: 117) noted some years ago, the effect of e-communications on 'efficiency, on their users, and on the overall power structure vary, depending crucially not so much on technical specifications as on social and political factors: how they are introduced and who has access to and control over them'. Thus, Flanagin (2000) pointed out that anxiety associated with any increased level of technical complexity reduces the likelihood of employee adoption. In similar vein, Damsgaard and Scheepers (2000) noted that technological innovations are most successful when maximum corporate support is in place, especially in terms of training and back-up. In essence, staff are more likely to embrace new technology if it is user friendly, readily accessible (for example, on their desk), employed by colleagues, seen to be effective, and has fringe benefits (for example, can be used for personal matters).

The two key tools for facilitating e-communication are the Internet and e-mail. We will examine each of these in turn.

The Internet

The Internet is a system of networked computers. It had its beginnings in the 1960s in the form of the Arpanet, commissioned by the Department of Defense to promote the sharing of super-computers amongst researchers in the United States. Since then it has metamorphosed into the World Wide Web (WWW), becoming an almost indispensable source of information globally. The Internet has been the platform for the increasing media convergence of telephone, TV, publishing and computing (Atkin, 1998). Internet usage has grown exponentially. Its tentacles now reach into almost every element of society, facilitating the purchase of all kinds of merchandise (even babies!), and providing masses of advice and information on useful as well as esoteric topics. There is little we cannot discover through our computers from the warmth and comfort of our own homes and offices. In essence, the world is opened up for organizations, particularly smaller ones who can use the Internet as a tool to enter a larger market.

In its early stages the Internet was seen as an optional tool that could help to create a competitive advantage. Now, however, it is an expectation, not an addition. The corporate Internet site enables organizations to decide on the messages they want to distribute directly to their publics, without going through mass media 'gate-keepers' such as journalists and broadcasting bodies (Ihator, 2001). This can be updated quickly because the information is in real time. Communication can therefore be at its swiftest and most accurate. It is the public face of the organization and increasingly the first port of call. Research by Sullivan (1999) suggests that image creation is the major function of a corporate home page and therefore the design of this is important.

Website design

A corporate website should be easy to navigate, provide relevant information and represent the company image. This does not mean that all the current information can simply be lifted from brochures and uploaded onto the website. The net has its own distinctive personality, due to its richness in graphics, sound and picture, navigational functionality and interactivity, so that what works in other forms of media, or with personal contact, will not necessarily transfer directly to it (Pruter, 1998). Appropriate content needs to be devised. Organizations design their website in one of three main formats (Leichty and Esrock, 2001).

1   *Static*   This type of site is seen as a one-way tool to provide fixed messages. In essence the site is the web equivalent of a basic promotional brochure. Many small firms adopt this approach, since it gives them the perceived prestige of a 'cyber presence' for a relatively small outlay.
2   *Broadcast*   Here the communication role of the site is still one-way, but its content is continually changed and refined. Hyperlinks are provided so that the visitor can navigate specific areas of interest. Many tourist sites, for example, offer regularly updated information on special events, weather, opening times, maps, etc.
3   *Interactive*   These sites encourage two-way communication, and are designed so that publics can interact with the organization. E-mail addresses are provided to allow specific corporate staff members to be easily contacted. They may also contain bulletin boards, feedback questionnaires, and so on. Leichty and Esrock (2001), in a study of Fortune 500 companies, found that over a one-year period almost all of the company sites had undergone changes in visual elements, hyperlinks and textual content. Some 84 per cent had e-mail links, and 75 per cent had these on the front page. These authors sent an e-mail enquiry to 111 sites and tracked the replies. Just under half of the companies replied (47 per cent), and two-thirds of these did so within 24 hours. However, over 50 per cent of companies did not reply at all, showing a schism between interactivity and corporate responsiveness. An important point here is that if an organization adopts an interactive site, it must be well managed, and this may require quite substantial resources. For example, Xerox has four employees whose sole job role is to deal with some 1,000 e-mail enquiries per day (Sterne and Priore, 2000).

Three key factors that organizations need to bear in mind are their audience, available resources and products.

Audience

An organization's website can be designed in a number of ways, depending on the needs of its publics. Industries such as manufacturing or engineering may require an information site with basic feedback and contact options, whereas others, such as selling or banking, look upon it as a business transaction tool requiring high levels of interaction with the user. Additionally, younger audiences will probably appreciate receiving information on the latest music scene, business customers tend to find share information useful, and fitness enthusiasts are likely to enjoy up-to-date facts on healthier lifestyles.

Resources

Opening the door to the Internet market does not just require the addition of a website. Companies must have the resources to deal with extra orders they may receive. As the web transcends boundaries and barriers, this may include being au fait with the difficulties associated with overseas selling, such as exchange rates and tax tariffs. Other issues include continual maintenance of the website, and training staff to deal with this new form of customer communication.

Product

The fact that sales of items such as books and CDs have been very successful online is due in no small part to the nature of the product. Being able to sit in your own home and browse through the selection is seen by many (especially the 'massive passive') to be more convenient than standing in a shop. More and more traditional industries are moving some or all of their business functions onto their Internet site. In order to be successful this needs to be carefully implemented. C.S. Lee (2001) suggested five steps to successfully transform traditional business practices to e-commerce:

1 Redefine the competitive advantage – decide what the company can offer that no other can.
2 Rethink business strategy – how does this need to change in order to capture the cyber market?
3 Re-examine traditional business and revenue models – integrate the figures for doing business on the net in order to assess financial viability.
4 Re-engineer the corporation and website – the company needs to be behind the proposed changes. Encourage this and ensure that the site meets the company needs.
5 Re-invent customer service. The unique needs of the Internet customer must be met.

E-marketing

Recent e-communication trends have been towards relationship and direct marketing. The main driving force here is fiscal. Costs have dropped dramatically as online retailers focus on niche marketing rather than on more expensive mass-market advertising campaigns. In order to target their market the company must build a profile of their public. The database should contain not only traditional demographic information but also psychographic details such as interests, hobbies, etc., which can be used to ensure that customers receive tailored information. A personal profile can be built up by tracking which areas a customer investigates on the site and what is purchased, but the collection of this information can lead the company to ethical dilemmas regarding its use. (The issue of ethics is fully discussed in Chapter 14.) Ways to market Internet business include:

- *Affiliate programmes*   These allow other people to sell your products from their website or newsletter, receiving a payment only when the item is purchased.
- *Links*   Here one business places a link on another's site, either by convincing them of the advantages of having your link or paying for the privilege. For the best results the associate company should be relevant to your product, but you also need to be aware that any adverse publicity they attract could affect your organization by proxy.
- *Traditional advertising*   Businesses should include their website address on all literature, livery and advertising, so that it is easily located.

Creating a site in which the customer has a unique, personalized experience increases its potential. The provision of consumer desired content, such as games, jokes and gossip is one method of encouraging a visitor to return to your site (for example, hotmail.com provides horoscopes and up-to-date news), as can providing customer specific-information quickly and easily (www.bbc.co.uk allows registered users to create a page called mybbc in which they decide on the content they view upon entry). This form of *virtual marketing* both draws people to the site and keeps them there. It also encourages them to tell others about it (which is of course the most effective form of advertising).

The Internet differs from other forms of customer communication in that it requires the individual to make the first move – this is known as the pull strategy. They must sign up to a service provider and log onto a site. Therefore the consumer has a choice about the information that they receive (although this boundary is crossed when we consider the influx of pop-up windows which now permeate our web experience). Organizations must build a relationship with the client, and this can be achieved in a number of ways:

- *Regular e-mail contact*   For this strategy to be successful the content must be relevant and up-to-date, such as Amazon's regular e-mails to customers. Increasing relevance through personalization can increase the click through

rate with the effects growing over time (Postma and Brokke, 2002). Customers should only be contacted if permission is given and the option to
revoke it should always be available. Doubleclick's (2001) Dartmail study
revealed that 88 per cent of consumers had made purchases as a result of
this permission-based e-mail strategy. In contrast, sending uninvited junk
e-mail ('spam') is likely to lead to client alienation.

- *Prompt response*   Many questions can be answered through browsing, but
  according to a Forrester Research report in January 2000 online shoppers look
  to e-mail first for customer service (Bloom-Mirski, 2000). From a global
  perspective, 'for advisors working with long distance clients, e-mail is a vital
  link' (McCarthy, 2000: 64). Therefore when a member of the public chooses
  to e-mail the organization on any issue, the response can dramatically affect
  customer opinion. Reply promptly, with more than just an acknowledgement
  of the received e-mail and customer opinion will be good. Leave it longer than
  48 hours, or never reply at all, and the impact can be extremely damaging.
- *Provide a medium for personal contact*   The Internet reduces the level of face-
  to-face contact with customers. This creates a psychological as well as
  spatial distance. As Drury and Van Doren (1999: 56) pointed out, 'self-
  service doesn't always work. Many transactions require contact with a live
  human being to clarify information, close a sale, correct an error or discover
  something not covered on the website'. Therefore a company must always
  provide some form of personal contact in case a customer requires this.

While the Internet has opened up a whole new market to many companies,
their existing customer base should not be ignored in favour of what the Internet might bring. The choice of medium is dependent on those with whom we
wish to communicate. Therefore an organization needs to assess both their
existing and potential customer base when deciding upon the level of technology they wish to employ. Provided each customer is given the same level of
service regardless of whether they choose to visit in person, e-mail, telephone,
or write, the value of e-communication is enormous. An important part of this
is monitoring the effectiveness of existing facilities. Tourish and Hargie (2000b:
152) noted that 'audits can help organizations decide if rational and productive
choice are being made, or whether people have purchased the latest gear for no
better reason than that it was there'. They emphasized the importance of monitoring a website's accessibility, utility, timeliness and potential for feedback.
One example is the 15-point scale Murgolo-Poore *et al.* (2002) have developed
to measure the effectiveness of a company's intranet site. In a similar vein Cox
and Dale (2002) have a proposed a measurement tool which designers can use
to assess the quality of websites. Likewise, e-mail communication should be
investigated in terms of the volume of e-mails sent and received, how it compli-
ments or substitutes other communication media, the uniqueness of the
information available, the quality of messages transferred, the frequency of
'flame' mails (irate e-mails from colleagues) and whether targets for responsiveness have been set and achieved.

The Internet is not just about what the organization says to the public, since anyone can put information about the corporation on the net. Companies need to engage in media monitoring to counteract any problems that may arise from information that is posted about it on the web. Many now hire teams of private investigators and lawyers to clamp down on damaging claims (Goodley, 2002). These include malicious comments on chatrooms or bulletin boards, as well as spoof or hate websites – the latter of which often have 'parallel' names (for example www.nthellworld.com as the hate site for NTL). The sources range across dissatisfied customers, special interest groups opposed to the company, investors wanting to influence the share price, and disgruntled former employees. For example, in December 2001 the US medical systems company Varian won $775,000 in damages against two former employees who had posted some 14,000 malicious messages on 100 bulletin boards over a three-year period.

Not only does the Internet represent an information-giving and selling tool for businesses, as mentioned earlier it is a method of sourcing suppliers and resources. This gives the organization an opportunity to investigate and gain information on many different producers and products in order to select the most relevant. Martin and Hafer (2002) found that, although companies used the Internet to research product information, only 14 per cent actually conducted a transaction online, partly because they were not confident with Internet usage, thereby not taking advantage of the cost reductions associated with e-procurement. It also provides an opportunity to investigate competitors' products and services in order to remain current. Of course, what is sauce for the goose is also sauce for the gander, and so your organization can be researched by competitors. This means that companies have to be careful about what is revealed on their site.

Finally, the Internet presents a new opportunity for training. E-learning enables employees to manage their own education timetable and encourages 'bite-sized' learning which breaks it into manageable chunks that can be undertaken at the employee's convenience. Cost savings can be realized in reduction of travelling expenses and time off work but the system requirements need to be in place to ensure a positive e-learning experience. Planned well and tied into business objectives this form of training can provide a more effective learning solution as it can allow for differences in employee experience and learning curve, as well as providing resources, such as simulations, not available from traditional training. From an organizational viewpoint it is easier to manage and assess training programmes as the facilities are in place to allow reporting of progress. Additionally, remote supervision, through e-mail, chat rooms and telephony, provides employees with the backup they may need to conclude the course successfully.

Intranet and extranet

An *intranet* facilitates increased collaboration among employees, as it flattens the organizational structure and introduces 'any-to-any' connectivity within the company. An *extranet* extends this to encompass external stakeholders such as specific customers or shareholders. The increased information flow created by these media can lead to strategic advantages such as improved decision making and innovation. As will be illustrated later, these benefits are tempered by issues surrounding security, privacy, management commitment and training.

The intranet, although symbiotic with the Internet in terms of technology, has a different role to play in the field of organizational communication, and as such differs in the way in which it should both be designed and managed. The mountain of information that can be made available through the intranet site, from both the organization and its employees, needs to be controlled to ensure that it provides not only accurate but also timely information. Head (2000) recommended the following guidelines when designing an intranet site:

1   *Know your audience* As the intranet audience is much smaller there are fewer needs to be catered for. 'Visitors' enter in order to find work-related information and need only be wooed by its facility to make their job easier.
2   *Deliver work productivity* Discover what users frequently do and use this as a basis to build a successful site. This should encompass *inter alia* a directory, search facility and corporate news.
3   *Emphasise breadth over depth* Intranet sites should allow employees ready access to the important information and applications. Therefore, links to these pages should be available as early as possible.
4   *Minimize the graphics* It is more important that intranet sites can be accessed quickly than have exciting graphical capabilities. If a reader needs to urgently find out the internal phone number of Jo in Supplies, s/he will only get irritated having to firstly watch colourful psychedelic displays or wade through virtual pages of corporate news.
5   *Colloquial labelling can work* An intranet audience is more defined and therefore specialized, and so industry- or company-specific labels can be incorporated to aid understanding.

The extranet is becoming a more common feature in corporate websites with, for example, companies allowing customers to track their order or access their accounts online. Corporate information can be limited to particular people, thus providing a cost-effective method for delivering specific information to customers, or special information for 'members only'. If a company already has an intranet site it is relatively inexpensive to extend this to an extranet. The concept is similar to that of intranet and Internet – keep the information relevant, accessible and up-to-date. Key issues for companies are to anticipate and alleviate any security issues and ensure that the experience is made as accessible as possible, with sign-up and sign-in procedures kept secure but simple.

E-mail

One of the most striking offshoots from the Internet has been e-mail. The central advantage of e-mail is that it enables the 'instant transfer of messages and documents world-wide between people on the same private network, or with access to the same public network' (Samuels, 1997: 35). Not surprisingly, it has overtaken telephone and written communication to become the main form of mediated communication in organizations (Hargie and Tourish, 2000). The advent of the new millennium witnessed e-mail becoming the dominant force in written communications, both in the office and at home. Indeed, so great has been its impact that traditional 'snail mail' postal delivery services in all western countries have been very severely affected. For example, in January 2002 the Royal Mail handled 258 million letters for domestic customers in the UK, while over twice as many e-mails (550 million) were sent and received from family homes. One consequence was that the UK Post Office was losing £1.5 million per day in 2002 and responded by shedding over 40,000 jobs.

Two-thirds of US companies reported that sales increased in 2001 as a result of using e-mail marketing (DMNews, 2002). It provides a vital link with customers, which can reduce the down time in both contacting clients and replying to enquiries. The asynchronous nature of e-mail means that customers do not find themselves caught in the 'voice-mail jail' associated with automated telephone systems. As mentioned earlier, the time taken to respond to a client's query can mould opinion about the company. Organizations should set realistic and achievable targets for response times.

E-mail content

The informal nature of the medium can lead to problems such as misunderstanding and conflict. The time devoted to writing e-mails is usually lower than that allocated to letters or memos, and therefore the content is often less precise. Spelling and grammatical errors that would be frowned upon in memos or letters are more readily accepted in e-mails. Indeed, with the epidemic of texting from mobile phones, e-messages are becoming even less formal. But confirming by e-mail a formal appointment with the CEO with 'OKCU4T&Jaw@3' is clearly not appropriate! In business contexts, words and phrases need to be chosen carefully. Box 5.1 presents guidelines for e-mail composition, which should be incorporated into employee training.

Crystal (2001) pointed out that 'netspeak' is neither written nor spoken language; instead it relies on characteristics of both, forming a 'third medium' for communication. Employees should be cognizant that the way in which they communicate through e-mail is unique and as such they have to respect the boundaries of this new language. This has been recognized in many corporations. For instance, the New Jersey Hospital Association adopted a proactive approach, by providing training for all new recruits, encompassing the basics of

Box 5.1   Ten rules for the composition of business e-mails

1   Decide that e-mail is definitely the most effective medium. Would face-to-face, telephone or 'paper' communication be better?
2   Be aware of your audience. Tailor the style to the person to whom it is being sent.
3   Always use a signature as this gives vital contact details for follow-up.
4   Select the 'subject' line carefully to reflect the content.
5   Only prioritize or mark 'urgent' when it really is.
6   Keep the message brief and to the point.
7   Keep emphasis to a minimum.
8   Check for spelling and grammar – this is often overlooked in casual e-mails.
9   Re-read messages to check for clear understanding.
10 Do not get involved in 'flaming'. There is a natural temptation to respond to rude e-mails in kind. But remember, if you lose your temper you lose the argument.

communicating quickly but courteously, being careful not to write e-mails which could come back to haunt the sender, and the importance of proofreading (Poe, 2001).

Overarching issues

When an organization embarks upon the process of introducing new technology for communication purposes it must look both at issues surrounding cost, time and storage and the underlying consequences which include changes in organizational structure, legal, security and privacy issues, and technostress.

Cost

One of the primary motives that drives the adoption of most new working practices is cost reduction. E-communication offers such benefits. For example, sending messages via e-mail is cheaper than using either written communication, which incurs paper, postage and internal mail costs, or telephone calls. The Credit Union estimated that if just 10 per cent of members, in a union of 50,000, chose to accept electronic statements they would save $36,000 annually (Schooler, 2001). Cost efficiencies are also realized with the Internet. Research involving IT and corporate managers has shown that investments are resulting in improved productivity, increased revenue and lower costs (Violino, 2001). As an example, Joe Signorelli of First Union Corporation reported that by publishing two key documents via Adobe Acrobat on the web, print and distribution costs were reduced by $400,000 annually (First Union Corporation, 2002).

E-communication allows companies to collapse the supply chain by using the

Internet to sell goods and services. This not only produces economies for the organization, it in turn brings the possibility of price reductions for the consumer as well as opportunities for improved customer relations (Jones, 2000). The cost of an e-mail campaign is about $5–7 per thousand, significantly less than a traditional direct mail campaign, which costs between $500–700 per thousand (Garcia, 2002). When estimating savings, of course, cognizance must be taken of the costs involved not only in introducing new technology into the workplace, but also in providing support, maintaining the site, and training staff.

Time

On the credit side, e-mail reduces the time for both internal and external transfer of messages and the Internet provides a quick way to source information about the company both for the employee and the customer. On the debit side, while e-communication has changed the way in which people operate their working day, time wasting is one of the largest associated problems. Thus, some 30 per cent of the time an employee spends reading e-mails is related to gossip, jokes and other unproductive material (Grey and MacDonald, 2001). Internet misuse, through excessive web-surfing, and problems associated with the technology, can lead to loss of productivity. Of course, much of the former may merely be a replacement for the traditional joke telling and banter that has long characterized organizational life. Having said this, the Internet offers many and varied temptations (whether licit or otherwise) for staff, and its use has to be carefully monitored.

Information flow

A core advantage of e-mail has been in the realm of information transmission. Documents sent as attachments save time, not only over geographical areas, but also in larger offices, as it negates the need to physically carry files from one place to another (Anderson, 1998). Bulk mails, which can be distributed company-wide, customer-wide, or be specifically targeted, mean that all parties can easily be kept up-to-date with what is happening. Many on-line companies regularly send their customers tailored information about special offers. The ease and speed with which information can be updated on the Internet has led to an increase in information exchange. From an organizational viewpoint this has meant that people have more relevant material available to them. It can therefore assist in periods of uncertainty, such as during major change, because employees and customers can be quickly and cheaply kept informed (Jones, 2000). However, this can also lead to an increase in staff expectations because of the awareness that information is readily available should management so wish to share it. If they decline this opportunity, the information shortfall can be even more frustrating and alienating for employees.

This picture of information as the secret to organizational success needs to be tempered with the reality that if the systems are not managed appropriately the level of material available to employees can become overwhelming. The ease with which information can be exchanged often leads to overload (Edmunds and Morris, 2000). The popularity of e-mail means that one's 'e-tray' can be many times larger than would have been a traditional mail in-tray. The reality of this was illustrated by one survey in which one-half of the 2,600 respondents stated that work would be more effective if information overload was reduced (Bray, 2001). Indeed, we have witnessed employees who were so snowed under by the cyber blizzard that they simply printed off all of their e-mails and piled them in an in-tray. The benefits of e-mail rapidly disappeared. Such overload can be circumvented by training employees how to use features such as the priory status on their e-mail programmes, including an informative subject line, and preventing, identifying and deleting 'spam' e-mails.

Storage and retrieval

Computer applications are helping to solve the growing information storage problem – bulky filing cabinets and cupboards are fast disappearing. To take but one example, in 2002 Encyclopædia Britannica was available either in print as a 32-volume set containing 44 million words, or on a single CD-ROM (at a fraction of the price) containing additional material with a total of 55 million words. The Internet has also greatly facilitated information searches, for everything from staff contact details to details about travel destinations. Information stored either in the form of PDFs (such as Adobe Acrobat or Real Page), or on the website, reduces the possibility of it being lost, because the information cannot be removed by an individual, and it can usually be retrieved much quicker than from a traditional filing system. Additionally the information is concurrently accessible to staff.

Organizational structure

New technology has impacted upon the structure of organizations. Employees now have instant access to senior managers via their e-mail address (although some organizations actually forbid staff from sending e-mails to levels higher than immediate line manager). Likewise, Jo Public can immediately hit the CEO of a company with a direct message to his or her e-mail address gleaned from the web-site.

The old adage 'information is power' is particularly relevant to the changes that have occurred in employee communication. The ability of e-communication tools to provide employees with high levels of access to information coupled with the intranet concept of 'encouraging people to pull information towards them rather than pushing it at them' (Rogers, 1996: 35) can invoke a sense of staff empowerment. This is because they feel more in control of their communications and their individual working environment (Phaneuf, 2000). With different roles being created and others redefined this can lead to greater responsibility for individual members of staff and more accountability for information transfer, leading to a positive sense of being valued in the organization.

Employees spend much of their working time using technology and so their evaluation of it is strongly related to job satisfaction. Technology influences the ease and ability with which they complete tasks and so influences their self-identity as effective employees (Sergeant and Frenkel, 2000). It has led to higher levels of collaboration, because information sharing between members of the same community has become more readily available through such features as bulletin boards on the intranet (Marshall, 1999). This has also enabled relationships to develop that may not otherwise have been possible. Greater communication between colleagues has positive benefits for both the individual and the organization. In this way, as discussed by Filipczak (1996), an intranet can be relatively easily turned into a very accessible collection of corporate knowledge (the issue of knowledge management is fully discussed in Chapter 6). Indeed, Andersen (2001) found that in companies with low levels of dynamism and complexity an increased use of the Internet and intranet led to increases in organizational innovation. It can help to spur ideas in the company but it also needs to be implemented with an air of caution. Negative messages can be generated, and so prior vetting of information may be necessary.

The increase in communication across all levels that has resulted from the introduction of e-communication has impacted upon the internal mechanisms of most companies (Coombs and Hull, 1996). One interesting problem is the threat to management jobs, because decisions are increasingly becoming the responsibility of employees (Langnau, 2000). This could lead traditional managers to view e-communication with an air of mistrust. The loss of power may be associated with a concomitant feeling of loss of status. One of the time-honoured roles of managers is to act as gatekeepers. Consequently, if they feel threatened by new technology this could lead to significant adoption problems. They are unlikely to be highly motivated to help build a communications technology platform if they see it as a form of electronic scaffold upon which they will later be hanged. Harrington and Ruppel (1999: 234) investigated this issue and concluded that 'lack of management trust of employees acts as a barrier to ... adoption and diffusion and has slowed its growth'. Changes in management style have had to occur because employees expect higher levels of information about the organization and therefore a greater input into its future. Organizations must be sensitive to management fears when implementing new communication technology, and instigate procedures, such as retraining and open discussion, to overcome them.

Media richness theory, social presence and channel utilization

It is clear that computer-based interactive media facilitates information exchange, while also having the potential to create interpersonal distance. For example, people may opt to exchange e-mails with colleagues in adjacent offices rather than engage in face-to-face encounters. This raises important issues about social presence, media richness theory and channel selection and utilization.

Social presence is conceptualized as the salience of the other persons involved in an interaction, and the consequent salience of the interpersonal relationship (Short *et al.*, 1976). In essence, the argument here is that the more we are aware of the other person's actual presence the more likely it is that interpersonal relationships will result. Various media provide greater or lesser auditory and visual cues to simulate the 'presence' aspects of a dyadic encounter. The research suggests, overall, that there is a sliding scale of social presence decreasing from face-to-face contacts, to video meetings, then audio encounters, with e-mail and written communications offering the least presence (Westmyer *et al.*, 1998; Fulk and Collins-Jarvis, 2001).

The importance of social presence, in turn, reflects what is known as *media richness* (Daft and Lengel, 1984, 1986). Media richness refers (Suh, 1999) to a channel's capacity to carry information based upon:

- availability and speed of feedback
- ability to communicate many cues simultaneously, including voice tone and nonverbal behaviours
- use of language rather than statistics
- ability to transmit affective components of messages.

Thus, social presence is diminished when few communication channels (for example, a computer screen only) are available. In turn, this means that such communication is less able to reduce uncertainty and handle equivocation. For simple information exchange this is not a problem. But the richest medium (face to face) is best when:

- issues are inherently complex
- conflict is involved
- uncertainty reduction is a priority
- building interpersonal relationships is an urgent requirement.

However, face-to-face communication is not without its problems – an obvious constraint, for example, is that everyone has to be in the same place at the same time. Especially with larger groups, this means that a few people are speaking with everyone else passively listening (Rice and Gattiker, 2001).

Thus, managers must make intelligent and informed choices about channel and media selection, depending on a multitude of variables, including the purpose of the information exchange, the existing level of uncertainty on the items under discussion, and the extent to which people are savvy with the various communication options available. Carlson and Zmud (1999) noted that it takes time for e-mail users to be able to engage in rich communication, and the newer the task or contact the less rich e-mail communication becomes. This means that the multitude of new options opened up by technology make the acquisition of communication competence more difficult than in the past. Relational competence is generally defined by *appropriateness* and *effectiveness* (Rubin, 1990). Communication competence therefore requires the selection of the most appropriate or socially acceptable channel, and the one that will be most effective in the accomplishment of relational and informational goals (Westmyer *et al.*, 1998). With those strictures in mind, managers will be more likely to function effectively if they:

- Determine the informational purpose behind communication episodes – for example, is the primary purpose to transmit uncomplicated information, reduce uncertainty or resolve interpersonal conflicts?
- Consider the logistical issues involved in bringing parties together for face-to-face encounters. Often, this is just not possible (or may be prohibitively expensive).
- Evaluate the familiarity of the individuals concerned with the techno-logical options available.

In addition, e-communication has enabled some employees to make the decision to work away from the office for an extended period of time. The result can be a better balance between the demands of work and family life, and more flexible working hours (Boyett and Boyett, 1995). This has been found to increase productivity, significantly reduce overheads and enhance employee recruitment and retention (Evans, 1993). Such distal employees have virtual managers, whom they see only occasionally. However, as the Swiss novelist and playwright Max Frisch noted, technology can also be viewed as 'The knack of so arranging the world that we need not experience it'. People can become conditioned to mediated communications to the extent that they start to shy away from face-to-face contacts. There is a clear 'isolation effect' associated with a remote working environment, which can cause employees to feel distant from the organization and result in decreased job satisfaction (Gainey *et al.*, 1999). Advantages, such as reduced office space and employees' enjoyment of running their own timetable, may lure company leaders to rapidly adopt this alternative without adequately considering the long-term implications of isolating workers from the traditional office setting (Weisband *et al.*, 1995). These aspects must be fully investigated before the decision to introduce such a working practice is made.

It should certainly not be the case that communication channels or altern-ative working arrangements are selected solely by such criteria as the speed of information transmission, and the quickness with which the communicative episode can be concluded. This would reduce the amount of human encounters people experience. As the discussion above suggests, this might ensure some gains in efficiency, but result in overall lowered effectiveness. Thus, the extra choices generated by technology have added a layer of complexity to the man-agement decision making process.

Legal, security and privacy issues

As a company is responsible for its e-mail and Internet system, it has to protect itself from the legal and security problems associated with their usage as well as ensuring both employee and customer privacy (see Box 5.2). Employees should be made fully aware of the legal parameters surrounding e-communications. The informality of the medium can be seductive. People often e-mail messages that they would never send in a formal written paper document. They forget that the 'delete' button is not a destruct button. Messages have a permanency in the system and can be tracked and traced. Additionally, in order to protect the company from legal and security issues 'firewalls' using specialized software can be installed to monitor e-mail messages sent through a company's system for dubious content. E-mail monitoring is undertaken not only for legal and security reasons but also to prevent spam blocking an employee's inbox and to mini-

Box 5.2   Privacy, legal and security issues

Legal
Cognizance must be taken of the following legal possibilities:

- copyright infringement
- corporate espionage
- harassment and discrimination
- admissions against interest
- adverse uses – liability for company
- defamation
- invasion of privacy.

Security
Here, protections should be developed against:

- hackers – e-communication exposes the company to external hackers
- viruses – these can lead to the theft, destruction or alteration of vital data
- unauthorized access to confidential information – can be illegally transferred by employees.

Privacy
An 'electronic trail' is left from which it is possible to identify the source of the message and view the contents. This can allow organizations to:

- track worker productivity
- monitor e-mail content
- monitor web usage.

mize the drain on company resources from both unimportant information and unproductive or personal e-mails. Employee access to the Internet also brings its own set of problems, such as accessing inappropriate or offensive materials. Again, monitoring can help to counteract this.

The dangers of e-mail were realized by a large Wall Street Bank when it was successfully sued by a group of African American employees because allegedly racist jokes were e-mailed among employees (Kirshenberg, 1997). Likewise BG (formally British Gas) found themselves paying a £101,000 plus costs libel suit after a senior manager sent an internal defamatory e-mail about a rival company.

Given these legal matters, most businesses send formal correspondence, such as contracts and sensitive information, through traditional mail. McCarthy (2000) noted that the majority of a firm's e-mail to clients is to do with routine administration. It tends not to be employed for formal or contractual matters, and most avoid sending sensitive files as message attachments. For example, Amoco Corporation has a clear policy of limiting e-correspondence to issues that are not 'mission critical' (Sipior et al., 1998). A number of key recommendations for managing employee e-mail have been identified (Sipior and Ward, 1998), and these are summarized in Box 5.3.

There is a necessity to monitor employee actions in terms of e-mail content and websites accessed in order to protect the company. Most staff will readily accept that they should not be surfing porn sites or e-shopping during working time. But to what extent should employees be monitored? Research is limited but 'several studies of telecommunications and clerical workers suggest that electronically monitored workers experience higher levels of depression, tension and anxiety, lower levels of productivity, and more health problems than unmonitored employees' (Boehle, 2000: 58). If an organization chooses to engage in employee monitoring they should, from the outset, inform staff of the extent to which they are being scrutinized and ensure that an end-user

Box 5.3 Ten recommendations for managing employee e-mail

1 Develop an e-mail system plan.
2 Formulate an e-mail policy.
3 Identify who will put this e-mail policy into practice.
4 Appoint an e-mail system manager.
5 Implement technical forms of privacy protection within the e-mail system.
6 Consider the consequences for employees.
7 Understand the implications for the organization.
8 Take cognizance of the wider external consequences.
9 Clearly communicate to all employees the e-mail policy and system protection facilities.
10 Undertake regular audits and reviews of the e-mail policy.

agreement is signed, stating what is acceptable usage and what is not. As discussed earlier, monitoring for legal reasons is an inescapable reality of e-mail usage.

Technostress

Technology can add stress to the workplace. This phenomenon has been variously termed 'technostress', 'information fatigue syndrome' and 'mutiphrenia' (Hargie *et al.*, 1999). The challenge of learning new and ever-developing technology, changes to existing work routines, 'time saving' expectations not being met, systems problems and computer errors have been found to be the most stressful aspects (Weil, 1997). Physical problems include backache, eye strain and headaches. An organization's health and safety strategy should address these somatic complaints and provide the relevant equipment and information to help alleviate them.

The emotional aspects are more complicated. Within the workforce there are still those who grew up before the advent of the VDU. Some have embraced the computer age with relish, while others still find it rather alien. However, in most organizations, employees now have to cope with, if not master, e-communications. An inability to use the equipment, due either to technophobia or ineffective training, can cause stress. This may be at a fairly basic level. For example Gordon (1993), in his study of the relationship between computer anxiety and keyboarding skills, found that poor typing ability led to higher anxiety. Negative experiences, such as losing important documents or contracting a virus, can also increase stress levels (Hemby, 1998). These problems should be identified and either prevented or remedied. Careful consideration needs to be paid to technosensitive or inexperienced users, in terms of expectations as well as training. With sufficient encouragement to use the technology, and appropriate support, these difficulties can be overcome.

Facilitating group communication

The Internet, e-mail and their applications have a key role to play in enhancing group communication. Using technology for discussions over distance and time results in greater flexibility in the structure of task groups and enables appropriate employees to have their say without the costs and inconvenience associated with meetings. For example in one survey, 29 per cent of the 2,600 respondents stated that their work would be more effective if they spent less time travelling to meetings (Bray, 2001). The area where the benefits have been greatest is in what Teich *et al.* (1999: 230) described as 'same-time, same-place decision rooms', where distal employees use mediated communication to come together to form virtual teams.

Group discussion using e-communication can take the form of text, audio or video. Research in this field has concentrated on text-based interactions in areas such as the quality of decisions reached, how the group performs, and factors that influence the way in which decisions are reached (Ulrich *et al.*, 2001). Managers need to be aware that the dynamics of e-groups differ from those that operate face-to-face. At the same time, there are no hard and fast findings regarding computer mediated communications, as a number of factors have been shown to impact upon the efficacy of the interaction (Ramirez *et al.*, 2002), including:

- the technology being employed and how familiar and at ease particular individuals are with it
- the purpose of the encounter
- how many people are involved
- total number of locations and number of people at each
- time available for the interaction
- time of day
- physical distance between people
- extent of cultural similarity between participants.

Therefore a decision to conduct a meeting using technology must be made with the following factors in mind.

Time and relationships

The time required to make a decision becomes longer in mediated groups (Kiesler and Sproull, 1992) but this has to be tempered by the fact that it reduces travel time and costs. The extended time can be explained by *social information processing theory*, which asserts that e-communication forces both task-related and social information into a single verbal/linguistic channel, and therefore it takes more 'real time' to exchange the same number of messages than it would with face-to-face interaction (Walther, 1992). This also means that relationships take longer to develop in e-groups than face-to-face groups (Walther, 1993). However, the former groups have been found to develop in relationally positive directions over time. With the anticipation of future inter-action associated with longitudinal groups, members are more likely to make an effort to form interpersonal bonds (Walther, 1994).

Participation and status

E-group discussion has been shown to promote status equalization, due to the reduced perception of social differences and this tends to result in greater participation by peripheral members (Kiesler and Sproull, 1992). However, when status cues do become available they tend to be more dominant in mediated than in face-to-face groups, as the participants have less evidence or opportunity to correct stereotypical ideas about the others (Weisband *et al.*, 1995).

Conflict

Disagreements can occur in any group situation, but it has been found that those occurring in electronic interactions promote deeper conflict than those in face-to-face encounters. In e-groups, it has been shown that flaming remarks doubled (Kiesler and Sproull, 1992). This is partly due to the lack of non-verbal contact with other members, which causes higher levels of misunderstandings to occur. It is also because the risks of overt aggression or violence from the other person are removed in mediated communication. Thus, it has long been known that people are more aggressive in telephone than in face-to-face exchanges (Hargie *et al.*, 1999). To facilitate groupwork, it is necessary to ensure that participants are aware of the dangers of heightened conflict, and engage in steps to counteract it. Another feature of e-groups is that risk-taking tends to be higher. The physical presence of others seems to make people more cautious in relation to decision making. This needs to be borne in mind when organizing virtual teams.

Group performance

The choice of medium can affect the quality of the decision reached by the group. It has been found that compared with groups that interacted face-to-face, e-groups seem to share less information of all types and reach poorer decisions (Hollingshead, 1996a). Moreover, in another study by the same author, it was shown that electronic communication, as well as suppressing information exchange, reduced the perceived influence of all members, regardless of status, which led to decisions being of poorer quality (Hollingshead, 1996b). This means that e-groups have to be *managed*. Those involved need to be warned of the potential pitfalls and of the steps needed to overcome these. For example, initial working arrangements should be agreed about how and in what ways communication will take place. In particular, methods for maximizing information exchange should be promoted. Mediated communications are facilitated if employees can meet face-to-face before the first electronic encounter. This facilitates the process of human bonding.

Conclusion

The electronic revolution has affected all organizations, and its influence will continue to expand. It has impacted upon all aspects of the business process from sourcing supplies to selling products. It has also affected the way in which employees communicate with one another. The previously ever-ringing office telephone is becoming quieter as messages silently sail through space into the desktop computer. As the paper trail diminishes, the size of the e-tray increases concomitantly. Companies need to recognize both the benefits and the possible dangers that this brings. There are substantial costs involved in terms of equipment and training requirements, and these are ongoing. Like children, technology grows and develops at a very fast pace and what fits or suits today is unlikely to do so next year. The key consideration is not which technology to implement, but rather how to use it and combine it with other channels of communication. Especially after the events of 11 September 2001, many corporations prefer to use technology rather than send executives on long plane journeys. However, virtual groups are not the same as actual groups, and the differences must be dealt with if the time-saving potential of distal teams is to be harnessed. This chapter has addressed the core issues of the Internet, intranet and e-mail that need to be borne in mind when employing these electronic tools.

6 Knowledge management and/as organizational communication

Theodore E. Zorn and James R. Taylor

In 1973, Daniel Bell (Bell, 1973) wrote that we were moving towards a post-industrial society (and a post-industrial economy). More recently, Peter Drucker similarly observed that 'we are entering the information society in which the basic economic resource is no longer capital ... but is and will be knowledge' (Drucker, 1995: 42). It is far from evident, almost thirty years after the publication of Bell's book, that we have left industrialism behind, but it is clear that there has been, as he foresaw, a remarkable growth in importance of the knowledge sector. The salience of the knowledge sector is reflected not so much in sheer numbers of people in the workforce, as in the influence the sector wields (Thompson *et al.*, 2001). Knowledge 'is increasingly regarded as the critical resource of firms and economies' (Lam, 2000). Knowledge (sometimes referred to as 'intellectual capital'), rather than traditional resources such as fixed assets and capital, is said to be 'the critical resource in the determination of competitive advantage' (Dunford *et al.*, 2001): a 'strategic asset' (Narasimha, 2000). In short, 'a knowledge-based economic revolution is taking place' (Neef, 1999).

It is a 'revolution' fuelled by science, technology, as well as rising standards of education. It is materialized in a dazzling array of telecommunications and information-processing enablers, the product of a telecommunications/IT convergence promised more than half a century ago, but realized only in the 1990s, when the Internet and the World Wide Web became a commonplace of daily interaction. But, although it may be rooted in technology, the 'revolution' that now preoccupies management, and management science, is centred on people (McAdam and McCreedy, 1999). When the technology is available to everyone in general, it no longer confers a strategic advantage on anyone in particular. What now determines 'competitive advantage' is the know-how (practical knowledge) and know-what (formal or cognitive knowledge) of the people who develop and use knowledge in organizations: part specialized training, part hard-won job savvy. The knowledge community is a reality. Not surprisingly, this reality is reflected in the literature on management.

Certainly one of the more prominent features of the organizational landscape in the early years of the twenty-first century is a focus on a cluster of related ideas such as information, knowledge, and learning. There is much talk about the knowledge economy, the learning organization, and the information superhighway. At the centre of this discussion for many organizations is the notion of knowledge management, or KM. While this term is used in a variety of different ways, the general notion is an effort to define, develop, control, and exploit the organization's expertise. KM has become a major management trend, similar to earlier trends such as Total Quality Management and Business Process Re-engineering, in that it has become both a way to reconceptualize the management of organizations and has become a major 'programme' promoted by management consultants.

Our goal in this chapter is to explore the concept of KM and its relationship to organizational communication. Specifically, we will attempt to (a) define KM and its key components, (b) explain why it has become such an important issue for contemporary organizations, (c) suggest some important ways that KM relates to and can be informed by organizational communication scholarship, and (d) identify some key implications of organizational communication theory and research for KM practice.

What is KM and how is it relevant to organizational communication?

Consider the following scenarios:

Scenario A   You are reading this chapter as part of a class on organizational communication or something similar. Based on this chapter and others, your instructor asks you to write a paper demonstrating your understanding of the readings. To get an A, you must carefully organize your ideas, develop coherent arguments, support your arguments with evidence from the readings, use competent academic writing practices, and so on.

Scenario B   A young man, Dan, has a part-time job with an inventory company. This job requires him to work with a team of people who are contracted to go into retail stores after hours to count, record, and report on the inventory of the stores. They must work quickly and accurately, and they must coordinate their efforts in order to provide an accurate report on the stores' inventory and do so in a way that is cost-effective.

Perhaps compared with software designers or engineers, the jobs in these two scenarios may appear fairly simple. However, in both scenarios a substantial amount of knowledge is required to perform competently. The writer in Scenario A and the inventory clerk in Scenario B each apply knowledge and skills they have developed over a period of time in order to complete their assigned tasks. Each has to coordinate the completion of the task with others in the organization (you with your instructor, at least, and Dan with his supervisor and coworkers). Furthermore, it is easy to imagine that if you and Dan are good at your tasks, others may want you to explain how it is that you are so effective. They are likely to ask you to do so based on a desire to learn to be more effective themselves or a desire to share your expertise with others. For example, your university is likely to have developed guidelines, classes, and tutoring sessions based on an analysis of effective paper writers such as yourself, in order to help those who are less skilled at writing to be more effective. And Dan's supervisor is likely to want to pass on lessons learned from Dan to new employees or others who are not as skilful as he is. What we have just described are some simple examples of knowledge management. In both cases, knowledge important to the organization is identified, codified, and exploited by the organization.

However, like many major management trends, KM is both ambiguous and multifaceted. Given the diversity of origins of the concept of knowledge management, it is not surprising that the field has failed to arrive at a clear understanding of exactly what KM means: 'passing fad, significant trend, or paradigm in its own right ... toolbox of techniques or philosophy?' (McAdam and McCreedy, 1999: 94). Neef (1999: 71), for example, reports on the puzzlement of one senior executive he met, who complained that he could make neither head nor tail of KM: ' "Where's the beef," he demanded.'

Knowledge has always been important to organizations, so when a member of an organization today claims to have implemented KM, what exactly is meant? We see at least four major uses of the KM label. The boundaries between these four uses are somewhat fuzzy, yet they seem to capture the primary uses of the term.

First, and most typically, KM is used to describe a relatively comprehensive programme or strategy intended to manage an organization's 'intellectual capital' or expertise. We will refer to this use of the term as KM_1. Flanagin describes this use of the term:

> The dominant strategy has been to identify and develop technologies for the capture, storage, retrieval, and dissemination of explicit knowledge. The chief concern has been how to extract an individual's knowledge, place it in a format and location that are accessible to relevant others, and ensure that this knowledge is utilized in the achievement of organizational goals.
>
> (Flanagin, 2002: 243)

As is apparent in his description, such programmes make prominent use of information and communication technologies (ICTs). So, if the inventory company in Scenario B above got serious about implementing KM_1, they might codify the best practices of inventory clerks and other workers, along with other valuable information such as client profiles, and develop software to deliver such information to their workers when they need it to perform. However, KM gurus are quick to explain that a full-scale KM initiative means not only utilizing ICTs but also changing the organizational culture to one that encourages sharing – rather than hoarding – knowledge. KM_1 programmes are often introduced into organizations with substantial fanfare, framing KM as a major new strategy that will help the organization achieve competitive advantage or 'world class' performance.

A second prominent meaning for KM (KM_2) is specific software applications that are marketed as KM solutions. IBM Lotus's Lotus Notes is perhaps most well known, but there are many others sold by IBM Lotus and a host of other vendors (Barker, 2000). Consider the sales pitch from IBM Lotus's website: 'Our Knowledge Discovery products and solutions can help you rapidly achieve your KM vision by capturing and organizing knowledge in the form of content, expertise and communities so it can be easily managed, located, evaluated and reused to drive responsiveness, innovation, efficiency and learning.' (IBM Lotus Software, 2002). In KM_2 the KM initiative is largely based on the functions of the particular software. As we discuss below, such applications vary in the specific functions they serve. For example, Dan's inventory company might purchase an off-the-shelf software application that allows him and his coworkers to input suggestions for solving problems then, when needed, access the suggestions. While such off-the-shelf applications may be featured within KM_1, this is not necessarily the case. Organizations introducing KM_1 often have internal or external specialists develop specific organization-specific ICT solutions, or may simply use or adapt existing software.

The third use of KM (KM_3) is to reference relatively small-scale initiatives that manage information in some way. This may be a centralized database that is created or reorganized for easier access, or an intranet that attempts to manage document maintenance and access. For example, several years ago, the Waikato Management School (where the first author is employed) implemented a form of KM_3 by renaming its School Librarian as the 'Knowledge Manager' and charging her with bringing KM to the School. This initiative largely focused on using the School's already existing intranet more fully for storing and accessing internal documents and taking advantage of the web for accessing external sources of information such as journal articles.

Finally, the fourth use of the term (KM_4) is in reference to what knowledge workers do, often without labelling what they do KM. Researchers, lawyers, and scientists, for example, all 'manage knowledge' in the course of doing their work, yet 'knowledge management' is typically only used to label their work by someone external to the work – for example, a manager or consultant looking to intervene in work processes. Good examples of KM_4 are reported in a study by Heaton and Taylor (Heaton and Taylor, 2002) of software designers in Denmark and Japan. While the designers' work is almost entirely a process of creating and using – thus, in one sense, *managing* – knowledge, neither the designers nor their managers would be likely to point to KM as a programme they have initiated.

We do not argue that these four uses are exhaustive, nor that they are watertight, mutually exclusive categories. Rather, they are intended to give a sense of the most common meanings intended by the KM label in the contemporary work place.

Reasons for the emergence of KM today

It is important to consider why particular management trends such as KM emerge at a particular time in history. While the notion of knowledge management has been around at least since the 1970s (Henry, 1975), it is arguably only in the past five years that it has become a widespread management 'buzzword'. KM's emergence may be seen as arising due to a number of contemporary trends in organizations, technologies, and discourse. The explanation includes both rational and non-rational elements.

First, KM may be seen as part of the general trend towards an increase in what is commonly referred to as knowledge work, that is, work such as that done by scientists, consultants, and physicians, which is largely dependent for its success on access to knowledge or expertise. With the recognition of the importance of knowledge in getting work done comes the concomitant recognition of the need to create processes and structures that enable workers to have access to knowledge resources.

Second and closely related to the rise of knowledge work is the recognition of intellectual capital as a source of organizational success. A concern with intellectual capital is most likely in for-profit organizations concerned with achieving competitive advantage within their industry, although many government agencies and not-for-profit (NFP) organizations also have begun to consider intellectual capital in accounting for their resources. For example, a CEO of an NFP organization explained the development of a centralized, web-based database system (an example of KM_3) thus: 'One of the major reasons for doing this [was that] the knowledge base was appalling. We needed knowledge to make good decisions' (Zorn, 2002b). Essentially, many organizations have recognized that a resource essential to their success is the collective expertise they have to do their work. This recognition often prompts KM efforts. That is, it prompts managers to attempt to identify, develop and retain intellectual capital.

A third reason for the emergence of KM is the fallout from organizational trends of the past decade. Downsizing and Business Process Re-engineering (or BPR, which often resulted in downsizing) became enormously popular business strategies in the 1990s, particularly as organizations began to value the ability to become quicker to respond to customer demands and competitors' moves. These strategies led directly and indirectly to organizations' loss of expertise. That is, many knowledge workers were terminated by the organization as part of downsizing efforts, whereas many others exited from organizational environments that were perceived to be less stable and secure as a result of downsizing. Subsequently, organizational strategists recognized that the mass exodus of expertise made organizations vulnerable. KM became attractive to these strategists as a way to protect the organization's intellectual capital from the whims of employees (Martensson, 2000; Zorn and May, 2002). The logic is that, if employees' knowledge could be captured and stored in computer databases, the organization would be less dependent on its people.

Fourth, KM has emerged in response to the explosion of information and the subsequent problem of information overload. Recent decades have seen dramatic increases of available information, such that knowledge workers have difficulty keeping up with developments in their fields of expertise. Thus, organizations see the need to find ways to manage information such that knowledge workers have access to useful information and are not overwhelmed by less useful information.

Fifth, KM is in part a response to problems created by globalized, networked organizations, including the problem of distributed expertise. Large (and even not-so-large) multi-national organizations today find themselves with workforces distributed across the globe. In many cases, workers need to coordinate their efforts with each other, or draw on expertise that may not be easily accessible. For example, international consulting firms such as Accenture or Price-Waterhouse Coopers must provide their consultants with the resources needed to offer comparable services in Jakarta, Berlin, or Hong Kong. Thus, such organizations rely increasingly on KM systems that provide general industry information as well as 'best practice' solutions to specific problems.

Of course, underlying many of these explanations for the emergence of KM is the fact of advances in information and communication technologies (ICTs). Developments in ICTs have indirectly contributed to KM's emergence by enabling and encouraging globally networked organizational forms, the explosion of information and even, to some degree, the trend towards BPR and downsizing. In the latter case, technological solutions were often used to 're-imagine' organizational processes and structures and the replacement of some manual processes with automated ones. In addition to the indirect effects, ICT advancements have contributed more directly to the emergence of KM by enabling methods of capturing, storing, and processing information, and making information immediately available to workers, as well as by suggesting possibilities for collaboration. In other words, the emergence of KM is made possible by advanced ICTs.

Finally, we cannot discuss the reasons for the emergence of KM without considering the 'faddishness' of KM. That is, as a bit of historical reflection and the recent research on management fashion (Abrahamson, 1996; Abrahamson and Fairchild, 1999; Jackson, 2001) suggests, KM is the most recent in a long line of management trends that have emerged with great fanfare as the 'next big thing' in management practice. Jackson (Jackson, 2001) argues that knowledge management (KM) is the most recent of a long string of management fashions that include Total Quality Management, Learning Organizations, and Business Process Re-engineering. The characteristics of a management fashion include (a) a collective belief that it is leading edge of management progress; (b) it has its own distinctive jargon; (c) over time it demonstrates a bell-shaped popularity lifecycle; and (d) it is actively promoted by management fashion setters such as business schools, consultants, and the popular press (Rigby, 2001). Certainly most of these characteristics apply to KM; the one question mark is whether KM will decline in popularity, although there is some evidence that it has already peaked (Jackson, 2001).

Core concepts and concerns in KM

Understanding KM and its relationship to organizational communication requires a review of some concepts central to KM. In this section, we review several clusters of related concepts.

Perhaps the most central concept to KM is knowledge itself, particularly its distinction from and relationship to similar concepts such as data, information, and wisdom. As Flanagin (2002) stated, 'A central issue within the knowledge management literature is what constitutes knowledge. Traditional information processing perspectives distinguish between data (raw numbers and facts), information (processed or analysed data that takes on relevance), and knowledge (applied information endowed by experience)' (p.242). There is a clear hierarchy inherent in these definitions, in that data is necessary but insufficient to produce information, which in turn is necessary but insufficient to produce knowledge. Wisdom (knowledge applied with good judgment) is a step further up the hierarchy. For example, many grocery store chains gather data on customer purchases, often tracking the purchases of particular customers, for example through automated systems that use bar code scanners and some form of customer identification (such as a frequent shopper card) to identify the customer and his or her purchases. The data is transformed into information when it is analysed to identify shopping patterns at particular stores or by particular categories of customers. This information becomes knowledge when it is interpreted by marketing professionals to enable them to make decisions, for example about which products to promote or discontinue. The marketing professionals' knowledge may be seen as wisdom when it is applied in ways that are particularly insightful or when it leads to decisions that prove to be beneficial.

Figure 6.1 illustrates these relationships, demonstrating that each level in the hierarchy requires the lower levels as a foundation, but is itself a different phenomenon, due to human interpretation and judgment. However, as Brown and Duguid (2000) remarked, when people use the term 'knowledge' what they typically have in mind is actually information. If knowledge is no more than information then the temptation is to underestimate the embodied, contextually situated, practical knowledge of people at work: a kind of knowledge that is not easily captured in a database.

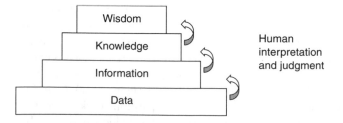

Figure 6.1 Knowledge and related concepts: a hierarchy

Distinguishing these concepts from each other is important to the management of knowledge, and equally important is understanding the possibilities for conversion of one level in the hierarchy to the next. The attempt to convert data to information, information to knowledge, and knowledge to wisdom is at the heart of KM efforts, and also points to the limits of ICTs in KM and, more generally, the possibilities for *managing* knowledge. Walsham (Walsham, 2002), among others, has argued that 'knowledge resides in human beings, not in computer systems, and communication is a complex process of human sense-reading and sense-giving, not the simple "transfer" of knowledge from one person to another' (p.267). Other scholars go further, arguing that knowledge resides not in the individual but in the interaction between or among individuals as they conduct their work. Thus, Heaton and Taylor (2002), among others (Wenger and Snyder, 2000), invoke the concept of communities of practice in explaining the creation and sharing of knowledge in organizations. Thus, while ICTs may be useful support, human interpretation and judgment are required, at least in the higher stages of such conversion processes.

A closely related distinction that is made in the KM literature is that between tacit and explicit knowledge, concepts borrowed from Polanyi (Polanyi, 1966) by Nonaka and Takeuchi (Nonaka and Takeuchi, 1995) in their widely cited model of knowledge creation and dissemination. Nonaka and Takeuchi argued that tacit knowledge is 'deeply rooted in an individual's action and experience' (p.8); when it is codified and externalized, it becomes explicit knowledge (i.e., written, drawn, or programmed) and only at that point does it become useful to the organization as a whole. In its explicit form, knowledge lends itself to re-combination, and becomes transmissible. Explicit knowledge, in turn, may subsequently be internalized, that is, merely part of what everyone in the community of work knows. Individual knowledge is transformed into organizational knowledge (and vice versa) by combining four processes: tacit-to-tacit, tacit-to-explicit, explicit-to-explicit, and explicit-to-tacit. Nonaka and Takeuchi consider the objective of knowledge management to be the enablement of a knowledge creation spiral – a sequence of steps that includes (1) socialization (tacit-to-tacit) to (2) externalization (tacit-to-explicit) to (3) combination (explicit-to-explicit) to (4) internalization (explicit-to-tacit).

The steps in the knowledge creation spiral are a fairly accurate depiction of what many knowledge management programmes *attempt* to do. Thus, KM practitioners (and managers more generally) have found it, and the tacit-explicit distinction, particularly useful in understanding the KM process and conceptualizing their objectives. So, for example, a KM manager might see her goals as: (1) identifying the tacit knowledge that employees have and that, if made explicit, would be helpful to others in the organization in making better decisions; (2) figuring out methods for collecting the tacit knowledge and making it explicit, such as putting it in a procedures manual or a database (i.e., *externalization*); (3) combining the externalized knowledge with knowledge of best practices from other sources; and (4) figuring out methods for making the combined knowledge accessible to other employees so that they may use it and, in doing so, make better decisions or perform their jobs more effectively (thus *internalizing* the explicit knowledge).

However, critics argue that Nonaka and Takeuchi's conceptualization of tacit and explicit knowledge is oversimplified. Polanyi (Polanyi, 1969), in his later writing, argued that the notion of explicit knowledge is self-contradictory. As Walsham (Walsham, 2002) argued, 'Polanyi was clear that there is no objective, explicit knowledge independent of the individual's tacit knowing' (p.268). Thus, according to Walsham, databases and other so-called knowledge repositories will be useful 'only if they connect well to the tacit knowledge of the user, and offer something new or interesting to that person' (p.268).

Two closely related concepts often invoked in the knowledge management literature are organizational learning and the learning organization. Organizational learning may be seen as a label for the process of acquiring and making use of knowledge by members of an organization, whereas the learning organization may be seen as a label for organizations that exhibit characteristics such as valuing and routinely nurturing the acquisition of knowledge (Pace, 2002). Watkins and Marsick (1997) defined the learning organization as 'one that learns continuously and transforms itself' (p.4). The close connection between knowledge management and learning may be seen in Marsick and Watkins' (1996) argument that 'a learning organization must capture, share, and use knowledge so its members can work together to change the way the organization responds to challenges' (p.4).

KM from the perspective of organizational communication: knowledge as resource

In what sense can it be said that the issues of KM are illuminated by taking an organizational communication perspective? Or, to put it differently, what is the role of communication in the management of knowledge?

Knowledge as a resource within communities of practice

We argue that KM is a process of organizational communication primarily because KM is fundamentally concerned with sensemaking: the construction of meaning by people who are caught up in a practical world of work, with its multiple, and frequently immediate, concerns. Knowledge is not, from a communicational perspective, abstracted from the domain of work, but rather it is how people are enabled to accomplish tasks, and a shared resource they continue to develop and use as they do their work. From this perspective of enablement, knowledge-as-resource has three characteristics that need to be kept in sight: (1) it is directed to an object (Suchman, 1987), (2) it develops and is elaborated on within a community of 'knowers', through normal processes of interaction, and (3) it is expressed in the discursive practices of that community.

We can illustrate these three characteristics using the example of a study by Suchman (Suchman, 1996) in which he described the activities of an operations control team in a small airport when an incoming flight is unable to unload its passengers because of malfunctioning disembarkation equipment (a set of mobile stairs). By *object*, we simply mean that on which the attention of people in the community is focused. Thus, the object of concern in this case, in the material sense, is the set of mobile stairs, but the real object (or objective) is to get the passengers off the plane, and to maintain the normal operation of the airport. It is this need to solve a present problem that focuses the attention of members of the team. The *community of knowers* is the team itself, but Suchman argues that the knowledge needed to deal with such emergencies is lodged, not only in the human actors, but also in the physical environment they have constructed for themselves, with its multiple technologies (Hutchins, 1995; Cooren and Fairhurst, 2002). Finally, the sharing of knowledge needed to resolve the crisis calls upon the group's discursive practices – that is, the all-important resource of speech. Without speech, the distributed resources of knowledge needed to deal with the situation could not be mobilized. The combination of these three characterisitics defines a *community of practice* (Lave, 1988; Lave and Wenger, 1991; Wenger, 1998).

Identifying knowledge-as-resource as located within communities of practice (CoP) highlights the central role of communication in KM. That is, people become members of a CoP when they have mastered not only its relevant skills in dealing with its usual objects, but also its modes of making sense of events, and its discursive practices, or shorthand ways of talking. For example, here is how Orr reports the recorded talk of a Xerox photocopier repairman, describing a problem he has dealt with:

> First time with the new boards, the new XER board configuration, it wouldn't cook the board if you had an arcing dicorotron. Instead, now it rips the 24-Volt Interlock in the Low Voltage Power Supply, and when it comes back ... the machine will crash and when it comes back it will give you an E053. It may or may not give you an F066 that tells you the short is in, you know, check the xerographics. Etc.
>
> (Orr, 1996: 137)

Only another experienced repairperson in the same CoP would ever be able to comprehend what he was talking about, much less do what he did, unless they had a translator. His report on his solution to a problem makes sense when the listener is not only familiar with the jargon, but is also in possession of the same fund of tacit knowledge as the speaker – a knowledge that is developed in the practice of a trade or profession. It is the tacit knowledge that accumulates with time as a result of being exposed to the same kinds of dilemma, and coming up with the same kinds of solution, that makes the sharing of knowledge among members of a community of practice so unproblematic. It is also what complicates the sharing of that knowledge with others who do not possess the same fund of tacit background understandings.

Large organizations of the kind that are characteristic of industrialized economies are actually networks of CoPs. The knowledge resources of each of these CoPs may be quite opaque to others in the same organization, even though they seem transparent to those within the community. It's important to recognize that the CoP members may be located either within or outside the organization – or both – as Brown and Duguid (2000) point out. To use an expression coined by Weick (1985), such organizations are held together by a mixture of 'tight' and 'loose' coupling: tight within the boundaries of a given CoP, loose between them.

The tight coupling that is characteristic of a single CoP, from a managerial perspective, is what we have called KM_4 – at least when that CoP is comprised of knowledge workers. As a number of empirical studies have shown (Goodwin and Goodwin, 1996; Heath and Luff, 1996; Hutchins and Klausen, 1996; Suchman, 1996), such tightly coupled professional communities function on the basis of a well-understood distribution of responsibility and authority, mediated by verbal channels of communication. Paperwork is largely absent. Oral modes of interacting are the prevailing style. In other words, managing knowledge happens reasonably easily and 'naturally' within many such communities.

Managing knowledge within large organizations

It is the effectiveness of loosely coupled forms of organizing, by comparison, that is more problematical from a KM perspective, and here again, communication is the central issue. Knowledge sharing in loosely coupled organizations is problematic since there is necessarily a translation from one CoP to another, given their different discursive and disciplinary practices. The conventions of the traditional bureaucratic form of organization are oriented to written reports, often using standardized formats, and to briefings, reports and meetings that frequently follow a pre-set agenda. Such forms of communication, which adequately served the needs of a society less oriented to knowledge as a key resource, are instruments for the maintenance of centralized control much more than they are means for effectively communicating knowledge. Reporting procedures impose a language of their own, the effect of which is to transform locally situated knowledge into data (where standardized forms are concerned) or information (where more elaborate written and verbal reports are the mode of reporting). Such traditional modes of knowledge transfer actually encourage the strategic hoarding of information, and promote bureaucratic politics (much of it behind the scenes of the façade of formal meetings). This is so because such practices enable knowledge (converted to data and information) to be stored, accumulated, and then differentially interpreted and reframed by those controlling the bureaucratic communication practices, typically managers.

It is precisely these bureaucratic conventions that KM, as it is typically envisaged, is meant to supercede. However, while the overall goals of KM are clear enough, the means to arrive at them are not. There appear to us to be two principal schools of thought in this respect. Each is associated with a different idea of what communication is and does. In one of them the goal is to arrive at a means of translating a variety of different knowledge bases into a single common language, thus facilitating easy access by many different communities of practice to a pool of collective organizational knowledge. As described above, Nonaka and Takeuchi (1995) envisage this process as a transposition of the knowledge that is locally situated in a community of practitioners (skilled bakers, for example), and dependent on tacit knowledge acquired in the practice of that profession, into what they call explicit knowledge. Once made explicit, it is assumed, its subsequent integration into other communities of practice (the engineers who are designing a large bakery, for example) is non-problematic. Underpinning this view of KM is a theory of communication that perceives knowledge as encoded into symbols, and views communication primarily as the transmission of information.

As against this first view of KM, a second school of thought questions the realism of assuming that so-called 'explicit' knowledge is objective in a way that tacit knowledge is not. As we have already observed, the tacit-explicit distinction as it is explicated by Nonaka and Takeuchi, and their interpretation of Polanyi as well, has itself been questioned (Walsham, 2002). In effect, Nonaka and Takeuchi are proposing that the transformation of knowledge acquired by the members of a community of practice, and embedded in the multiple unspoken understandings such members acquire through experience, becomes 'explicit' when it is expressed in symbols, that is, in text. On the surface, this seems straightforward: tacit knowledge is stored in our heads as thoughts, then is codified into explicit knowledge, or *texts*. But this is to introduce a misunderstanding, Heaton and Taylor (2002) argued, as to the role of text. All communication is mediated by text-construction, either expressed orally or in one or another graphic medium, such as writing, pictures or diagrams. That is, regardless of how we communicate – writing, speaking, or drawing – we are in the process of creating a product (albeit sometimes an ephemeral one). The process is text construction and the product is text. The important distinction is thus not tacit-explicit, but process-product. As process, text construction and interpretation are the means by which people establish and maintain their local organization. In this theory of communication, speech is more than a device for the conveyance of information; it is to act, to mobilize, to explain (Austin, 1962; Searle, 1969; Taylor and Van Every, 2000). As product, text is simply a record of someone's communicational activity. But here's the rub for KM: text, in the sense of product, has no inherent meaning *per se*, until it is read and interpreted by someone.

The interpretation of text, whether in the context of a conversation or in an individual reading of it, is invariably *situated* and *indexical*. By 'situated' we mean that it takes on meaning within a particular situation and in relation to particular objects; by 'indexical', we mean that a text

> communicates because it indicates, or points to, an object of attention that is already framed for the listener or reader by shared, unspoken understandings. It is the existence of those understandings that characterizes a

community of practice and discourse, and constitutes its tacit knowledge. Such tacit understandings do not, however, travel well.

(Giroux and Taylor, 2002: 500)

In fact, what seems intuitively obvious in one situation may seem completely meaningless in another.

Thus, this view assumes, there is no organizational *lingua franca* – no single objective meeting ground on which the various communities of practice comprising the organization can come together to unambiguously share their knowledge. Text interpretation – that is, reading and making sense of information stored in documents or computer files – is as much a creative process of text construction as is the process of creating the written text document in the first place. With this in mind, most forms of KM as practiced today – in our terms KM_1, KM_2, and KM_3 – become much more problematic. KM as simply a matter of collecting, organizing, storing, and distributing documents or information seems fundamentally misguided from this perspective. Of course, we are not the first to point out that KM efforts are problematic because of the problematic assumptions typically made by practitioners and theorists regarding the codification of knowledge and its subsequent interpretation. Polanyi (1969: 195) himself argued that 'The ideal of a strictly explicit knowledge is indeed self-contradictory; deprived of their tacit coefficients, all spoken words, all formulae, all maps and graphs, are strictly meaningless' (quoted in Walsham, 2002).

What we and our colleagues (Giroux and Taylor, 2002; Heaton and Taylor, 2002) are attempting to demonstrate, however, is that such problems are fundamentally communication problems – that is, problems resulting from the process and product of text construction. Until practitioners come to grips with the implications of text as process and product, KM efforts will continue to run into problems.

A simple illustration may help here. In a recent investigation, Zorn (2002b) reported a case study of a not-for-profit organization that implemented a centralized, web-based database that was used by its multiple offices around New Zealand – an example of KM_3. One important goal of the initiative was that social workers would input their knowledge – or, more accurately, information – about particular clients to whom they had or would provide services, and then this could be accessed by other social workers who might interact with that client. Yet there were multiple instances in which local interpretations of the information on the database differed from what was intended by the person who input it, largely due to the differing circumstances of their work locales.

Now of course, the fact that we cannot treat texts as objective, explicit knowledge does not mean that various KM systems are without value. In the same way that a textbook, documentary film, or website can be useful tools for learning, so can KM systems that store useful information and make it accessible to workers. However, our analysis does point to the limitations of such efforts, and it suggests that, for KM systems to be effective, attention will need to be paid to communication processes that enable different CoPs to engage in dialogue that focuses not on converting local, subjective understandings into objective texts, but into intersubjective understandings.

Barriers to communicating knowledge in organizations

Another aspect of the ways CoPs manage knowledge (that is, KM_4) is worth mentioning here, for its relevance to organizational communication: the way that the process of interpretation, or sensemaking, occurs and becomes constructed as knowledge. Sensemaking is dependent on pattern recognition. Within the bounds of a particular CoP, members confront similar phenomena, and evoke similar processes of pattern recognition. As Orr (1996) suggests, the members of such a community then recount to each other their pattern-recognition experiences in the form of 'war stories', and, as they do, they collectively develop a common fund of experience-based understanding, that both reinforces and informs their subsequent search for patterns when they are next confronted with ambivalent stimuli. As the process of interactively accounting for the recognition of patterns continues, they increasingly become confident in the legitimacy of their knowledge, to the point, finally, of a certain dogmatism. They become resistant to other interpretations that they have not themselves validated by trial and error. This resistance, given the inevitable solidarity that comes to characterize well-established communities of practice, becomes a barrier to innovation and a barrier to the transfer of knowledge across CoPs.

The problem is well illustrated by Silverman's (1999) study of the New York Police Department (NYPD). Although police departments may present themselves as bureaucratically organized (Manning, 1997), they actually function as a collection of locally situated communities of practice. Within the bounds of a single community, the usual processes of pattern recognition and sharing of experience are active, and police officers become expert in reading features of their local area. Crime, however, may be operating in patterns that do not conform to the structure of police districts. To deal with the larger configurations, a different mode of pattern recognition is required – one that takes account of inter-district connections. ICT provides the kind of information infrastructure that makes this possible. But police organization, with its characteristic defence mechanisms and inter-sector rivalries, is an effective barrier in preventing the use of ICT for inter-district pattern recognition.

In 1994, New York invited a new man, Bratton, to be its police commissioner. His first act was to request undated letters of resignation from fifteen of the department's highest-ranking officials. Within two weeks, he had dated four of those letters, and announced to his department that the era of complacency, in the face of record crime statistics, had ended. In the weeks that followed, he shook up his administration from top to bottom, getting rid of some, promoting others, and demanding levels of performance that were, for NYPD, unprecedented. The core component in his campaign, however, was a piece of information technology called 'Compstat'. What it enabled was the piecing together of the vast information resources that police automatically record in the course of their daily rounds, in order to uncover patterns of criminal activity that were not strictly local. In the current Washington jargon, they were learning 'how to connect up the dots'. The result, when this knowledge was accompanied by new kinds of organizational configurations of officers, was a dramatic decline in New York crime in the years that followed.

The tension between locally situated and centrally managed does not, however, disappear. In a postscript written in 2001, Silverman found that as the reforming fervour that Bratton's arrival stimulated cooled, the department was already showing signs of returning to its old modes of organizing and bureaucratic politicking. Like the Business Process Re-engineering that was so popular in the 1990s, the transformation of bureaucratic modes of managing proved to be easy to promise, hard to deliver. As the Hawthorn studies conducted in the 1920s illustrated, the influence of CoPs does not disappear in a rational administration; it just goes underground.

The upshot of all this is that without a sophisticated understanding of communication processes, knowledge management in its most typical forms – KM_1, KM_2, and KM_3 – is doomed to failure. The practice and study of KM may be enhanced by seeing KM as a process of managing meanings, or, as we prefer, managing the process of text construction and interpretation. The notion of communities of practice captures the complexities of how knowledge is created and shared by those who work and talk together regarding shared objects and in shared situations, and simultaneously it captures the difficulties of attempting to transfer that knowledge to others.

Challenges of KM for communication researchers and practitioners: A communication research agenda for KM

Our analysis suggests a number of key challenges of KM for communication researchers and practitioners. In this concluding section, we point to a few of the challenges that we consider most important for researchers and practitioners to address.

First, a fundamental question to address is that of where knowledge is located. While this may seem primarily a question for theorists, it has immense pragmatic importance. If there is any hope of truly managing knowledge, we must have clarity regarding what it is we are attempting to manage and where it is located. While the goal of practitioners is often to capture and store knowledge in ICTs, achieving this goal is highly problematic when one considers that theorists have argued that knowledge resides in individuals (Walsham, 2002), groups, networks (Contractor and Monge, 2002), discourse (McPhee et al., 2002) or CoPs (Heaton and Taylor, 2002). What is very apparent is that the tacit-explicit distinction, while useful, is quite limited. Clearly knowledge is not simply either in the heads of individuals (i.e., tacit) or in written texts (i.e., explicit). As we have argued above, this distinction fails to account for knowledge that is embedded in the interaction of workers as they do their work. Furthermore, it suggests a simple conversion process that masks the complex interaction of individual knowledge, shared knowledge, context, and artefacts.

Second, following Giroux and Taylor (2002), both researchers and practitioners should consider the role of text more fully and consider how texts are used to *justify* knowledge within organizations. By this they mean to draw attention to the *rhetorical* dimension of all text, namely its capacity to organize and display information in a way that makes it convincing to others: highlighting some facts, underplaying – even hiding – others. Text, in a larger organizational context, should not be simply regarded as an objective representation of explicit knowledge, but as a strategic intervention into the managerial conversation on the part of actors, each of whom is also located within at least one CoP (Robichaud *et al.*, in press). This perspective also highlights the fact that management is itself a CoP. Thus, rather than management's role being the unproblematic administration of knowledge, the focus becomes the managerial processes that result in justifying some kinds of knowledge, and not others.

Third, our analysis suggests that we may need to re-think *management* in the context of knowledge management. Lam (2000) has advocated the idea of a J-form organization, where the 'J' stands for Japan. In this organization, managers are moved around so that they become sensitive to the different CoPs' perspectives. This is more than simply MBWA (Management By Wandering Around), which became so popular in the 1980s. Rather, it involves working closely within CoPs such that their discursive practices related to pattern recognition, knowledge sharing, and knowledge justification become familiar to the manager. With this sort of intimate familiarity with various CoPs' practices, managers have a greater chance of successfully managing knowledge beyond the level of a CoP.

Finally, we would argue that the ethical dimensions of KM need to be considered more fully. The term 'knowledge management' has an ominous ring to it for people concerned about the surveillance activities of contemporary organizations. The idea that something inherently human – knowledge – may somehow be controlled for organizational uses is disturbing to many. The discourse of KM, with its emphasis on 'capturing', 'extracting', and 'harvesting' knowledge raises such concerns even more. As Zorn and May point out:

> [KM] is in part an attempt to 'extract' or 'capture' and commodify that part of the employee that is valued (his or her knowledge), thus making the organization less vulnerable to the employee's loss and making the employee more expendable. Indeed this rationale is offered by consultants who simultaneously promote a 'people-centered' approach to KM and warn organizations of the necessity of KM to avoid losing their intellectual assets to competitors.
>
> (Zorn and May, 2002: 239)

Since much information in KM systems may be collected through various forms of surveillance, Trethewey and Corman (2001) argued that KM can be conducted ethically by a consideration of two dimensions: transparency-opacity and inclusiveness-exclusiveness. The former focuses on the degree to which KM systems and their applications are visible or hidden, whereas the latter is concerned with whether such systems are designed for collective good, with all stakeholders involved in design decisions. Transparent and inclusive systems are most desirable from an ethical standpoint, yet Trethewey and Corman argue that various trends point to pressures to move towards exclusive and/or opaque systems. The challenge for communication scholars and practitioners is to find ways to encourage ethical practice.

In spite of our criticisms and concerns about KM theory and practice, we see KM as an important and, to some degree, necessary development in contemporary organizations. Furthermore, we are cautiously optimistic about the possibilities that interest in KM may hold for improving organizational communication practice and furthering our understanding of organizational communication processes.

Acknowledgements

This project was supported by a grant from the (New Zealand) Foundation for Research, Science, and Technology (contract number UOW X0016, Programme Title: The Socio-Economic Impacts of ICT).

7 The tyranny of trends?

Towards an alternative perspective on fads in management

Monica Rolfsen

Introduction

In December 2000 the management guru Tom Peters visited Norway for the first time, to conduct a seminar about his latest book (Peters, 2000). The seminar was presented in the business press with the rhetoric of rock concerts: 'Tom Peters performs live in Norway for the first time', 'release of his latest book'. The only difference from a rock concert would be the price. Not even old Rolling Stones fans would be willing to pay £1,000 for a concert ticket.

It was curiosity about the extreme popularity of such management gurus and ideas that initiated a book project upon which this article is based (Rolfsen, 2000). In a research project on business development in Norwegian industry, fads and fashions had been a recurrent theme. We wanted to investigate the most popular concepts used by the participating companies.

The title of this chapter, 'The tyranny of trends', is a metaphor for the normal view on this field: the managers as slavish followers of new fashions. Until recently, the field has not been given serious consideration among organizational researchers. Fads and fashions in management have been arrogantly rejected as mere pulp literature. Since the mid 1990s, however, the theme has been investigated with increased interest.

I will start the chapter with a brief summary of the literature on organizational concepts, and present the 'tyranny approach' upon which much of the literature is based. Second, I will focus on the communication issues and success criteria, trying to explain the extreme popularity of these textbooks. Third, I will present an alternative perspective where the different actors in the organization play an active part in the implementation process, based on one of our case studies.

The literature on organizational concepts

There are many different labels on the phenomenon I will investigate in this chapter. Although the theme has received considerable academic attention during the last ten years, not many authors have tried to come up with a definition. Abrahamson (1996: 257) is an exception, defining a management fashion as 'a relatively transitory collective belief, disseminated by management fashion setters, that a management technique leads to rational management progress'.

One of the early authors in the field adopts the term 'business fads' from the business press (Pascale, 1990). Huczynski (1993) uses the neutral 'management ideas' as a general term, and 'guru theory' as a more specific term for the popular ideas which first appeared in the 1980s. Abrahamson (1996) and Kieser (1997) choose to call the phenomenon 'management fashion', while Micklethwait and Wooldridge (1997) prefer 'management theory'. Collins (2000) uses the term 'fad', defined as 'the tendency of management gurus to proffer "peculiar" and eccentric accounts of management and organisation which retain their plausibility only because the gurus have been successful in enforcing a particular "grammar" and inquiry upon their customers' (Collins, 2000: 15).

In this chapter I want to focus on the relation between the concept and the organization implementing it, and de-emphasize the individual relation between a guru and a manager. With this intention, I find it useful to adopt 'organizational concept' as the main term, as defined by Røvik (1998): 'A legitimised recipe on how to shape parts or elements of an organisation. It is a recipe filled with enthusiasm, and is an ideal to other organisations' (Røvik, 1998: 13). However, I will also use some of the terms mentioned above when discussing the literature.

In recent years, there has been a growing debate on such concepts. What can be labelled 'the guru industry' has boomed ever since Tom Peters launched his first book (Peters and Waterman, 1982), which sold more than five million copies. Iacocca's account of his managerial career (Iacocca with Novak, 1985) became the best-selling business book that year, and Steven Covey has sold six million copies of his book *The Seven Habits of Highly Effective People* (Covey, 1989).

In the American fashion-setting community, production of management fads and fashion concepts has become a business in itself. Some companies specialize in ghostwriting potential management bestsellers (Benders and van Veen, 2001). The consultant business is increasing. American firms alone now spend $20bn. a year on outside advice. Jackson (1996) draws a picture of a guru pyramid, using Business Process Re-engineering as an example. At the top of the pyramid are the main authors Hammer and Champy, at the next level a number of 'gurus-in-waiting', on the third level the big management consultant firms who have developed major practices on the basis of the concept. At the lower level is a veritable army of consultants from medium-sized to small consultant firms.

Although there has been an immense and rapid growth in the field during the last two decades, the phenomenon is hardly new. The first recognizable guru was Frederick Taylor (1911), the father of stopwatch-based 'scientific management'. In the early 1900s his book sold millions of copies, and Taylor's seminar fees were high for their time (Micklethwait and Wooldridge, 1997; Collins, 2000).

The 1980s represented a watershed both in the United States and in Britain.

Business books were suddenly more successful than they had been in the past, and sold more than books about food, diets and sex (Huczynski, 1993). The popularity of the different concepts can be described by bell-shaped curves, where the cycles of the management fashions are getting shorter at the same time as their peaks are getting higher (Kieser, 1997). This tendency was shown already by Pascale (1990), who drew a picture of management fads and their popularity over the years. A distinct difference can be noticed around 1980, when the number of new concepts every year started following an exponential curve.

Over the last years, an interesting new trend has developed. There is apparently a huge market for 'anti-guru' bestsellers, offering harsh criticism of the different writers in the genre. Jackson (2001) mentions a few of the critical titles:

- *The Witch Doctors*
- *Fad Surfing in the Boardroom*
- *Dangerous Company*
- *Consulting Demons*

These titles indicate unfriendly attitudes towards the concepts. Ironically, the guru industry grows as fast as ever, in parallel to this equally expanding 'anti-guru' industry.

This literature focuses mainly on the gurus who have written bestsellers. However, as Clark and Salaman (1998) demonstrate, the gurus are part of a larger 'management fashion-setting' community that also includes consultants, business schools and business press organizations. And the gurus are more than just successful writers, they are also successful orators, and their performances incorporate theatrical behaviour, anecdotes, challenges, threats and humour.

Seminars like Peters' performance in Norway constitute one of the important arenas for producing and reproducing management fashions and myths (Kieser, 1997). All the players in such arenas (consulting firms, publishers and academics) can promote their different, personal goals. Kieser's conclusion is that the theatrical seminars concerned function as purely symbolic actions: 'The participant who hopes for enlightenment at such seminars is mostly disappointed' (1997: 64). Success is dependent on the charisma and fame of the guru. But, as Jackson shows, such seminars are just as important as the books in the creation of a guru myth (Jackson, 2001).

The 'tyranny approach'

As previously mentioned, most of the literature analysing organizational concepts has a critical starting point. The agenda is to describe the guru as someone offering more or less good ideas, but with brilliant communication abilities that convince the user of their exceptional value. The manager, on the other hand, is described as a slavish follower. Abrahamson can serve as a good example. In his analysis, he uses theories of fashion in women's clothes as a basis for his critique, describing managers as fashion victims. In Kieser's (1997) summary, one of three different fashion theories is called the 'marionette theory', conceptualizing fashion as the 'natural' outcome of the capitalist economy.

I define the tyranny approach as a view of management fads and fashions where the suppliers – the gurus – are seen as the strongest component. The gurus tyrannize the consumer by continually offering new fads and fashions. The consumers are manipulated by the gurus, and are eventually transformed into what could be described as dedicated followers of fashion.

Clearly, this approach has considerable explanatory power. Much of the literature is presented in religious, bombastic ways which aim to convince the reader by way of the concept's persuasive force (for instance Covey, 1989; Peters, 2000). However, the tyranny approach is not sufficient by itself to fully explain the relationship between a concept and how it is ultimately applied. Therefore, this chapter will seek to develop another approach that also deals with the manager and the organization in this process. Before I present this alternative I will describe the content of the tyranny approach further.

Pascale (1990) describes the target group as consisting of managers who are confused and overwhelmed by new trends and fads. The problem, according to Pascale, is that companies apply concepts in a piecemeal fashion and shift from one to the next too frequently, without taking a larger context into consideration. This tendency makes management life a tough one, as this interview with a marketing manager shows:

> In the past eighteen months, we have heard that profit is more important than revenue, quality is more important than profit, that people are more important than profit, that big customers are more important than our people, that big customers are more important than our small customers, and that growth is the key to our success. No wonder our performance is inconsistent.
>
> (Pascale, 1990: 18–19)

This citation paints a picture of the passive manager as a victim in the manipulative guru's hands, as the tyranny approach indicates.

Many of the critics argue that the concepts are nothing more than 'old wine in new bottles' and just empty rhetoric. Micklethwait and Wooldridge are among the most critical authors:

> Even in self-conscious, cynical Britain some forty companies now provide adventure-based management training courses where fat merchant bankers and balding bond traders swing across rivers and tell their colleagues what they really think about each other around camp fires.
>
> (Micklethwait and Wooldridge, 1997: 9)

In their view, the term 'guru' is used because most people are too well-mannered to call them 'charlatans' in public. Others call the management fashion producers 'snake oil salesmen' (Collins 2000: 5). Other terms in use are fad, panacea, fashion, myth or hype, all used in a pejorative way (Benders and van Veen, 2001: 33).

The critical literature on management concepts tries to explain the popularity of these texts and performances in different ways. Clark and Salaman (1998) have divided these different explanations into three groups: those who focus on management users, those who focus on the gurus themselves and those who focus on the socio-economic and cultural context.

The first group of explanations focuses on aspects among *the managers* that make them predisposed to management fashions. The majority of such explanations use psychological explanations, showing in what way the concepts satiate their needs, assisting the managers in controlling a world that is unordered and unstable. The guru theories help the managers to 'create a sense of order in the face of the potential chaos of human existence' (Watson, 1994: 904). The search for control makes the managers vulnerable to quick solutions. In this category, Clark and Salaman place the work of Byrne (1986, 1992), Huczynski (1993), Watson (1994b) and Jackson (1996). Besides, the concepts are often formulated in a form that is attractive to managers because of their tendency to prefer quick and easy solutions, as Conrad (1985), Freeman (1985) and Zibergeld (1984) argue.

The second group of explanations sees *the guru performances* as the most important part. They argue that the success of the guru is related to his or her public performance. Thus, it is not only the ideas but the form in which they are presented that become influential and so important (Huczynski, 1993; Clark and Salaman 1998). Clark and Salaman (1998) argue that the guru performance has major elements of display and conversion with a focus on the irrational, emotional and symbolic aspects of organization. Similarly, Huczynski argues that the public performances of management gurus are exercises in persuasive communication.

The third group of commentators has highlighted the importance of the socio-economic and cultural context within which management concepts emerge and become widely adopted. They are able to capture the 'spirit of the times', resonate with wider political programmes and correspond with core national values. A number of commentators note the affinity between organizational concepts and the values of the politico-ethical projects of developing an enterprise culture fostered by the Reagan and Thatcher administrations (for instance de Guy, 1990; Miller and Rose, 1990). Guest (1990) similarly argues that the success of guru ideas is due to their close link with core ideas in American society – optimism, simplicity, the focus of a dream and the view of a leader. For instance, the 're-engineering guru' Michael Hammer has explicitly said that the re-engineering movement suits the American national spirit better than many other, collectively oriented theories (Jackson, 2001).

Explanations of the gurus' influence

The main issue in all the analyses is to explain the huge sales figures for the books through which gurus communicate and sell their ideas. Cialdini (2001) proposes that people have a tendency to act according to so-called 'controlled responding' (2001: 8). In essence, in certain situations we react according to fixed-action patterns. The automatic behaviour patterns tend to be triggered by a single feature of the relevant information in the situation. The trigger feature can prove valuable by allowing an individual to decide on a correct course of action without having to analyse the situation carefully. The disadvantage of such responding lies in its vulnerability to silly and costly mistakes (Cialdini, 2001).

According to Cialdini (2001), the tendency to react according to fixed-action patterns is increasing in modern life because information, choices and alternatives are expanding, and knowledge is exploding. Although we all wish to make fully considered decisions in any situation, the accelerating pace of knowledge acquisition forces us to make interpretive shortcuts. The positive response towards organizational concepts can be understood as a fixed-action pattern. There is a need for change in organizations, and the advertising of books, seminars and concepts plays on the psychological dimensions described by Cialdini.

In analysing the communication and influence of the gurus, I have chosen some of the most common issues in the relevant literature: the guru's *rhetoric* developed in Kieser (1997), the use of *narratives* (Clark and Salaman, 1998) and *emotional effects* (Pattison, 1997). In the discussion, I will relate these to Cialdini's psychological categories that direct human behaviour.

The guru's rhetoric

First, a lot of the textbooks focus on the guru's *rhetoric*, such as those by Pascale (1990) and Huczynski (1993). Abrahamson (1996) and Kieser (1997) developed this perspective further. In Kieser's view, it is impossible to separate the management fashion from its rhetoric, as Abrahamson implies. According to Kieser, the organizational concept is not available in a pure form. Management fashions are started with rhetoric, and are transmitted via rhetoric (Kieser, 1997: 53).

Thus, successful management books focus strongly on simplicity, identifying one single factor as the most crucial one for success, for example culture, lean production or business process re-engineering. Moreover, the implementation of this single factor is presented as unavoidable, because the old principles are bound to fail. The key factor is linked to highly treasured values, such as efficiency, enrichment of jobs, full employment, flexibility and innovation. It is invariably reported that those implementing the new concept have made enormous improvements in business performance. For example, re-engineering experts typically promise cost reductions of between 30 and 90 per cent (Kieser

1997: 60). The new principle is always presented as having been based on empirical research, while efforts are made to ensure that at least one of its major proponents holds a prestigious academic position.

In developing the particular rhetorical story behind a given management fashions rhetoric, a consistent trait is the promulgation of myths and the creation of heroes. Of particular importance is the name of the new concept. Business Process Re-engineering, for instance, is a good name for an arena of myths and fashions, because it simultaneously suggests feasibility and an activity and is not simply addressing a goal (Kieser, 1997: 62).

Stephen Covey uses agricultural metaphors and rhetoric to convince his audience. He sets up a dichotomy between the 'natural system', which is good, and the 'social system', which is unnatural. In seminars, he elaborates what he calls 'the law of the farm':

> Cramming doesn't work in a natural system, like a farm. That is the fundamental difference between a social and a natural system ... In the short term, cramming may appear to work in a social system. You can work for the 'quick fixes', and techniques with apparent success. But, in the long run, the Law of the Farm governs in all arenas in life.
>
> (Covey et al., 1994: 55)

Relating to Cialdini's categories, the *authority dimension* is surely something the gurus utilize in their rhetoric. There is a strong pressure for compliance with the request of an authority. It is frequently adaptive to obey authorities, because they possess high levels of knowledge, wisdom and power.

The linkage to science, empirical proof and academic legitimation is important, and much space is used to tell the success stories. For instance, the use of Toyota as an ideal would be a crucial success criterion for the lean production movement. Also, the *liking dimension* can be used as explanation. People prefer to say yes to individuals they know and like. Liking is influenced by physical attractiveness, similarity, increased familiarity through repeated contact and association. In the gurus' books there is always an immense focus on case studies, using successful firms that other managers identify with and want to copy. Of course, unsuccessful case studies are never reported, creating an illusion that the technique concerned has a 100 per cent track record of success.

The misleading reliance on examples of successful implementation efforts can also be seen as a sort of *social proof*; others have been successful when implementing the guru's wisdom. This principle states that one important means that people use to decide what to believe or how to act in a situation is to look at what other people believe or are doing. It can be used to stimulate a person's compliance with a request by informing the person that many other individuals have complied with it. It is most influential when people are unsure and the situation is ambiguous, and when the situation is characterized by similarity: People are more inclined to follow the lead of similar others. As Cialdini argues, this is most efficient in uncertain situations.

Use of narratives

Clark and Salaman (1998) claim that *narratives* are important tools in the guru's contribution to the management role. These narratives are told in textbooks, on videotapes and in seminars. The ability to act as organizational storytellers is the gurus' real expertise. Clark and Salaman call these stories 'rationality-surrogated'. They compensate for the uncertainties generated by the absence of 'true' expert knowledge in the field. The use of the guru is a powerful and convincing symbol of an organization's status and aspiration.

The narratives consist of miraculous strategic virtuosity, of heroic organizational turnarounds, of battles with organizational monsters such as poor quality and service levels, and about necessary virtues and how these virtues may be gained. Above all, the narratives are about heroes who made success possible. The form is usually interactive, encouraging responses from clients and audience when presented in seminars. The stories claim authority by referring to other famous successful senior clients.

One example is Stephen Covey. The rhetorical potency of his argument, as shown in the previous section, is reinforced by a number of metaphors rooted in an agricultural heritage, and named 'the law of the farm'. In seminars, he starts with showing an idyllic short video of a potato farmer earnestly discussing his respect for 'unforgiving Mother Nature', which drew nods of recognition from some members of the audience (Jackson, 2001: 102).

In his first book, *The Seven Habits of Highly Effective People*, Covey uses a narrative to explain what he calls the 'natural law':

> This principle can be easily understood by remembering Aesop's fable of the goose and the golden egg. The fable is the story of a poor farmer who one day discovers in the nest of his pet goose a glittering golden egg. At first, he thinks it must be some kind of trick. But as he starts to throw the egg aside, he has second thoughts and takes it in to be appraised instead.
>
> The egg is pure gold! The farmer can't believe his good fortune. He becomes even more incredulous the following day when the experience is repeated. Day after day, he awakens to rush to the nest to find another golden egg. He is fabulously wealthy; it all seems too good to be true.
>
> But with his increasing wealth comes greed and impatience. Unable to wait day after day for the golden eggs, the farmer decides he will kill the goose and get them all at once. But when he opens the goose, he finds it empty. There are no golden eggs – and now there is no way to get any more. The farmer has destroyed the goose that produced them.
>
> I suggest that within this fable is a natural law, a principle – the basic definition of effectiveness. Most people see effectiveness from the golden egg paradigm: The more you produce, the more you do, the more effective you are. But as the story shows, true effectiveness is a function of two things: What is produced (the golden eggs) and the producing asset or capacity to produce (the goose).
>
> (Covey, 1989: 53–4)

According to Jackson (2001), Covey suggests in seminars that wise executives should learn from Aesop's farmer before it is too late. The metaphor is symbolically reinforced with the presentation of golden eggs to successful Covey training programme participants (2001: 103).

Another bestseller, *The One-Minute Manager*, is nothing other than a long narrative starting out like this:

> Once there was a bright young man who was looking for an effective manager. He wanted to work for one. He wanted to become one.
>
> His search had taken him over many years to the far corners of the world. He had been in small towns and in the capitals of powerful nations.
>
> (Blanchard and Johnson, 1983: 11)

In his search, he met 'tough' managers, but he did not like them. He had met 'nice' managers, whose people seemed to win but their organizations lost. At last he met a manager who was interested in both at the same time. He presented himself as a One-Minute Manager, and explained his basic principles. Then the young man talked to all the subordinates that confirmed what the managers explained about the 'One-Minute Principles'. And, not surprisingly, the story ends happily:

> 'I like you, young man,' the manager said. 'How would you like to go to work here?'
>
> The young man put down his notebook and stared in amazement. 'You mean to go to work for you?' he asked enthusiastically.
>
> 'No. I mean to go to work for yourself like the other people in my department. Nobody ever really works for anybody else. I just help people work better and in the process they benefit our organization.'
>
> This was, of course, what the young man had been looking for all along. 'I'd love to work here,' he said.
>
> And so he did – for some time.
>
> The time the special manager had invested in him paid off. Because eventually, the inevitable happened.
>
> He became a One-Minute Manager.
>
> (Blanchard and Johnson, 1983: 98)

According to Cialdini's dimensions, the *liking* aspect with regard to the guru is important. The readers identify with the story and the values presented because the alternative is presented in an unfavourable way. When stories are told orally, the guru's appearance is important. Experiments have shown that in seminars, only little attention is paid to the content. The most important aspect is the speaker's looks and appearance (Huczinski, 1993: 249).

Emotional effects

A third important aspect of communication is the use of *emotional effects*. Although the concepts at one level are justified on rational-technological grounds, they also rest on a more emotional basis (Oliver, 1999). This is noticeable in textbooks, but even more so in the guru seminars. I participated in a few seminars on lean production during the early 1990s, and the resemblance to religious revival meetings was striking. For instance, in a German seminar, a picture of a fat German eating bratwurst was contrasted with a lean Japanese, and the rhetorical question posed was: 'Which one do you want to be?'

Oliver (1999) gives an analysis of a guru seminar with Eli Goldratt, the founder of a management concept called 'OPT' (Goldratt and Cox, 1986). What Oliver finds to be most important is that seemingly rational engineers were influenced through the use of quasi-religious language and behaviour, and how emotion and faith rather than reason and data appear to shape key beliefs and behaviour. Important in such seminars are personal characteristics, for instance speaking without a script. Oliver exemplifies this point:

> Between 60 and 70 people attended the seminar. Goldratt appeared punctually at 9.15 a.m. All the delegates were wearing suits: he wore neither a jacket nor a tie but an open-necked shirt, a skullcap and open-toed sandals. He began by stating that he had no pre-prepared slides, or notes.
>
> (Oliver, 1999: 8)

The format of the day was a mix of presentations by Goldratt and simple exercises for the participants. The expression 'cost world' was used to denote the old order and 'throughput world' to denote the new one (Oliver, 1999: 9). Goldratt argued that his thinking represented a tremendous revolution via an 'expansion of thinking'.

In the afternoon, the session consisted of working through simple problems set by Goldratt. Whenever there was a wrong answer, Goldratt would point out that the audience represented a cross-section of British industry, and that there therefore was little justification for optimism. 'I give you a simple problem, and look at what you do to it' (Oliver, 1999: 11). His further remarks during this session included:

> 'It will not be easy to move from a cost world to the throughput world. We have to throw away much of what we have learnt over the last thirty years.'
>
> 'We've met the enemy. It's us.'

Towards the end of the session, Goldratt threw out the question: 'Where shall we begin the improvement?' The audience responded with a chorus of cries of 'us' and 'ourselves' (Oliver, 1999: 11).

The final session took the form of a discussion of how to implement the principles in the participants' organizations. The quotations from Goldratt represent, according to Oliver, the spirit of the discussion, the main theme of which concerned obstacles to change and improvement posed by formal training and 'emotional resistance':

> 'Why is it that something so good encounters something so bad as emotional resistance?'

> 'Do you really think that you can overcome emotional resistance with logic? If you do then you've not been married. No, you need a stronger emotion. We're fighting fire with fire and getting burned.'

> 'Slaughter, kill, the perceived solutions. Otherwise people will not think.'

The seminar concluded with Goldratt's question: 'Don't you want to leave a better world behind?' There was a general cry of 'Yes' from the audience.

The seminar was also confronted with a 'false prophet'. Goldratt was asked for his opinion about the work of a consultant in the area, whose ideas were similar to those of Goldratt. Goldratt was dismissive of the consultant, describing him as a 'charlatan', and his ideas as 'pure bullshit'.

Oliver concludes that the imagery of religious conversion was evident, embodied in Goldratt's style of dress and presentation, the language used, and the way the audience responded to him. Oliver sees this as consistent with the argument that the conversion to the new orthodoxy may have as much to do with faith and emotion as with logic and evidence (Oliver, 1999: 13).

Discussing the similarities between management theory and theology, Pattison (1997) finds many analogies. He argues that the management guru offers a vision of a world polarized between good and evil, heaven and hell, salvation and damnation. More importantly, he offers 'easy-to-grasp principles of salvation' (Pattison, 1997: 135).

Caricaturing Tom Peters' argument, Pattison (1997) suggests that his book *Thriving on Chaos* (Peters, 1988) may be summed as follows: The 'Promised Land' is under threat by foreigners. The foreign challenge has arisen because those in charge of the industry have failed to realize that the old order is passing away. But salvation is at hand. Those who would protect the 'Promised Land' rising up to meet the invaders need to embrace the 'new order'. Do not delay, tomorrow it may be too late. And those who fail to 'convert' will die.

The gurus playing on emotional effects use what Cialdini (2001) calls *the contrast principle*. By showing some unfavourable alternative in contrast to the concept you want to sell, it seems more favourable than it would have done without the opposite – for instance, the German and the Japanese mentioned above, or the contrast between the 'cost world' and the 'throughput world'.

The success criteria

Different authors give different explanations for why some management concepts become a 'hype' or a 'fad' while others do not. In our project, we came up with the following seven, which I will call success criteria for creating a management fashion (Rolfsen, 2000).

Timing is perhaps the most important requirement for success. Most of the authors identifying success criteria for organizational concepts focus on timing, but all of the authors find it hard to define this concept precisely. Kieser phrases it in the following way: 'All other ingredients are useless if the timing is not perfect. The book must hit the "nerve of today's managers"' (Kieser, 1997: 61). Huczynski (1993) has as his first success criterion that it must be 'timely, that is, it should address itself to the problems of the age' (1993: 1).

Timing may include the occurrence of economic crisis, which makes managers more receptive to changes (Benders *et al.*, 1998). The most distinct example is Peter Senge's success in writing *The Fifth Discipline* (1990), which dealt with organizational learning. He recalls in an interview why he decided to write a book: 'That morning as I meditated it dawned on me that it was not OK to sit on the sidelines this time. It was time for a book on the subject of learning organizations' (Senge, 1991: 37–8). Even though many similar publications had already appeared, for instance Argyris and Schön (1978), 1990 was obviously the right year for the learning organization. Another example, the lean production movement, was introduced at the same time as the German auto industry was in a big crisis, and it was an enormous success in that country, even though the principles were already known.

The next criterion for success is that the presentation must *describe the alternative in an unfavourable way*. More than that, the alternative to the new paradigm must be frightening, dreadful and characterized by horror. The jacket description of the Danish translation of the organizational concept 'lean production' (Womack *et al.*, 1990) reads as follows: 'If we in the west do not run our companies in the same effective way, our future will look very dark' (Womack *et al.*, 1991). In their best-seller, Hammer and Champy state that 're-engineering is the only thing that stands between many US corporations – indeed, the US economy – and disaster' (1993: viii). As previously described at a German seminar the opposite of lean production was visualized as a fat German eating lots of hot dogs.

Third, the concept must be *easy to remember*, for instance in acronyms of three letters, which is quite common. Many of the successful concepts have certain simple rules, such as Steven Covey's '7 habits', McKinzey's '6 S', the quality movement's '6 Sigma' or Senge's five disciplines. If the different rules begin with the same letter, it makes them even easier to remember. Many managers, according to Huczynski (1993), live in an orally-based world where storytelling is popular. Simple rules, simple phrases with a lot of case stories are efficient, as Tom Peters demonstrates in his latest books and his 'Wow-movement', where participants (besides buying T-shirts and baseball caps) are invited to join his 'Wow-camp' (see: http://www.tompeters.com).

A fourth criterion is to describe a *concrete recipe for action*. It is hard to change the way people think, and even harder to make thinking result in concrete action. A perspective for doing that was described by Kurt Lewin (1951) with his three-step model: 'Unfreeze, change, refreeze'. Following up is their main problem. Concrete programmes for action, 'how-to' books and recipes such as *The Lean Toolbox* (Bicheno, 2000) are ways of refreezing. Many of the later gurus are good at this; at the time when they published *The Balanced Score-card* (Kaplan and Norton, 1996), Norton's consulting firm had all the courses and training programmes ready.

The fifth criterion may appear to contradict the previous two: a successful concept should, besides being easy to remember and followed by a concrete recipe, be *vague and ambiguous*. Huczynski (1993) explains this with the need for ownership, to make the management ideas be partly created by the managers themselves. An effective way to make this happen is that 'the guru can make the idea a little opaque so as necessitate the individual to "unpack" it' (1993: 85). The concept of 'team work' in lean production is, for instance, very vaguely described (Rolfsen, 2000). Another example is the important term 'process' in Business Process Re-engineering, which is never defined precisely, even though it is the most essential notion in the books (Harrison, 1995).

Benders and van Veen (2001) call this criterion *interpretative viability*. In an earlier work, Benders shows that implementation of the management concept lean production can be loosely coupled to the original, but the label is nonetheless always used. This is also a reason why concepts wear out after use. The practice is different from the promise, which is very likely to happen when the definitions and descriptions are vague but at the same time characterized by simplicity (Kieser, 1997; Benders and van Bijsterveld, 2000; Benders and van Veen, 2001).

Criterion number six is the need to *appear to be academic*. Not all trends meet this criterion. As Huczynski shows, some of the early trends appeal to the logic of common sense. He uses Peters and Waterman as an example in their statement that their concept 'management excellence' works because it makes excellent sense (Huczynski, 1993: 101). Huczynski claims that there is a tendency towards favouring more academic gurus, because the educational level of managers is increasing. Therefore, an important basis for idea authority is scientific research. Often, prominent display of the authors' qualifications and background is enough. Some of the later management fashion concepts show that the most successful recipe is to have two authors operating as a pair, one professor (like Hammer and Kaplan) and one head of a consulting firm (like Champy and Norton).

The last of our success criteria is perhaps more controversial than the others: it seems important to launch the fashion concept with the *East Coast of the US as a geographical base*. Modern management ideas in general, and guru theory in particular, are American inventions (Pascale, 1990). All the main fads stem from the US, and the American dominance in the international consultant trade is increasing. Many of the concepts are inspired by success in other countries, especially Japan. But both the quality movement and lean production became bestsellers at a point in time when they were published in the US. They came to Europe via the US, or, more specifically, Boston, the capital of management fashion (Björkman, 1998).

This scenario applies to most of the concepts: they are launched in Boston by professors from MIT or Harvard. Seen in this light, it is not surprising that the Balanced Scorecard (Kaplan and Norton, 1996) won the game rather than similar competitors developed in Sweden or Australia.

Huczynski (1993) notes that British managers have a strong tradition of learning from experience, which makes them less receptive to the 'quick fix' solutions offered by outsiders. This would also explain why the three British gurus Edward de Bono, Charles Handy and Reg Revans all focus on encouraging managers to learn and think for themselves (Jackson, 2001).

An alternative approach: Creating communication arenas

The preceding types of explanation of guru impact in what I have called the tyranny approach are important and necessary, but also incomplete. The main problem, as Clark and Salaman (1998) argue, is that this approach assumes a simplistic, one-way conception of the guru–user relationship. The guru is defined as the dominant, initiating party who sells the users fads and empty slogans, and confuses them through rhetoric. Managers, on the other hand, are conceived as passive, docile consumers of the guru's ideas.

These explanations rely implicitly on a formalistic, academic and rationalistic conception of knowledge. Clark and Salaman offer a more interactive conception of the relationship where both parties benefit from the interaction. In this sense, gurus do not only constitute the organizational realities but also constitute managers themselves, by offering attractive conceptions of their role, which in turn define their identity: 'They tell managers why they are important, why they matter, why their skills are critical' (1998: 153). In this perspective, the guru serves an important role, but more so for the manager than for the organization.

Other authors point to the fact that most of the literature only theorizes about management fashions, giving few detailed empirically grounded examples (Newell *et al.*, 2001). Benders and van Veen (2001) focus in their article on the followers more than on the 'suppliers' of management fashions, which is quite unusual. All the critical articles focus only on the writers and their faddish language.

In my opinion, these are two closely linked shortcomings of the literature: the one-sided picture of the slavish user, and the lack of descriptions of implementation. Both point in the same direction: the focus has with few exceptions been on the supply side, on the gurus and the concepts in themselves, disconnected from the practical use.

As previously mentioned, the literature on organizational concept lacks examples and focus on implementation. In developing a new perspective, I want to use an example of a long-term implementation process of organizational concepts in a Norwegian company. I will then develop an alternative perspective on the relation between concepts and users.

Implementing by means of 'the snake'

Øyum (1999) shows a unique way in which new concepts and management fashions can be implemented without wearing out people. The object of study is a Norwegian aluminium reduction plant. In 1986, a team of senior executives and production engineers decided to start a quality process and to hire external business consultants. The main goal was to improve the quality of manufactured goods and thus reduce customer complaints. This approach represented a major redefinition of operational focus from production orientation to customer orientation. This was a novel approach for the organization.

During the quality process, the company's head office introduced a new organizational concept: 'Programme for Operational Understanding'. It was supposed to be implemented in all the firm's aluminium plants. There was some local resistance to this decision, because the plant was still in a 'quality mode' and it proved difficult to mobilize people behind another concept. The managerial challenge was to communicate to people that both the quality concept and the new concept were important at the same time. Since every plant could implement the new concept in their own way, the local managers chose to use many of the quality methods familiar to the organization when implementing the new concept.

A few years later, a new organizational change was approaching. The same strategy was chosen, using some of the best methods from earlier projects, and integrating the new ideas in the way that the organization was accustomed to organizing its improvement projects.

To explain their thinking the local managers developed a figure: 'the snake'. This was a visual image of their formalized change activities that had been accomplished since the first quality project in 1986. The snake shows the implementation of the different concepts as 'curls' where one improvement project follows the previous, without giant steps in work methods.

The snake's lessons

One important lesson learned is that the change processes are more likely to be successful if implemented as a continuum, instead of bell-shaped curves. This is a long-term process, and the company has developed its own teaching material, models and slogans, instead of copying outside concepts.

On the other hand, they have been inspired by outside ideas, but adapted them to their own models. This implies that there have been really strong 'insiders' available to carry out the process. Strong insiders are also essential to keep control over the process. A consequence of the snake is that external consultants should not be the driving forces in the implementation process, as they usually are. As an example, Benders et al. (1998) found that 80 per cent of Dutch insurance companies hired external consultants when carrying out a BPR project.

In the process of building an organization's self-confidence it is also important to *accept the past* and earlier actions, instead of rejecting them. Most organizational concepts have the opposite starting point. As Clark and Salaman (1998) put it, an important characteristic of guru theories is to offer 'a magic cure or transformation that rejects the past, and reinvents the organisation, its employees, their relationships, attitudes and behaviour' (1998: 138).

Taking Business Process Re-engineering as an example, Hammer and Champy (1993) identify the only solution as starting from scratch, and explain that re-engineering means 'the fundamental rethinking and radical redesign of business processes (1993: 32)'. The book stresses radical breaks with prevalent ways of working (Benders *et al.*, 1998). To be able to work with the snake as a guide, the Norwegian company had to work differently, re-defining the concepts in their own terms.

Towards a new perspective

As the snake illustrates, organizational concepts in practical life can turn out to look quite different from their origins. This is not surprising in itself. The interesting question is how one reflects on this difference. The fashion's fundamentalist advocates will claim that the practice is dysfunctional, because it differs from the original ideas. The strong believers will hold a position of faithfulness to the written text, and such a position can create controversies (Rolfsen, 1994).

In my view, the practical use of a concept is more interesting than the original idea. All concepts can to a certain degree be seen as socially constructed and reconstructed (Berger and Luckmann, 1966). Taking this position, the interesting discussions are moved towards the implementation, the practical constitution of the concepts and in what way the users identify with them. The implementation of management fashions can then be seen as a dialectical reflection process between the concept and the users. Instead of producing passive, alienated consumers of management fads, the change process can then function as a liberation of human potential by being a co-generative process (Elden and Levin, 1991). One crucial point in this thinking is to create *communication arenas* (Greenwood and Levin, 1998).

Communication arenas can be seen as rooms for learning processes resulting in meanings that participants trust. These are simply locations where the involved actors encounter each other in a material setting for the purpose of carrying out some change process, e.g. the implementation of a new fad.

The arenas represent an opportunity to make use of the participants' *local knowledge*, which is practical reasoning in action, and reflection on these actions. This is a different type of knowledge from that used to develop organizational concepts (Greenwood and Levin, 1998). A third key element is the importance of building on the past, of reflecting the organization's history instead of starting all over again with the new concept.

In the case of the aluminium company, all three of these points were considered. From the early TQM process, some communication arenas had been created to reflect on the local knowledge and to bring up experiences from the past instead of the rejecting what had formerly been done.

Conclusion

My main point in this chapter has been to focus on the relation between concept and organization, instead of the relation between guru and manager. This relation can be viewed as a social construction instead of a single one-way implementation. This position represents a dialectical interaction between concept and organization that liberates human potential instead of producing fashion victims. My argument is that such a process produces new praxis instead of reproducing doctrines.

In this sense, the purpose of the concept is to bring new ideas into the organization, because every fad, fashion or concept has some good points. And if in this way the focus is moved from fads and fashion in the management literature to practical use, the concept in itself can be as faddish as it wants to be. It is not the point any more.

8   Intelligent emotions management

Charmine Härtel, Leigh Kibby and
Michelle Pizer

Introduction

Human beings are a complex combination of thoughts, emotions, and physiology. To deny this means denying what makes us human. Workplaces who refute this, or fail to incorporate these ideas into their practices, are open to questions about their ethics. In contrast, embracing the full gambit of the human condition can assist organizations and their employees reach new levels of social and task performance or, at the least, reduce dissatisfaction and disharmony (Pizer and Härtel, 2004). The key to the development of ourselves and our organizations, therefore, is to work with thoughts and emotions in a way that liberates without chaos, accepts without judgment, and enables without commanding. These are the elements of what we refer to throughout this chapter as *intelligent emotions management*.

In this chapter, we explore the pervasiveness of emotions in organizational life. We begin by discussing what emotions are and how they affect us. Then, we explore the range of emotional responses and their communication. Next, we discuss organizational culture and argue that a culture's power is derived from the emotional needs of individuals. The way in which culture interacts with these emotional levers influences people, we argue, for better or for worse. This discussion establishes that humans' emotional needs are powerful leverage points, which can be exploited intentionally or unintentionally if not managed intelligently and ethically. While culture shapes the types of interactions likely to occur between individuals, intelligent and ethical management of emotions at the individual level is an important way in which a positive organizational culture can be fostered and maintained. We conclude the chapter in this vein by introducing a model relating language, emotions, and thought and outlining a specific strategy that managers can use to ensure the ethical and intelligent management of emotions, and consequently, organizational and personal health.

Emotion: What is it and how does it affect us?

Despite the fact that emotion was defined as early as Darwin (1872/1985), its definition is still debated today (Ashkanasy *et al.*, 2000, 2002b; Lord *et al.*,

2002). This confusion reflects not only the different perspectives scholars have taken towards emotion, ranging from social to biological explanations (Fraisse, 1968; Hochschild, 1983), but also the variety of emphases within perspectives (Schachter and Singer, 1962; Mandler, 1984). Despite attempts to combine these approaches, no single definition of emotion has been embraced by the academic community (see Strongman, 1977 for an in-depth review of emotions definitions and Ashkanasy *et al.*, 2000a for a recent discussion of perspectives on emotions).

Although scholars continue to passionately debate the relative emphasis that genes and socialization have on human behaviour (Rose and Rose, 2000) and point to the dangers of overemphasizing genetic role (Rose and Rose, 2000; Sapp, 2000), no scholar completely dismisses the evolutionary basis of emotions (Rose, 1998; Sapp, 2000). Thus, the evolutionary perspective of emotion continues to be one of the oldest and most influential definitions published.

Darwin's (1872/1985) primary contribution to the definition of emotion was to identify emotional expression as an adaptive mechanism. In other words, emotions help humans survive and adapt by signalling to one's self and to others when a situation is likely to be beneficial or harmful. For example, feeling a positive emotion, such as excitement, signals to us that something desirable is about to happen. Negative emotions such as frustration, on the other hand, signal to us that something undesirable is about to occur. Not only do emotions provoke us to draw closer or pull away from a situation, their display enables us to signal to others what we want to convey about ourselves, and to interpret the motives and needs of others (Jones and Rittman, 2002). This signalling function of emotions highlights the importance of the social context.

At the same time that Darwinism points to the social function of emotions, it fails to consider that the complexity of the human brain means that it can shape and alter the social norms in which these emotions play out (cf. Rose, 1998). Indeed, the large body of evidence accrued on human cultures shows that societal norms sometimes mirror the behaviours that evolutionary theory would predict and sometimes they stand in contradiction to it (Rose, 1998). Further, humans differ from animals in that they experience not only the primary emotions (for example anger, fear, surprise), but also the secondary emotions or thought-imbued emotions arising from internal causes and the person's sense of morality (for example hope, disillusionment, respect) (Vaes *et al.*, 2002; Demoulin *et al.*, in press). These secondary emotions motivate humans towards pro-social intentions and behaviours (such as to be nice and helpful for reasons of morality rather than for reasons of biology).

Human culture, we know, derives its power by interacting with the emotional needs of individuals through offering belonging to those who heed its norms and exclusion to those who do not (Pizer and Härtel, 2002, 2004). Culture influences the emotional experience by identifying what interactions take place, how these take place, what emotions can be displayed and how, and what emotions can not be displayed (cf. Earley and Francis, 2002; Pizer and

Härtel, 2002, 2004). Thus, while it can be said that emotions have a biological basis, it must also be said that that biology interacts with the societal norms humans themselves create and honour (cf. Lord *et al.*, 2002).

While the functional aspect of emotion is unlikely to be debated, the process by which it occurs is. Much research has been devoted to testing whether thought precedes emotion or vice versa, drawing heavily upon the early work of Schachter (1971) and Schachter and Singer (1962). Centralist theories like Schachter's (1971) admit that physiological reactions are precursors to emotion. However, without cognition, such reactions will not transform into a specific emotional experience. In other words, physiological arousal stimulates us to think about the source of the arousal. We experience an emotion only if our thought processes identify the cause as an emotional stimulus.

Besides emotions being viewed as a product of thought processes, many authors view emotions as also having a motor component. Izard (1993), for example, identified facial expression, posture, vocalizations, and head and eye movements as evoking emotions. It is no wonder then that individuals place primary emphasis on nonverbal body language and verbal tone in their interpretations of others' words and actions (Mehrabian, 1981).

What these multiple conceptions of emotion indicate is that emotion comprises many components and expressions, including cognitive processes, physiological changes, emotional displays, and feeling states (Izard, 1977, 1993; Plutchik, 1980). Each component and each expression is but one indicator of emotion. Therefore, learning to communicate about emotions will involve skill in recognizing and expressing emotion in all its dimensions.

The range of emotion and its communication

Humans are capable of experiencing and expressing a wide range of emotions. A well-recognized list of emotions identifies 135 emotion words (Shaver *et al.*, 1987). These emotion words are grouped under the categories of anger, love, joy, sadness, fear, and surprise. Further, recent research found evidence of 70 of these emotions being reported by individuals affected by an organizational issue (McDonald and Härtel, 2002). We list these in Table 8.1.

Emotional states can also be described in terms of three independent emotional response dimensions (Mehrabian, 1981):

- pleasure–displeasure, such as satisfied–unsatisfied
- arousal–non-arousal, which refers to the combined level of activity and alertness
- dominance–submissiveness, such as controlling–controlled and influential–influenced.

As we discussed earlier in this chapter, the communication of emotions is crucial for survival and adaptation (Darwin, 1872/1985). For example, expressing happiness at receiving a gift by smiling may encourage the person giving the

Table 8.1 Emotional responses to organizational issues

Compassion	Panic	Contempt
Fondness	Apprehension	Disgust
Shock	Disappointment	Outrage
Amazement	Hopelessness	Resentment
Elation	Helplessness	Jealousy
Pride	Sympathy	Bitterness
Relief	Regret	Loathing
Satisfaction	Insecurity	Resignation
Anxiety	Despair	Scorn
Distress	Dejection	Vengeance
Concern	Annoyance	
Dread		

gift to repeat the behaviour. In contrast, expressing displeasure at someone's late arrival with a frown may discourage repeat behaviour from that person.

Communication of emotions also underlies self-knowing and social bonding (cf. Buck, 1984; Kelly and Barsade, 2001). Thus, failure in communicating effectively about emotions to one's self frustrates one's sense of individuality, while failure in communicating effectively about emotions to others frustrates a sense of belonging. The negative emotions of individuals tend to be 'contagious', leading to a negative emotional climate (Hatfield *et al.*, 1994; Joiner, 1994; Härtel *et al.*, in press). Hence, individuals and groups require effective emotions communication to achieve and maintain emotional and social health (Spiegel, 1999). Models of emotional development, however, indicate that not all individuals and groups will be competent at doing so.

In order for people to understand the ways in which people communicate emotions, it is important to become aware of the range of emotional development. Figure 8.1 depicts emotional development as an affective hierarchy, where the most basic development form is emoting, or feeling, and the most advanced development form is self-noeticism or full acceptance.

More specifically, the affective hierarchy of emotional development comprises five building blocks:

- *Emoting* At the basis of the affective hierarchy is the exhibition of emotions.
- *Emotional awareness* The next significant step in emotional development is the ability to label emotions with words or connect emotion to language. This constitutes emotional awareness.
- *Emotional intelligence (EI)* Once individuals are able to integrate cognition and affect or connect emotion with thought, they have achieved a

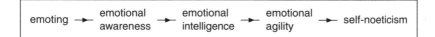

Figure 8.1 The affective hierarchy

level of emotional intelligence. EI involves the ability to describe emotions, to see them in context, and to take ownership of one's responses to emotions.

- *Emotional agility* Emotional agility refers to the ability to move through emotional states until one reaches a resolution that is congruent with the genuine self (Frankl *et al.*, 1967). Emotional agility enables goal achievement through developing new perspectives and beliefs (Lazarus, 1991; Stein and Devine, 1991), by challenging irrational thoughts and beliefs (Ellis, 1977, 1996) and by removing values and beliefs that are triggering/causing distressing emotions.
- *Self-noeticism* The penultimate developmental step is self-noeticism, a concept based on Frankl *et al.*'s (1967) concept of Noös, which refers to spirituality and a state of self-acceptance, i.e. acceptance of oneself as a human being, not for what one does, achieves or even whether one is loved (Albert Ellis, in Dryden 1991: 27). Self-noeticism refers to an individual's ability to resolve emotional states based on values aligned with one's genuine self even in those instances where the resultant choices garner disfavour with others.

Moving up the affective hierarchy requires insight, reflection, and understanding. Language will facilitate this, and, perhaps, is the only vehicle for enabling conscious emotional development and adaptation. Before exploring this point, we consider how emotions impact upon the workplace.

Research on emotions in organizations

The examination of emotions at work is a relatively recent and growing field. Proponents of its study argue that it has much to reveal about organizational behaviour. Kahn (1992, 1995, 1998), for example, found a powerful layer of emotions and relationships beneath observable organizational behaviour that exerts significant influence on shaping how people think, feel, and behave at work. These 'emotional undercurrents are powerful, moving people towards and away from one another, their tasks, and their organization' (Kahn, 1998: 72).

According to Mastenbroek (2000) and Fineman (1996, 2001), over the course of history, the mechanisms of emotion control have moved from explicit (for example, written rules) to implicit or unspoken norms. At the same time, expectations for emotional control have increased (for example, displaying politeness to an angry customer). Today, the mechanisms for emotional control are so embedded in societal expectations that rules for good behaviour need not be scribed. As a result, emotions have been driven under the surface of organizational behaviour (Pizer and Härtel, 2004), all too often forgotten by those who design and manage organizations.

Culture, which is one approach to describing organizational context (Schein, 2000; see also Chapter 13 in this volume), has important implications for the types of emotions most likely to be experienced and expressed in organizations (Triandis, 1994; Härtel *et al.*, 2002). Organizational culture is a form of social control or way of structuring social behaviour that operates on the emotional level (Van Mannen and Kunda, 1989). Culture control is, in effect, emotion control (Van Mannen and Kunda, 1989; Pizer and Härtel, 2004). It challenges the notion of the inherent freedom of individuals, and has important implications for the types of emotions most likely to be experienced and expressed in organizations (Triandis, 1994; Pizer and Härtel, 2002, 2004).

The way in which culture can be used to achieve a particular outcome is through the promise of offering belonging and identity and, at the same time, the threat of withdrawing these (Casey, 1999; Pizer and Härtel, 2002, 2004). In this way, culture sets the stage for certain behaviours, thoughts, and feelings while denying others (Pizer and Härtel, 2002, 2004). Culture's power, therefore, is derived from the emotional needs of individuals and the way in which it interacts with these emotional levers (Pizer and Härtel, 2002, 2004).

One basic need employment provides for people is a sense of belonging (Maslow, 1970). De Dreu *et al.* (2001) argue that, at the emotional level, a sense of belonging results in experiencing positive emotions such as happiness, elation, contentment and calmness. Conversely, feeling rejected is associated with negative emotions such as anxiety, depression, grief, jealousy and loneliness. Thwarting our basic need for belonging is at the core of most psychological disorders (Maslow, 1970). Thus, our need to belong is a very powerful leverage point, which can be exploited intentionally or unintentionally if it is not managed intelligently and ethically (Pizer and Härtel, 2002, 2004).

Real, potential, or imagined belonging or exclusion affects the quality of our social relations at work and the extent to which we attack, withdraw or approach others (De Dreu *et al.*, 2001; Pizer and Härtel, 2002). Given the interdependent nature of work, this will, in turn, influence our capacity to perform tasks and consequently influence, to a certain degree, the success of the organization.

A healthy organization will, therefore, be one in which our needs for belonging are met (Pizer and Härtel, 2002), and will be evidenced, among other things, by a higher proportion of felt *positive* emotions and fewer felt *negative* emotions (see Ashkanasy *et al.*, 2000, 2002b for a compilation of articles relating to this topic and Ashkanasy, Härtel and Daus, 2002 for a review).

It is because culture operates on the emotional level that it can have a significant impact on an individual's experience of work, affecting personal development and even the degree of one's psychological health or disturbance (cf. Jordan *et al.*, 2002; Pizer and Härtel, 2002; Härtel *et al.*, in press). Organizations, therefore, through the management of their cultures, have a crucial role and responsibility in contributing to the emotional needs of employees (Pizer and Härtel, 2002, 2004). As such, organizations assisting employees in developing their emotional competencies may enable these employees to develop higher quality work relationships (Pizer and Härtel, 2002, 2004).

There are several implications for managers. First, they need to increase their awareness and skill in developing, assessing, and managing organizational culture so that it provides employees with a sense of psychological safety (Van Buskirk and McGrath, 1999; Pizer and Härtel, 2002). Second, they need to be aware that because the organization's culture provides ways to express emotions through cultural practices, attempts to change such practices represent a threat to employees and will, consequently, be resisted (Beyer and Niño, 2001). Therefore, support through such changes is essential. Third, it is through the organization's culture that employees learn what specific emotions are appropriate to experience in different situations (Pizer and Härtel, 2002, 2004). Organizational culture must therefore be changed when changes in emotional expression are desired. Fourth, culture provides organizational members with a social identity and hence an emotional bond to other members and the organization itself (Beyer and Niño, 2001; Pizer and Härtel, 2002). Such commitment enhances motivation, satisfaction and retention. Weak affective commitment, on the other hand, fuels absenteeism, turnover and resistance (Jordan *et al.*, 2002). Fifth, culture produces ethnocentrism or likeness in thoughts, feelings, and behaviours (Beyer and Niño, 2001). This lack of diversity and lack of openness to diversity needs to be managed for the well-being of employees and the competitiveness of the organization (Härtel and Fujimoto, 2000).

The need to manage organizational culture intelligently and ethically

The extent to which control in organizations results in positive or negative consequences for employees depends partially on the legitimate and transparent use of those leverage points for outcomes that include the well-being of the employee (Pizer and Härtel, 2002, forthcoming 2004). If the use of those leverage points in situations of importance is perceived as fair, then organizational justice theory indicates that people will tend to respond positively. Conversely, if their use is perceived as unfair, then the affective and behavioural response will tend to be negative (Paterson and Härtel, 2002). This, in turn, can result in positive or negative consequences for the organization, such as positive or negative word of mouth about its value as an employer.

Drawing on the work of Buller and McEvoy (1999), and Gottleib and Sanzgiri (1996), Pizer and Härtel (2004) identified four characteristics of intelligent and ethical management of organizational culture:

- leaders who manage with integrity and a strong sense of social responsibility
- the fostering of dialogue and dissent
- the willingness to reflect on and learn from its actions
- the development of emotional communication skills in employees.

Because this last point is of particular relevance to this chapter, as it links the concepts of emotions and communication, it is our focus in the next section.

The skills underpinning effective emotions communication

Before we can outline a specific strategy that managers can use to ensure the ethical and intelligent management of emotions in organizations, we must identify first what we mean by effective emotions communication. This is necessary because, although communication theory does discuss work relationships, the assumption often is that these work relationships are there to produce what the organization desires, while the 'subtexts of emotional connections and disconnections running alongside our task-related conversations with one another' are ignored (Kahn, 1998: 71).

Emotions are reflective of environments, contexts, and internal states (Lazarus, 1989). Emotions, therefore, become tools for insight and understanding to one's self and others, and the interactions we have (Pizer and Härtel, 2004). Emotions as indicators of unfulfilled desires or wants provide information that can enhance the effectiveness of managers of people. Thus: 'Job satisfaction has been found to depend on the satisfaction of needs, in relation to what is wanted or valued' (Argyle, 1987: 147). One's emotional state can indicate one's job attitude (Fisher, Ashkanasy and Härtel, 2001) and provide an avenue for interacting and forming solutions. The key to opening the door that will release another's emotions and enable the intelligent management of them is understanding what the other is truly feeling and knowing how to enter into the closed room which holds the hidden (though perhaps outwardly rampaging exhibition of) emotions. We introduce the Language–Emotion–Thought Model[1] as a tool for assisting managers to using the right key for opening the emotions door.

Overview of the Language–Emotion–Thought Model

The Language–Emotion–Thought Model depicts the relationship between language, thought, and emotion (see Figure 8.2). It illustrates that this relationship is dynamic; that the elements interact with, foster, and create one another; and that each can and does impede, sustain, or facilitate the other.

For the purposes of this chapter and to provide a starting point, 'thought' is defined as the process of human mental activity related to ideas, understandings, concepts, and cognition, all of which can be used interchangeably. Language is defined as the words that express either thought or linkages to thought (Carroll, 1967; Kucaj, 1999). In this chapter we, like many other contemporary scholars (for example Lord *et al.*, 2002), consider emotions to have a specific cause (Frijda, 1993; Forgas, 1995; Weiss and Cropanzano, 1996), to be short in duration (Lord *et al.*, 2002), to manifest as an action, tendency or a feeling state (Lord *et al.*, 2002), and to be defined by social and cultural settings in addition to human biology (Oatley, 1993). For these reasons, we adopt

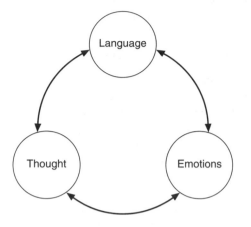

Figure 8.2 Conceptual model of language–emotion–thought

Frijda and Mesquita's (1994: 51) definition of emotion, 'Emotions are complex, structured phenomena … They are affective responses to what happens in the environment and cognitive representations of the event's meaning for the individual.'

Vygotsky (1971) postulated an inextricable connection between thought and word, thought and language, meaning and word, and meaning and language. Whilst thought and language may be linked, language might also govern thought, thus determining how the world is perceived and/or perception governed (Gopnik and Meltzoff, 1997). In fact, there may also be an inextricable link between thought, language, and action. 'Insofar as language is impossible without thought, and language and thought are impossible without the world to which they refer, the human world is more than mere vocabulary, it is word-and-action' (Friere, 1985: 50).

Language can govern the perception and interpretation of the world (or a reality that can be perceived) and in that way it governs an individual's reality or what is knowable or can be interpreted about an event (De Rivera, 1977). Although language expresses and reflects thought and in some cases facilitates it, language is not essential to thought (Diamond, 1989; Carruthers, 1997). Nonetheless, language may moderate, control, or govern thought or, at least, the outward expression of thought (Barrett, 1999).

Because language enables expression of an individual's reality and sharing of that reality through mutual expression, it is a tool for either social connection (Dunlop, 1984) or social disintegration. In fact, both thought and language represent experience and provide a tool for establishing, building, and maintaining social relationships (Olson, 1980) because relationships and interactions are an experience, which can be externalized and shared with others via language.

Emotions enable coping and development, which is achieved via a thoughtful process (Kibby and Härtel, 2002). There is some evidence that emotional intelligence (Salovey and Mayer, 1990) enables development, understanding of self, life, and others (Blanchard-Fields, 1996). 'Feeling involves a natural process of emergence and development ... Given that people cannot control these affective experiences, it is best that they learn from them' (Greenberg, 1996: 315). To learn from them means to link emotions and thought, 'To integrate the two is to help man realize what he might be' (Brown, 1976: 108). Because 'emotions in part result from beliefs ... consist of beliefs and engender beliefs' (Frijda, 1996: 21), effective emotions communication means recognizing not only the emotions, but also the beliefs that may be driving them.

Through words we try to express, describe, and label our own and others' emotions (Wierzbicka, 1992). Language is linked to ideas and to associated emotional states, and thus frames emotional states and whether, or how, the individual understands them. Not only is language then essential for human beings to consciously reflect on feelings, thought and perception, its ability to do so influences the level of our emotional communication skills (Kibby and Härtel, 2002).

The language–emotion connection is important because it reveals an interrelationship that governs how we are understood by others, the nature of our relationships, the internal relationship we have with ourselves and, eventually, what we believe. 'In most arenas of daily communication, speakers convey not only information about some state or event, but their feelings about that state or event as well' (Ochs, 1986: 256). And so, through language and a language interaction, we provide both content (i.e. information regarding thought and ideas) and affective messages.

The Language–Emotion–Thought Model provides a foundation upon which strategies for emotions communication can be formulated. Language expresses thought and emotion as well as shapes it (Kibby and Härtel, 2002). Emotions and thought can enable, create, or disable each other. Relationships with others and ourselves are shaped by these processes, as are beliefs. For organizations, leaders and managers alike, there are numerous implications to the model. We believe that some of these are as follows:

- Interpersonal skills need to be developed to address the Language–Emotion–Thought Model.
- Dialogue and thought processes need to be fostered that enable the labelling of events and others such that emotions and cognition generate action that builds respect, tolerance, appreciation of others, non-judgmental attitudes and social cohesion rather than diminishing it.
- The choice of dialogue in interactions can influence emotional states and hence well-being and workplace performance.
- Managers and leaders should be trained in a way that models an understanding of, and the skills related to, the Language–Emotion–Thought Model.

- Emotional intelligence, and any measure of such, must include aspects of dialogue and cognition.
- Self-management, coping and well-being, will involve language (for example, words to label emotions and associated thought).
- Language will determine what people think and their emotional responses. Therefore, the labels used in an organization for work and for people will determine how managers perceive people (their staff) and react towards them, i.e. is work only business, profit and process or are people human beings (rather than human capital)?
- The way we label via the words we use to describe external events or circumstances can govern emotional states and thinking processes.
- Language development, or at least language proficiency, in the predominant culture of the workplace, can impact upon the ability to manage emotions.
- Emotional development, or a model for such, can provide a reference for understanding and/or facilitating, emotions management.

We now outline some strategies that address the implications above. First, because language is a vehicle for expressing emotion and thought, individuals need to develop their skill in labelling emotions. A simple technique for managers to attend to the emotions of employees without delving into the psychotherapeutic domain is the ERA[1] communication/interaction strategy. ERA is the acronym for:

- Empathic listening or emotive tone listening
- Reflective listening
- Action based communication.

The ERA approach views an interaction as being between two people where:

- a speaker experiencing the emotion gives voice and expression to the emotion and the need or want linked to that emotion; and
- a listener (in business terms, the manager or leader) uses language in a way that assists the speaker in integrating thought and emotion.

The first phase of ERA, Empathic Listening, is based around the ideas of Carl Rogers (1966) (Frick, 1971; Nye, 1975). It is also based on the notion that using words to label or provide a label to describe an emotional state will make the emotional state conscious, which enables the individual to examine and reflect upon the emotion. Specifically, once the speaker finishes talking, the listener (or a manager/leader/mentor) says, 'You feel', followed by a single word that identifies a feeling/emotional state. The delivery, as in all aspects of the ERA approach, needs to be almost 'flat' in terms of body language and tone in order to avoid the judgmental messages that can be conveyed by nonverbal behaviour (Culley, 1992: 138).

The second phase of ERA, reflective listening, initiates once the speaker agrees with the emotion/feeling state identified by the listener. Reflection is achieved by the listener restating the feeling label followed by 'because you want to', after which the listener either leaves a silence or describes a strategic direction for action.

At this point, it is important to draw attention to the grammatical structure of the reflective phrase. The 'because you want to' implies a goal to be attained which becomes the focus, and in fact the grammar requires a conscious attention to goals (Church, 1961: 199). This phraseology is preferable to more open interactions which can lead to psychoanalysis and which requires further expertise in psychotherapy as it is not within the scope of ethical management behaviour.

The final stage of ERA is action based communication, which focuses on goal attainment that will alleviate the emotional intensity or volume. This is enacted after the speaker agrees with, or states, the goal that is identified through the reflective phase. During this final action focused stage, the strategy is for the listener to ask firstly questions like, 'How will that happen? How would that look for you? How would that work for you?' In the ensuing discussions of options, actions and outcomes can be tested with a value position, because 'a person's satisfaction depends in part on how well his values find expression in daily life style' (Yukl, 1981: 82–3).

A second strategy for dealing with the implications identified earlier in this section is to foster an organizational culture where emotions are recognized and dealt with in a way that has positive outcomes for the organization and the individuals involved. As we have shown, while culture shapes the types of interactions likely to occur between individuals, intelligent and ethical management of emotions at the individual level is an important way in which a positive organizational culture can be fostered and maintained (Pizer and Härtel, 2002, 2004). In addition to the four characteristics of intelligent and ethical management of organizational culture we identified earlier, the following measures need to be addressed.

- Employees become closer as they experience emotions together, and therefore work better together as a team (Huy, 1999, 2001, 2002). If they deal with these emotions in a manner that aligns with organizational goals, then this promotes affiliative behaviour – both with the organization and peers. In order to create an environment where emotions can be managed, managers need to acknowledge that people have to deal with emotions as well as help them to do so.
- As George (2002) notes, emotions serve to manifest and reinforce roles and status differences amongst groups. Consequently, if emotions are managed effectively, the effect that teams generate can have long-term positive effects on group development, group dynamics, group performance, and group effectiveness (George, 2002). Knowledge and acknowledgement of emotion processes is one aspect of effective emotion management (Glomb

et al., 2002). Further, rather than suppressing or ignoring emotions in the workplace, emotion can be integrated into worklife, not just into homelife, which creates a balance between the two (Ashforth and Humphrey, 1995; Grandey and Brauburger, 2002).

- A cultural audit can be undertaken to identify how the organization's vision, norms, policies, and practices lead to organizational behaviours prompting the expression or arousal of certain specific emotional states (Pizer and Härtel, 2004). Such continual monitoring will enable the identification of potential problems in the organization as well as the modification of the organization's culture and practices so that a positive, healthy organization is fostered.

A third and related strategy for dealing with emotions in the workplace is the development of emotional capability. *Emotional capability* refers to the organization's ability to acknowledge, recognize, monitor, discriminate, and attend to emotions at both the individual and collective levels (Huy, 1999). Skilful emotion management is necessary to create organizational environments that foster creativity and rapid change. If managers do not manage emotions appropriately, counterproductive work behaviour can have a detrimental effect on both the employee and the organization's culture (Liu and Perrewe, forthcoming). In contrast, as we have shown, organizations assisting employees in developing their emotional competencies may enable these employees to develop higher quality work relationships. One way to develop such skills is to train people in the theory and skills associated with the Language–Emotion–Thought Model discussed earlier. Other ways managers can develop emotional capability that attends to the employee's emotional responses to strategic change and innovation are:

- The identification, during strategic change, of the variety of emotions that can be aroused. Once known, the organization needs to accept and internalize these, and then act upon them. This may involve altering the course of the change or strategy, or assisting people to cope with the change in a healthy way.
- Because middle managers are closer to frontline workers and are more attuned to employees' needs, they need to be recognized and used by the organization as the key loci for emotion management during strategic change (Huy, 2001, 2002).
- Emotion management must be customized to the individuals and the situation in order to be effective (cf. Huy, 2001, 2002). For example, in culturally diverse settings, differences in the way people display or do not display emotion must be identified, and strategies modified to reflect these differences (Earley and Francis, 2002).

Conclusion

In this chapter we have presented theoretical frameworks that lay people can use to communicate emotions and develop tools, skills, and interaction and communication strategies for the intelligent and ethical management of emotions. Most organizations have yet to appreciate the full importance of these issues. Typically managers receive relatively little training in people management issues, and even less in such communication skills as empathic listening. Without this, organizations will be less likely to develop strategies designed to deliver intelligent emotions management, despite the gains that we believe could be accrued.

On the other hand, the communication strategies we identify in this chapter, if put in use by organizational members, can assist in fostering a healthy organizational culture where employees are viewed as autonomous and self-managed, where a variety of emotions are experienced and expressed, where psychological safety is present even during times of change, and where both organization and employee benefit.

Acknowledgements

We would like to express our gratitude to Victoria Strybosch, who provided invaluable assistance during the latter stages of the development of this chapter.

Note

1 Note that the Language–Emotion–Thought Model, the Affective Hierarchy insert diagram and the theoretical grounding for the ERA technique were developed as part of the Ph.D. thesis of the second author, Leigh Kibby.

9 Blending attitudes and motivation
A key cocktail

Harald Valås and Olav Sletta

Introduction

Motivation theories and motivation-enhancing strategies and techniques have attracted considerable interest in the organizational and management sciences. However, management science is 'notoriously faddish', which means that theories and strategies tend to move in and out of favour (Furnham, 1992: 152). While enjoying popularity, they are adopted by organizations, perhaps based on unrealistic or even naive expectations of success. In that case the result is disillusionment, dropping of strategies, and replacement by others. Little is known about the long-term effects of jumping from one fashion to another. This is hardly a pleasant state of affairs, as indicated in Norwegian educational literature by the term 'kangaroo organization'.

During the last few decades the nature and conditions of work have changed. The national and international competition in industry requires hard-working, flexible, creative, highly work-motivated and competent employees, who are also a company's most important capital. Thus, the company needs a staff with positive attitudes to their work and their workplace to maintain the company's competence and productivity, and to be able to meet future competition.

Within this world of work, motivation is an important concern, and few things are more urgent or more troubling for managers in their efforts to promote organizational effectiveness than the job satisfaction and motivation of their subordinates. Consequently, the important question is how to promote the workers' job satisfaction and motivation and thus keep the company's skilled labour.

According to organizational scientists, attitudes play a central role in their discipline (Brief, 1998). However, the definitions of attitude on which their research is founded tend to be narrow, in the sense that focus may be on one attitudinal component only (for example on feelings). This state of the art means that our 'blending of attitudes and motivation' requires a conceptual clarification as a starting point. Our conceptual and theoretical discussions will be based on educational psychology and the social psychology of education in combination with organizational studies. To date, relatively little of the social psychology literature on attitude formation has been applied by organizational scientists (Brief, 1998: 69)

The concept of attitude is popular, but the understanding of attitudes in society is limited. Thus when difficult problems are discussed with politicians, one of the most frequently heard conclusions is that a change of attitudes is necessary. But how this is to be attained is at best only vaguely indicated, and attitudinal change may be an empty phrase. Attitude refers to something that, once formed, tends to persist. Indeed, changing attitudes may require considerable effort. To suggest attitude change as a solution may actually communicate that one does not know what to do. Obviously people tend to believe that attitudes influence behaviour, and that a change of attitudes will affect action. But this is also a far more complicated matter than one might expect.

Definition of attitude

The widespread everyday usage of the attitude concept may make people think that they have the same notion in mind when they talk about attitudes, although their conceptions may differ in important ways (Berkowitz, 1986). Even in social psychology, where the study of attitudes has its disciplinary home (Brief, 1998), several different definitions are offered. An early definition was given by Gordon W. Allport:

> An attitude is a mental or neural state of readiness, organized through experience, exerting a directive or dynamic influence upon the individual's response to all objects with which it is related.
>
> (Allport, 1935: 810)

According to this definition, an attitude is a 'state of readiness', or predisposition to react in a particular way when confronted with the attitude object or issue. Attitudes always have a *referent*, they are attitudes towards something.

People are not born with their attitudes, they are acquired along the way. Attitudes can arise from single and multiple experiences (Rajecki, 1982). Most attitudes we hold are not the results of our own analysis or logical thinking, they are more likely to have been taken over from significant others (such as parents, teachers, friends and colleagues) as part of our socialization. In the long run we will develop attitudes that dominate important aspects of our social life, such as religion, marriage, politics, work and leisure, and they will tend to be long-lasting and difficult to change (Oppenheim, 1982).

Currently most social psychologists define or describe attitudes as evaluations of people, objects and ideas (Aronson *et al.*, 2002: 217). Attitudes are evaluative in that they consist of favourable or unfavourable reactions to something. Aronson *et al.* elaborate on this definition by referring to the components or parts that attitudes are made up of – feelings, beliefs, and behaviour. Most writers include these components in their definitions of the concept, thus emphasizing the affective, behavioural and cognitive nature of attitudes. By way of a handy mnemonic these have been termed the ABC of attitudes (Rajecki, 1982). However, there is some disagreement on the idea of the ABC of attitudes, and also some confusing formulations. Some researchers (for example Fishbein, 1963) prefer to define the attitude concept as single-dimensional, simply as positive or negative affect towards some object. Also, organizational scientists concerned with job satisfaction, which is considered to be an attitude, tend to define the concept in affective terms only (Brief, 1998). Other writers argue that attitudes have two components, one affective and the other cognitive. The reasons for omitting the behavioural component are either not given or only vaguely indicated. Thus Brief (1998: 53) says that he tends to rely on the two-component model 'largely for pragmatic reasons'.

In the 1980s and early 1990s cognitive social psychologists had a dominating position, and the role of affect was not adequately attended to (Brief, 1998). Research on attitudes did not fully recognize that people feel as well as think and act. Also, research on motivation was affected. According to Aronson (1990: 8–9) the concept of motivation became unfashionable: 'During the cognitive revolution in social psychology, researchers not only lost interest in the concept of motivation, they seemed to forget that it existed'.

The behavioural component of attitudes refers to *a predisposition to act* in a certain way (Greenberg and Baron, 1997: 53) or to social objects (Secord and Backman, 1964); also described as a *state of readiness* (Oppenheim, 1982). A failure to include this component means that the 'directive or dynamic influence' (in Allport's terms) is lost. However, there is some confusion about the behavioural component in the literature. Thus Aronson *et al.* (2002) describe the behavioural component as consisting of actions or observable behaviour, and Brief (1988: 53) states that the behavioural or cognitive component is 'how one acts or intends to act' towards an attitude object. According to most definitions attitudes are inner components of mental life that may express themselves through verbal statements, anger or satisfaction, selective learning and recall, and a variety of other types of behaviour (Oppenheim, 1982). However, the links between attitudes and behaviour are complex, and numerous empirical studies have demonstrated that attitudes are not directly predictive of behaviour. This lack of a strong direct relationship is explained by most writers in terms of *situational or social constraints* that prevent the person from acting out her/his attitudes. When assessments of attitudes are combined with measures of situational or social variables, such as visibility of behaviour or the effects of social norms (including expectations of significant persons), the prediction of behavioural outcomes is at its best.

Attitudes and norms

Norms specify beliefs, feelings, and behaviour that is expected from members of a group or an organization, or from people in a society. They tell us what we ought to do and, conversely, what we ought not to do in given situations. Social control through norms is necessary for any group, organization or society to function and continue to exist (Stensaasen and Sletta, 1996). Norms are established formally, sometimes as written rules, or informally, as group definitions of appropriate beliefs and behaviour in given situations. Ideally norms are widely accepted. If not, norms are often enforced through sanctions or threat of sanctions, in the form of approval, praise, scorn, or punishment. Powerful organizations may demand strong conformity, and individuals may then be strongly pressured into a homogeneous 'corporate culture' behavioural repertoire (Furnham, 1992: 344–5). Organizations can equally reward group activities, individual self-development, or creativity. But no matter how powerful organizations are, they cannot control people's attitudes.

A general tendency in people to follow norms (to conform) is explained with reference to two needs: the need to know what is 'right', and the need to be accepted (Aronson *et al.*, 2002). Particularly in new, confusing or crisis situations people look to the behaviour of others to know what is the correct (or best) thing to say or do. Experts, popular managers, and other significant or highly esteemed persons may be powerful sources of influence, i.e. norm senders, since they typically have the most appropriate information. The need to be accepted, and to remain a member of the group, makes us follow rules for acceptable behaviour, i.e. to conform to what we perceive as the conduct expected and considered appropriate by others.

Research on attitudes in organizations

In the organizational sciences research on attitudes has its focus primarily on work-related attitudes, and especially on job satisfaction. The results of more than half a century of intensive study in this field are not impressive. In his review of the literature on job satisfaction, Brief (1998) points to several questions that have not been attended to, or have not even been previously posed. Details will not be discussed here. Our critical comments on this research tradition can be summed up in three points:

1 Job satisfaction is commonly defined as how people feel about their jobs, i.e. as an affective reaction only (Greenberg and Baron, 1997; Brief, 1998). This definition is unsatisfactory, as a three-dimensional conceptualization of attitudes is generally preferred by social psychologists.
2 To define a person's job as an attitudinal object is meaningful, but problematic, considering the breadth of experiences associated with job situations. A great range of variables are applied in research on job satisfaction, in combinations that seem to be related to different attitudes, without focusing explicitly on any particular attitude. Job satisfaction is itself multidimensional. According to Furnham (1992) there may be as many as ten different dimensions of job satisfaction, like satisfaction with working conditions, with co-workers and with reward structure.
3 The research on attitudes in organizations calls for development of theoretical models that may be tested empirically, in order to identify predictive links between variables in comprehensive networks, and thus to make concomitant and longitudinal predictions possible. Until now, few studies have used this approach.

Attitudes as 'hidden motivation'

Human motives and attitudes reside in the private experience of individuals. Therefore we cannot directly observe each other's attitudes or motives. However, there are various self-evident reasons why people work: work provides a source of income, a source of social contacts, a means of structuring time, and a source of self-fulfilment and self-actualization (Furnham, 1992: 127). The amounts and types of work motivation that people experience are shown through the quality, quantity, enthusiasm, and productivity at work. Thus several aspects of work motivation are relatively open to observation.

In this sense attitudes are more complicated. Attitudes can be viewed as 'a psychologically based form of motivation' (Rajecki, 1982: 5). The motivational effects of attitudes, even when being strong, may not be open to observation. Because of the situational, social and organizational constraints described above, the behavioural component of attitudes, that is the predisposition or readiness state, will often not be acted out. Thus the formal and informal norms that cement the organization and keep it running, may effectively prevent the open expression of attitudes.

Consistency in and between attitudes

The motivational strength of attitudes rests partly on the consistency of attitudinal components within individual attitudes, and in the way different attitudes are related to each other. An implicit statement of consistency across the A-B-C components, is revealed in Allport's definition (Allport, 1935), and this has subsequently been elaborated on by numerous writers. It seems to make sense that when our cognitions about an attitude object or issue change, our affects and predispositions to act should be revised accordingly.

Different attitudes form patterns, they are not isolated boxes but are linked and intertwined. Underlying attitudes may be values or philosophies-of-life, organized in coherent systems, which guide beliefs and behaviour in many situations, at work and elsewhere (Furnham, 1992). To the extent that special attitudes are rooted in people's general value systems, they are likely to be long lasting and change-resistant. The patterns are not always logical, they may be irrational as well (Oppenheim, 1982).

Several theories have dealt with these ideas of attitude organization. Although humans may have some tolerance for inconsistency, the common assumption is that individuals attempt to maximize consistency among the various components in an attitude and between attitudes that are related to each other. If the components or attitudes are not consistent, the person will experience psychological stress, referred to as imbalance, incongruence, inconsistency, dissonance, and so forth (Albrecht *et al.*, 1987).

Among the consistency theories the theory of cognitive dissonance has been, and still is, the most influential.

Cognitive dissonance theory is concerned with the relations between attitude components and between attitudes and behaviour. The theory was presented by Festinger (1962), who was named 'the Picasso of social psychology' by his student Elliot Aronson. Festinger started with a proposition 'that if a person held two cognitions that were psychologically inconsistent, he would experience dissonance – and would attempt to reduce dissonance much like one would attempt to reduce hunger, thirst – or any drive' (Aronson, 1990: 3). Thus when cognitive dissonance occurs, that state will make one uncomfortable, and there will be a motivation to reduce the discomfort, primarily through attitudinal or behavioural changes designed to re-establish consistency.

Aronson describes it as a theory about sense-making, i.e. how people try to make sense of their behaviour 'and thus try to lead lives that are (at least in their own minds) sensible and meaningful' (Aronson, 1990: 3). Initially, social psychologists believed that dissonance could be caused by any two discrepant cognitions, but subsequent research made it clear that not all cognitive inconsistencies are equally uncomfortable (Aronson *et al.*, 2002). Dissonance was found to be most upsetting when people behave in ways that threaten their image of themselves. In his elaboration on the centrality of the self concept in the experience and reduction of dissonance, Aronson suggests three things that most individuals strive for: (1) to preserve a consistent, stable, predictable sense of self; (2) to preserve a competent sense of self; and (3) to preserve a morally good sense of self (Aronson 1990: 5). 'As a result, such acts as lying, advocating a position contrary to one's beliefs, or otherwise acting against one's principles, will arouse dissonance in most individuals' (Thibodeau and Aronson, 1992: 592). Accordingly, one way that attitudes change is when people behave inconsistently with their attitudes and cannot find external justification for their behaviour. Thus when individuals are induced to state publicly an opinion that runs counter to their own attitudes, their attitudes will tend to move in the direction of the public statement. This tendency is termed 'saying is believing' (Aronson *et al.*, 2002: 223).

In its heyday, cognitive dissonance theory generated more than a thousand experiments. In the decades that followed, the theory proved to be an extraordinarily fruitful and powerful explanatory concept (Aronson, 1990), and numerous principles and techniques for attitudinal change were suggested. Details will not be given here. Suffice it to say that dissonance techniques have proved to be powerful, and that they are applicable in groups and organizational contexts. On a mass scale, however, they are difficult to carry out. In order to change many people's attitudes in an organization or in society, such as when carrying out an anti-drugs campaign, for instance, persuasive communication is more frequently used. According to Hargie *et al.* (1999: 23), the ability to influence and persuade others is 'the main attribute of good management'.

Details about persuasive communication, with a special view on communication in organizations, are given by these authors, who define persuasion as a process of 'guiding people towards the adoption of some behaviour, belief or attitude preferred by the persuader through reasoning or emotional appeals' (Hargie *et al.*, 1999: 23).

Numerous examples of how persuasion is (or should be) used are given in social psychological literature. Sometimes high-pressure tactics are applied to get people to adopt (or not to adopt) a particular attitude or type of behaviour. When the pressure becomes so blatant that it threatens individuals' attitudinal or behavioural freedom, the persuasion attempt will often fail. According to reactance theory (Brehm, 1966; Brehm and Brehm, 1981) an unpleasant state of reactance is aroused when people feel that their freedom to act or to hold particular attitudes is threatened. Reactance is defined as a motivational state to restore a threatened or lost freedom. The greater the reactance, the more likely the person is to stick to his initial attitude or behaviour (Brief, 1998: 82), or even to rebel or boomerang, as when teenagers assert their freedom and independence by doing the opposite of what their parents ask. A classical example of reactance is Romeo and Juliet, whose love was intensified by their parents' opposition (Myers, 1996; Aronson *et al.*, 2002).

The implications of this line of reasoning seem to be that in organizational settings which facilitate individual autonomy, employees are not likely to be excessively preoccupied by hiding or defending their attitudes or by the need to justify their actions. In turn this freedom may increase the employees' initiative in self-development with future favourable outcomes. A controlling, under-stimulating environment is not likely to benefit either the employees or the organization.

Thus the effects of control versus autonomy or self-determination seem to be a highly relevant area of research in organizations, and since this serves to link attitudes and motivation, we have chosen this area as the main focus when we turn to motivation theory.

Theory of self-determination

Self-determination theory (see Deci and Ryan, 1985, 1992) is an integration of three sub-theories: cognitive evaluation theory (which describes the effects of events that initiate or regulate behaviour on motivation and motivational relevant processes); causality orientation theory (personality influence of motivation); and organismic integration theory (motivation and development – where the internalization of extrinsically motivated behaviour is of special interest), of which the first and second will be mentioned here. The coherence and broad applicability of these ideas have elevated self-determination theory to a position of prominence among contemporary theories of human motivation.

Cognitive evaluation theory is based on three fundamental human needs. These are the needs for autonomy, competence, and relatedness, all of which are innate.

First, human beings have *a need to maintain a sense of self-determination*, the feeling that actions are based on personal choice (perceived intrinsic loci of causality) rather than on obligation or coercion (perceived extrinsic loci of causality). External events relevant to the initiation or regulation of behaviour will affect a person's intrinsic motivation to the extent that they influence the perceived locus of causality for that behaviour. Events that promote a more external perceived locus of causality will undermine intrinsic motivation, whereas those that promote a more internally perceived locus of causality will enhance intrinsic motivation (Deci and Ryan, 1985: 62). However, it should be emphasized that in this connection self-determination refers to the extent to which a person perceives or feels self-determinate, and not to objective realities. Self-determination is a question about maximum autonomy support within well-defined limits. Here, autonomy support involves leaders understanding and acknowledging their subordinates' perspectives, providing meaningful information in an informational manner, offering opportunities for choice, and encouraging self-initiation (Deci and Ryan, 1985). In this connection important questions refer to opportunities to make inputs into deciding how to do the job, to express one's ideas and opinion on the job, to what extent one feels pressured at work, if one's feelings are taken into consideration on the job, etc. (Deci and Ryan, 2000).

Several studies have shown that autonomy-supporting leaders tend to promote the intrinsic motivation and job satisfaction, while controlling leaders tend to undermine intrinsic motivation and promote extrinsic motivation or amotivation (learned helplessness). Thus, research reveals a positive association between autonomy supportive management and level of trust in the corporation and overall job satisfaction (Deci et al., 1989), trust and loyalty (Pajak and Glickman, 1989), greater job satisfaction, less absenteeism, and better physical and psychological well-being (Blais and Briere, 1992) and intrinsic motivation (Gagne et al., 1997).

A second issue in cognitive evaluation is that people have an intrinsic need to feel competent and to master optimal challenges. As early as 1959, White (1959) proposed a need for effectance as a basic motivational propensity that energizes a wide range of non-drivebased behaviours, and suggested that there is an inherent satisfaction in doing activities which exercises and extend one's capabilities. The energy behind these activities was named *effectance motivation*, and the corresponding affect feeling of efficacy, while the term competence was used to connote the structures through which effectance motivation operate. Competencies are thus the accumulated results of the interaction with the environment, of exploration, learning, and adaptation. In a biological sense, competence refers to the capacity to interact effectively with the environment that ensures the maintenance of the organism. Human beings, unlike lower animals, have few competencies innately provided and need to learn a great deal about how to deal with the environment. The motivational counterpart of this capacity is often called competence motivation, effectance motivation, or mastery motivation (see Kagan, 1972). According to White, the development of competence is in part maturational and in part learned, and the need for competence provides the energy for this learning. The feeling of effectance that follows from competent interaction with the environment is the reward for this type of behaviour and can sustain behaviour independently of any drive-based or other form of reinforcement (in psychoanalytic theory referred to as independent ego energy).

In short, White's theory (White, 1959) provided the foundation for other theories focused on personal agency beliefs and the intrinsic desire for a personal agency. Inherent in human beings is a general desire to explore and master our environment, in other words to be competent, with manifestations of this general motive varying in strength across domains as a function of emotions, self-referent thought concerning one's competence, and contextual support for exploration and mastery. A sense of personal competence/mastery advances feelings of pleasure, while a sense of incompetence advances feelings of anxiety, despondency or distaste. One condition that is critical for effectance motivation is an optimal challenge given the person's capacities.

Thus, external events will affect a person's intrinsic motivation for an optimally challenging activity to the extent that they influence the person's perceived competence, provided that the context is autonomy-supporting. Events that promote greater perceived competence will enhance intrinsic motivation, whereas those that diminish perceived competence will decrease intrinsic motivation (Deci and Ryan, 1985: 63).

The *competence* concept, as used here, is in a way like the concept perceived *probability of success* from an expectancy-*value* point of view, as conceptualized by, for example, Atkinson (1964) or the concept *perceived self-efficacy* as defined by Bandura (1977). However, in accordance with White (1959), the theory of self-determination considers feeling competent as an intrinsic need that is inherent in human beings.

Three conditions must be fulfilled to satisfy the need for feeling competent. First, the task or activity must be optimally challenging. Very easy jobs or routine work will not promote the feeling of competence. On the other hand, when activities are unmasterable, perceived incompetence tends to occur. Second, the person must feel some self-determination or autonomy with respect to the activity. If these two conditions are met, success or positive feedback will increase one's feeling of competence and thus promote intrinsic motivation.

The association between perceived competence and intrinsic motivation, optimally challenging tasks and a context of some self-determination, is supported by several studies (for example Anderson *et al.*, 1976; Fisher, 1978; Blanck *et al.*, 1984; Valås and Søvik, 1993). However, most of these studies refer to college students or school children. Concerning adults at work, typical questions are whether they feel competent, get positive feedback, are able to learn interesting new skills at work, feel a sense of accomplishment from working, have a chance to show their capability, etc. (Deci and Ryan, 2000).

The third condition that must be fulfilled in order for people to feel competent relates to the human *need to maintain a sense of relatedness*, i.e. a sense of mutual respect, caring and reliance with others. Building or maintaining attachments, friendships, intimacy, or a sense of community, and avoiding feelings of social isolation or separateness are important for fulfilling this need. Many of the theories of human motivation and development incorporate some sort of innate process by which people seek to establish and maintain satisfying relations with other people (see Reis and Patrick, 1996 for a review), as well as relatedness, in addition to autonomy and competence, which are included in several recent studies by Deci and Ryan (for example Deci and Ryan, 2000; Ryan and Deci, 2000a, 2000b).

Causality orientation theory deals with the personality influence of motivation and people's general tendencies to behave as autonomy oriented, control oriented or interpersonally oriented across situations, activities, or contexts.

Self-determined behaviour is initiated and regulated by an individual's own choices, and using information from internal or external sources, one chooses how to behave in anticipation of achieving self-related goals and satisfying organismic needs (self-determination, competence and relatedness). When autonomy oriented, people tend to use available information to make choices (consciously or intuitively) to regulate themselves in pursuit of self-selected goals, and thus feel self-determined. They seek out opportunities to be autonomous and initiate in the situations they are in, and tend to interpret environments as informational and use the information to make choices about when and where to initiate.

Control-determined behaviour is initiated and regulated by environmental control, such as reward contingencies, external demands, or by internally controlling states (sense of duty, guilt, fear of failure, etc.). The control orientation involves experiencing initiating events, such as pressure to behave in accordance with the demands of the environment (feelings like should, have to, ought to, or must). Typically, control orientation involves a conflict between the controller and the controlled, a conflict that may be suppressed and unconscious (without experiencing the sense of conflict) or conscious, in which case the person would be either compliant or rebellious. In both cases the sense of choice or self-determination is lacking, and the person tends to rationalize and reduce the cognitive dissonance by aligning his or her thoughts and cognitions with actions.

From Deci and Ryan's (1985) point of view, control orientation may be associated with high levels of performance. Through learning how to achieve desired, contingently offered approval, a person may become competent and effective, but as the person's sense of self-worth depends on continued good performance, the activity becomes instrumental and a means of protecting the sense of self-worth, and thus promoting ego involvement (see, for example, Nicholls, 1979, 1983).

Amotivated behaviour is initiated and regulated by forces beyond the person's intentional control and is neither intrinsically nor extrinsically motivated. Thus, such behaviour is almost identical with Abramson's personal helplessness (see Seligman, 1974, 1975; Abramson *et al.*, 1978; Abramson *et al.*, 1989).

The impersonal orientation promotes amotivated behaviour and involves the belief that behaviour and outcomes are independent and that forces are uncontrollable. The results are the experience of incompetence and, like personal helplessness, the impersonal orientation is often followed by anxiety, hopelessness, and depression.

In sum, autonomy orientation together with psychological needs satisfaction (self-determination, competence and relatedness) seem to be necessary (but not sufficient) conditions for work motivation, work satisfaction, positive attitudes to the workplace, psychological adjustment, health and well-being. However, it remains to be seen what factors are affecting need satisfaction and thus intrinsic motivation.

Is causality orientation a stable and general trait of the personality? Evidence indicates that individuals' causality orientations are partly general and stable, and partly dependent on the environment and the context. It seems reasonable that controlling environments and authoritarian leaderships will promote control or impersonal orientation and external motivation (see Deci *et al.*, 1981), while on the other hand informational environment will promote autonomy orientation and intrinsic motivation.

Controlling events are those that are experienced as pressure to think, feel or behave in specified ways, and thus facilitate an external locus of causality. Situations or contexts that make an activity instrumental relative to a desired outcome (such as receiving rewards, or avoiding criticism from the supervisor) will often be interpreted and felt as controlling. Similarly, evaluation may be experienced as pressure and therefore controlling. However, it is possible to administer both instrumentality and evaluation in an informative way and thereby prevent undermining the feeling of self-determination.

The term informational should be clarified. According to Deci and Ryan (1985), informative events are those that allow choice and autonomy and provide information that is useful for an individual to interact effectively with the environment. However, informative environments should not be confused with permissive environments, which are without control and lack structure. On the contrary, informational environments are structured, and set informed, clear and plain limits, which are explained, understood and accepted by the employees. Within these structures and limits the employees are given maximum opportunities to make choices and feel self-determination. According to Deci and Ryan (1985) and Ryan and Deci (2000b), four factors make an event informative: first, opportunity to make choices, which means absence of unnecessary control, and thus promotes a sense of self-determination; second, availability of efficiency relevant information concerning optimally challenging activities; and third, possible implicit conflicts with a person's needs or feelings must be acknowledged. A fourth factor, as stated in Ryan and Deci's later publications (Ryan and Deci, 2000b) is a sense of belonging or a feeling of relatedness. Thus, an event is informative to the extent that it promotes feeling of relatedness.

To create an informational environment and thus contribute to the employees' experienced satisfaction of their needs for autonomy, competence and relatedness, the leadership's ways of communicating are essential. Thus, positive informative feedback concerning the job will increase the employee's feeling of competence and thereby increase their intrinsic motivation and job satisfaction. On the contrary, negative controlling feedback may decrease the employee's job satisfaction, promote extrinsic motivation or, at worst, induce learned helplessness. However, the employee's feeling of competence is best taken care of if they succeed in their jobs, provided that the jobs are challenging. Routine jobs are often tedious and boring and will not give the employees a feeling of competence. Consequently, the supervisors have to provide, as far as possible, for their subordinates a chance to show their capabilities and also express that they are recognized.

Moreover, for a work environment to be informative, supervisors' communication should bear evidence of respect and esteem towards their subordinates. Informal talks with their subordinates about ordinary subjects like leisure activities, hobbies, family, etc. in addition to subjects concerning the company, should enhance subordinates' feeling of relatedness. In addition, much of the work in modern industry is based on team activities, especially in high technology industry. Thus, conditions for high productivity and work satisfaction are positive interpersonal relations.

Finally, an informational work environment is also contingent on autonomy-supportive supervisors, that is, supervisors who understand and acknowledge their subordinates' perspectives, and provide meaningful information in an informational manner, offer opportunities for choice, and encourage self-initiation. Support for competence and relatedness seems to be implicit in the concept of autonomy support. Hence, autonomy support is also expected to facilitate satisfaction of the needs for competence and relatedness. Consequently, supervisors should make their subordinates feel that they can contribute and make suggestions when decisions that affect their jobs are taken, feel little or moderate pressure, strain, and stress, and feel free to express their ideas and opinions at work.

To summarize, an informational work environment is a necessary condition for need satisfaction, particularly the three innate needs competence, autonomy, and relatedness, which are necessary for work satisfaction, task engagement, psychological adjustment, and well-being, and for the employees to develop positive attitudes to their jobs, work colleagues, supervisors, employer, and to the company. Thus, organizational and communicative factors within the company should be evaluated and reconsidered in the light of self-determination theory.

Conclusion

Can a blending of attitudes and motivation be accomplished, and in case it can, where will it get us?

The starting point for a discussion can be found already in the conceptualizations of attitude, where the blending should be, and often is, inherent. The 'state of readiness' and the 'directive and dynamic influence' (in Allport's terms) clearly point to the motivational strength of attitudes. So do the three-dimensional definitions of attitudes that have subsequently been preferred in social psychological research.

In organizational literature the number of attitudinal components are often reduced to two or even one. In the case of defining attitudes as feelings (for example the feelings one has to one's job), 'attitude' seems to be included in and become part of motivation, which means that there is no need for an attitude concept. This is not the sort of blending we are aiming at. To stick to a narrow attitude concept is like removing the spirits and juice when mixing the cocktail.

To our knowledge no successful attempt has been made to integrate theories of motivation and social psychological theories of attitudes. Clearly, the theories are not mutually exclusive; they are, or should be, compatible. This chapter has aimed at pointing to ties between the two academic areas, and hopefully it will serve as an argument for the advantage of considering both.

When organizations are planning activities with a view to motivating their employees, or to developing favourable attitudes to some aspects of their policy, their programmes and strategies should be based on research in both areas. However, the immediate and long-term success of such efforts depends on the competence of programme supervisors, more specifically on their mastery of the subject matter, their communication skills, including the skills of persuasive and autonomy-supporting communication, their sensitivity to self-determination needs, and their understanding of the subtle and complex links between attitudes and their expression. Activities should be planned with a long-term perspective, partly to avoid over-application of principles based on experiences from an early phase (while enthusiasm is high), and partly because participants' commitments to longitudinal processes are likely to prevent faddishness. In the long run, participants may forget the distinction between attitudes and motivation, or realize that the distinction is artificial (which of course it is in real life), and the blending has taken place.

Such experience might be the point of departure for theory development, which, if it worked, would serve to bring new perspectives into organizational thinking and practice.

10 Communication competence in cross-cultural business interactions

Oluremi Ayoko, Charmine Härtel, Greg Fisher and Yuka Fujimoto

Introduction

Evidence abounds of an increasing escalation of business globalization (Bartlett, 1989; Nadesan, 2001; Prince, 2001; Sands, 2001). Increasing competitive pressure is being placed on international firms to develop worldwide communication networks within their own firms, as well as with their suppliers, customers and their external constituencies such as government agencies and special interest groups (Babcock and Babcock, 2001; Fisher et al., 2001b). This phenomenon is compounded by the constant development in technologies that allow a rapidly expanding number of messages to be exchanged within a short span of time and across large geographical distances. Communication skills that bridge cultural boundaries are therefore critical to both employee and organizational effectiveness.

These trends mean that today's organizations must find effective ways to manage the increasing heterogeneity in their workforces and consumer bases (Ashkanasy et al., 2002a). Research indicates environments where diversity creates *productive* conflict result in organizational effectiveness such as greater innovativeness (Jackson et al., 1992), improved problem solving and decision making, and higher levels of creativity (Härtel and Fujimoto, 1999). On the other hand, failing to equip employees with the skill to deal with diversity runs the risk of promoting *destructive* conflict in the organization (Watson et al., 1993; Ayoko et al., in press), which results in reductions in team performance and increased turnover and absenteeism (Hambrick, 1994), as well as negative effects on individuals' emotional well-being (Fujimoto and Härtel, in press).

The organizational implications of diversity mean that individuals who come from different cultures and possess different language competence levels will require specific strategies that can help them achieve effective communication during business interactions. This is because it is anticipated that their roles as producers and customers will add value to interrelated global business networks (Porter, 1985). This is, however, no easy task. The diversity literature paints conflicting pictures of the effects of cross-cultural (compared to mono-cultural) interaction (for example Milliken and Martins, 1996; Chatman et al., 1998;

Härtel and Fujimoto, 1999). Specifically, studies show that, in comparison to homogeneous workgroups, diverse workgroups suffer from:

- greater conflict
- more turnover
- higher stress
- more absenteeism
- greater communication problems (O'Reilly *et al.*, 1989; Zenger and Lawrence, 1989; Alder, 1991; Tsui *et al.*, 1992)
- less trust
- lower job satisfaction
- low cohesion
- poor social integration (Hambrick 1994).

While the greater likelihood of these difficulties occurring in diverse workgroups is well established, research in this area has offered organizations little information upon which management practices for interactions for culturally diverse workforces and customer bases can be formulated (cf. Pelled *et al.*, 1999). One of the goals of this chapter is to examine the issue of communication competence in cross-cultural business interactions. To begin this journey, we must first understand what culture is.

Culture

Culture has been studied widely within the cross-cultural management arena and refers to the symbolic dimension of human action. As discussed in Chapter 13 in this volume, it refers to the sum of the learned values, beliefs, attitudes, practices and customs of a group, which are passed from one generation to another (Collier, 1989). Culture is, therefore, a historically derived system of shared symbolic ideas and meanings that a community uses to interpret and give meaning to their experience (Gudykunst and Kim, 1984; Collier, 1989).

Individuals' dispositions are informed by their early social and cultural experiences and, consequently, with respect to communication in groups and organizational contexts, culture shapes our interaction goals, which in turn, have implications for our styles of interaction, our interpretation of behaviours and communications, and our management of cultural conflict (Hofstede, 1995; Zorn and Violanti, 1996; Kozan and Ergin, 1998; Weaver, 1998). For example, national culture was found to influence organizational managerial values in twelve Thai-owned companies and thirteen Amercian-owned companies in Thailand (Sorod, 1991). Communication competent strategies were also found to vary by organizational type (for example, government, state enterprise, or private business) in Thailand (Komin, 1995). These findings illustrate that conflict management skills may not only vary across cultures but also across organizational types (Komin, 1995).

The salient differences among cultures have been classified according to Hofstede's (1980) research on individualistic and collectivist societies (Triandis, 1990), which are sometimes referred to as low and high context cultures (Hofstede, 1980, 1991). On the one hand, collectivist cultures place greater emphasis on group goals, co-operation, and interdependence of self within the group (Triandis, 1990; Cox and Blake, 1991). On the other hand, individualist cultures place greater emphasis on personal goals, competition, and independence of self from groups (Triandis, 1990; Stipek, 1998). Numerous studies have demonstrated that the effect of these differences in workgroups is multifold (for example Smith *et al.*, 1995; Selmer, 1997; Hall *et al.*, 1998; Pillai and Meindl, 1998; Tinsulanonda, 1998; Von Glinow, 1998; Gibson, 1999; Jung and Avolio, 1999; Kuntonbutr, 1999; Scandura *et al.*, 1999; Ayoko and Härtel, 2000; Drost and Fisher *et al.*, 2000). Namely:

- culture tends to lead to different preferences and responses to leadership style
- leaders tend to hold more positive views and interactions with employees similar to themselves and more negative ones with employees different from themselves
- trust tends to be more difficult to achieve among members of diverse workgroups
- decision making tends to be more innovative when diverse perspectives are used
- decision making tends to be diminished and slower when diverse perspectives are ignored or argued over without resolution
- job satisfaction and organizational commitment, especially of minority members, tends to decrease when diversity is not valued
- job satisfaction and organizational commitment tend to increase when diversity is valued, which improves performance
- turnover of minority members tends to increase when diversity is not valued, which increases the homogeneity and 'groupthink' in an organization
- task performance tends to diminish when the differences in a group are responded to with destructive conflict and communication patterns, whereas it tends to increase when the differences in a group are responded to with constructive conflict and communication patterns.

Although studies abound comparing collectivist and individualist cultures, the factors that foster effective communicative interactions between individualist and collectivist cultures are not thoroughly documented in the literature. This chapter attempts to fill this void by examining communicative competence in business interactions across cultures.

The relationship between culture and communication

The communication literature has documented the interdependent relationship between culture and communication well (Gudykunst, 1997). *Culture*, as defined earlier, provides the structure of the communication process (Birdwhistell, 1970) whereas *communication* involves the verbal and non verbal transmission of information (Keesing, 1974, in Gudykunst, 1997). Therefore, the relationship between culture and communication has been described as a point between the two extremes of these constructs, that is, between culture and communication itself (Keesing, 1974, in Gudykunst, 1997). In other words, the way in which people communicate is influenced by their culture and, in turn, their culture is influenced by the way they communicate. As such, academics and scholars alike must be aware that culture plays an important role in the communication process. (See Gudykunst, 1997 for more extensive discussion.)

Skills needed to communicate cross-culturally

There are a myriad of skills and competencies that facilitate cross-cultural communication (Lloyd and Härtel, 2003). A communicatively competent individual has both the knowledge of the appropriate communication patterns for a situation and the ability to apply that knowledge (Cooley and Roach, 1984: 25). Researchers have also used a rule-based approach to conceptualizing communication competence (Harris and Cronen, 1979), identifying both *strategic* and *tactical* communication competence (Jablin *et al.*, 1994) as vital components in the process. Strategic communication deals with knowledge of organizational realities, what things mean in the organizational context and how they differ between organizations. Tactical communication competence, in contrast, is defined as an individual's ability to follow and manipulate regulative rules. Tactical communication competence, therefore, includes communication skills and performance capability to achieve personal, group, and organizational goals.

Based on theories of social cognition (Sypher 1984, Sypher and Zorn, 1986), tactical communication competencies, as opposed to strategic communication competencies, are viewed from a skill/performance perspective (cf. DiSalvo, 1980; DiSalvo and Larsen, 1987). Such skills include advising, persuading, instructing, interviewing, exchanging information, public speaking, leading discussions, delegating, problem solving, and listening (cf. DiSalvo, 1980; DiSalvo and Larsen, 1987). Underlying these skills are communication skills and knowledge communication. While these dimensions are generally germane across cultures, the specific characteristics of each dimension are likely to vary from culture to culture. Thus, cultural variability may be a major factor for which members from different national cultures develop their understandings of the strategic communication knowledge and tactical skills needed for communication competence.

Business communication is a dynamic, two-way, multiple influenced, and transformational translation process (Sherblom, 1998). The complexity and variety of the translation process is intricate given that individuals send and receive messages via multiple languages and cultures in varying business and social environments. Skills that enable individuals to be open to differences in interaction preferences are therefore critical to achieving positive outcomes in cross-cultural business interactions (Härtel and Fujimoto, 2000). This set of skills is what we call business communication competence (BCC) across cultures. Our BCC strategies are firmly anchored in communication accommodation theory (CAT) (Giles, 1973; Giles and Powesland, 1975) and specifically refer to an individual's capability to use CAT communication strategies such as approximation, discourse management, interpersonal control, and interpretability to achieve effective interactions in a cross-cultural business environment. We propose in this chapter that these BCC strategies are a useful tool that can lead to effective cross-cultural business interactions both external and internal (i.e. cross-cultural co-worker relationships) to the organization. In the next section, we present the theoretical underpinnings of the proposed BCC strategies.

Theoretical background: Communication accommodation and categorization theories

Communication accommodation theory (CAT) examines the attitudes, motivation, intentions, and identities that intervene between objective social and contextual variables and the individual's language behaviours. Designed to explain the cognitive and affective processes fundamental to speech convergence or divergence (Giles, 1973; Giles and Powesland, 1975), CAT clarifies and describes the communicative behaviours arising in interactions and their subsequent effects.

CAT rests on the premise that group interactions and goals are driven by the interpersonal history between the interacting parties and the individuals' propensity to view an encounter in intergroup terms (Watson and Gallois, 1998). The type and course of an ongoing discourse is then shaped by these predispositions, attitudes, and views. In other words, the participants' perceptions, speech behaviour, language use, and subsequent responses are influenced as they negotiate meaning. In this way, each participant develops and evaluates the other in order to gauge and modify his/her initial perception and orientation for further interactions.

Specific strategies are employed to communicate modifications to speech behaviour during interactions. Participants, for example, approximate or converge on their counterpart's language use (i.e. using the same language structure, accent, dialect, speech rate, and lexical diversity as their interlocutors) to gain acceptance or approval and close the social distance between them (Coupland et al., 1988; Gallois et al., 1988). Such movement is explained, as we show next, by social identity theory (Tajfel and Turner, 1986), social categorization theory (Turner, 1987) and the similarity attraction paradigm (Bryne, 1971).

Social identity theory (Tajfel and Turner, 1986) asserts that individuals identify themselves with respect to group memberships and tend to classify others into one or more categories in order to identify similarities and differences. Therefore, an employee's perception of who they are, based on cognitive and social evaluations, can determine who they seek to interact with in their organization (Ashforth and Mael, 1989). Individuals establish a positive social identity and confirm association by showing preference to members of their own social category, which has the effect of disadvantaging out-group members. The differential treatment, in turn, disrupts group interactions (Jehn et al., 1999).

Categorizing individuals in a workgroup into different groups can aggravate hostility or animosity within the workgroup, evidenced by relationship conflicts (Jehn, 1995, 1997). Outcomes of studies in this area also show that people employ demographic characteristics (basing salient social categories on demographic attributes) to categorize others and predict their likely behaviours (Allport, 1954). Since individuals seek situations which reinforce their self-identity, it is argued that a threat to individual self-identity (through categorization) impacts negatively upon self-esteem, which in turn results in the individuals' withdrawal from the context to avoid further threats and declines in self-esteem. It is our contention that employees interacting with co-workers, customers, and clients who are culturally different from the majority group in the local culture may perceive threats to their self-identity, which may lead them to avoid or minimize contact with culturally different others or to seek alternative work. Skills in communication competence across cultures may minimize perceived threats and assist in resolving this dilemma (Ayoko et al., in press).

Like social identity theory, the self-categorization paradigm refers to the process by which people define their self-concept in terms of their membership in various social groups. In this case, a salient social category functions psychologically to influence a person's perception and behaviours of another individual (Turner et al., 1987). Members of a salient group are more likely to co-operate with in-group members and to compete against out-group members.

In the same vein, the similarity attraction paradigm (Bryne, 1971) postulates that interpersonal attraction and liking is heightened by similarities in attributes, values, and demographic variables such as race, ethnicity, and gender. In particular, individuals who are similar in ethnicity may share common values and attitudes and may find the experience of interacting with each other easier, positively reinforcing, and more desirable (Williams and O'Reilly, 1998). Given the predictions of social identity, social categorization and similarity attraction theories, it is anticipated that interactants in business environments are more likely to engage in communications with business partners whose communicative behaviours and styles are similar to theirs, thereby leading to the exclusion of business colleagues that are dissimilar.

CAT also proposes that participants in an interaction use a divergence strategy, heightening the speech differences between themselves and others to increase social distance (Beebe and Giles, 1984) and to distinguish in-group and out-group membership (Giles et al., 1987; Gallois et al., 1988). In addition, speech accommodation levels are associated with the extent to which people identify with a salient in-group (Gallois et al., 1988), so that speakers who identify highly with a salient in-group are more likely to maintain their language style or even to diverge from an out-group member to signal differences in their identity. Furthermore, participants maintain communicative behaviours so that there is no movement towards or away from other speakers. Street (1991) argues that where there is role, power, or status between interlocutors, complementary behaviour may occur where parties mutually maintain their social differences through their communicative interactions.

To model the overall communication process, CAT now incorporates additional conversational strategies such as interpretability, discourse management, interpersonal control, and relational needs (Coupland et al., 1988). Interpretability refers to attention to others' interpretative competence or ability to understand. Modification processes for complex speech include decreasing the diversity of vocabulary, increasing clarity by changing pitch and tempo, clarifying and repetition, as well as selecting topics that are safe and familiar areas for the other person. However, strategies are subject to constant changes as participants negotiate meaning through the interpretative competence of their partners (Giles et al., 1991).

Discourse management strategy, on the other hand, involves judging and responding to the conversational needs of others (Giles et al., 1987), such as making decisions about the discourse, and the management of communication breakdown (cf. Hamilton, 1991). In addition, it includes the willingness by participants to facilitate others' contributions to conversation repair and dealing tactfully with threats.

Interpersonal control is concerned with role relations between interactants. It decreases or increases the flexibility to change roles during an interaction (Gallois et al., 1988). Thus, role relations can be positive (keeping a person in a role to reduce uncertainty) or negative when interactants use language devices to place a person in a role they can control, or suppress their own disclosure to offer the floor to their partners (Giles and Coupland, 1991).

Drawing from the work on face dualism, positive face, negative face, and face threatening acts, the newest addition to CAT models the strategies for relational needs of the interactants. It includes the ability to influence the relational and emotional aspects of the relationship with the other interlocutors (Gallois and Giles, 1998). Based on a framework integrating the theories described above, this chapter explores the communication issues, skills, and interventions required for cultural heterogeneity in the contemporary business interactions environment. In this chapter, we apply a unique approach to examine cross-cultural business interactions *outside* the organizational environment (cross-cultural client collaborations), *inside* the organizational environment (cross-cultural coworker relationships) and at the *interface* of the internal and external organizational environment (cross-cultural service provisions). This holistic approach is depicted in Figure 10.1.

Finally, communication competence within a speech community exists when the systematically possible, the feasible and the appropriate are linked to produce and interpret naturally occurring cultural behaviour. Sectors of competence involve the degree to which something is formally possible, feasible (given the means of communication available), appropriate (for example, adequate, happy, and successful in relation to the context in which it is used and evaluated), and performed. Communication competence and membership of a

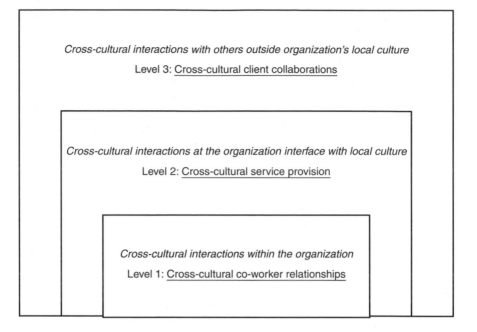

Figure 10.1 Multi-level analysis of cross-cultural business interactions

given culture can, therefore, combine to cause poor group processes. We propose that the CAT-based business communication strategies (BCC) are useful in disentangling the communication difficulties in business interactions. Next, we discuss in detail the three levels of cross-cultural interactions depicted in Figure 10.1 and the communication competence and strategies that are likely to produce effective intercultural business interactions at these different levels.

Communication competence for cross-cultural co-workers within the local culture

As previously described, the operation of social identity processes and similarity attraction tends to activate negative stereotypes and prejudices, causing group members to make biased attributions (Jackson *et al.*, 1993). Hence, within groups or organizations having employees from both the cultural majority and minority, minority group members are likely to report higher levels of differentiation, and in-group favouritism by majority group members, leading to intergroup anxiety and negative social identification (Brown and Smith, 1989). Consequently, key outcomes for the self and the organization will suffer, which in turn, will result in organizations systematically and organically driving out culturally dissimilar members (Byrne, 1971; Schneider, 1987).

Heterogeneity, particularly observable heterogeneity, more often than not arouses responses founded on biases, prejudices, or stereotypes (Milliken and

Martins, 1996). Biases, prejudices, and stereotypes themselves originate from social identity and self-categorization processes, bringing about discrimination and self-segregation, which in turn, disrupts group interaction (Jehn *et al.*, 1999).

Integrated threat theory addresses the potential causes of negative attitudes towards culturally dissimilar others. Stephan and Stephan (1996) identified four types of threats that act as predictors to the attitudes towards the out-group, namely realistic and symbolic threats, intergroup anxiety and negative stereotypes.

A threat to the very existence of an in-group is referred to as a *realistic* threat, whereas a *symbolic* threat refers to threats concerning the in-groups' 'way of life' (Stephan and Stephan, 1996). Intergroup anxiety describes feelings of threat, based on interactions with the in-group whereas negative stereotypes directed towards the out-group are another cause for threat and conflict. Research has shown that inter-group anxiety and negative stereotypes are stronger predictors of prejudice towards immigrants when compared with realistic and symbolic threats (Stephan *et al.*, 1998).

Social category membership provides a platform to activate the triggers of conflict. Perceived dissimilarity, for example, is based on observable attributes, which are likely to produce negative short-term effects driven by evoked stereotypes and prejudice (Härtel and Fujimoto, 2000). These, in turn, may lead to negative conflict, thus inhibiting optimal performance. Conflict, in turn, negatively affects innovation, decision making, and group outcomes (Tannenbaum *et al.*, 1996). Isolating the participant's capacity to effectively communicate and manage conflict in a business environment in a particular culture (as manifested by their communicative behaviours) should significantly impact the quality and efficiency of such interactional outcomes. We propose that the principle hurdle to successful business interactions and negotiations is conflict, and that skills and strategies in communicative competence are the key to effective interactions across culture.

Our research has demonstrated that the triggers of conflict in culturally diverse groups are often related to cultural differences such as values, beliefs, and different interpretations of space (Ayoko and Härtel, 2002). Interview respondents indicated that cultural differences underpinned member differences in work orientations and views of how individuals should interact with one another. They also identified that the way people talk, and communication styles, triggered conflict. Interviewees indicated that speakers of English as a second language used English differently, which led to misunderstandings from English speakers.

Communicative competence for cross-cultural service provision within the local culture

This chapter examines not only the skills required to work effectively in multicultural workgroups, but also the skills required to interact with a multicultural customer base and engage in cross-cultural client collaborations.

Research suggests that service providers attract customers of nationalities identical to themselves (Harrison-Walker, 1995). The reciprocal can therefore be assumed, namely that service providers are more attracted to customers who match their own cultural background (Härtel et al., 1999).

As the core source of business, customers provide a stimulus for achieving and maintaining a sustainable competitive advantage (Schuler, 1996). In particular, customer service and satisfaction are the main areas where organizations can set themselves apart from their competitors (Bowen, 1996). Failure to better understand the changing customer market and their specific needs puts organizations at risk of losing their competitive edge (Wah, 1999) as unsatisfied customers readily take their business elsewhere (Schneider and Bowen, 1985).

Although the behaviours of the service provider are influential in a customer's evaluation of service quality (Mohr and Henson, 1996), to date little attention has been given to the challenges faced by frontline employees interacting with culturally diverse customers. As highlighted by Strauss and Mang (1999), there are two causes of deficiencies in intercultural service encounters, namely *provider* and *customer* performance gaps. An intercultural provider performance gap occurs when foreign customers' expectations are not met by the performance of the provider, which can be attributed to the physical environment, service personnel, or delivery systems (Strauss and Mang, 1999). In contrast, the intercultural customer performance gap illustrates situations where the behaviours of the foreign customer do not meet the expectations of the service provider (Strauss and Mang, 1999).

Studies show that the greater the distance between the cultural and behavioural norms of the provider and customer, the greater the likelihood that expectation differentials will occur (Strauss and Mang, 1999). Because our focus is on the skills required by organizational employees, our research addresses the intercultural provider performance gaps that arise from the behaviours of service personnel. In other words, such gaps emerge when a 'provider does not show the level of competence, empathy, politeness, or assistance that foreign customers expect' (Strauss and Mang, 1999: 332).

The underlying assumption here is that the behaviours of the service provider, including what is said and how they behave, impact upon repeat purchases (Berry and Parasuraman, 1991). Particular focus is placed on the communication patterns adopted by service employees when interacting with culturally dissimilar customers. Therefore, it is proposed that the characteristics of a provider's verbal and non verbal behaviours and the subjective meanings customers attribute to these behaviours can be linked to customer satisfaction and repeat patronage. Further, we argue that service providers dealing with customers of different cultural backgrounds might experience cognitive dissonance. Research shows that providers are friendlier in terms of smiling and being more pleasant when interacting with culturally similar customers in comparison to interaction with culturally dissimilar customers (McCormick and Kinloch, 1986).

In an Australian study undertaken by Barker and Härtel (2002), white customers rated provider behaviours significantly higher than non-white customers and were more satisfied than non-white customers. The results provide strong evidence of inequity and variable quality in cross-cultural service provision, underscoring the need for organizations to train and monitor the communication competence of service providers.

Communication competence for cross-cultural client collaborations outside the local culture

Upon examination of research in the diversity arena, it is apparent that most diversity research has been conducted within the context of the internal organization, specifically in relation to enhancing the effectiveness of heterogeneous groups (see Milliken and Martins, 1996 for a review). Of the organizational studies of cultural diversity in the external environment, most have focused on expatriate adjustment. Recently, however, attention has turned to cultural differences in short-term employee collaborations with clients abroad (Fisher *et al.*, 2000) or in customer service contact (Barker and Härtel, 1999). In this section, we summarize the literature used in the analysis of communication competence for cross-cultural client collaborations outside one's local culture.

Early research on communication competence in different cultures focused on the identification of traits that contributed to intercultural effectiveness (for example, Bochner, 1973). However, the lack of strong empirical support for the link between traits and communication competence has now led to an emphasis on behaviour.

Today, intercultural communication effectiveness is generally identified as comprising three abilities: (a) the ability to communicate effectively; (b) the ability to establish interpersonal relationships; and (c) the ability to cope with psychological stress (Gudykunst and Hammer, 1984; Hammer, 1987; Dean and Popp, 1990). Our research indicates, however, that there may be differences across cultures in the relative importance of each ability to being interculturally competent, and the skills that are associated with each ability (Fisher *et al.*, 2000; Fisher and Härtel, 2002).

A number of issues limit the applicability of most research on intercultural communication effectiveness to contemporary intercultural encounters. First, there are concerns that the Western managers described in the research, and their relationship with others in the organization, do not reflect the full scope of the relationships that exist in the current international business environment.

Second, the organizational context within which businesses operate is dramatically different from that of earlier decades. In particular, the growth of information technology has changed the nature and style of communication (Fisher *et al.*, 2001b). The impact of geographic distance, for so long a key aspect of research into the head office–subsidiary control relationship, has been reduced by technology. The use of technology has allowed the growth of virtual teams in a number of organizational areas, most notably in research and development, marketing and customer service. There is evidence that virtual communication influences trust, decision making, and leadership (Gibson, 1999). In international business contexts, culture further adds complexity to virtual communication relationships.

Finally, there are questions related to the relationship between intercultural communication effectiveness and effectiveness in intercultural contexts. Frequently, in communication research, these terms are used as synonyms. However, effectiveness is a broader construct than communication effectiveness. Achievement of organizational and management goals need to be taken into account.

Managers and their relationship to others

Research conducted on cross-cultural interaction needs to be broadened. To date, much of the research on interactions with persons outside one's local culture is based on either the working experiences of male Western expatriate managers who have stayed abroad for an extended period, working for a Western home country multinational operating in a host country, or the intercultural communication and management experiences of international students in Western countries.

Expatriates are proposed to gain intercultural communication skills and, consequently, intercultural effectiveness through a cultural learning process (Furnham, 1987). Generally, the research addresses only the behaviour of the expatriate, from the expatriate's viewpoint, and their opinion on how this behaviour contributed to their intercultural communication success. This focus on the expatriate manager appears to be out of harmony with modern communication theory (Berlo, 1960; Limaye and Victor, 1995), which discusses sender and receiver transactions, rather than the information-giving focus subscribed to by the traditional models of communication (Shannon and Weaver, 1949).

Haworth and Savage (1989), Limaye and Victor (1995) and Asante (1980) cite the importance of considering the host country national as an active participant in the communicative process. The host country national brings with them perceptions, biases, and expectations, as well as task specific skills, communication skills, and knowledge of the organization and national cultural environment in which the communication is occurring. All of these can contribute to the degree of effectiveness of the communicative process. Another underlying theme in the literature is that the expatriate is the more senior member in the organization. This contrasts with the diversity literature, where the cultural minority is generally the junior organizational member. Fisher *et al.*, (2000) note that the power relationship in cross-cultural client relationships do vary, and that with the growth of globalization, expatriates will increasingly be the subordinate rather than the supervisor or advisor (Fisher *et al.*, 2001b).

Intercultural communication effectiveness and effective performance in cross-cultural contexts

The intercultural communication literature frequently uses a single measure of performance of expatriate effectiveness that is often a self-rating by the expatriate. The importance or contribution of various characteristics to overall performance is then rated, again by the expatriate alone. Thus, the link between intercultural communication items, and actual performance, relies on the link between item importance and a potentially biased self-assessment of overall performance.

More recent research shows differences between the weight placed on the importance of intercultural items and their actual contribution to overall performance of Western expatriates as rated by both the expatriate and non-Western counterpart (Fisher *et al.*, 2002a). The existence of either a cross-vergence or mutual adaptation in perceptions of communication expectations can also be inferred from this research of Western expatriates in a non-Western setting (i.e. Thailand). Put simply, it appears that the Western expatriate manager adjusts to the non-Western business environment, while at the same time the non-Western counterpart adjusts their expectations of the Western expatriate manager. This finding should not be surprising given the globalization of business, the increasing mobility of qualified managers and professionals, the growth of international education, and the emergence of world class universities in non-Western countries. Nonetheless, additional research is needed to clarify if this creates a new, unique cultural environment, as crossvergent theorists would argue, or is evidence of mutual adaptation only. Notwithstanding this, it is important for researchers and practitioners to be aware of the need to take into account the values, attitudes, and contributions of all people in a communication process, not just the Western expatriate manager.

Communication issues raised by diversity

There are at least seven communication issues raised in the foregoing sections. These include:

* knowledge of organizational rules and norms regarding communications within and across hierarchical boundaries, including face-to-face and e-mail exchanges, public speaking, dissemination of information, negotiating, interviewing, giving directions, and chairing meetings
* communication skills necessary to achieve personal, group, and organizational goals in the context of the employing organization
* knowledge of cultural differences in interaction goals
* knowledge of cultural differences in conflict management
* understanding that culture may impact on the way in which the primary spoken language is used

- understanding the triggers of conflict including different work orientations, different value orientations, and different interpretations of space
- understanding the impact of technology on communications between diverse persons.

Communication competencies for a diverse world

The communication issues associated with cross-cultural business interactions can be effectively dealt with if one possesses the appropriate competencies or knowledge, skills, abilities, and personal characteristics. We suggest that the core competencies required are:

- cultural awareness
- emotional competence
- openness to dissimilarity
- conflict management skills.

In order for individuals to interact effectively in the cross-cultural situation, they need to possess self-awareness of the influence of their own culture on their attitudes, perceptions, values, and behaviours, and awareness that people from different cultural backgrounds have also been socialized by these types of influences in their local culture. Such cultural awareness, coupled with an empathetic perspective, will help motivate individuals to enact BCCs.

Emotional competence means that an individual has the ability to accurately detect their own and others' emotions and regulate both to keep communications productive (Härtel et al., 1999; Huy, 1999) and to maintain emotional well-being (Fujimoto and Härtel, in press). This competency includes the ability to interpret both verbal and nonverbal behaviour and to do so nonjudgmentally (Kibby and Härtel, 2002). More detail on developing these skills can be found in Chapter 8 in this volume.

Openness to dissimilarity is the term coined to describe individuals, groups or organizations who see difference as an opportunity rather than a threat, are willing to interact and have relationships with dissimilar others, and are not prone to making in-group/out-group distinctions (Härtel et al., 1999; Fujimoto et al., 2000; Härtel and Fujimoto, 2000; cf. Hargie, 1997). Openness to dissimilarity is a prerequisite for appreciating and adapting to cultural differences (Lloyd and Härtel, 2003), and has been linked with non-discriminatory behaviour (Härtel et al., 1999), conflict resolution and group cohesion (Ayoko and Härtel, 2000). Consequently, a key BCC is to be aware of the inclination to be attracted only to similar others and to take personal and social steps to overcome this (Härtel and Fujimoto, 1999). In other words, social norms need to be established that value diversity of backgrounds and perspectives and that discourage sub-groupings. Individuals need to accordingly solicit views from all parties related to the interaction goal, ensure information exchange among all relevant parties, and seriously consider all viewpoints.

As we have demonstrated throughout this chapter, one of the crucial stumbling blocks diverse interactants are likely to face is conflict. Without conflict management skills, such conflict is likely to degenerate into destructive conflict. Therefore, a key BCC comprises understanding the conflict cycle, understanding conflict management skills, and knowing how and when to implement them (Ayoko *et al.*, in press). This competency would also include adopting a collaborative negotiation style and dealing with all interactions with tact, diplomacy, and respect.

Conclusion

In this chapter, we have explored the communication issues, skills and interventions required for cultural heterogeneity in the contemporary business environment. We examined cross-cultural business interactions at three levels:

- inside the organization
- at the interface of the organization and its external environment
- in the environment outside the organization.

Our interest was to identify communication competence in an intercultural context as a means of managing diversity, the term we use to refer to situations involving employees from both cultural majority and minority groups.

We proposed that BCC derived from CAT offers insights into the communication competencies and strategies that are likely to produce effective intercultural business interactions at these different levels, thereby increasing organizational efficiency at individual, group and organizational levels.

11 Conceptualizing involvement, participation and workplace decision processes

A communication theory perspective

Stanley Deetz and Devon Brown

Introduction

Numerous writers have argued that we have entered an 'age of participation', suggesting a distinctively new way of managing and making decisions together. In discussing communication more generally, the various essays in this volume have outlined the many conditions pushing increased participation in workplace decisions, the forms and practices of participation, and the consequences for business and society. Still, workplace participation has been constrained (Heckscher, 1997; Wisman, 1997). And, where it has occurred it has been most often limited to employee participation. Institutional relationships, vested interests, and both overt and subtle power relations, have provided clear barriers to widescale productive participation in business decisions. We, among many others, have tried to address such issues in other places (for example, Deetz, 1992, 1995b; Wagner, 1994; Cheney *et al.*, 1998; Seibold and Shea, 2001). In this chapter, we wish to present a theoretical perspective on the issues involved. Our focus is upon what might appear to be more benign communication conceptions and practices that nonetheless have tremendous impact on the success and viability of participation programmes. The form and practices of participation, not just its existence, matter (Russell, 1997). Communication is an integral part of any form of participation.

Workplace participation of various forms is important for all types of organizations. The core concepts of stakeholder representation, enhanced creativity, and positive communicative practices apply to for-profit businesses, public agencies and not-for-profit groups. The central questions – 'Whose objectives should count?' 'How much should they count?' and 'How will they be accounted for?' – arise in all modern organizations. And, the problem of managerial control directed towards a limited set of objectives is common to most.

Much of this analysis grows out of the social/political/legal/economic conditions in the United States. The US model is significant in the ways that it has spread throughout the world. With so-called free trade agreements and the globalization of business, the world economy increasingly works structurally like the US economy. As governments are weakened in relation to commercial organizations, public goods and public values lose their primary means of representation. As governments are further restrained, democratic societies are hard pressed to find ways to represent public values. But not only is state governance stressed in global economies, macro-level governmental intervention even where it has existed has created its own dislocations and is often not terribly productive.

Wider member and public involvement in organizational decisions is important for purposes of efficiency, effectiveness, and social good. Concerns with the representation of social values and economic success are rarely necessarily contradictory and are most often mutually supportive, especially in the long term. A careful look at communication practices, however, is critical to positive outcomes. Even in countries with strong co-determination models and structures like Germany, Sweden and Denmark, the communication model and practices may be fairly traditional and greatly reduce the impact and benefits of participation.

First, we wish to briefly address in a broad way the reason, hopes and goals of workplace participation. The ways these are conceptualized make a great difference to the conception and practice of participation. Second, we will argue that communication has been largely treated as unproblematic, thus leading to a focus on developing participation *forums* and higher levels of involvement with uneven consequences for decisions. Much of this results from dominant 'enlightenment' conceptions of communication that overlook critical aspects of interaction processes whereby meanings and interests are produced. Managerial driven forms of participation based in these older conceptions are often strategic attempts to increase loyalty and commitment or decrease resistance, rather than seeking genuine decisional input. The lack of *voice* even with appropriate *forums* results from constrained decisional contexts, inadequate or distorted information, socialization and colonization activities, and the solicitation of 'consent' where stakeholders 'choose' to suppress their own needs and internal value conflicts (see Deetz, 1998). Even team-based decision making is often filled with self-generated limits to open participation (Barker, 1997). Finally to overcome these problems, we will advance a collaborative constitutive view of communication that offers great potential for transformative practices. New conceptions of interaction are likely to improve collaborative decision making within corporations.

Why workplace participation now?

Despite general ignorance about the benefits of participation and the lack of a clear corporate or political agenda supportive of participation, many companies and communities have gradually recognized the need for, and value of, increasing the representation of different stakeholders (Wisman, 1997). Numerous new programmes have been proposed. Most of these have been aimed at employee participation, but an increasing number have begun to include important other stakeholders. Partnering arrangements are becoming increasingly common. This work is not intended to be simply another review of these programmes. Excellent reviews exist in both academic (Cheney *et al.*, 1998; Seibold and Shea, 2001) and professional (McLagan and Nel, 1995) literatures. Most of these programmes have resulted more from pragmatism than democratic ideas. Such pragmatism has been based in both business and social concerns.

Business concerns

From a business (though not necessarily managerial) standpoint, the primary justification for wider-spread participation is that diverse group participation in organizational decisions will lead to better decisions than are currently being made. Thus, any concept of management superiority and centralized authority is economically inadequate. Several claims advance this position. Diversity can enable greater creativity. The use of distributed expertise can lead to faster, higher quality decisions. Members at the point of the business activity are often in a better position to innovate and improve processes. Coordination through shared values is often more effective than supervision. People can make good collaborative decisions if given the chance.

One of the fundamental ironies of our democracy, however, is the relatively weak faith that people have in the ability of their groups to make joint decisions. Jokes about committees, team meetings, and decisional processes are so common as to hardly be funny. All of us have been frustrated at times in trying to make decisions with others. The cost of meeting time in most corporations is astounding. Yet, despite the sometimes weak models and inadequate implementation, and the experiences and common deprecation of working together, evidence on decisional quality, effectiveness, and efficiency consistently favours participatory decisional forms over traditional hierarchical alternatives (McLagan and Nel, 1995; Jones, 1997; Lawler, 1999). Where participation programmes have been less successful, the lack of managerial acceptance and inadequate participation processes have been largely responsible (Cotton *et al.*, 1988).

While decisional quality may appear to be an obvious reason for participation, many current programmes actually start from very different assumptions. Many worker participation plans, for example, have been guided by the desire for more commitment to the organization and greater compliance to standards and authority (Whitty, 1996). These are important concerns. Surveillance and evaluation of work activity is very difficult and often costly in many industries. Reduced commitment and increased possibility of employee exit can be very expensive, especially in industries where employee-held social and intellectual capital is of great value. These assets can go out the door with the employee. But emphasis on these is often at the expense of the larger 'quality of decision' issue as well as many benefits not measured well by traditional organizational standards (Rothchild-Whitt and Lindenfield, 1982).

Increases in the diversity of the workforce, the need for customized products, and internationalization of markets and operations, and social interdependence and complexity will continue to increase the value of participatory decision making.

Social/political concerns

Greater involvement in corporate decision making appears warranted by political as well as business conditions. If an increasing number of the decisions affecting our personal, social, and national well-being are made in corporations, the public has a right to be represented in them. And as governments move away from successful involvement in commercial choices, new ways of public involvement need to be found. Corporate actions and decisions are value-laden, reflecting a particular kind of culture and way of life and they entail large social (though often uncharged) costs (Deetz, 1995a, b). On this basis alone, even if greater public representation was economically less efficient, it might still be important. But it is also an economic necessity today. Managerial control and the focus on short-term profitability create dislocations and costly inefficiencies. New systems of decision making can increase the effectiveness of existing companies, improve long-term economic health, and provide important social benefits.

The possibility of public value guidance is not great unless people come to see commercial corporations as political institutions making political decisions. Fortunately, more people have increasingly come to share this view. Historically in market-driven economies people conveniently divide decisions into private ones and public ones. Public decisions usually concern governance and the general welfare and tended to be democratic, based on an assumption of citizen rights and guided by public conceptions of 'the good'. Corporate decisions were put on the private side and were seen as primarily economic. Most democratic rights were suspended in the workplace in the US, for example, because of accepted contractual relations of subordination and ownership rights. Consequently, decisions were guided by consumption and profit. With such conceptions, relevant democracy disappeared as commercial corporations made more of the significant public decisions. In the standard treatment, the corporate organization was treated as a non-governing institution engaged in private decision making. But to a large extent major businesses reneged on their side of the implied social contracts with both employees and societies. Employees feel a greater right to participation when they know the company has no commitment to them; the society feels a greater right of participation when the quarterly report has replaced any sense of stewardship. In Europe, the public generally has more representation in even private enterprise, but limits exist here too.

The private–public distinction does not serve well today. With the legitimacy and perhaps even power of governments in decline worldwide, the commercial corporation can easily be seen as the more potent elitist political force and as having a greater interest in extending influence over the vast majority of people. Significantly, commercial corporations even in democratic states do not routinely operate by democratic principles. The inequitable distribution of political, economic and social power supports a narrow and distorted system of interest development and representation in most democratic societies. The commercial corporate influence on and control of the mass media furthers these relations.

Corporations have come to overshadow the state, the civil community, and the moral community in making decisions directing personal lives and general social development (Deetz, 1992). The State's power is exercised primarily through restriction and crude guidance through taxation and environmental protection, while corporate organizations make most proactive decisions regarding technology development, utilization of natural resources, product development, working relations among people, and distribution of income. Many of these decisions are based primarily on the social values of corporate leaders rather than simple market and other economic conditions.

But further, corporate values and practices extend into life outside of work, providing personal identities, structuring time, constraining child rearing practices, influencing education and knowledge production, directing entertainment and news production, rewarding personality types, influencing availability of the arts, and defining and preferencing consumption-based lifestyles. While economic reasons are often given for corporate choices, they have clear political motives and consequences. And even the state's relatively limited restrictive power is restricted by massive corporate influence on legislative processes and policy boards. Commercial corporations function as public institutions but without public accountability. Economic capital is not the only investment deserving rights. And, corporations are not economically rational in any strong sense. Even when not intentional, the nature of decisional routines and the inevitable gap between information and the need to make a decision leaves values central to all decisions. Information formation processes and accounting practices themselves are inherently value-laden. More and more we ask whose values are these? Values are not just a concern in high-profile responsibility concerns, they are deeply embedded in all organizational practice.

Despite a growing conviction that public values have a right of representation in corporate decisions, the current means of representation through the marketplace and through governmental guidance are limited in effect (Deetz, 1995a, b). Stakeholder, rather than 'economic', models of corporate decision making are essential. The conception of commercial corporations as autonomous private enterprises and the resultant removal of the corporation from public accountability is no longer very useful in light of the decisions that they make and the value-laden nature of reaching decisions. Positions that radically separate the corporate from other institutions by being centred on economic rationality softened only by a goodwill social responsibility leave no accountability for the massive public effects of corporate decisions and the self-interested and value-laden bases of their actual internal decisions.

Corporations can, in contrast, be understood as complex political sites. Corporations are political in process and outcome. The modern corporation has a variety of stakeholders with competing interests within and between each of them resolved in internal decisions. Corporations could be a positive social institution providing a forum for the articulation and resolution of important social conflicts regarding the use of natural resources, the production of meaningful goods and services, and the development of individuals. These political processes are often closed, however, owing to a variety of practices that produce and privilege certain interests – principally managerial – in both public decision making and in the production of the type of person that exists in modern organizations and society. Recognising the existence of multiple stakeholders with competing legitimate interests is not to make corporate organizations more political, but to explore the politics that is already there, a politics that is often denied or obscured to the benefit of particular group interests. Corporate practices and decisions are already value-laden rather than simply economic. But structural changes alone are not sufficient; even with more stakeholder participation, value debate has not and will not necessary resulted.

The concept of communication and the concept of participation

Understanding the forces driving the move to greater workplace participation aids the establishment of clear goals for these new forms of governance and advances the development of assessment processes that identify the relation between specific practices and goal accomplishment. From the business side the hope is for more creativity impacting on new product development and greater efficiency and effectiveness in personal and organizational goal accomplishment; higher levels of mutual commitment; and greater product and service customization. And from a social side, the hope would be for an active consideration of personal and social values beyond those of the management group, which are often reducible to basic profitability measures.

The success of participation is directly linked to the quality and character of communication (Cheney, 1995; Cheney, *et al.*, 1997; Russell, 1997). Legal structures of co-determination do not assure communication practices that lead to creativity. The core question is whether our dominant concepts and practices of communication are capable of aiding organizational members in accomplishing these goals even if the forces towards participation prevail. But perhaps an even more important question is whether available alternative communication perspectives offer additional hope and can be implemented.

The first question is fairly easy. Most managers' approach to communication grew out of specific concepts of hierarchy and control. Business schools more often require public speaking and presentation skills rather than listening and negotiation skills. 'Leadership' training is still primarily conceived in the form of directing or taking charge of others (Calás and Smircich, 1991; Chrislip and Larson, 1995). Theories of control, persuasion and motivation are treated more centrally than cooperation, facilitation, and group creativity. Direction and compliance-gaining have characterized the communication in relation to internal groups, and similarly with advertising and public relations to external ones. Clearly such conceptions and skills of communication cripple rather than aid participation.

The second question is more complex. With the increased use of and talk about team decisions, dialogue and forms of participation generally, alternative ways of communicating have been advanced. Often these 'participative' alternatives have not been theoretically or empirically investigated and have been presented in a vague, unproblematic way as simply 'democratic' communication or 'dialogue'. And frequently these communication practices have been seen as requiring little training or development. If we build a trusting team, members will communicate well; if we develop participatory attitudes, appropriate skills will spontaneously arise. But all democracies are not alike and native intuitions and skills can be less than positive (Deetz and Simpson, 2003). Anyone hanging around most corporations will hear a lot more complaint about the endlessness and frustrations of meetings than the lack of opportunity to participate. This results not just from the limited nature of participation tasks but from the inability to participate well. Our biggest task may not be overcoming the autocratic tendencies of many managers and the communication structures, principles and practices fostered by this, but in providing new ways to think about and do communication in places where participation is genuinely favoured.

Common views of democracy and communication were never designed to accomplish the type of participation that can deliver on the promises laid out above. Common native understandings are largely based in an enlightenment conception of 'liberal democracy' as institutionalized and advanced by Western state institutions. Barber (1984) provided one of the more complete analyses of the consequences for state practices and decisions given this view in contrast to more participatory forms of democracy (see also Bachrach and Botwinick, 1992). While he focused more on issues of structure and representation than forms of communication, his initial distinction between liberal and participatory democracies is instructive to understanding the limits of productive participation in the workplace even when it is desired.

Liberal democracy is core to the justification of contemporary forms and institutions of communication. The weakness of its communication conceptions may partly account for the poor regard people have of political processes and the general cynicism in many societies.

Liberal democracy rests on three essential communication conceptions:

1   Freedom of speech and the existence of speaking forums are adequately available for equable participation in decision making.
2   The autonomous individual is the origin of perceptions, thoughts, and feelings, thus communication is about the expression of these.
3   Persuasion and advocacy are seen as the preferred mode of communication leading to decisions in cases of differences and conflict.

Such perspectives enable the narrow US conceptualizations where democracy itself is reduced to freedom of expression and 'free' markets, rather than a form of deliberation and decision making where people can collectively make decisions for the good of all. But even outside of the narrow US version, all three conceptions provide limits on the capacity of liberal democracy to provide for an effective method of discussion and decision making. Let us consider difficulties with each of these three conceptions.

Places to talk together

Liberal democracy is greatly dependent on both the freedom of speech and the having of places or forums in which to speak. In the demographic and cultural context of the development of liberal democracy, having speaking forums was relatively unproblematic. Scale and the massive growth of mediated communication have had great consequences for the availability, quality and nature of spaces of talk. Even in state processes, more attention has often been given to the defence of the freedom of speech than to the preservation of meaningful places to speak. Often the extent of the inequality of access to speaking forums and the difference in 'megaphone' size has not received adequate attention. The problem is not just one of having places and access, but also what happens there. Forums plus freedom does not equal positive productive participation.

Despite the massive attention to discussion of the public sphere, largely initiated by Habermas (1974), much of the debate has focused on places rather than forms of talk and relatively little has been directed to organizational life. The logic behind the focus on the freedom of expression is that good decision making requires that all relevant perspectives should be known by all. But guaranteeing places where everyone has their say does not assure this outcome. If we consider choices from the point of view of outcome, several conditions are necessary beyond simply assuming a place of expression. Contemporary communication environments in organizations do not assure all perspectives are known by all, or even thought by someone. Freedom of expression is meaningless if there is no one to represent relevant positions, if the one with the biggest megaphone can drown out the chorus of free voices, or if, as in the case of the Internet, the proliferation of opinions allows no place for meaningful discussion. Expression has exceeded deliberation in most contexts (Forester, 1999).

As companies imported liberal democratic conceptions in their development of participation plans, much of the focus has been on developing forums. Whether these are low engagement sites like suggestion boxes and town hall meetings or more engaged forms like cross-functional teams or Board of Director membership, they have been often justified and marked principally by giving people a chance to have a say. In this sense they focus more on being 'involved' than 'participating' in decision making. In some sense it is no surprise that meetings have become so long and inconsequential when the intent is for all to have their say. To the extent that people do not become cynical, such an approach may increase commitment but rarely creativity. Talking to have a say is very different from talking to invent a choice to which all can commit. More meetings, more chances for expression, do not mean better decisions. Forums are necessary for decision making but not sufficient. A different kind of talk freed from expressionist ideals is necessary to make decisions there.

The primacy of personal experience

Part of the reason participation plans have focused on providing communication forums arises from their theory of meaning. Liberal democratic models of communication have treated meanings as already existing, and as having been worked out in the private life of the individual. Communication was seen as arising out of already formed experience and viewed as the means of giving expression to them. In the enlightenment conception of experience grounding this, little consideration was given to the possibility of the social formation of experience. Contemporary communication theory based in critical and constructionist work reverses this relation (for example, Hall, 1985; de Guy, 1996; Weedon, 1997). Experience is more usefully seen as an outcome of communication rather than the basis for it. Two, rather than one, is the smallest unit of communication. Experience is always social before it is personal. Hence, the 'personal' can be formed either in open communication processes or in closed ones. Most workplace participation assumes that positions, interests and meanings are fixed and simply brought to expression, rather than exploring the processes of their formation.

Thinking through this concept of experience is essential to analysing communication for the purpose of more participatory democracy. In a constitutive view of communication, the core questions regard the processes of experience formation rather than their expression. Taking time to explore a theory of communication and experience may seem a bit abstract and philosophical for a paper looking at management and participation. But in the absence of a fundamental reconception, native theories of communication and experience ultimately undermine the opportunity for more productive participation (Deetz, 1990; Deetz and Simpson, 2003). Much of the practical advice for better communication fulfils common normative ideas in society but may work against productive forms of participation. For that reason we will focus more on the theoretical position necessary for evaluating practices than on suggesting specific context free practices.

From a constitutive view, human beings always find themselves embodied in social configurations. They act within this context in ways that reproduce particular selves and realities and produce new possibilities. Human beings are interpretive creatures. They live and work in a world that is formed in particular manners given their specific sense equipment, manners of comportment, and routinized practices. In this way, they respond to a world external to them, but this is a world that is only known in regard to specific characteristics and activities of the subject. In this sense the world and subject are co-constituted. The particular socially/historically derived way that a person encounters the world can be described as an 'I' position. The 'I' is a perspective or standpoint in a social/historical rather than biographical or psychological sense (Harding,

1991). An 'I' and a real but not yet determined world must both be present to have a specific experience or experience the world as filled with specific objects. Experience is thus always socially and historically situated; socially constructed in specific power-filled conditions.

For human beings, unlike most living things, much of this interpretive mode of being is provided socially rather than genetically. Social routines, linguistic distinctions, and institutional structures operate for humans much like instincts do for other creatures. The body is extended through space and time as the position, point of view, or subjectivity within various technological extensions of the senses and limbs, and as concretized in buildings, landscapes, and patterned practices.

A series of prior more or less participatory social interactions and social decisions thus constitute the conditions of every 'personal' perception, feeling or need in organizational life. Language, as the primary mode of interaction, is a particular form of institutionalized sensing that directs the attention of other senses, that strikes and recalls differences in the inner and outer world that make a difference, and that provides system reflexivity (Weedon, 1997). Issues related to language, institution, and routine practices thus have both a political and moral dimension since they ultimately determine the character and survival of the species (and perhaps all others) (Deetz, 1995b). Our very condition provides a moral foundational rather than simply pragmatic grounding for participation.

Each psychological state and conception of personal identity arises out of a background of social practices in which such things are constructed as possible, 'feelable', and imaginable (Henriques et al., 1984). Every social structure can be seen as an arbitrary, routine, habitual way that social interactions have come to be played out. As such they have no stature except as reproduced and legitimized in ongoing social interaction.

Common contemporary organizational conceptions of free agents, knowledge and decision making are based on eighteenth-century conceptions of the individual and reason, views which both help to sustain managerial domination in corporations and hamper the development of alternatives. The very development and importation of the language of psychology, for example, has political consequences. Modern HRM, for instance, is in the culture and meaning business, its focus is on the production of a specific type of human being with specific self-conceptions and feelings. And, equally importantly, much of the work promotes concepts of the person that make the critical investigation of the individual and his or her experience less likely and seemingly less important. The very notions of free contract, social relations, and agency as well as personal identity as a manager, secretary, or worker that are core to HRM can be seen as corporate productions and reproductions needing investigation (Rose, 1990; Townley, 1993; Jacques, 1996; Holmer-Nadesan, 1997). All of these finally work against open and productive participation, putting in its place repetition of known positions formed in conditions of domination.

The most common conceptions of the human character and the communication process are thus 'imaginary', that is, they are constructed as real within particular social/historical systems of domination. And corporate processes like those organized as HRM actively support and reproduce these images. If we understand this imaginary nature we can displace the constructed-as-presumed-free subject as centre and origin of meaning and better understand how the subject is produced. And if discourse itself is understood as power-laden rather than neutral and transparent we can better reveal the sites of power deployment and concealment and hence advance participation.

Persuasion and advocacy

Finally, liberal democracy operates with a specific notion of how talk should occur in situations of differing positions. Liberal democracy embodies a faith that if all engage in self-interested expression, good collective decisions arise through some invisible hand mechanism. Persuasion and advocacy become prized and institutionalized at the expense of other ways of working with difference. Other forms of communication such as collaboration and mediation enable creative solutions that never arise in adversarial situations (Gray and Wood, 1991; Wood and Gray, 1991; Forester, 1999). Part of the problem of endless meetings in many organizations rests in the focus on expression rather than decision making. The rationale here is that it is better to ensure that all have made their case rather than assure a committed agreement. As argued earlier, a communication process in which there is a discussion where everyone merely has a say is quite different from one where all reach and commit to a decision together.

Leadership skills often include the individual's ability to advocate and persuade. Would we chose the same leaders if those aspiring to upper management positions were required to sit down and solve problems together rather than simply displaying the capacity to advocate their position (Chrislip and Larson, 1995)? But all this requires a different communication model. Participation is hampered by the implied model of communication both in the selection of leaders and the way a participation model of communication is supported throughout the organization. Our current conditions provide complex negotiation sites, the model of communication built for rather simple issues with constrained contestations is less than useful.

Conceptualizing participatory communication

As social conditions change, liberal democracy provides a less than adequate way for people to interact and make decisions together in organizations as well as other places. Enriching participation requires working out alternative concepts and practices of communication for decisions to be made together (Kapoor, 2002). Wider and more equable participation requires a model that attends to the systemic ways communication can be productive rather than simply reproductive. This requires constructing workplace forums that optimize difference, a mode of interaction that investigates and 'deconstructs' experience enabling an open process of reformation, and a model of decision making that focuses on the invention of mutually satisfying decisions.

Building better forums

Productive forums require not only expanded places of interaction, but spaces that enhance equality and optimize diversity (Zoller, 2000). In general, more complex and important issues require greater diversity in participants. This is a type of 'requisite diversity'. The goal is to create groups with differences (whether in terms of race, gender, or opinion, etc.) and to use those differences to foster creativity. In most workplace participation, relevant stakeholders are not included in decisions because of values and structure. For example, most businesses resist inclusion of external environmental groups in decision making processes that have consequences for the environment. Generally they will choose to make decisions on narrowly conceived economic grounds, choosing strategic implementation and eventual legal battles down the road (Lange, 2002). The inclusion of environmental groups early on, however, can help generate creative decisions that are economically more viable and lack the long-term social and economic costs. But exclusion may also occur because the nature of productive communication is not itself understood. Fear of impasse may also occur because the communication processes leading to creativity are not understood. Communication is often directed to attempts at consensus arising out of discovered 'common ground', hence the fear that if common ground is not found then time and strategic advantage are lost.

The presence of diverse goals, rather than creating costly conflicts and impasse, however, can create the conditions whereby limited decisional frames are broken and the company learns. In the process the faulty bases of recurring conflicts are exposed and synergistic energy is created. Some of the best-known examples of this process come from the Saturn Corporation where co-management by labour and owner representatives has assured a more diverse value basis for decision making (Rubinstein *et al.*, 1993). For example, in the early 1990s Saturn Corporation needed to increase production to meet higher than expected product demand. Owner representatives proposed a short-term cost containment solution, a decrease in quality control. Union representatives with a greater interest in long-term employment security and quality did not concur, a concurrence that was required in the co-management arrangement. While a temporary impasse was present, the difference of interests here coupled with the need to make a decision without following typical managerial routines led to improved production processes and the maintenance of high quality. If the standard management response had been implemented, they would not have pursued the more innovative solution, which had both social values and greater economic value. Unfortunately, most representation forums are used by management to suppress or defuse conflict arising from stakeholder groups rather than foster genuine conflict and productive interaction for the sake of company improvement.

Communication as a formative process

Most participatory discussions even in the best forums take the existing thoughts, feelings, experiences, information and interests as given rather than explore their formation. More recent communication theories represent our 'personal' meanings and experiences as reproductions of earlier formations (Deetz and Simpson, 2003). These formations are produced by someone else to serve their purposes at a particular time, and are then uncritically taken on as our own in this time and place. Usually these meanings are those of dominant groups (Bourdieu, 1991). The world is understood based on particular distinctions while distinctions that would organize the world differently are hidden and suppressed. While the reproduced experiences are clearly 'ours' they are not formed by us but borrowed from earlier formative processes. Most often organizational members merely acquiesce to the 'personal' understandings available to them, as opposed to actively selecting them or even exploring how they were formed (Jacques, 1996; Deetz, 1998).

These social constructions *could* be the result of prior open interaction or held temporarily and continuously revised in ongoing micro-negotiations in the present. Genuine participation would enable this to occur. The constructions, however, limit participant voices to the extent that they were formed in distorted communication processes. Alternatively they simply become fixed and taken for granted, and closed to reconsideration and choice. In these cases the stakeholder accepts meanings and positions constructed by others as one's own and, hence, demonstrates complicity in his or her own disregard.

A constitutive theory of communication focuses on the production of specific meanings and experiences. From this standpoint, everyday notions of discussion based in liberal democracy simply reproduce meanings. The constitutive orientation, however, recognizes that meanings and experiences initially form in the relation between a goal directed activity and the not yet determinant stuff of the world, including people and events.

Constitutive communication studies focus on the social processes by which meanings, identities, psychological states, and social structures are produced and reproduced. In both its constitutive and reproductive modes, communication processes are central to how perceptions, meanings, and routines are held in common. In all interactions, perception, meaning and data transmission are complex, multileveled phenomena produced out of and producing conflicting motives and structures. Communicative relations can be either open and productive or closed and reproductive in relation to both others and the world. Participation in organizational decisions accomplishes positive economic and social ends to the extent that communication is productive. In productive relations the unity of the 'I' is risked as the 'otherness' of the external interrogates the fixed position of the 'I', opening the possibility of new experiences. Thus, the fixed self/other/world configuration gives over to the conflictual, tension filled antagonisms out of which objects are differentiated and redifferentiated, and preconceptions are given over to new conceptions (Weedon, 1997). In such relations both the power in the web-like configuration and the presumed self-directive power of the individual as produced by the web, are challenged. At this constitutive level a communication perspective draws attention to a politics of perception and person formation.

Productive interactions are responses from a relatively stable set of practices and linguistic forms that constrain variety to an actual set of events that could have been described and responded to in a variety of fashions (i.e., that potentially demand variety). In productive interactions, these identities are utilized improvisationally to provide a moment of articulation which is freely transformed into another, constantly moved by the excess of meaning and possible experience over that which is momentarily present (Laclau and Mouffe, 1985). But when identities are protected from examination in interactional systems, often through either invisibility or processes of discursive closure, they distort the development of each participant and the consensus reached on the subject matter at hand.

Various forms of communicative micro-practices may unwittingly but actively close off the possibility of the type of discussion that can surface values and reclaim important conflicts while appearing to have an open and sensitive conversation (Martin, 1990; Clair, 1993). These have been described in detail as acts of discursive closure (Deetz, 1992). These include various ways individuals are qualified and disqualified as experts, the ways social constructions become naturalized (given in nature) and neutralized (called objective or value-free), the inclusion and exclusion of topics of discussion, and the valorization of opinion as an expressive form.

Communication as a collaborative process

Even if 'otherness' is present, challenging existing ways of experiencing and outcome possibilities, certain forms of talk are required to turn differences into productivity. Advocating a difference may give it a space, but only collaborative talk can give it a consequence. A 'successful' presentation of one's own meaning can limit rather than aid productive communication. To the extent that the object or other is silenced by the success, we limit the capacity to engage in reclaiming difference and conceptual expansion towards a more open consensus on the subject matter. The 'otherness' before us shows the one-sidedness and suppressed conflict in current perceptions.

Much has been written about collaborative communication processes (see Wood and Gray, 1991). Unfortunately few companies appear to use collaborative processes as part of their participation process. Often collaboration is reserved for only their most serious conflicts. In fact, collaboration is often only discussed as a conflict resolution process rather than a normal way to make complex decisions. But as a conflict strategy, collaborative processes are so well known as to require little discussion (for example, Fisher and Ury, 1991). Bringing this logic into participatory processes, however, remains very important.

Two key characteristics separate collaboration from other forms of communication. First, most discussions tend to focus on the airing and advocacy of known positions rather than the exploration of unknown ones. Second, most discussions often focus on saying rather than doing. At best they may end with a vote, but often the discussion ends with simply the need for more discussion. Collaboration focuses on the reaching of a common understanding and mutual commitment to a decision by focusing on the ends to be achieved rather than the preferred means of achievement or present positions. It requires a different attitude going into meetings and a different form of interaction in meetings. As shown in Box 11.1, these differences are well characterized in the comparison between adversarial and collaborative communication (see Gray, 1989).

Conclusion

Productive participation in organizational decisions requires both *forums* – places for occurrence – and *voice* – the capacity for differences to be vividly, 'demandfully' present. Participation thus requires spaces for encountering 'otherness', a model of productive interaction that recovers indeterminacy and suppressed discord and conflict across a broad spectrum of differences, language processes that avoid discussion blockage and promote free and open discourse, and collaborative interaction skills designed for creative fulfilment of multiple goals.

Perhaps one of the greatest challenges and most exciting potential contributions of organizational communication today is to recognize the role that we

Box 11.1 Adversarial and collaborative communication

Adversarial communication	*Collaborative communication*
Members are adversaries.	Members are joint problem solvers.
Speaking comes from a position or preferred means of accomplishment.	Speaking comes from an outcome wishing to be accomplished.
Discussion becomes polarized around positions.	Dialogue focuses on complex underlying interests.
Discussion narrows options.	Dialogue broadens field of options.
Facts are used to support positions.	Joint search is used to discover the facts.
Seeks winning arguments.	Seeks workable options.
Definition of the problem is accomplished before meeting.	Definition of the problem is a joint achievement.
Final responsibility for the decision rests with others.	Final responsibility for the decision rests with the group.

can play in challenging native, common-sense assumptions about communication and participation that privilege the self at the expense of the other. Failure to attend carefully to the 'otherness' around us limits our own perspective, produces incomplete and inadequate decision-relevant information, and does violence to those others whose positions are often already institutionally and culturally marginalized. Encounters with another must go beyond notions of exchange, move past understandings of communication as the transmission of internally located meaning, and revitalize conceptualizations of participation that recognize the central importance of radical difference to our own capacity for growth in understanding.

Native actors in organizational contexts already believe in participation as a powerful tool rich with promise. Yet the commonly held assumptions about communication derived from liberal democracy inherently privilege the already dominant set of understandings. Participatory communicative processes perpetually recover a space for exceeding personal and systemic restraints and distortions. Responsiveness is greatest in chance and transformative events that defy routines and standard recipes. Such chance events make possible reclaimed conflicts and transformations. But openings can also be encouraged, especially in periods of transition.

12 Motivating critical upward communication

A key challenge for management decision making

Dennis Tourish and Owen Hargie

The temptation to tell a Chief in a great position the things he most likes to hear is one of the commonest explanations of mistaken policy. Thus the outlook of the leader on whose decision fateful events depend is usually far more sanguine than the brutal facts admit.

(Winston Churchill, 1931)

Introduction

Communication in organizations involves the transmission of information (*messages*) between senders and receivers (*sources*), utilizing a variety of means (*channels*). Such information can flow horizontally (across similarly placed levels in the organizational chart), vertically (from managers to non-managerial staff, or vice versa) or diagonally (from non-managerial staff to managers, bypassing intermediate layers, and vice versa). The meanings of the messages are affected by the cognitive set of the individuals who receive them and the context in which they occur. Organizational communication research has therefore often been construed in terms of an *information exchange cluster*, involving information, networks, uncertainty, messages, load and (more recently) technology (Conrad and Haynes, 2001). The purpose of this chapter is to suggest that important issues involving information transmission from those without managerial power to those with such power have been insufficiently explored in the literature. Power itself is a frequently unacknowledged variable in organizational science (Clegg, 2000), while it has been argued that, whatever other changes have occurred, 'corporate organizations have remained largely autocratic in form' (Deetz and Mumby, 1990: 19). In particular, the need for upward communication that is critical of organizational goals and management performance has been little recognized, or researched. Primarily, researchers in the general area of feedback have been concerned with the nature and efficacy of appraisal systems. Here, we argue that this is no longer sufficient.

Feedback and knowledge of results have long been known to be essential to effective human performance in any task (for example, Annett, 1969). The more channels of accurate and helpful feedback we have access to, the better we are likely to perform. Likewise, if channels are cut off, performance deteriorates. As Dickson *et al.* (1997) noted, practice does not make *perfect* – it makes *permanent*. If we carry out a certain behaviour often enough it merely becomes habituated. It is practice with apposite *feedback* that steers us in the direction of perfection. Most businesses recognize the importance of obtaining feedback from key markets to assess how their product is being received, yet in relation to staff communications many implicitly or explicitly take the view that feedback is only required from the top down. Often, no more than lip service is paid to the notion of 'addressing staff concerns'. Our intention in this chapter is to explore the extent of upward feedback at present, what organizations gain if they institutionalize systems for critical upward feedback into their decision making process, the main barriers that often impede efforts to implement such ideas, and the most important lessons that can be drawn from the research into how practice in this area can be improved.

Benefits of upward feedback

Research into upward feedback in organizations has burgeoned over recent years (Atwater *et al.*, 2000), although most of this has focused on upward appraisal. One survey of 280 Midwest companies in the USA found that 25 per cent used annual upward appraisals, 18 per cent peer appraisals and 12 per cent used 360-degree appraisals (De Nisi, 1996). Companies such as AT&T, the Bank of America, Caterpillar, GTE and General Electric have been pioneers with 360-degree appraisals (Hargie *et al.*, 1999). Nearly all the Fortune 500 companies have now embraced the approach, while it is rapidly gaining ground in the UK (Mabey, 2001). Thus, upward feedback itself seems to occur mostly as part of the appraisal process, rather than through the daily utilization of informal communication channels (Atwater *et al.*, 1995; Waldman and Atwater, 2001). The relatively low profile of the issue, from a research perspective, itself suggests an extreme sensitivity to the whole question. Nevertheless, the notion that managers might benefit by obtaining feedback from those traditionally classed as subordinates is no longer regarded as revolutionary. It has even become part of the mainstream in terms of management practice.

It has been argued that upward feedback, upward communication and open door policies deliver significant organizational benefits (see Box 12.1). Such findings are consistent with perspectives that see organizations as information processing entities (O'Reilly *et al.*, 1987). Moreover, as uncertainty and complexity increase it is likely that the need for information processing will grow (Brashers, 2001). An upward flow of information is therefore likely to become an increasingly important issue. Yet it is also clear that a smooth flow of critical upward communication does not always occur, and that this failure exacts a significant toll on organizational functioning (Tourish and Robson, 2001). What, therefore, tend to be the obstacles in the way of its development?

Box 12.1 The benefits of upward feedback

> - the promotion of shared leadership, and an enhanced willingness by managers to act on employee suggestions (Moravec *et al.*, 1993)
> - a greater tendency by employees to report positive changes in their managers' behaviour (Hegarty, 1974)
> - actual rather than perceived improvements in management behaviour following on feedback, beyond what could be attributed to regression to the mean (Reilly *et al.*, 1996)
> - a reduced gap between managers' self-ratings and those of their subordinates (London and Wohlers, 1991)
> - the creation of improved forums for obtaining information, garnering suggestions, defusing conflict and facilitating the expression of discontent (Shenhar, 1990)
> - an enhancement of organizational learning (Belasen 2001; Weick and Ashford, 2001)
> - better decision making (Nutt, 2002)
> - enhanced participation (Stohl and Cheney, 2001)

Fear of feedback

As identified by Morrison (2002), and summarized in Box 12.2, there are a range of considerations that influence the extent to which we actively look for feedback. Not all of these are positive, since negative feedback can both be personally upsetting and may impact adversely upon one's public image. Thus, people at all organizational levels are often fearful about seeking feedback on their performance (Ashford and Northcraft, 1992). For example, feedback to the effect that a cherished course of action is failing is unpleasant. People may also worry that seeking feedback is a sign of weakness.

It can therefore be suggested that managers discourage critical feedback. The effect is to distort both downward and upward communication processes. To deny fault and avert the possibility of blame, senior managers sometimes conceal negative organizational outcomes (Abrahamson and Park, 1994). Managers suppress information (Ashforth and Gibbs, 1990), they cover up negative financial data (Whetton, 1980), they deny failure (Sutton and Callahan, 1987), and they have been shown to 'launch propaganda campaigns that deny the existence of crises' (Starbuck *et al.*, 1978: 118). Such campaigns are the equivalent of an out of form marksman deciding that whatever he hits will be declared the target. Improvements in performance are unlikely, while the necessary suspension of disbelief requires the elimination of critical feedback. As Clampitt (2001: 17) has observed: 'Sending the good news up is only natural for those who wish to get ahead in the organization.' No one wants to be a dead bad news messenger!

Box 12.2   Feedback considerations

Reasons for feedback-seeking

- high level of uncertainty and the desire to reduce this
- the goal of becoming competent in a task
- a wish to correct perceived errors in performance
- wanting to regulate and improve one's performance.

Factors that influence the decision to seek feedback

- the perceived credibility and expertise of the feedback source
- receptivity of the source – the extent to which the person is likely to be available, and willing, to give considered feedback
- the importance of achieving a definite set target or goal
- concern about *developing* rather than *demonstrating* competence
- level of self-esteem – those higher in self-esteem seek more feedback
- performance expectations – those with high expectations seek more feedback
- going with the flow – if significant others are seeking feedback, the probability is that we will follow suit
- tactics – we are more likely to ask for feedback if we think our performance is good as this shows us in a good light.

Potential costs of negative feedback

- damage to one's ego
- a less positive public image in the organization
- the effort involved in having to change one's performance.

It seems that 'we are left with a paradox: the most successful leaders appear to be those who cultivate the least compliant followers, for when leaders err – and they always do – the leader with compliant followers will fail' (Grint, 2000: 420). Nevertheless, research has shown that when managers openly solicited and accepted negative feedback they gained a more accurate picture of their actual performance and were rated more favourably; when they looked for positive feedback they acquired no insight into their true performance and were viewed less favourably (Ashford and Tsui, 1991). Clearly, followers who are less compliant are more likely to deliver upward and critical feedback. Unfortunately, managers may be more likely to fire such recalcitrants than to encourage them.

Groupthink

Problems with upward feedback have consistently been shown to be a key part of what is known as 'groupthink' (Janis, 1982). This proposes that groups insulated from critical outside feedback develop illusions about their own invulnerability, excessive self-confidence in the quality of their decision making and an exaggerated sense of their distinctiveness from other groups. Furthermore, as a result of groupthink, groups:

- deny or distort facts (Janis, 1982)
- offer rationalizations for their activities (Laughlin, 1970)
- use myth and humour to exaggerate their sense of worth (Filby and Willmott, 1988)
- attribute the failure of their decisions to external factors (Ross and Staw, 1993).

It follows that a group so inclined will also have a tendency to disparage criticism from outside its own ranks, since it will conflict with the group's ideal self-image and depart from its well-entrenched norms.

The absence of critical feedback may become a vicious rather than a virtuous cycle, in which:

- poor decisions result
- the group responds by belittling or denying the existence of crisis
- feedback pointing to the crisis is disparaged as coming from tainted sources outside the magic circle of key decision makers
- those attempting to offer feedback respond by minimizing much needed future critical feedback.

In turn, this is likely to reinforce the conviction of those at the top that (rogue indicators aside) things are much better than they are, and that the group does not require additional outside input.

Problems of ingratiation

One of the most potent explanations for difficulties with upward feedback can be found in ingratiation theory. This proposes that those with a lower level of status habitually exaggerate the extent to which they agree with the opinions and actions of higher status people, as a means of acquiring influence with them (Jones, 1990). Studies conducted with students in hypothetical situations indicate that decreased power among subordinates is accompanied by an increased tendency to employ some form of ingratiation (Michener *et al.*, 1979) and an increased use of 'politeness' strategies (Baxter, 1984). A culture of sycophancy has been identified as a key factor in the profits collapse that afflicted one of the UK's best-known businesses, Marks & Spencer, in the late 1990s (Bevan, 2001). The company chairman's direct reports have confessed that they actively avoided bringing bad news to his attention, fearing his wrath. However, as De Vries (2001: 94) has put it: 'Effective organizational functioning demands that people have a healthy disrespect for their boss, feel free to express emotions and opinions openly, and are comfortable engaging in banter and give and take.' Otherwise, the CEO may end up like Hans Christian Andersen's Emperor, left exposed as a result of obsequious and totally misleading feedback from subordinates.

Particularly when contemplating dissent, employees consider whether it will result in retaliation, or whether it will be perceived as constructive (Kassing, 2001). Trust, or its absence, is therefore a key issue in determining the availability and efficacy of upward feedback. Without trust, such communication is limited. Moreover, the frequency and openness of inter-organizational communication is a vital precondition for the development of trust (Sydow, 1998) – a construct which is itself increasingly acknowledged as a positive contributor to business effectiveness (Sako, 1998; O'Brien, 2001). It has been noted that 'subordinates who do not trust their superior are willing to suppress unfavourable information even if they know that such information is useful for decision making' (O'Reilly *et al.*, 1987: 612). The result is yet more ingratiation behaviour, and a further weakening of critical upward feedback.

Managers' own behaviour is not immune to these dynamics. One review concludes that 'managers are less likely to employ "assertiveness" with superiors than co-workers, less likely to employ "sanctions" with superiors or co-workers than with subordinates, and less likely to employ "exchange" with superiors than co-workers' (Krone, 1992: 2). In addition, self-efficacy biases suggest that most of us imagine we are better on various crucial dimensions of behaviour than we actually are (Hill *et al.*, 1989; Myers, 1996). Accordingly, researchers have generally found that managers view the defective and uncritical feedback they receive from subordinates as accurate, sincere, and well meant (Rosenfeld *et al.*, 1995) – it is in line with their self-efficacy biases. Since they are therefore inclined to think that the inaccurate and ingratiating feedback they receive daily is accurate, they grow even less inclined to seek mechanisms that institutionalize critical upward feedback into the decision making process.

Single loop versus double loop thinking

Single loop learning has been defined as asking a one-dimensional question to get a one-dimensional answer (Argyris, 1994). This is in contrast to taking several additional steps, to explore context, causes and underlying rationales. Thus, managers might seek people's input in terms of identifying a particular problem, and how it might be solved – single loop learning has occurred. However, they might not explore such additional questions as: how did this problem arise in the first place? How come nobody either told us about it or did anything about it before? What systemic problems does it reveal, and what must be done to correct them? As defined here, the tendency towards single loop learning limits the range of issues on which organizations seek people's input. If the only tool you want to use is a hammer everything starts to look like a nail. It is better to employ the full range of implements in the managerial toolbox, so that the shape of problems can be accurately assessed.

Likewise, employees often resist asking these hard questions, contenting

themselves with blaming other departments, management or nameless procedures for their own inertia. We have conducted many communication audits, in
a variety of organizations. One of our most consistent findings has been that
although employees regularly complain that little information is circulated, they
also do not believe that they themselves should transmit much more (for
example, Tourish and Hargie, 1998)! The need for more and better communication is widely acknowledged, but so also is the tendency to assume that it is
someone else's obligation to provide it. Argyris (1994) identified many reasons
for such mindsets, including a profound human need to save face, an excessive
diplomacy couched in terms of the need to be thoughtful and caring towards
others, combined with the urge to blame others rather than engage in critical
self-analysis.

Narcissism and group identity

This chapter suggests rather more than that upward feedback is hard to come
by. It is systematically distorted, constrained and eliminated. This finding is
consistent with the notion of a narcissistic group identity. As Brown (1997:
643) has pointed out, groups may be as prone to this problem as individuals,
through such ego-defence mechanisms as 'denial, rationalization, attributional
egotism, sense of entitlement, and ego aggrandizement'. People have a need to
nurture a positive sense of self, and they embrace ego-defensive behaviour in
order to maintain self-esteem. Eliminating or disparaging critical feedback is
one obvious means of doing so.

   Furthermore, there is an interaction between employee responses to upward
communication opportunities and the facilitative/constraining role of management, creating major paradoxes. A number of studies have explored how social
actors discursively develop organizational identities that are simultaneously
constraining and enabling, debilitating and empowering (for example
Collinson, 1988). Likewise, we often see a simultaneous affirmation by senior
managers that they want an empowered staff to take decisions and feel liberated
to transmit upward feedback. This co-exists alongside the elimination of dissenters from the ranks of senior management teams; fear by dissident members
of such teams and other groups to openly express their critical views (views that
the evidence suggests will either wither, or see the person leave the ranks of the
group); and a number of management behaviours widely perceived as hostile to
dissent, and hence punitive in nature. The danger is that top managers can
become like rock stars surrounded by a sycophantic entourage – they may fall
for their own propaganda. A narcissistic self-image can result (Maccoby, 2000).
The solution requires experimentation with power sharing, and a downsizing of
entourages. However, it has been pointed out that 'Relinquishing power and
control does not come easily for many leaders' (Kirkman and Rosen, 2000: 55).
The evidence suggests that the first steps in such a direction (for example the
acknowledgement of problems and an open discussion of mildly critical
information) are frequently never taken.

Irrational belief systems and naive story construction

People have a fundamental need to make sense of the social word around them, and indeed spend a great deal of time constructing plausible-sounding narratives to achieve this end. It is a question of structuring the unknown (Waterman, 1990). However, the process is fraught with error. In particular, sense-making is often driven by plausibility rather than accuracy (Weick, 1995). Here, we suggest that irrational belief systems and naive story construction contribute to a limited understanding on the part of managers, so that they often have serious problems with upward communication.

Many irrational beliefs (i.e. unfounded assumptions about the nature of the physical and social world) take deep root because people construct plausible sounding stories that posit causal relationships between what are actually unrelated variables (Dawes, 2001). The inherent motivation appears to be the reduction of uncertainty, through the construction of convenient stereotypes into which unpredictable or mostly unrelated events, people or physical attributes can be slotted (Tourish and Wohlforth, 2000). In particular, it appears that unusual events stand out in our minds, because they are atypical. However, in the process of retelling, they acquire an added vividness. Those involved in the discourse gradually become convinced that what they are describing is more typical of the category than is actually the case (Dawes, 1994). This is a good illustration of what has been termed the availability error (Sutherland, 1992) – information that is more readily available to us (such as an unusual event) influences our perceptions much more than information that is harder to access. The effect, however, is that implausible stories become widely circulated, correspondingly more available to our minds and hence deeply believed.

The point, in relation to upward communication, is illustrated in a case study by Tourish and Robson (in press) of one senior management team's (SMT) response to critical feedback. The SMT had appointed a layer of important general managers within the previous eighteen months, but still encountered problems with slow decision making, delegation, communication and over-work at senior levels. In particular, critical upward communication, from any level of the organization, was wholly absent. Other researchers have also found that middle managers frequently have little influence, either upwards or downwards, and that business planning processes can be of an exclusionary and top-down nature (Currie, 1999). In the Tourish and Robson case study, the main narrative developed by the SMT to explain this state of affairs was the alleged incompetence of the general managers they themselves had recently appointed. Without exception, all were deemed to be failing. In line with what has been described as the ultimate attribution error (Pettigrew, 1979), which posits a tendency to over-ascribe the behaviour of others to their personality while explaining our own problematic behaviours to the situation in which we find ourselves, this was viewed exclusively as a personal failing. The possibility that it reflected an inherently impossible job description or unsupportive management structure was not considered. It suggests a tendency on the part of busy managers to:

- look quickly for causal explanations of organizational problems
- construct such explanations through the dynamics of story construction rather than empirical exploration
- create such narratives with minimal awareness of attribution processes (and thus with a strong tendency towards error)
- develop an environment characterized by extraordinarily limited feedback from outsiders.

This further strengthens the alluring power of a narrative that both explains events, and exonerates the managers themselves from responsibility for organizational problems.

Tourish and Robson (in press) suggest that a *blame realignment theory* can be posited as shedding further light on this dynamic – a tendency of people in a failing or difficult situation to realign blame in such a manner that it is placed on others rather than the self.[1] Such a dynamic may underlie the attribution difficulties discussed here. It also seems likely that this misdirects management attention from the real sources of their problems and so intensifies the spiral of crisis. Thus, managers may perceive some of the problems thrown up by limited upward feedback, but attribute these to the personal failings of subordinates rather than systemic weaknesses in their own practice, or in the design of their own organization (Tourish and Vatcha, 2003). With the deeper issues ignored, underlying problems can only grow worse. In turn, this lends illusory substance to narratives that extol the personal inadequacies of hapless underlings. The opportunity to grapple with the real problems recedes ever further into the mist.

Over-critique of negative feedback

Research suggests that feedback tends to flow mainly from persons in authority to their subordinates (Luthans and Larsen, 1986). Significant problems have been reported with the delivery of upward feedback. Moreover, the limited feedback that occurs tends to be flawed. As discussed earlier, positive upward feedback is a more common occurrence than negative upward feedback (Baron, 1996). Baron's study also suggests radically different perceptions between managers and staff on this issue. The managers concerned perceived many more instances of negative feedback than their subordinates. However, both managers and subordinates perceived the same level of positive feedback. In essence, each instance of negative feedback acquired a heightened sense of vividness for its recipient. Managers then assumed that their heightened awareness of the event rendered it more typical of the feedback category than was the case. Moreover, for most people, negative feedback is less accepted and is perceived as less accurate than positive feedback (Fedor *et al.*, 2002). It thus appears that people are especially sensitive to negative input – what has been termed the *automatic vigilance effect* (Pratto and John, 1991). Intentionally or otherwise, it is therefore likely that their less than enthusiastic response will discourage it. This manifests itself in various ways.

For example, the case study by Tourish and Robson (in press) cited above suggests that senior managers have a tendency to over-critique negative feedback, while instantly agreeing with positive feedback. The SMT of the organization concerned rejected any feedback that implied weaknesses in their performance, while instantly accepting feedback (derived from the same methods) that praised their actions – thus, the data were simultaneously regarded as prescient, but fatally flawed. Schutz (1998) analysed the strategies that people use to account for negative outcomes. One of these is termed *dissociation*, wherein the individual rejects any responsibility and someone else is blamed for the failure. Interestingly this is associated with a change in the pronominals employed to associate or dissociate with the event (for example, '*I* succeeded' but '*They* failed').

It is evident, however, that unless senior managers adopt an equally rigorous approach to both forms of feedback they will inevitably acquire a lop-sided view of their own organization. We would describe this process as one of *unconscious feedback distortion*. For example, Waldron and Krone (1991) found that some subordinates who had experienced extremely negative emotional encounters with their supervisors edited their communication to make it more formal, superficial, task-oriented and devoid of personal messages (for example, self-disclosures). The consequence is likely to be that the only people surprised by critical results from research investigations are a SMT, nominally the people best placed to have an overall view of their organization. Thus, motivating truthful upward communication is widely recognized as a serious problem (Chow *et al.*, 2000).

Characteristics of top teams and communication networks

Top teams 'refers simply to the relatively small group of most influential executives at the apex of an organization' (Hambrick, 1995: 111). How this apex is defined varies widely from organization to organization, but is not correlated with its size. Nevertheless, top teams are responsible for setting strategic direction, and communicating it widely among teams, team members and other emergent communication networks. Communication networks are widely regarded as the patterns of contact between those engaged in a communication exchange and who transmit messages though time and space (Monge and Contractor, 2001). However, larger organizations have greater distances between team members, between teams, and between teams and senior managers. Nevertheless, strategic alliances in general, and inter-organizational collaborations in particular, have grown in importance, in response to such management initiatives as delayering, downsizing, re-engineering and empowerment (Cravens *et al.*, 1996). In essence, communication networks are more important than ever.

Krackhardt (1994) has pointed out a number of problems with the emergence of rich communication networks. The 'law of N-squared' proposes that with more and more people in a given organization the number of potential links in a network organization increases geometrically, and soon exceeds everyone's capacity for communicative action. The law of propinquity also recognizes that 'the probability of two people communicating is inversely proportional to the distance between them' (Krackhardt, 1994: 213). Thus, the number of communication options, as well as obligations, combined with such prosaic matters as physical distance, renders contact between senior managers and those further down the hierarchy increasingly problematic. Although much can be done to at least partially compensate for these difficulties (including the use of e-communications), it is unlikely that anything will be done if senior managers themselves do not recognize the absence of upward communication as a problem.

Dominant models of leadership

Managers are influenced by general trends. It has been shown that feedback seeking is less likely when individuals believe that significant others do not seek such feedback (Morrison, 2002). Thus, if there is a general ethos in society of managers being expected to 'take the lead' and 'make the tough decisions', the individual manager is less likely to take cognizance of what employees think or say. In recent decades, the study of leadership has been heavily influenced by the distinction drawn between transactional or transformational leadership (Tourish and Pinnington, 2002). With transactional leadership, the independence of both leaders' and followers' goals is a given (Flauto, 1999). The resultant culture is likely to be one characterized by dissent, which may be more or less tolerated, and possibly reduced cohesion.

Transformational leadership (TL) is different. Here, the leader changes the goals of followers, subordinates or devoted members. Put in its most positive form, the new goals are assumed to be of a higher level in that, once transformed, they represent the 'collective good or pooled interests of leaders and followers' (Burns, 1978: 426). By definition, transformational leaders need more power rather than constraints (or 'regulation'), presumably in order to restrain the power of their potential dissidents.

However, from the standpoint of critical upward communication, the dangers are considerable. Research has long shown that new group members, or those with low status, only acquire influence within a group by over-conforming to its emergent norms (Brown, 2000) – i.e. they minimize the amount of critical feedback that they are prepared to offer. If they are perceived not to be 'fitting in', they are penalized, usually through the withdrawal of valued social rewards. Leaders, on the other hand, have greater status, authority and power. They therefore have more freedom than followers to violate long-established norms. The risk for non-leaders is of followers prematurely complying with destructive forms of action, thereby ingratiating themselves with leaders (Jones, 1964). The leader, meanwhile, takes the absence of overt dissent as assent, and moreover views it as supplementary evidence that the given course of action is correct – what has been termed consensual validation (Zebrowitz, 1990). TL is liable to exacerbate these problematic processes yet further, with negative consequences for decision making.

The handling of dissent, and hence of critical upward feedback, is one of the most problematic aspects of TL theory. Even managers introducing change who are not explicitly guided by the precepts of TL theory frequently view resistance as something to be overcome, rather than as useful feedback (Lewis, 1992). Researchers into TL are especially prone to this conceptualization (Yukl, 1999a). An alternative perspective, based on the institutionalization of feedback into organizational decision making, is rarely considered (Tourish and Hargie, 2000a). The problem is inherent to myths of heroic leadership, and the behaviours that are associated with it. As Yukl (1999a: 40) has argued: 'expressing strong convictions, acting confident, and taking decisive action can create an impression of exceptional expertise, but it can also discourage relevant feedback from followers.'

The problem is that influence is conceived of in unidirectional terms – it flows from leaders to subordinates, rather than vice versa (Yukl, 1999b). These issues relate to the questions of corporate culture (see Chapter 13). Within the rubric of theories that prioritize transformational leadership, the implied ideal state is one of monoculturism (Tourish and Pinnington, 2002). Difference, dissent, debate and critical feedback are banished to the margins of the group's tightly policed norms. Critics are perceived as party poopers, injecting venom into what might otherwise be a celebratory occasion. It has long been known that in a coercive environment, instead of facilitating dissent, 'tremendous overt and covert pressure is brought to bear on everyone to conform publicly, to participate actively, and to work hard, while a façade is maintained that such conformity and dedication is entirely voluntary or the product of successful ideological persuasion' (Schein *et al.*, 1961: 80).

The consequences of such defects are clear. They include:

- the elimination of dissent
- an insufficient flow of critical upward communication
- the accumulation of power at the centre
- a failure to sufficiently consider alternative courses of action, when they appear to conflict with a centrally ordained and divinely inspired vision
- a growing belief on the part of the leader that, other evidence notwithstanding, he or she is ever more essential to the organization's success.

In any event, a deliberate attempt to seek out critical upward communication would seem unlikely.

Implications for practice

Many senior managers are clearly aware that the feedback they receive is limited. Hambrick cites one CEO as follows:

There's a lack of genuine debate. Sometimes there's a half-hearted 'devil's advocate' gesture, but they really don't confront each other or me on the big issues. We're too comfortable, too self-congratulatory. It's gotten obvious to me in the past few months. I have to find a way to shake things up.

(Hambrick, 1995: 115)

The question is: what can senior managers do to 'shake things up'? Based on the available research, we tentatively offer the following suggestions:

1   Experiment with both upward and 360-degree appraisal. Such practices are no longer regarded as revolutionary, and as we have pointed out are commonly employed in many leading corporations. They are a powerful means of institutionalizing feedback. Moreover, there is now growing evidence to suggest that they genuinely stimulate more focused self-development activities (Mabey, 2001). It is of course vital that the underlying organizational culture is genuinely supportive, and that the feedback obtained is utilized to shape changes in behaviour. Feedback without follow-up action is akin to diagnosis minus a treatment regime. The malady has been identified but nothing is done to remedy the complaint. Eventually, both sides grow discouraged and give up on their relationship.

2   Managers should familiarize themselves with the basics of ingratiation theory. They should recognize that they will be subject to its effects, whatever their intentions. This suggests the need for a quizzical attitude in the face of all feedback obtained from those with a lower status, particularly when such feedback is positive in tone. Jonathan Swift, author of Gulliver's Travels, expressed it best: 'The only benefit of flattery is that by hearing what we are not we may be instructed what we ought to be' (cited by De Vries, 2001: 89).

3   Positive feedback should be subject to the same, or greater, scrutiny than negative feedback. Otherwise, positive feedback will come to predominate, and managers will develop a dangerously rose-tinted view of the climate within their own organizations. In turn, this means that key problems will remain off the agenda, and will therefore grow worse. Management meetings should regularly focus on such questions as:

- What problems have come to our attention recently?
- What criticisms have we received about the decisions we are taking?
- How are we going to respond to them?
- How can we get more critical feedback into our decision making processes?

4   Managers should seek out opportunities for regular formal and informal contact with staff at all levels. This should replace reliance on official reports, written communiqués or communication mediated through various management layers. A key focus during such contact should be the search for critical feedback. As a rule of thumb, the more reliant a manager is on official channels of communication the more likely it is that s/he will be out of touch with the mood of his or her people.

5   *Promote systems for greater participation in decision making.* Participation inevitably involves the creation of structures that empower people, and enable them to collaborate in activities that go beyond minimum co-ordination efforts characteristic of much work practice (Stohl and Cheney, 2001). Organizations that do not sufficiently utilize upward communication systems which includes positive and negative comments pay a considerable cost. In particular, it seems certain that the quality of decision making by the top management team suffers, and this has a detrimental impact upon the whole organization. For example, Nutt (2002) studied 400 decisions in medium to large organizations over a twenty-year period. He concluded that half the decisions made within such organizations failed. Nutt's analysis suggested that among the key factors explaining such failures were a tendency by managers to impose solutions, limit the search for alternatives, and use power rather than influence/persuasion to implement their plans. Successful decisions were more likely when managers made the need for action clear at the outset, set objectives, carried out an unrestricted search for solutions and got key people to participate. However, participation was used in just one of five decisions. Nevertheless, on this crucial issue, many communication efforts remain rudimentary. In working with senior managers, we have frequently been astonished by how many admit that their organizations do not even have a formal suggestion scheme in place. Its benefits have been documented over several decades. Yet a recent survey of members of the Institute of Management in the UK found that no more than 42 per cent of them made significant use of what is an elementary practice (O'Creevy, 2001). A more creative and determined application to this issue is clearly required.

6   *Create 'red flag' mechanisms for the upward transmission of information that cannot be ignored.* Organizations rarely fail because they have inadequate information. It is clear, for example, that the spectacular bankruptcy of Enron in 2001 (one of the biggest in corporate history) occurred in spite of the fact that many people who worked for the organization fully realized the weakness of its position and the unethical nature of its practices. One other aspect of the Enron scandal was the fact that whistle-blowing occurred. This was a good example of how, when they feel that they cannot safely feed back negative information up the hierarchy, employees are liable to leak this information outside the organization (Hargie *et al.*, 1999). To circumvent such a state of affairs, organizations should create the type of mechanisms we propose in this chapter. We give one example of a communication system that achieved at least some of these aims in Box 12.3. These have been found to help organizations make the transition from being merely good in their field to achieving sustained greatness (J. Collins, 2001). Organizations need to develop similar mechanisms, appropriate for their own circumstances, and rigorously pursue their implementation.

Box 12.3   Creating systems for information flow that cannot be ignored

An excellent example of a robust system for internal communication is provided by Tompkins (1993). Tompkins interviewed engineers at Marshall Space Flight Centre in the 1960s, when Werner von Braun was its director. Repeatedly, people told him that the communication device that worked best was 'The Monday notes'. This referred to a practice that had sprung up when von Braun had asked twenty-four key managers across several units to send him a one-page memo every Monday morning, in which they described the preceding week's progress and problems. Von Braun read their comments, initialled them, and added his own questions, suggestions and praise. The collected notes were then arranged in the order of the authors' names and returned as a package to all contributors. Closer investigation showed that the key managers involved had compiled their own Monday notes by asking their direct reports for a 'Friday report' about their activities. Some of them even organized meetings to gather the required information. Many of them also circulated von Braun's eventual report back down the line. In short, a simple request had triggered a robust mechanism for the transmission of information, and ensured that whatever was contained in the Monday notes was not ignored.

7   *Existing communication processes should be reviewed to ensure that they include requirements to produce critical feedback.* With very few exceptions, team briefings tend to focus overwhelmingly on the transmission of information from the top to the bottom. This is akin to building an elevator capable of travelling only in one direction – downwards. Team briefings should also include a specific requirement that problems and criticisms be reported up. Targets should be set for precisely such feedback, and closely monitored.

8   *Train supervisors to be open, receptive and responsive to employee dissent.* It has been suggested that when supervisors behave in such a manner they are signalling receptiveness to entire workgroups (Kassing, 2001). However, training in the appropriate skills is often lacking. As with many other vital communication skills, it is frequently just assumed that employees will have access to the right toolkit. This optimistic assumption is unwarranted. Even if people have some notion of which tools are available to them, training is required so that they select the right one for each task. Otherwise, those trained only in how to use a hammer may instinctively reach out for it, even when a screwdriver is more appropriate.

9   *The CEO, in particular, needs to openly model a different approach to the receipt of critical communication, and ensure that senior colleagues emulate this openness.* Repeatedly, studies have shown that when people are asked to gauge the efficacy of communication in general and the role of senior managers in particular

they personalize the issue into the role of the CEO (for example Young and Post, 1993). Without a clear lead at this level it is unlikely that progress on the issues we have discussed can be made.

Conclusion

This chapter has revealed fundamental problems with critical upward communication, illuminated some of the mechanisms whereby it is obstructed and suggested means by which the problem can be addressed. Upward feedback, especially of a critical kind, would seem to be generally inadequate. This conclusion is consistent with the observations of Heller (1998: 1425), based on two twelve-country studies on industrial democracy and a five-year longitudinal programme in seven companies in three countries: 'organizational influence sharing appears to have made only limited progress during the last 50 years'. A workplace industrial relations survey conducted in Britain in the late 1990s concluded that: 'Britain is approaching the position where few employees have any mechanism through which they can contribute to the operation of their workplace in a broader context than that of their own job' (cited by Caulkin, 1997: 6). Even the minimal influence that comes from being able to articulate different perspectives is often lacking. Evidently, those with power hang on to it, while frequently lamenting the reluctance of subordinates to exercise more initiative. On the other hand, we have argued that senior managers receive plenty of positive upward communication – much of it inaccurate. The problem is not with upward feedback *per se*. It is with ensuring that the feedback is open, honest, dissenting and, above all, critical.

The issues raised are fundamental to the theory and practice of management. No one individual or any one group has a mastery of problems, as a result of organizations' inbuilt interdependence and complexity. Thus, the search for solutions to problems that are multi-causal in nature involves creative input from different disciplines, departments and from people of varied managerial rank. Openness is therefore critical to organizational learning (Senge, 1994). However, as Weick and Ashford have noted:

> Not only do executives often prefer to hear good news but, in fact, subordinates often get promoted up the career ladder because they tell only good news. Thus, as managers move up in the organisation, it becomes more difficult for them to get honest feedback on their efforts as their subordinates are busily portraying every effort as a success. These processes in which learners defend their own egos or their subordinates do it for them would seem to impede organisational learning since they create an impoverished and distorted information base from which to take action.
>
> (Weick and Ashford, 2001: 716)

Without a willingness to even acknowledge the existence of problems, it would seem unlikely that managers can engage their people in a wider debate on strategic direction and how to build an impregnable competitive advantage. Thus, the difficulties discussed here are a recipe for chronic organizational decline.

An organization without a coherent and cohesive system for facilitating upwards feedback is like a bird with one wing. Under certain circumstances it can survive, and even thrive. However, in adverse conditions, especially when predators are circling, it will experience severe difficulties. It will certainly fail to take off and reach the heights it could have. Internal communication is indispensable for organizational learning, corporate cohesion and the achievement of business objectives. We have suggested that many of the obstacles to the emergence of good internal communication do not arise from external environmental considerations, but rather from the approach that senior managers often display towards critical feedback. The challenges posed are considerable, but need to be met for optimal organizational functioning.

Note

1 Oscar Wilde, who was asked by a friend how the first performance of a new play had gone, once provided an amusing illustration of blame realignment. Wilde replied: 'My play was a complete success, but the audience was a disaster.' The SMT of the HCO in this case study seemed to have a similar approach to analysing their problems.

13 Organizational culture
Liberation or entrapment?

Ashly Pinnington

Introduction

Over the last twenty years, organizational culture has become a topic of everyday conversation. To talk about the previous place where one worked as having a 'different' culture to the present establishment is unlikely to surprise anyone, so long as the respective organizational cultures are then distinguished through either general explanation or by giving examples. For instance, we might say that in organization A, the management–employee relationship is characterized by an 'us and them' culture, whereas by contrast in organization B culture is such that 'your manager is your friend as well as the boss'.

Research studies of companies reputed to possess 'strong' cultures have found the employees don't just talk about it, but their firms establish meetings and workshops on culture and culture change (Kunda, 1992; Stiles, 1999). The concept of organizational culture can, therefore, at the beginning of the twenty-first century, be considered to be part of our common sense reality, although clearly the term is a relatively recent addition to popular discourse. Indeed, references to culture, and more rarely concepts akin to 'organizational culture', would have tended to focus, during the nineteenth and twentieth centuries, on distinguishing such things as: the organization of agriculture and manufacturing labour (Carlyle, 1941; Kropotkin, 1974); or civilized and uncivilized manners and the state (Arnold, 1978; Elias, 1978a, 1978b); or class, high brow and popular taste (Williams, 1961; Hoggart, 1977; Adorno and Horkheimer, 1989).

So, given that people nowadays readily talk about organizations as having a culture, do they all possess one? Assuming further that there may exist several cultures in most organizations, will there invariably be one which is predominant? And if there is a dominant organizational culture, to what extent might it be a source of freedom on the one hand and a prison cage on the other? In this chapter, the aim throughout is to answer these questions and make some recommendations for communication practice. This is done with the conviction that people can influence their organizations to become more liberating and less constraining places than they presently are.

Do organizations invariably have an organizational culture?

Culture is a many-headed phenomenon applied routinely in the management literature to organizations, occupations (notably professions), ethnic groups and societies (Eisenberg and Riley, 2001). Further, we talk more and more about an emergent 'global' culture, usually meaning by this term 'compression' of the world and intensification of our consciousness of it as one totality (Robertson, 1992). Some writers speak of the 1980s as a period for the 'cultural turn' when academe and management practitioners proliferated new and rehashed concepts of organizational culture. Much of the jargon and terminology for speaking about changing the culture of an organization bears analogy with traditional religious discourse: organizational culture in crisis but with an idea of the way forward (in hell with a 'vision'); a new culture of high performance (in heaven and 'mission' achieved); employee resistance to change and no clear way forward (in hades and lacking 'charismatic', 'transformational' leadership). As a concept, culture essentially encourages us to consider collective properties and groups of people, and, for the purposes of this chapter, culture will be defined as:

A collective (for example society, organization, group or sub-group) interpreted for its sense of social integration, differentiation, and fragmentation.

The above definition is taken from mainstream qualitative research on culture exploring issues of *consensus, conflict* and *ambiguity* (Martin and Meyerson, 1988; Frost *et al.*, 1991; Martin, 1992; Alvesson, 1993, 2001). It has been chosen for its emphasis on a range of sources of cultural consensus and dissensus.

Culture and organizational performance

In the 1980s, partly in response to the rising strength of companies from Asia and the Pacific Rim, management interest in culture grew rapidly. Amongst others, Ed Schein (1992: 12), from the Massachusetts Institute of Technology, has been influential in the management field, defining the culture of a group as the pattern of shared basic assumptions learned as it has 'solved its problems of external adaptation and internal integration, that has worked well enough to be considered valid and, therefore, to be taught to new members as the correct way to perceive, think and feel in relation to these problems.' Schein believes leaders have the capacity to create group culture, as do Deal and Kennedy (1982). Their recommendations on changing organizational culture met a clear need amongst senior executives in the 1980s, many of whom were running organizations that were facing difficult business conditions.

Deal and Kennedy's (1982) portrayal of culture change in *Corporate Culture* focuses on symbolic aspects of management, highlighting differences in performance and their possible relationship to organizational culture. They especially extolled the virtues of charismatic leadership, entrepreneurialism, vision and values, and the rites and rituals of corporate workplaces, which were part of a new wave of thinking on the management of change emerging in the USA during the 1980s. They proposed that management and employees should distinguish 'strong' from 'weak' cultures. America's great companies, they claimed, were high-performing and successful human institutions. High performers ascribed by Deal and Kennedy the status of 'strong' cultures included such organizations as 3M, GE, IBM and Hewlett-Packard.

In the same year, Peters and Waterman (1982) produced a set of anecdotal case studies on a group of high-performing US corporations, which they considered were successful organizations because they had the right culture. Their set of stories about excellent companies published in the book titled *In Search of Excellence* popularized the approach of managing culture. The 'excellent company' and 'strong culture' approaches emanate from a similar network of people affiliated to high profile educational establishments such as Harvard Business School and consulting companies such as McKinsey. One measure of the considerable interest at the time in the 'excellent company' approach was that, at the height of its popularity, the book was selling more copies than the bible. During the 1980s, advocates of the 'excellent company' approach appeared to become increasingly convinced by the argument that a strong culture is the major key to business success. However, events have called this into question. The following companies were among those held up as exemplars, but which then experienced profound problems:

- Walt Disney: it produced a string of films that were failures
- Caterpillar: it experienced declining demand for its heavy plant machinery
- Atari: its name was once synonymous with computer games, but it has now disappeared
- Hewlett Packard: it underwent considerable downsizing during the 1990s.

A possible explanation for the appeal of these 'guru writings' on culture lies in the simplicity and cultural acceptability to US organizations of the 'strong' and 'excellent' culture messages. The overall tenor is rigorously individualistic, pragmatic, optimistic and uncomplicated, as is the vision of successful leadership, management and culture. However, evidently the link to performance was not a reliable one nor was it especially sustainable.

Societal culture – liberation or entrapment?

In theoretical and empirical research on culture the notion of entrapment often still figures strongly. This dilemma remains apparent in much of the case study research by people who don't subscribe to the positivist scientific paradigm, but their findings nevertheless reveal ways in which culture is a regular constraint on our freedom of action (Jones *et al.*, 1988; Kunda, 1992). Recent qualitative research studies majoring on culture, as far removed from one another as a division of a major UK multinational conglomerate (Watson, 1994a), a UK

Midlands-based building society, a manufacturing company and a North of England town hospital (Parker, 2000) and a Swedish computer consultancy (Alvesson, 1995), all reveal the capacity of a small group of fallible, but powerful, senior executives to influence the daily working lives of their employees. Even at those very moments when the three researchers – Watson, Parker and Alvesson – are at pains to emphasize limits to managerial control by highlighting the autonomy, localness, individuality and specificity of organizational culture(s), the perceptive reader cannot help but notice trends across Western societal contexts (Ulizin, 2001). Often, their observations on specific details of organizational culture – its symbols, languages, ideologies, beliefs, rituals and myths (Pettigrew, 1979) – highlight commonalities running across many organizations. We will return to the contribution of recent qualitative research on organizational culture, including the above three mentioned studies, later on in this chapter.

Organizations entrapped by uncertainty and change

In their book *The Cultures of Work Organizations* (1993) Trice and Beyer argue against the entrapment perspective by emphasizing the liberating forces of organizational uncertainty and change. They observe that there is research evidence that cultures in organizations are being changed, and therefore can in principle be changed. With regard more specifically to corporate culture, Trice and Beyer propose the chances of success increase whenever managers are clear-headed about their approach to cultural innovation – replacing an 'old' culture with a 'new' one.

Trice and Beyer (1993) define human cultures in general terms as arising from people's dealings with uncertainty and attempts to create order in social life. They observe that there exist many problems of uncertainty and order in organizations, and propose that, as in other cultural contexts, people will thus seek to create cultures in organizations. Trice and Beyer's approach to organizations as cultures concentrates on the cultures of modern capitalist corporations in both the private and public sectors. Their ideological presentation of culture is one that takes for granted many current developments in the globalization of business. They prioritize the roles of top executives and managers in leading change and implementing cultural innovation. Returning to the question of whether or not there are organizational cultures, these authors resolutely answer in the affirmative and provide evidence in their favour through a substantial review of the management and organization studies literatures.

Trice and Beyer offer prescription and aphorisms for the proactive management of change. Whereas their research approach for studying management might be accused of liberation on the surface but entrapment within its ideological framework of American capitalist democracy, some of their general proposals for changing culture apply to other societal cultures because, as they observe, in principle organizational cultures can always be changed. More specifically, in terms of measuring and changing culture, a variety of tools and techniques are available for use in organizations (Ashkanasy *et al.*, 2000). In so far as Trice and Beyer can be seen as advocates of cultural change that is liberating for managers and for employees, then they can be considered promoters of organizational culture as a source of liberation.

Organizational cultures contain a multiplicity of voices

Notwithstanding Trice and Beyer's views on corporate culture change, the question as to whether organizations routinely possess a distinctive organizational culture is hard to answer. What the disciplines of cultural anthropology and sociology advise us, then, is to be cautious whenever ascribing to organizations notions of culture that are individual and unique properties. An organization's culture is complex and contains a number of societal influences, which may be tantamount to culture (Geertz, 1973).

Our age, gender, education, ethnicity, religious, occupational, professional and family allegiances are all potent sources of culture. Nelsen and Barley's (1997) work, for example, is interesting for its exploration of how groups of employees promote and exploit occupational cultures through what the authors call 'occupational mandates'. Occupational affiliations can play a critical role in whom people associate with inside and outside the organization, and the relative social status of occupations almost invariably affect monetary and social rewards. The role of gender specifically in organizational culture has been researched in companies such as Body Shop International. Martin *et al.* (1998) found that organizations staffed by a high proportion of women may dispense with some communication practices typical of a male-dominated organization that places high significance on an impersonal, technical and emotionally constrained style of interaction. They argued that Body Shop International encouraged a different sense of workplace community, tolerating more open expression of emotions, expecting greater self-disclosure and taking private life concerns as being central to personal well-being.

Alvesson (1995, 2002) has argued persuasively for a 'plurivocal' conceptualization of culture. He noted the tendency of some people to associate culture with unitarism, whereby we perceive everyone in the organization has the same ultimate interests and goals. This refusal to accept there might be a plurality of valid alternatives is frequently accompanied, he says, by a concentration on culture as a metaphor for instilling harmony, integration, clarity and consistency (Alvesson, 1995). Unfortunately, it is only a short step from here to institutionalized intolerance where other perspectives are stereotyped as not 'fitting-in' with the dominant or desired organizational culture (Tourish and Pinnington, 2002).

Alvesson's (1995) solution to over-simplification of cultural realities in organizational life is to treat cultural meaning and symbolism as involving on the one hand, 'consensus, consistency and clarity' and on the other hand, 'dissensus, inconsistency and confusion'. Examples of the consensus side of culture include: shared meanings and understandings within the organizational culture, unquestioned assumptions in the company, normative agreement on the 'right' and 'wrong' ways of doing things, harmonious ways of working together, and non-contentious forms of coordination and control. Whereas examples of the dissensus side of culture would be: unharmonious social conflict and organizational politics, aggressive turf wars between departments or cliques in the organization, lack of common understanding between groups, unfair discrimination, widespread cynicism, long-term resistance, strongly contested forms of coordination and control, and fundamental disagreement over the core values, basic assumptions and priorities of work.

Embedded in this research perspective is the idea that cultural phenomena are deep and multifaceted. Alvesson offers a helpful framework for research on culture that places organizational culture on a continuum located in between two poles. On the one side culture, he suggests, can be seen in very broad, macro-level terms as a 'form of life', and on the other side it can be narrowly conceptualized as denoting solely artistic activity. Positioned somewhere towards the middle, he proposes, is organizational culture conceptualized as a collective consciousness or, alternatively, as a set of common values, ideas and norms.

To sum up the argument so far. Organizational cultures are rarely going to be entirely original and unique; possibly a historical period of isolation from the host societal context may be the most likely way that an idiosyncratic individual culture might develop, such as religious communities and political groups (Tourish and Wohlforth, 2000). This is because organizational culture comprises an amalgam of sources of culture, most of which are shaped within societal contexts rather than solely being the product of individual cultural histories. Therefore, it makes more sense to consider organizational culture as constructed out of a plurality of sources of cultural identity (Hall and du Gay, 1996).

It may be useful to close this section by inviting the reader to consider communication and culture within an organization where you work now, or have worked in the past (see Reflective Exercise 13.1).

Organizational culture as multiple sources of culture

The previous section has argued that cultures are composed of 'a multiplicity of voices'. It has been argued that research on organizational culture must distinguish the organizational collective – its organization-specific ideologies, symbols and cultural forms – from general societal change. A review of the literature soon reveals that many of the techniques of managing culture change have been in use for over two decades and some for considerably longer. For instance, Biggart (1977) tells the story of the creative–destructive process of organizational change in the US post office, involving the replacement of old ideologies, cultural forms and symbols with new ones. The changes included the following:

Reflective exercise 13.1 Exploring communication and culture in your organization

> - Select a group employed in your organization, or one in which you have previously worked, and distinguish those values and behaviours which are specific to the culture of the organization from those that you might find in many other similar organizations.
> - Describe the culture of your organization in a few sentences. Jot down three short stories which demonstrate its culture of, on the one hand, 'consensus, consistency and clarity', and on the other hand, 'dissensus, inconsistency and confusion'.
> - Select three individuals who seem to you to be very different people. Make a list of the sorts of things you would expect them to say about the 'old' culture and the 'new' culture of your organization.
> - Identify what aspects of your organization 'cause' people to behave in ways that are harmful or unproductive.
> - Make a list of key things that should change in your organization and what should stay the same. Then, identify what changes may need to occur in the organizational culture for this to happen.

- a new chief executive
- name changes, new logos, new stationery
- early retirements with 'happy exit' ceremonies
- birthday celebrations for anniversaries of new parts of the organization.

A question that immediately has to be asked is, together do these constitute a unique culture or are they 'generic techniques' applied across a variety of organizations? Whichever organization instituted these cultural changes for the first time in all probability would have had a highly distinctive organizational culture, and there is evidence that some original organizational cultures will endure for a long period of time. To give one example, Gratton *et al.* (1999) found that Hewlett Packard in the UK had a very resilient culture when compared with other large corporations in their research sample. This company had the most committed and flexible workforce, which was part of its cultural heritage created by the views of the founding partners and reinforced through consistent ownership by line management of responsibility for 'people management'. Consequently, the company's business strategy was implemented within an organizational culture of genuine and continuous investment in employees. Interestingly, even a severe period of organizational downsizing did not destroy employees' commitment and loyalty (for more on this topic see Chapter 2 by Tourish and Hargie).

Mats Alvesson (1995), nearly twenty years after Biggart's article was published, tells a somewhat different story of the creative–destructive process of organizational change in Enator, a Swedish private sector, computer consultancy company. Enator was a 'knowledge intensive firm' that was characterized by its reliance upon rare, specialist, esoteric expertise and idiosyncratic knowledge and skills (Starbuck, 1992; Alvesson 2001). He recounts a story of growth, not unlike the one typified in Greiner's (1972) well-known article on issues of leadership, autonomy and control, in what might be thought of as those inevitable growing pains when making the cultural transition from the relatively small business concern to a massive corporation. Alvesson's (1995) story of culture change in Enator is not 'revolutionary'. However, it similarly involves the replacement and modification of old ideologies, cultural forms and symbols with new ones. The changes related include:

- growth of a cohort of senior managers steadily increasing over time their power and influence in Enator relative to the original three owner-directors
- personal leadership, especially during the early years of business operation, by three owner-directors
- name changes following merger with another company, joint ventures and creation of new international subsidiaries
- glossy promotion photographs of managers shot in impressive landscape settings
- publicity stunts and gimmicks at get-togethers and company conferences, such as having the plane seats removed to enable dancing 'in-flight entertainment' for employees travelling from Scandinavia to London
- talk of plans for 'happy exits' by senior staff
- birthday celebrations for the main company and its subsidiaries
- regular informal company socializing, such as five o'clock beer, and so on.

Alvesson characterizes Enator's corporate culture as open, positive, loyal, generous, informal, non-bureaucratic, friendly and participative. These are all familiar qualities recommended in prescription in texts on managing culture change (for example Deal and Kennedy, 1982, 1999). Alvesson is adamant, however, that they genuinely distinguish Enator as a unique organizational culture. In keeping with his concept of culture as containing positive and negative aspects, he does though draw attention to the reverse side of these positive attributes:

- anti-unionist culture
- thorough-going public criticism and debate being sanctioned in socialization events such as the induction training
- discussions on pay being taboo except in private on a one-to-one basis with an appropriate manager
- employees being expected to (over)work compulsively for long hours on projects and to have a limited private life with regular company socializing being an obligation during non-work time.

Both of the above stories on organizational culture, related respectively by Biggart and Alvesson, convey ideological change in societal-level culture. In Western countries, this ideological move from a paternalist, and sometimes autocratic culture to a more managerial culture has been well-documented in the practitioner and academic press, and in both private and public sector contexts (Hinings *et al.*, 1991; Morrill, 1991; Whittington *et al.*, 1994; Greenwood and Hinings, 1993, 1996). Ideological pressure to become more 'business-like' has influenced people employed within traditional as well as the new professions (Cooper *et al.*, 1996; Brock *et al.*, 1999). Enator had been in the IT and consultancy business for about ten years before Alvesson studied it, and he asked the question: 'How long does it take for culture to develop?'

If we understand organizational culture as being enmeshed within societal culture(s), then a liberating perspective might suggest its development can be almost instantaneous. This may not suit the palate of those people who view the development of organizational culture as being analogous to that of a maturing, local and unique wine. However, if we accept that any culture comprises a selection from many potential sources, then there are reasonable grounds for assuming that individual identities and a collective culture can fuse together rapidly to form a new organizational culture. Such change is unpredictable, but is thought more likely to occur during moments of fundamental crisis (Pettigrew, 1985; Bourdieu, 1988).

Culture as craft

A more recent and similarly intriguing study of culture is Tony Watson's (1994) one-year participant observation study of ZTC-Ryland, titled *In Search of Management*. The overall corporation, of which ZTC-Ryland is just one business unit, is a massive British manufacturing conglomerate that has been criticized over the years in the financial press for being risk averse in its core markets and not investing sufficiently in new high-growth businesses. Watson (1994) adopted a political treatment of culture, portraying the organization as a coalition of interests in contest with one another, although less of the documentary history of the organization was related than has been done in other case studies of organizational culture such as Pettigrew's (1985) well-known longitudinal case study of ICI.

During the study of ZTC-Ryland, Watson concentrated on reflecting upon managers' own experience and understanding of what they were doing. Culture, as observed from the outset of this chapter, is a collective phenomenon and thus the portrayal of organizational culture presented by the individual researcher should be appropriately explained and justified to others. Purposefully, to ground his own study of culture in their sense of culture, Watson therefore asked a number of managers who had been involved in culture change programmes what they thought the word 'culture' meant. They variously defined it as:

- acceptable behaviour
- getting people thinking on the same lines
- values

- below the surface patterns
- a valuable means of comparing one organization with another.

These ad hoc definitions of culture, it is worth noting, are not dissimilar to their basic idea of management practice, which, when asked by Watson, they described in consensual and prescriptive terms specifying how any manager should behave, especially:

- listening to people, treating them fairly and building trust.

Watson tried hard not to force the stories they told him into his own preconceived ideas (Gabriel, 2000), observing that his study was not meant to be delivered from 'on high', but be based on a sociable 'mixing-in' of the researcher with managers going about their daily business. He sees management as being an emergent, social and moral craft (Watson and Harris, 1999) and consequently his preferred research focus is on managers' continual involvement in enacting, thinking and learning about the craft of management. Watson's study of ZTC-Ryland conveyed a sensitive acknowledgement of the danger of researchers becoming entrapped within their own academic conceptualizations of organizational culture. His belief is that researchers do not convey 'facts' so much as construct 'fictions' (Czarniawska, 1999) that are of varying degrees of plausibility to the reader. Therefore, Tony Watson's story of ZTC-Ryland, sometimes revealed more about his assumptions than it uncovered the culture(s) of the researched.

Culture as an archipelago: unity and division

Martin Parker (2000) contends that organizational cultures should be seen as 'fragmented unities'. By this phrase he meant that culture is a complex process that is, at the same time, both inclusive and exclusive of people in the organization. Parker identified distinctive areas of cultural difference, which he argued can help us understand how organizational culture is a collective and divisive process.

In his book titled *Organizational Culture and Identity* Parker (2000) relates, in detail, three case studies of technology and culture. From this he identified several key influential cultural factors. His first case study was a hospital in which he concentrates on the 'us and them' relationships between different occupational and professional categories, namely doctors, managers and IT professionals. Problems of communication were compounded by distinctions arising from different positions in the hospital hierarchy and people working in different spatial locations, particularly different hospital sites. The second case, of a manufacturing company, illustrated cultural differences arising from locality (bottom and top sites) departmental divisions (production and marketing), age (older and younger engineers) and their related different allegiances to production technologies (mass production and flexible production systems). The third case, of a small building society, revealed cultural differences arising from tensions between HQ and branch offices. The organization had been led for a long period by a paternalist, domineering and rather autocratic traditionalist, creating cultural differences between an older group of nostalgic (Gabriel, 1995) conservative managers and a younger more radical set who had been appointed since his demise.

In summary, divisions internal to the organization, considered by Parker, are: spatial, functional (for example departments) and hierarchical. Divisions arising from outside the organization are: occupational and professional, generational, regional and gender-based. Members of the organization created culture, he argued, through understandings and identities that were local and specific on the one hand and societal on the other. Distinctive organizational cultures arose out of organizations having particular histories, geographical reach, key people and so on.

To conclude this discussion on the plurality of sources of culture making up an organizational culture, researchers and practitioners must focus on what is distinctive in the organization. The representation of organizational culture should be situated in an analysis of the local organization of broader culture, the organizational culture being a particular manifestation of societal culture. Mass media communications industries, for example, utilize sources of distinctive 'local' culture and contribute towards the production of collective or 'global' cultures. The twentieth century saw the rise of culture industries, and Bjorkegren's (1996) study of publishing, music and film production of popular culture highlights well the tension that routinely occurs whenever large sums of capital are involved between local innovation and the herd effect of global financing and promotion strategies. Research on organizational culture should attempt to understand what sources of culture are used, and attend to its obverse, what sources are discarded or silenced. Identities and allegiances arising from religion, occupation, generation, gender and family will likely be found to be important sources of culture. We should consider both the current situation and its historical development because organizations are at the same time embedded in culture and perpetually in transition (Hughes, 1992). It might be worth, again, checking this idea in the context of where you either work now, or have done in the past (see Reflective Exercise 13.2).

Returning to the issue of liberation and entrapment: a consensual view of culture that deliberately seeks to minimize difference for its own sectional group ends will tend towards entrapment of the majority. Mills *et al.* (2001) show just how sophisticated some corporate cultures have become at creating a sense of belonging and community, inclusive of members of the corporation, trading companies and end-consumers. Even the case research reported by Alvesson (1995) and Watson (1994) periodically slipped into the trap of accepting the status quo by not clarifying for the reader the extent to which an influential group of managers have moulded their organization's culture (Rose, 1996). By the end of their studies, it is unclear to the reader how far the dominant coalition of managers had successfully biased the organization's ideology, structure,

Reflective exercise 13.2   Analysing culture and communication practice

- Select a group of managers in your organization. How might they be encouraged to mix socially more with other employees? How might they be encouraged to reflect more on their management practice as an ethical craft?
- Assess how far demographic diversity creates a conflictual culture in terms of: gender, age, occupation/profession, ethnicity. How might this conflict be made more productive/creative?
- Assess how far divisions internal to the organization support a culture of conflict in terms of: spatial, functional (for example, departments, teams), hierarchical. How might this conflict be made more productive?
- Identify how your present organizational culture has been shaped by its history, geography and key people.
- Subdivide your organization into a dominant coalition and contender groups. In what ways do the dominant and dominated groups contribute to the present organizational culture? What interventions can be made to help these groups communicate more effectively with each other?

culture, systems, values and beliefs to suit their own social advancement, in preference to other members of the organization. On this point, Kallifatides' (2001) study of interaction between top management and selected fast-track managers provides a good example of how the organizational culture can be evaluated in terms of organizational interaction and interpersonal politics. It showed how interpersonal relationships in the company were socially constructed according to dominant societal and organizational cultural values that reinforced particular ways of behaving. Kallifatides identified a virtue of 'toughness' in the company, which determined managers' promotion chances, influenced their sense of managerial identity ('being made of the right stuff – i.e. tough') and regulated details of everyday social interaction, especially patterns of conversational turn-taking – who talks, when and for how long?

A contested view of culture, accepting the many sources of culture and encouraging people to make use of them, is likely to be more liberating than entrapment within a consensual viewpoint or a modernizing perspective (Foster, 1985). Parker's (2000) case studies portray specifically the contested nature of culture more so than the other studies by Watson and Alvesson. This is not to say that cultural sameness and unities aren't significant: they are. Essentially, the cultural perspective should be a varied one that can reflect issues of homogeneity and heterogeneity. In this regard Alvesson (1993) has offered a helpful framework for thinking flexibly about culture by viewing it in four distinct ways:

1   unitary and unique organizational culture
2   organizations as meeting points of 'fields' of culture
3   local subcultures
4   ambiguous cultural configurations.

Understanding organizational culture as *unitary and unique* means making the assumption that the culture really is not like any other and thus is different from the rest. By contrast, understanding organizations as *meeting points of 'fields'* conceptualizes all organizational culture as being composed of societal-level commonalities and divisions. An individual organization culture following this way of thinking therefore can never be entirely distinctive or unique because it is entirely a manifestation of macro-social phenomena. The *local subcultures* approach plays down the macro-societal issues conceptualizing the organizational culture as constructed out of a variety of local, contextual influences. The fourth approach, understanding organizational culture as comprising *ambiguous cultural configurations*, assumes a plethora of sources of culture, simple and unique, macro and shared, local and others, complex and confused. Alvesson recommended using all four approaches to gain a more informed and comprehensive insight into organizational culture.

So, on the question of liberation or entrapment, it is hoped that a liberating approach to organization culture can actively encourage ongoing democratic dialogue within a plurality of perspectives. Moreoever, it should challenge members of the organization to discuss various sources of culture as a way of assisting them with reformulating aspects of their cultural identity and under-standing of work. The next section explains how this liberating approach might be put into practice in organizations.

Re-invigorating workplaces by continuously challenging dominant organizational culture

In the spirit of Watson's (1994a) plea for management and organization researchers not to criticize from 'on high', this last section makes recommendations for how communication might be improved, building on the lessons of the research on organizational culture reviewed in this chapter. It has been argued that organizational culture conceptualized as the unitarist imposition of managerial prerogative in almost every aspect of working life – what employees think, feel, value and how they act – is a form of entrapment. It is unreasonable for employees to be expected by senior management to trust and accept the assertion of prerogative in critical decisions, such as on rewards, allocation of resources and organization of work (Reed, 2001). Extension of corporate culture across work and home life, and throughout networks of suppliers, producers and consumers, may be an effective way of maximizing shareholder wealth, but it grossly undervalues the diverse sources of available culture. What might, on occasions, be to the short-term advantage of some investor or managerial group is likely to disadvantage the majority, especially when there is a lack of

Table 13.1 Culture as entrapment, or source of liberation

Entrapment	Liberation
Seeing organizational culture as:	Seeing organizational culture as:
• conformity to senior management strategy	• capacity to reformulate senior management
• 'the way we do things round here'	• different ways of doing things around here
• forging a new culture	• creating a culture out of many sources of unity and difference
• a 'can do' (anything) outlook	• a 'some do' outlook
• corporate symbols	• democratic symbols
• corporate rites	• multiple dialogues
• one best way forward	• many roads to success
• managerialism	• pluralism
• performance-based rewards for all	• equitable rewards for all
• We don't talk about our pay and conditions	• we frequently discuss pay and conditions
• an environment of over-work	• place(s) of work
• a total corporate-consumer community	• a partial community in a network of communities and neighbourhoods

participation and involvement of the many voices inherent to the organizational culture. The recommendations in Table 13.1 present a challenge to unitarist, stereotypical 'old' and 'new' conceptualizations of organizational culture in management practice and research, and the reader is respectfully asked to interpret them within the context of the overall argument of this chapter for a pluralist conception of organizational culture.

Conclusion

It has been argued that organizational culture might be a source of entrapment in so far as it is shaped by societal 'forms of life', and it is often a social constraint and source of repetitive collective behaviours. The culture of management and employment practices in Western countries, for example, reveal many commonalities and patterns that seem unavoidable (Barley and Kunda, 1992). Culture also can be a source of entrapment in our communication by shaping theoretical assumptions and creating deep meanings, which then make it difficult for us to rise above them into other modes of cultural understanding (Heracleous and Barrett, 2001; Wicks, 2001). However, such characteristics of cultural entrapment do not add up to an inescapable cage. We are able to think and behave in ways that go beyond and contrary to the cultural context. Culture is a means of liberation in its very make-up because it is a plurivocal source of identity. Organizational culture is to an extent malleable as has been alluded to by the culture change typifications of 'old' and 'new' cultures.

This chapter has argued that it is rather idealistic to assume that culture is purely functional or that it is a causally determining nexus of variable influences on our behaviour and thought. Organizational culture is not all-encompassing, nor wholly liberating, nor a total trap. We need to understand more clearly its unitarist and pluralist elements, its rationalism and irrationalism, and its positive and negative processes of creation and destruction. From a communication perspective, our acknowledging that organizational culture is not a fixed entity, but a complex of sources of culture, will help to liberate us from a fruitless, over-simplified conceptualization (Burrell, 1997).

In favour of constructing a clear dividing line between organizational culture and societal culture, this chapter has provided some empirical evidence for organizations 'having a culture'. It also has drawn attention to the importance of people – both researchers and practitioners – reflecting upon the interplay of societal sources of culture when analyzing organizational culture. Further, it has been contended that conducting qualitative, single case studies does not absolve organizational culture researchers from considering in-depth, societal commonalities. Otherwise, they will inevitably fall into the trap of over-ascribing uniqueness to the organizational culture under study. Finally, it is proposed that more inclusive and consensual organizational culture flourishes when differences and pluralist sources of culture are given opportunity for voice and participation, rather than ignored or treated merely as 'employee resistance to change'.

14 Organizational communication ethics

Directions for critical inquiry and application

Matthew W. Seeger

Introduction

Questions of right–wrong, good–bad, and ethical–unethical are endemic to any purposeful human activity that affects others (Johannesen, 2002). Organizations, by virtue of their size, power, and prominence in society profoundly affect the lives and welfare of a wide variety of stakeholders. Organizations are, therefore, moral domains pregnant with ethical significance. Moreover, the ethical questions organizations face are highly equivocal and increasingly characterized by competing values of individuals, organizations, and a wide variety of stakeholders (Seeger, 1997). Communication is the fundamental process whereby organizations sort through this equivocality and reach consensus regarding what constitutes ethical conduct (Seeger, 2001).

Questions concerning the ethics and values of organizational communication have recently become more prominent in both the study and practice of organizational communication. Cultural and interpretive metaphors of organizational communication (Putnam, 1982; Putnam and Fairhurst, 2001), efforts to detail the moral dilemmas organizations face (Jackall, 1988) and dramatic cases of ethical failure such as the Prestige oil spill, the Archer Daniels Midland price fixing scandal, the continued deception and consumer harm caused by tobacco companies, and the Enron collapse, have pushed questions of right and wrong to the forefront of organizational inquiry.

The purpose of this chapter is to describe the role of ethics in organization communication. The position of ethics in the larger domain of organizational communication is outlined, including the kinds of issues explored. Three frameworks for facilitating communication-based inquiry into the ethical dimensions of organizations are presented. These include culture, sensemaking and applied ethics. Finally, future directions for ethics and organizational communication are offered.

Ethics and organizational communication

Organization communication, as a domain of research and practice, has typically privileged questions of effectiveness and efficiency over questions of ethics and values. Deetz (1992) for example, has suggested that organizational communication suffers from a management bias and that practices have emphasized hierarchical domination through language, access to information and voice. Redding (1996) has charged organizational communication scholars with culpable neglect for their failure to give even most modest attention to ethical questions. This neglect has occurred despite the fact that 'The preponderance of everyday problems that plague all organizations are either problems that are patently ethical or moral in nature or they are problems in which deeply embedded ethical issues can be identified' (Redding, 1996: 18).

This lack of attention has occurred in the presence of an impressive litany of ethical misdeeds with organizational communication implications. These include the Bhopal Union Carbide accident, Jack-in-the-Box tainted beef, the sex scandal in the American Catholic Church, Chernobyl, the outbreak of mad cow disease in Britain, and the WorldCom collapse, as well as many more mundane cases of deception, violation of employees' rights, exploitation of labour, violation of human dignity and environmental mismanagement.

One of the fundamental questions facing communication investigators concerns the relationship between ethics in organizational contexts and organization communication. This question may be addressed in two ways.

1 First, communication in organizations is a target of ethical reasoning and judgments. That is to say, the practice of communication in organizations involves a variety of ethical questions and issues.
2 Second, communication more broadly is the process whereby organizations constitute and reconstitute a moral frame or ethical climate. That is to say, communication is the process whereby organizations come to discover what they believe about ethics and whereby those beliefs and associated standards are both disseminated and reified.

Communication in organizations includes a wide variety of ethical issues (Redding, 1996; Seeger, 1997) associated with:

- employee privacy and voice
- free speech
- honesty
- deception
- social influence
- persuasion and coercion
- diversity
- whistleblowing
- change
- power, authority and control
- leadership
- legitimacy
- recruitment and socialization

- management style
- advertising
- public relations.

These issues may be clustered according to two general foci; those concerning ethics and values in internal communication with internal audiences, and those concerning ethics and values in external communication with external audiences. For example, a set of ethical issues including legitimacy, advertising and public relations, are principally external and concern the organization's larger role as a social actor. These issues also relate to the organization's position as part of a larger social structure with larger moral obligations and sense of social responsibility.

The concept of corporate social responsibility, or CRS I, has been a dominant part of business ethics since at least the early 1900s. It can be traced to the community chest movement, whereby organizations were expected to contribute to charitable efforts to offset the harms they helped create (Buchholz, 1990). CRS I programmes were criticized, however, for supporting narrow sets of middle class lifestyles and values, for their status as mere public relations, and for the influence they sometimes exerted on social policy. Organizational philanthropists also complained that they could not serve as social agency and that only government had the resources and social legitimacy to provide broad-based, long-term social services (Buono and Nichols, 1995). Following this criticism, a new orientation called corporate social responsiveness, or CRS II, emerged based on organizational openness, sincerity and flexibility. Closely connected to the stakeholder model of organizations, CRS II was grounded in processes that encouraged organizations to understand and accommodate the needs and interests of groups with a legitimate stake in the organization (Sethi 1987; Buono and Nichols, 1995).

Cheney and Christensen (2001) argue that the external organizational communication designed to create and maintain organizational identity includes several ethical and moral dimensions. These include:

> (1) the posited character or integrity of the source of the messages, (2) the defensibility of a particular message, (3) the legitimacy or pattern of campaign of messages, (4) the practical impact of messages or the cumulative effect of a series of message, (5) the openness of the structure of communication between an organization and its publics/audience, (6) the articulation or representation of general public interests and (7) the question of shared responsibility.
>
> (Cheney and Christensen, 2001: 259)

Ethics of external organizational communication are the most visible and generally garner the widest public attention. In fact, dramatic instances of managerial moral misconduct often result in widespread attention to issues of ethics and a heightened awareness of these issues.

The second general cluster of ethical issues involve essentially internal communication processes and audiences. These include employee privacy and voice, free speech, diversity, whistleblowing, change, power, control and leadership. These internal aspects of organizations represent a different moral domain because organizations generally have greater authority to establish and enforce internal standards. The principle of organizational legitimacy, however, suggests that there should be at least a general correspondence between internal and external standards. These internal ethical domains have been described as the moral climate or culture and relate to how values are modelled, communicated and enforced, and how rights of internal employees are framed and maintained. Ethical climate is the 'shared perception of what is ethically correct behaviour and how ethical issues should be handled' (Victor and Cullen, 1988: 104).

Although internal and external ethics may be viewed as distinct, they are also related. Ethical failures in internal communication, such as stifling employee voice and dissent, may lead to ethical failures in external communication, such as investor deception and fraud. In fact, this pattern of ethical decay was characteristic of the recent Enron scandal.

Research traditions and conclusions

Although questions of values and ethics have traditionally been at the fringe of organizational communication inquiry, recent efforts have been helpful in articulating basic issues and principles. These include communication and leadership, external responsibility and responsiveness, and questions of internal employee communication such as employee voice, free speech, whistleblowing, and democracy.

Leadership

Questions of credibility, honesty and truthfulness are traditionally described as components of leadership effectiveness in political or social contexts. Recent efforts have focused more explicitly on the communication ethics of organizational leaderships, primarily through the lens of virtue ethics (Seeger and Ulmer, 2001; Cavanagh and Bandsuch, 2002; Johnson, 2002). Virtues are a set of relatively fixed aptitudes, attributes, or traits that are broadly recognized within a society or community as ethical or moral. Johnson (2001: 50) suggests that 'The premise of virtue ethics is simple. Good people (those of high moral character) make good moral choices'. The virtuous person, then, serves as a model of appropriateness, credibility, suitability and character. Aristotle regarded a moral virtue 'as a form of obedience to a maxim or rule of conduct accepted by the *agent* as valid for a class of recurrent situations' (Smith, 1946: xiv, emphasis added). As a fixed attribute or rule, a virtue represents a moral touchstone of stability and order. Moreover, because the virtuous person models ethics, those in visible leadership positions, including CEOs, can be expected to exemplify admirable and laudable traits (Liebgig, 1990; Seeger and Ulmer, 2001).

Seeger and Ulmer (2001) examined the behaviour of two CEOs, Aaron Feuerstein and Milt Cole, following devastating fires that destroyed most of their companies. They argued that an underlying entrepreneurial ethic motivated the tendency of these leaders to act and communicate in highly commendable and virtuous ways. In both cases, these CEOs appeared to act out of habit or inner drive rather than through strategic and calculated consideration. The entrepreneurial ethic they described includes core values of corporate social responsibility, long-term obligations to diverse stakeholders, and a need to communicate immediately in ways that contained the harm and lead to rebuilding. Both CEOs discounted the importance of short-term profitability in favour of long-term issues of mutually supportive relationships with stakeholders and involvement in the community. Both had a well-developed sense of community obligation and commitment and saw their enterprises as closely connected to the community. The two cases they describe both involve private rather than publicly held corporations. Seeger and Ulmer (2001: 136) concluded that the 'ability to respond to a crisis in virtuous ways, with regard to the strategic implications for profitability, would likely not have existed in publicly traded corporations'.

Leaders are also generally seen as playing a central role in establishing an organization's ethical climate through modelling desirable behaviours (Simms and Brinkman, 2002). Gini argues that, 'The ethics of leadership whether they be good or bad, positive or negative affect the ethos of the workplace and thereby help to inform the ethical decisions and choices of the worker' (1996: 2). Leaders, their choices and behaviours are often very visible to other organizational members and are often widely publicized. Leaders also serve as spokespersons, describing and justifying organizational activities and decisions. Followers take cues from leaders (Simms and Brinkman, 2002) based on:

- what they pay attention to
- how they respond to crisis
- their behaviour
- how rewards are allocated
- how they hire and fire others.

Overall, then, organizational leaders are moral models, emulated by others.

Ethics and external communication

The ethics of external communication on the part of organizations includes a very broad set of principles, codes and standards largely because this form of communication confronts community, social and professional norms of ethics. Both public relations and advertising, for example, have well-developed codes of professional conduct and norms regarding what constitutes ethical practice. Moreover, responsibility and responsiveness described earlier both concern the ethical conduct of external organizational communication. Heath (1997) suggests that part of the strategic issue management activities of organizations should involve maintaining ethical conduct. In similar vein, Daugherty (2001) argues that to survive organizations must address issues of social responsibility through their public communications and public relations functions. Stakeholder theory (Freeman, 1984; Freeman and Gilbert, 1987; Deetz, 1995b) describes a set of ethical obligations organizations have to primarily external groups with a stake in the organization, including customers, suppliers and members of the community. These obligations concern the ongoing, mutual exchange of messages leading to representation of stakeholder concerns in organizational decision making. Organizations should solicit input from employees, customers, members of the community, suppliers, professional groups, governmental agencies, stockholders as well as other stakeholders so that their needs and values are represented in organizational decision making.

Organizations also have specific obligations to communicate with external stakeholders following accusations of wrongdoing, including cases of ethical misconduct. Apologia, a genre of apologetic organizational discourse, is grounded in these obligations. Benoit (1995) and Hearit (1995) have detailed the range of explanations for wrongdoing offered by both organizations and individual managers. These typically involve a set of strategies such as denial, evading responsibility, reducing the offensiveness of the event, corrective action, and mortification. Organizational apologia explicitly addresses questions of ethics and values including issues of blame, responsibility, culpability, and accountability. Strategies of apologia are designed to meet audience expectations by complying with ethical standards regarding taking responsibility for actions, apologizing and asking for forgiveness, offering restitution when harm has occurred, and offering plausible assurances that the offence will not happen again.

Finally, organizational legitimacy concerns the correspondence of organizational activities and processes with larger social values. This legitimacy, then, may translate into a broader basis of stakeholder good will and support (Metzler, 2001). Dowling and Pfeffer (1975: 122) explain that organizations are viewed as legitimate when they 'establish congruence between the social values associated with or implied by their activities and the norms of acceptable behaviour in the larger social system of which they are a part'. When organizations violate norms of legitimacy, they no longer meet 'certain expectations on the part of citizens with regard to the policies of the official order and its personnel' (Friedrichs, 1980: 549). To overcome such incongruity, organizations must communicatively engage stakeholders. This may involve actively promoting the organization's social record, discussing strategic changes made to accommodate social values, as well as creating opportunities for stakeholder input into organizational operations. Seeger argues that for organizations, the process of securing or regaining legitimacy is 'rhetorical and involves offering adequate justifications within a consensus producing dialogue concerning the value of the institution and its activities' (1980: 148). Much of the public discourse offered by an organization is at least partially designed to maintain or bolster legitimacy.

Employee voice, free speech, whistleblowing, and democracy

A third set of inquiries concerns a loosely related body of principles regarding internal communication issues and practices. Employee voice, free speech in organizations, whistleblowing, and workplace democracy relate to values of individual empowerment, freedom, participation and equality. 'Employees as citizens,' for example, 'should not just be compliant [sic] but should be influential in shaping the culture of their work place. They should engage appropriately in the dialectics of managing those institutions that significantly affect their lives' (Gorden and Mermer, 1989: 4). Free speech in organizations similarly suggests that when employees are free to express themselves, they are more likely to innovate, call attention to problems, and be satisfied (Seeger, 1997). Free speech is closely connected to both workplace democracy and employee participation. Democracy refers to 'those principles and practices designed to engage and represent (in the multiple sense of the term) as many relevant individuals and groups as possible in the formulation, execution and modification of work-related activities' (Cheney et al., 1997: 39). Democracy is grounded in values and practices of free expression and participation. Whistleblowing concerns efforts on the part of employees to call public attention to issues of organizational wrongdoing. Often, this requires reporting the wrongdoing to outside agencies or the press, usually at considerable personal risk to the whistleblower. In this way, whistleblowing spans organizational boundaries, and uses broader social values, norms and public opinion to correct some wrong. These views emphasize the positive values associated with the free movement of messages within organizations and the creation of more equitable power relations.

Internal conversations about ethics

A final body of work in organizational communication ethics more generally examines internal conversations and dialogue about ethics. A number of scholars have documented the fact that ethical issues are rarely discussed in most organizations. Toffler (1986), for example, concluded that managers avoid engaging employees in discussions of ethics so as to maintain ethical ambivalence. This ambivalence, then, translates into plausible deniability in case something goes wrong. Deetz et al. (2000: 125) describe an 'ethics code of silence' in organizations that drives ethical issues underground until they erupt as significant problems. Seeger (1997) offered a somewhat less jaundiced explanation as to why ethics are not part of the ongoing discourse of organizations, arguing that managers are usually not trained to discuss ethics and so often suffer from perceived powerlessness and general ambivalence with regard to ethical questions. Jackall (1988) similarly suggests that participants in organizations avoid discussions of critical values because these issues are politically sensitive. The fact that conversations about ethics are rare suggests that ethical questions often go unaddressed in systematic ways (Brown, 1990). Moreover, because ethics and values do not become part of the overt discourse of the organization, the ethical framework used to make decisions often remains hidden from view. Frequently, this means that the more prominent and habitually discussed issues of profitability dominate.

As Cheney and Christensen note: 'To talk about the value of behaving ethically in itself is frequently not persuasive. A measurable economic end product becomes the warrant for making a case for "good business". And "just business" becomes a short-hand justification for all sorts of questionable corporate practices' (2001: 262). Ethical issues are often positioned in opposition to the more dominant issues of organizational profitability in ways that privilege profitability. Value questions are secondary, a luxury only to be considered when economic goals are met. In fact, a significant body of work suggests that many managers view their jobs as necessitating moral compromise (Jackall, 1988; Deetz, 1995a).

Frameworks for organizational communication ethics

The recent surge in interest regarding organizational communication ethics and values is associated with the development of new research paradigms and frameworks (Seeger 2001). In some instances, these developments have followed other, more general, theories of organizational communication while other areas of research have emerged to focus specifically on ethical issues. These frameworks include cultural based views, sensemaking and applied ethics and professional codes.

Culture

As noted by Pinnington in Chapter 13, the term 'organizational culture' has now entered the everyday lexicon. Indeed, arguably, interpretive and cultural views of organizational communication have become a dominant paradigm for inquiry (Eisenberg and Riley, 2001). Culturally based metaphors and methodologies of organization emerged in the 1980s (Deal and Kennedy, 1982; Peters and Waterman, 1982) and interest in value dimensions of culture soon followed. This interpretive turn in organizational inquiry focuses on the organization as a symbolic and linguistic place where meaning is constructed and used to make sense of experiences (Eisenberg and Riley, 2001). Culture intersects with ethics in at least three ways.

1   *At the point of organizational values*   Conrad (1993) notes that while culture does focus on values, it treats them largely as straightforward, unproblematic and reflected in organizational operations and decisions. Values, from the cultural perspective, are underlying assumptions, guidelines and unifying themes for organizational life. Some investigations suggest that values are broadly and persuasively communicated in organizations and actively inform actions and decisions (Martin and Siehl, 1983; Valesquez *et al.*,

1983). Values may be encoded and communicated in stories, language, symbols, myths, and icons or more explicitly through codes, mission statements or corporate value statements. Beyer and Lutze provide an extensive review of the organizational values literature and model the relationship between individual and organizational values. They suggest that individuals hold complex sets of values before joining organizations and that 'through socialization processes inside an organization these values are moderated and transformed into shared internalized values' (Beyer and Lutze, 1993: 43). Feedback from the organization's environment, then, interacts with these values. Cheney's (1993) examination of value premises of discourse found in corporate documents and his detailing of the values processes at the Mondragon cooperatives (Cheney, 1999) provide clarification of both the larger value framework of 'business' and of how participatory values function within one specific organizational culture. At this Spanish cooperative, decisions have been made to 'promote social values of long standing importance' including the 'diverse expression of democracy' (Cheney, 1991: 141–2). Moreover, the Mondragon cooperatives have been stable and economically successful. Other investigations have focused on how values are encoded and transmitted in organizations (Pribble, 1990) and how values become part of the organization's larger cultural discourse (Waters and Bird, 1987). Pribble (1990) described ethical socialization as a rhetorical process using identification to evoke commitment to organizational values. Bird and Waters (1987) found that public discussions of moral issues and explicit, public agreement regarding the standards of appropriate conduct contribute to clarity regarding the moral dimensions of organizational culture.

2   *Over issues of organizational identity*   In addition to the focus on values, cultural approaches also explore questions of organizational identity and ethics. Drawing on issue management (Heath, 1997) and organizational rhetoric (Elwood, 1995; Hoover, 1997), identity concerns issues of image, reputation and legitimacy as organizations seek to craft a sense of 'what the organization "is" or "stands for" or "wants to be"' for both internal and external audiences (Cheney and Christensen, 2001: 233). Questions of identity and ethics merge in the larger ethical assessment of organizations. Those organizations assessed as good, worthy and appropriate, for example, may enjoy a stronger reputation, legitimate image and favourable identity. Cheney and Christensen (2001) identify a number of ethical concerns for communicating externally and building and managing organizational identity. They include '1) Integrity of the source of the message; 2) the defensibility of a particular message; 3) the legitimacy of a pattern or campaign of a particular message; 4) the practical impact of a message or the cumulative effect of a series of messages; 5) the openness of the structure of communication between an organisation and its audiences/publics; 6) the articulation/representation of genuine public interests; and 7) the question of shared responsibility' (Cheney and Christensen, 2001: 258). These issues

'represent an important basis for ethically informed criticism of the communication that organizations carry on between themselves and their environment' (2001: 262).

3   *At the level of cultural critique* A third trend within organizational culture is a small but growing body of work focusing on organizational critique from the perspective of critical theory. Deetz (2001: 26) suggests that of the general orientations to organizational culture, 'critical studies have the most explicitly stated value commitments and most explicit attention to moral and ethical issues'. Critical studies approaches organizational communication from a specific value premise that seeks to eliminate domination and create workplaces that emphasize equality and democracy (Deetz, 2001). This work often draws on feminist and cultural perspectives, labour studies, and multiple stakeholder views to promote diverse and genuine participation in organizations (Mumby, 1988, 1996; Deetz, 1995b, 1995c). As such, critical studies represents a radical shift in notions of organization from conceptualizations that emphasize issues of investment, technology, production and markets to those that privilege questions of participation, development, equality, self-determination and empowerment of diverse groups.

The study of organizational culture makes investigations of values, identity and critique central to understandings of larger systems of organizational meaning. Belief systems, norms, icons, symbols, language and values are the organization. Values are assumed to have a direct effect on organizational action and decisions as well as moral choices. Much of the cultural approach to organizational communication, however, views values as simplistic and unproblematic and fails to recognize how individual and organizational values intersect, how competing values are negotiated, how values shift and are appropriated, and how feedback, social influence, learning and reinforcement may affect values and their expression (Beyer and Lutze, 1993). Nonetheless, cultural approaches have helped clarify the role of values, provided insights about ethics and organizational identity, and provided an initial framework for the communication-based cultural critique of organizations.

Sensemaking

Closely associated with cultural approaches is the general theory of organizational sensemaking (Weick, 1979, 1988, 1995). In developing a communication-based theory of sensemaking, Weick (1979) approached the concept of organization from a unique stance. Rather than adopting a structural approach whereby an established strategic structure influences behaviour or where structure follows the behaviour of members, it is argued that structure emerges or is enacted from the collective efforts of members to make sense of or construct their informational environment (Sutcliffe, 2001). Organizing is, therefore, a dynamic and ongoing process of social construction. Weick summarized his broad view of the socially constructed nature of the organizing process as 'How can I know what I think until I hear what I say?' (1979: 133). This process is inherently retrospective as members look back on events and construct the meaning of those events. Communication is central because members must share their meanings to create a collective sense of the informational environment. The principle problem for organizations, Weick suggested, is resolving or reducing environmental uncertainty, or equivocality. There is an ongoing need to determine how to know what to think about information inputs. Equivocality, according to Weick, concerns the various possible interpretations associated with some informational input.

Organizational members must interpret or make sense of the informational inputs they receive. Communication processes allow for the development and testing of various interpretations. Those interpretations that are useful in allowing members to act are more likely to be adopted and retained in the form of organizational structures, procedures, policies, methods, assumptions, and responses. This process of reducing or resolving equivocality through shared interpretations, or sensemaking devices and responses, represents the ongoing process of enactment leading to organizing. Enactment, then, is a social process whereby a material and symbolic record of action is laid down and made available for subsequent action.

Sensemaking has particular utility in understanding the ways in which organizations make sense of issues with ethical implications (Seeger, 1997). Weick's view suggests that members must hear ethical issues and organizational values discussed in order to be able to engage in moral reasoning and action. Communication, therefore, is the process whereby a kind of ethical equivocality is resolved in organizations. Without the opportunity to hear what is said about ethics and values, members do not know what to think and ethical equivocality remains unresolved.

Sensemaking may 'problematize' ethics in three specific ways (Weick, 1988; Seeger, 1997).

1   *In failure to perceive.* For example, organizational members do not have the requisite background, experiences, or sensitivity to perceive or attend to some ethical issue. The ethical dimensions of an issue may simply not be recognized.
2   *In failures of rules and cycles.* Here, organizations do not have the retained rules or opportunities to communicate about ethical issues. There may not, for example, be established ethical codes, committees, fora or similar venues for examining and discussing ethical issues.
3   *In perceived powerlessness.* Weick (1988) suggests that when members do not believe they have the power to affect change in an issue, they cannot afford to pay attention to that issue. Ethical issues may simply be too politically sensitive for many members to attend to.

Finally, in stunted enactment, an unwitting collusion develops where members learn to ignore some issue. New members, for example, may be socialized into an organization culture that ignores ethical issues and values conformity with existing practices.

Sensemaking as a general theory of organizing and communication makes explicit the link between dialogue about ethics and values, moral reasoning and ethical conduct. As such, it suggests that enhancing the level of organizational conversation about ethics and values may help members reduce the moral equivocality of organizational life.

Applied ethics

One implication of sensemaking is that programmes and activities of applied ethics may help reduce ethical equivocality. Applied ethics, as an area of both inquiry and practice, focuses on issues of ethical decision making and problem solving in professional and organizational communities (Singer, 1986). Applied ethics typically focuses on moral issues or controversies with specific manifestations in professional or business contexts such as law, engineering, medicine and bio-ethics, research, government and communication. Specifically, applied ethics offers norms and guidelines of professional practice and methodologies for promoting ethical decision making. The role of codes of conduct in promoting discussion, informal decisions, and resolving practical ethical problems are explored (Rosenthal and Shehadi, 1988).

Ethical codes and guidelines have been popular in organizations since at least the 1970s and have become increasingly common among businesses and professional associations (Ethics Resource Center, 1997). In general, most large organizations will also have at least some form of ethics code. They were initially created by organizations and professional associations seeking to respond to specific ethical wrongdoings. Codes vary significantly in form and structure, from highly legalistic documents used to protect organizations from legal liability to much more general aspiration value statements (Stevens, 1994; Schwartz, 2001). Statements of core values or mission statements sometimes serve as the organization's formal declaration of ethics. They vary widely in functions, including protecting the organization from legal liability, constraining and focusing employee behaviour, and enhancing the image and reputation of the organization (Frankel, 1989; Schwartz, 2001). In addition, codes serve as a means of communicating value positions to stakeholders and as ways of facilitating discussions regarding ethics in organizations (Stevens, 1994; Seeger, 1997). It is relatively common, for example, for all new employees to receive copies of ethical codes. Codes and ethics programmes are related to an improved ethical climate and are particularly important during times of transition (Ethics Resource Center, 2000).

One of the interesting developments in the area of applied ethics is the adoption of professional codes of conduct for the communication discipline and proposals for codes of conduct in organizational communication (Montgomery *et al.*, 1995; NCA, 1999). These codes, although not without controversy, have helped identify important ethical issues, clarified the core values of communication, and suggested methods for avoiding and resolving ethical dilemmas. Moreover, they promote discussions of ethical issues and help broaden understanding. Associational codes for communication professions have been used for a numbers of years. These include codes for journalists, public relations professionals, marketing and advertising professionals, and broadcasters (Johannesen, 2002). Recently, the National Communication Association (NCA) also adopted a Credo for Ethical Communication. The credo includes ten principles regarding the ethical practice of communication. It notes, for example, that ethical questions occur whenever people communicate and that ethical communication is 'central to responsible thinking, decision-making, and the development of relationships and communities' (NCA, 1999). The NCA credo draws on a broad set of ethical traditions including honesty, truthfulness, free speech, condemnation of hate speech, the ethic of care, privacy, respect, social justice, protest, responsibility and responsiveness among others. It includes an explicit statement regarding responsibility; 'We accept responsibility for the short and long term consequences of our own communication and expect the same of others' (NCA, 1999). The credo also suggests a clear link between ethical and effective communication: 'We believe that unethical communication threatens the quality of all communication and consequently the well-being of individuals and the society in which we live' (NCA, 1999).

The applied ethics approach addresses issues of responsibility and accountability, limitations on ethical conversations, and the argument that ethics are not relevant when compared to issues of efficiency and profitability. Codes and guidelines, for example, function in part by explicitly clarifying issues of responsibility and accountability. Many corporate codes also clarify issues of conflict of interest. Some of the more legalistic corporate codes require that employees sign an affidavit indicating that they have read and agree to abide by the code. Some organizations develop elaborate programmes to train employees in the code, while others include ethics officers or committees, responsible for enforcement. Many organizations use codes and guidelines to foster conversations about ethics and values. Johannesen (2002: 201) suggests that codes serve an argumentative function, 'to stimulate public and professional scrutiny of major ethical issues'. Codes, along with ethics programmes, audits and reports can serve to make ethics and values part of the organization's larger agenda (Seeger, 1997). Finally, codes and guidelines, as applications of ethics to practical problems, often explicitly address the relationship between ethical issues and efficiency and profitability. Many codes, for example, discuss the value of a good or ethical reputation. Codes and credos, however, are not panaceas for ethical communication in organizations. Enron had an extensive ethical code, which included explicit provisions about ethical communication (Bowen, 2002). The Enron code obviously failed to prevent fundamental moral decay.

Research directions and issues of practice

Although questions of ethics have migrated towards the centre of organizational communication, understanding remains largely fragmented and a number of important areas are essentially unexplored. These areas of inquiry concern both how communication functions in the doing of ethics in organization and how communication practices may be a target of ethical standards.

Organizational communication scholars and ethicists, for example, should turn their attention to examining how values are manifest and communicated throughout organizational contexts. Although studies of socialization and codes of ethics have begun to explore some of these processes, investigations of more informal communication process such as modelling, storytelling, and learning have not yet focused explicitly on ethics. In addition, important questions concerning how practical issues of ethics are resolved and the role communication might play in that process require attention. There are also important questions about how the moral climate in organizations changes over time. How is it that a company can turn from a model of ethical conduct to corporate pariah in a few short years? The ways in which codes, guidelines and even ethics training are used and influence choices and behaviour represent potentially fruitful areas of inquiry. What processes, structures and training might facilitate conversations about ethics? Other than in the formal and stylized cases of whistleblowing and apologia, little is known about how, when and with what frequency organizational members discuss, question, explain and argue about ethical issues. These communication processes are at the heart of any comprehensive understanding of how ethics function in organizational processes.

Conclusion

The systemic failure of organizational communication scholars to examine ethics and values is slowly being corrected. Culture, sensemaking and applied approaches are facilitating this examination into a wide array of internal and external organizational communication phenomena. In the process, a much more complete understanding of both organizational life and the impact of organizations on society is emerging. This understanding includes a general recognition that fundamental moral questions underpin most organizational communication processes. Communication, in this way, is comprehensive to organizational ethics as both process and product. As Conrad noted:

> It is through discourse that individuals develop their own views of morality; through discourse that organizations develop and inculcate core values and ethical codes; and through discourse that incongruities within individual and organizational value-sets are managed and contradictions between the value sets of different persons are negotiated.
>
> (Conrad, 1993: 2)

Failure to talk about ethics, to discuss and debate values, to publicly question the ethics of decisions and actions promotes ethical equivocality and helps insure that many fundamental moral issues organizations face will be largely ignored.

15 How are we doing?

Measuring and monitoring organizational communication

Owen Hargie and Dennis Tourish

Introduction

This book has examined a range of communication issues that are central to effective organizational functioning. Running through all of these, however, is the necessity to evaluate the extent to which any measures introduced to improve communication are actually working. In this chapter, we explore the process of auditing an organization's communication performance, by examining the following questions:

- Why is it necessary to audit?
- What exactly is the audit process?
- How is the audit conceptualized?
- What methods are used in the audit process?
- Why don't all organizations audit?
- What do audits tend to tell us?
- Can the audit be used as a teaching tool?

Why is it necessary to audit?

In the UK, BBC television broadcast an insightful series entitled *Back to the Floor*, in which chief executives from a range of companies agree to spend a week being filmed while working on the shop floor. In one of these, screened in 2002, the chief executive of Hoover's vacuum cleaner manufacturing plant in Cambuslang, Scotland was shown interacting with employees on various parts of the production line. After hearing numerous very perceptive comments from these (mainly female) operatives about huge communication hiatuses, the visibly surprised chief executive concluded that: 'The big message today was communication. Issues that I thought we'd communicated pretty well on, and we had in fact put a lot of effort in, it's quite clear some of the issues are not getting through so I think it's how we can communicate more effectively.' This message was confirmed by one of the workers who commented about management: 'I think they live in cloud cuckoo land sometimes. Different planet from us. They see it from a different angle you know.'

This is not atypical of what happens in many organizations, in relation to the strategy of senior management teams. Communication initiatives are launched, like missiles, by central command. But the missiles are not guided, and there is no equivalent of mission control to track their performance. It is as if the wonder and ballyhoo associated with the grand spectacle of the launch is sufficient success in itself. How could anyone fail to be dazzled? The reality is likely to be that many employees will have never heard that there even was a launch, and the missile itself disappears into the corporate ether leaving little trace. George Bernard Shaw noted such difficulties when he remarked: 'The single biggest problem in communication is the illusion that it has taken place.' The female employee in the Hoover factory summed it up rather well in the above quotation. Managers and workers often do inhabit two different planets, and there may be very little contact between them. They speak different 'languages', have divergent priorities, and perceive the organizational world through deviating filters. As we will show in this chapter, this is a recipe for organizational dysfunction. A communication strategy must be something that is carefully thought through, widely disseminated to all employees, and its impact regularly and objectively monitored and evaluated at all levels.

There is now a great deal of evidence to show that effective communication is central to business success, and as such should form an integral part of the strategic planning process for all organizations (Clampitt *et al.*, 2000). In their research in this area, Morley *et al.* (2002: 69) found that 'Organizations that develop effective communication processes are more likely to both have more positive work environments and be more effective in achieving their objectives.' A great deal of research into what constitutes effective human resource management has also reinforced the role of communication, both directly and indirectly. For example, O'Reilly and Pfeffer's (2000) analysis of such top companies as Southwest Airlines, Cisco Systems and the Men's Wearhouse repeatedly highlights the methods used by the companies to maintain top quality communication systems between management and employees. Recurring communication themes in the general literature include:

- the need for adequate information flow concerning key change issues (Tourish and Hargie, 1998)
- the central importance of supervisory communication, as a preferred communication source (Synder and Morris, 1984)
- the importance of inter-departmental communication in promoting enhanced innovation (Tjosvold, 1991)
- the role of participation as a means of enhancing corporate cohesion (Brewer, 1996)
- the notion of communication as a foundation of teamwork and positive employee attitudes, and thus as an agency for enhancing performance (Rodwell *et al.*, 1998)
- the need to maintain face-to-face communication as a primary method of information transmission (Smith, 1991)

- the benefits obtained from conceptualizing dissent as a source of useful feedback, rather than simply as resistance to be overcome (Tourish, 1998).

The dangers of ineffective communication have also been well documented. As summarized by Hargie *et al.*:

> Problems caused by breakdowns in communication are legion and have produced effects ranging from, at one end of the continuum, job dissatisfaction and stress, through to damaging strikes, operating losses, bankruptcies, production line injuries, plane crashes, and, at the other extreme, mass slaughter in the field of battle.
>
> (Hargie *et al.*, 1999: 4)

To circumvent such negative outcomes, internal and external communications must be carefully and systematically monitored. Yet, in many organizations, managerial activity takes the form of fire-fighting rather than the provision of strategic leadership, while unstable communication systems create frequent and unexpected conflagrations (Tourish and Hargie, 1998). The sad reality is that communication is:

- all-pervasive, but often unplanned; in many instances communication is what happens to companies when they are busy doing other things
- widely touted as a panacea for organizational ills, but given minimal resources
- hailed as being of central importance in terms of what managers actually do, but rarely investigated with the same rigour as is reserved for such other functions as finance
- still seen as what managers do to their subordinates; in other words it is a one-way street with in effect a 'no entry' sign for upwards communicators.

The result is a disabling gap between theory and practice. This is clearly dysfunctional, and can impact adversely upon the workforce, resulting in reduced employee motivation, lower rates of production, greater industrial unrest, increased absenteeism, and higher staff turnover (Hargie and Tourish, 2000).

Managers cannot rely upon their own 'feel' for the state of communications, since this is notoriously unreliable (Huczynski and Buchanan, 2001). Research suggests that when two or more people interact, those with a lower level of status tend to ingratiate themselves with those of higher status by exaggerating the extent to which they agree with their opinions, and to which they value their performance (Jones, 1990). The research also suggests that most managers are inclined to take this defective feedback at face value, and assume it is accurate, sincere and well-intentioned (Rosenfeld *et al.*, 1995). This has been called 'the boss's illusion' (Odom, 1993). For example, our own work with audits over a number of years has found that the people most surprised by critical audit findings are the senior management team (Hargie and Tourish, 2000). The reasons for this were explored in Chapter 12, in that in the natural state of the organizational world employees are disinclined to reveal unsavoury information to managers. As a result, senior management are likely only to hear good news stories and be spared unpalatable truths such as woeful internal communications and rock bottom staff morale.

To avoid this vicious circle, systems must be put in place so that staff can openly and honestly express their true feelings. This requires an objective, confidential and anonymous mechanism for accessing and assessing employee views. There is, therefore, the necessity first of all, to accurately evaluate the organization's present communication performance in order to devise and implement worthwhile improvements.

What exactly is the audit process?

In broad terms, the key steps in measuring communication can be summarized as follows:

- audit current levels of performance
- disseminate the results of the audit widely across all levels
- implement an action plan tailored to rectify identified deficits
- conduct a follow-up audit to evaluate the effects of the action plan.

Accurate information about the state of internal communications can best be obtained through the implementation of a communication audit. The main advantage of an audit is that it provides 'an objective picture of what is happening compared with what senior executives think (or have been told) is happening' (Hurst, 1991: 24). The findings provide reliable feedback and this in turn allows managers to make decisions about where changes to existing practice are required. A communication audit sheds light on the often hazy reality of an organization's performance, and exposes problems and secrets to critical scrutiny. It enables managers to chart a clear course for improved performance.

The term 'audit' is ubiquitous. Financial audits are well established, and clinical audits, medical audits, and organization audits are also now widely employed. Three characteristics are, in fact, common to all audits (Hargie and Tourish, 2000):

1   *The accumulation of information* This is the *diagnostic* phase of the audit. In communication terms, managers need *information* about the quality and quantity of communication flowing between different sectors of the organization.
2   *The creation of management systems* This is the *prescriptive* phase of auditing. Once information has been gathered, *systems* must then be put in place to further develop best practice, and to remediate identified deficits.
3   *Accountability* This is the *functional* aspect of the audit process. Specific individuals should be made *accountable* for different aspects of internal

communication, so that when problems are highlighted someone is specifically tasked with ensuring these are swiftly dealt with. If a problem is everyone's responsibility it is usually no-one's responsibility.

All three of the above elements must be addressed within any audit. In essence, an audit is the organizational equivalent of a personal physical. It pinpoints those areas of the corporate body that are healthy, but also diagnoses if there is organizational hypertension, whether tumours of discontent are growing in certain sections, to what extent communication arteries are clogged, and the current state of emotional and psychological well-being. The results of the check-up then allow decisions to be made about how identified weaknesses can best be rectified.

This chapter argues that assessments of communication effectiveness should match the seriousness of intent evident when such functions as finance are audited. As such, a communication audit has been defined as: 'a comprehensive and thorough study of communication philosophy, concepts, structure, flow and practice within an organization' (Emmanuel, 1985: 50). Various techniques exist to achieve this outcome (Goldhaber and Rogers, 1979; Downs and Adrian, 1997; Hargie and Tourish, 2000; Dickson *et al.*, 2003), and these will be summarized in the next section. Typically, data emerges on information underload and overload, bottlenecks within the organization, examples of positive communication flow, and pressing communication concerns at all levels. For example:

- Do management and staff perceive the organizational world differently?
- What must be done to achieve and sustain significant improvements in communication?
- Where are the greatest threats and the greatest opportunities?
- When, how, and in what way, will future progress be monitored?

A key goal in all of this is to gauge the accurate views of employees. Thus, as noted by Furnham and Gunter (1993: 204), 'A communication audit is a positive and motivating exercise, being in itself an internal consultation process'.

How is the audit conceptualized?

Although the audit process attracted enormous attention and a large volume of academic publications in the 1970s, academic interest tended to wane thereafter (Hargie *et al.*, 2002). However, organizations continued to audit on a regular basis, and audit methods were consistently taught on most organizational communication courses (Zorn, 2002a). The number of publications declined in the 1980s and was reduced to a trickle in the 1990s. The reason for this was two-fold. First, among organizational scholars there was a general move away from what were seen as applied concerns, and a desire to embrace what were perceived to be more theoretical issues (Mumby and Stohl, 1996). Second, there was a growth of interest in iterative or interpretive collaborate approaches to organizational investigation (Scott *et al.*, 1999). The audit was regarded by some theorists as a mechanistic tool that was 'done to' employees, while many researchers preferred approaches that could be 'done with' them in a spirit of collaboration.

For example, Jones (2002: 469) argued that the auditor should be 'a skilled and committed listener to, and within, organizational communication processes' as opposed to 'an outside expert, a diagnostician of communication problems, and an enforcer of best practice standards'. Thus, auditing is often conceptualized as two poles. At one of these, the audit involves a scientist rigorously applying validated investigatory tools using a fixed, inflexible procedure to obtain answers to pre-determined questions. At the other the auditor is a keen-eyed and intrepid explorer on a free-flowing voyage of discovery around the organization, with employees as the informed guides. This perspective is consistent with the increasingly popular theoretical frameworks of critical management studies. These hold that there has been a 'near collapse of the positivist consensus within social science' (Grey and Willmott, 2002: 414), validating the role of different epistemological traditions in generating new insights into the contested and power dominated corridors of all organizations. Thus, Jones (2002) criticizes an emphasis on the diagnostic and prescriptive roles of communication audits as reflective of a simplistic conception of organization life, over-relying on an outdated metaphor of *the organization as a machine*. The argument is that traditional approaches to auditing have implicitly endorsed the privileged role of management in agenda setting, and therefore excluded competing and equally valid perspectives from the equation.

However, in our view many theorists have beaten the straw man of the mechanical auditor, who is portrayed as automaton-like, administering pre-set, standardized, 'one-size-fits-all' survey questions to employees who are expected just to acquiesce as passive participants in the process. Like extra-terrestrials, such creatures may exist, but we have not encountered them personally. Equally, the interpretive auditor could be portrayed as a rather naive 'touchy-feely' type of individual, who believes in mom and apple pie, and engages in much interaction with what are believed to be informed and informative employees, but in the end only produces the communication equivalent of pyrites (fool's gold) – the data collected looks fine at first sight but upon deeper analysis it is shown to be of no value. This, again, is a flawed stereotype.

The audit is itself a process of transaction and negotiation between those who commission it and those who conduct it. In the scores of audits that we have conducted we have experienced a wide variety of attitudes ranging from those who see themselves as 'paying the piper' and therefore wanting to call the tune, to those who enter the encounter with minds wide open, ready and willing to listen to advice about the best way forward. In some of the private sector manufacturing companies that we have worked with, the notion of the audit as an interpretive exercise in which the auditor is someone 'who can listen with a trained interpretive ear' and provide feedback 'in an open and tentative spirit' in a process of 'ongoing self and peer evaluation' (Jones, 2002: 469) would quite simply have been anathema to the CEO and senior managers. We would have been perceived as ivory tower academics and quickly and quietly shown to the exit. Furthermore, our experience in this sector has shown that many employees have a mindset that does not easily facilitate interpretive methods. For instance, one of our doctoral students attempted to use the critical incident approach in an engineering company. However, it rapidly became clear that this would be problematic. Managers and employees found it difficult to conceptualize the notion of remembering and describing positive and negative communication 'incidents'. One manager's response was, 'But I don't go around collecting incidents.' In this organization a combination of questionnaire and depth interviews then proved more appropriate. By contrast, the critical incident approach provided invaluable data in an audit we carried out with Catholic priests, who relished the prospect of detailing in great depth their world of experiences (Hargie and Lount, 2000).

One difficulty is that interpretive approaches are often vague in conceptualization – they are more of an 'exercise' than an audit. They can therefore be difficult to implement, especially in hard-nosed, hierarchical organizations, and are more likely to succeed in corporations with flattened hierarchies and forward-thinking management, and usually not in the manufacturing sector. For example, interpretive audits have been reported in people-centred organizations such as child-care centres and Alcoholics Anonymous (Meyer, 2002). However, flexibility is the key to success in auditing. We would concur with Salem (2002) that a combination of qualitative and quantitative methods is often the optimum approach, and that 'The final report is richer and more meaningful when it comes from both types of methods' (p.448).

Meyer (2002) produced a balanced overview of the two approaches. As he put it:

> Even many who are fairly sophisticated about and interested in communication look for the nuts-and-bolts kind of quantified data on communication flow and satisfaction that are typical and important parts of organizational assessments. Alternative methods of study like narrative or metaphor analysis generate ambivalence; such methods take more time, effort and expenditure than practical-minded organization members may have the patience for. However, eliciting the symbols that make up the day-to-day life-world of communicators in organizations is crucial for assessment, since they represent the key sense-making actions of organizational members.
>
> (Meyer, 2002: 472)

What methods are used in the audit process?

The answer to this question is that there is a wide variety of alternative approaches, and the ones selected should be the 'best fit' for the organization concerned. The methods used should be tailored for the corporate body under analysis, as 'off-the-peg' systems, like cheap suits, are rarely attractive and inevitably fail to fit along some of the required dimensions. Furnham and Gunter (1993) used the term 'organometrics' to refer to the methods used to measure the various dimensions of organizational functioning. We will now briefly review the alternative organometric tools relevant to communication audits.

Survey questionnaires

This is the most widely used approach to auditing. Indeed, Clampitt (2000) pointed out that organizational surveys are now as commonplace as weather forecasts. This was confirmed by Goldhaber (2002: 451), who noted, 'The survey, however, has become the dominant method chosen by academics and consultants – mostly due to its ease of development, administration, and inter-pretation – both for clients and for research publication'. There are several vali-dated audit questionnaires that can be tailored for specific organizations. The two main ones are the *Communication Satisfaction Questionnaire* (Downs and Hazen, 1977) and the *International Communication Association Audit Survey* (Goldhaber and Rogers, 1979; Hargie and Tourish, 2000). The questionnaire method allows the auditor to control the focus of the audit, enables a large number of respondents to be surveyed, and produces benchmark rating scores for various aspects (for example, 'communication received from senior man-agers'), against which future performance can be measured. The main drawback is that it is limited in the extent to which it can gauge the deeper level thoughts and feelings of respondents.

Interviews

Another popular audit approach is the structured interview. Indeed, in his text in this field Downs (1988) concluded that if he had to select just one audit method he would choose the interview. This is because it allows for communica-tion experiences to be explored in detail, and as such can often produce interest-ing insights that surveys may miss. Researchers have increasingly recognized that people form different impressions of the same events, and that chronicling the stories that typify organizational life is a key means of understanding what sense people are making of their environment (Gabriel, 2000). Interviews, and focus groups (discussed below), are an invaluable means of tapping into the stories, folklore, myths and fantasies that people develop as part of the organizational sense-making in which we all engage. On the down side, it is time-consuming and expensive. Interviews, which can last up to two hours for managers and one hour for non-managers (Millar and Gallagher, 2000), have to be recorded and transcribed for analysis. As such, it does not readily allow for large numbers to be involved in the audit. Furthermore, unlike surveys, interviews cannot be anony-mous and so may be vulnerable to social acceptability responses.

Focus groups

These are ubiquitous, and have permeated all walks of professional life, from politics to marketing. They can be used to develop insights at a macro level (such as the impact of strategic decision making) or on a micro level (such as detailed responses to particular communication messages) (Daymon and Holloway, 2002). In their comparison of audit methodologies, Dickson *et al.* (2003) argued that the open-ended and interactive nature of focus groups produce insights from respondents that are difficult to obtain through other methods. Participants spark one another into action by sharing and developing ideas. Two main disadvantages are that more introverted staff are reluctant to participate, and some staff may be unwilling to express honest views in the presence of colleagues.

These are the three most widely employed organometric audit tools, although there is a range of other approaches, such as critical incident analysis, ECCO, data collection log-sheet methods, constitutive ethnography, social network analysis, and undercover auditing (for a full analysis of these see Hargie and Tourish, 2000; Dickson *et al.*, 2003).

For those who conceptualize organizational assessment as a form of collaborative or employee-centred enterprise the two main methodologies employed (Meyer, 2002) are:

1   *ethnomethodology*, which seeks to understand how employees construct their interpretations of the organizational world through interaction
2   *textual analysis* (or hermeneutics), which involves the thematic analysis of written documents of all kinds (brochures, minutes of meetings, mission statements, etc.) as well as transcripts of interviews or group meetings.

In interpretive audits, three main types of data are collected: naturalistic observations, transcriptions of relevant texts, and recorded responses to researcher questions. These are, in turn, analysed using thematic analysis, metaphor analysis or narrative analysis, in order to achieve a symbolic interpretation of organizational communication (Meyer, 2002). The report produced from an interpretive investigation is also different from a traditional audit report, being more in the form of a narrative 'tale' of the researcher's experiences in the organization (Van Mannen, 1988; Gabriel, 2000).

Why don't all organizations audit?

Any proposal to implement a systematic analysis of an organization's communicative performance is not always met with wild cheering and whoops of delight from management. Some senior managers will initiate the exercise and warmly welcome the opportunity to ascertain their communication effectiveness. Others, however, regard the audit process with suspicion. They perceive it as akin to keeping an elephant as a household pet – an interesting challenge but not one they personally wish to undertake, especially given the potential dangers. As a result, there may be overt or covert resistance to the audit from managers at various levels. In relation to the latter, in our experience some managers who ostensibly seem to welcome the procedure, especially when the CEO is very upbeat about it, in reality harbour covert opposition and can be obstructive at various stages of the cycle. For example, at the operational level they may:

- create difficulties regarding the release of staff in their department for participation
- try to bias their staff against the audit by derogating its rationale
- attempt to achieve such bias by casting aspersions on the knowledge base or experience of the auditor
- be 'unexpectedly unavailable' for key meetings.

Given the benefits of the audit as outlined in this chapter, why should this be? One main reason is that managers may be fearful of being exposed to scrutiny and subsequently shown up in a negative light once the 'truth' is revealed. Or, they may genuinely believe that the whole exercise is simply a waste of time and that nothing of worth will come from it. In fact, following the large number of audits we have conducted over many different types of organization, we have identified the ten main attitudinal obstacles to the idea of an audit. The auditor should be aware of these and take steps to deal with them. We summarize these below, together with actual comments made by senior managers on occasions when we were discussing with them the possibility of auditing their organization.

1 Smugness

Here, there is a conviction, usually formed without evidence, that communication performance is already satisfactory. Researchers have documented the pervasive nature of self-serving biases, in which people exaggerate their effectiveness and the quality of their insights on all manner of issues (for example, Dawes, 2001). It has been repeatedly found that 'managements tend to credit themselves for positive outcomes and blame negative results on the environment' (Tsang, 2002: 51). Indeed, there is a view that to 'submit' to an audit is to admit shortcomings in the way one runs one's department. In essence, then, an audit would only tell managers what they already know anyway – that everything is hunky-dory. So the whole exercise is unnecessary. This problem was epitomized during one of our audits by the following comment: 'Things are fine in my department. Communications are good and everyone is very happy. I don't need an audit to tell me that. I already know it.' However, even if one's department is operating well (although in our experience smug managers usually have little grasp of the true reality), this is not a cause for inaction. As John F. Kennedy once said, 'The time to repair the roof is when the sun is shining.'

2   Conformity

Here, managers feel they should emulate what other successful companies are doing, rather than identifying the needs of their own organization and tailoring actions specifically to meet these. The desire to be in style and up-to-date with the current fashions and trends being embraced by one's peers is a very potent factor in determining behaviour from an early age (Hargie and Dickson, 2004). This phenomenon, termed *social proof*, whereby we validate the acceptability of something by dint of the fact that it is used by significant others, has been found to be a highly effective compliance-gaining technique (Cialdini, 2001). As shown by Rolfsen in her analysis of business gurus and fashionable 'fads' (see Chapter 7), managers suffer from this pressure no less than adolescents. The following quotation from a senior manager in a manufacturing company exemplifies this phenomenon: 'Why do we need to examine our own performance in detail? Is it not better to implement examples of best practice from elsewhere?' The problem here is twofold. First, insights into what constitutes best practice can only be generated through comparative analysis – in order to know what constitutes best practice in some companies we must have a measure of what many other organizations are doing against which to measure it. Second, every organization is different. Remedies that will cure the ills of one may actually cause damage to another. If I have a severe stomach ache I would be ill advised just to take tablets that were successfully prescribed for my spouse's abdominal pains. The ailment is likely to be substantially different.

3   Inertia

We have discovered this to be a major issue in many organizations. Managers often persist with what are essentially failing courses of action because this is easier than devising a new approach. As discussed by Dawson in Chapter 4, change is always problematic. Managers are happy just to leave things as they are, and any new proposal is perceived as a threat to the status quo. Many of them seem to be guided by the Latin maxim that was the modus operandum for the first British Prime Minister, Sir Robert Walpole: '*Quieta non movere*' (let sleeping dogs lie). To vary the metaphor, there is a concern that an audit may open a can of worms and so it is better to keep the lid firmly closed. A departmental manager in one organization used a well-worn phrase to sum up this approach: 'If it ain't broke, don't fix it.' One wonders how these same managers would feel about flying with an airline company that adopted a similar policy towards their aeroplanes.

4   Authoritarianism

Many managers have set views about what the corporate structure should be. They believe that there is a preordained order to the organizational jungle, and this is the way things are meant to be. Therefore, there is no point in auditing, since employees do not have the authority to make any worthwhile contribution to the state of communication. Managers of this 'Me Tarzan, You Jane' school make comments such as the following from a CEO at a conference we ran on the audit process: 'Managers should manage and workers should work. What you are proposing is tantamount to the lunatics running the asylum.' Such an attitude is increasingly untenable and dysfunctional. At times of high unemployment, when employees fear for their jobs, they may endure this style, although they are also likely to covertly retaliate by using various forms of sabotage. Sooner or later, however, they will either leave or openly rebel.

5 Cynicism

Some managers go beyond authoritarianism, and perceive workers almost as 'the enemy'. McGregor (1960) famously argued that managers are guided by the assumptions they hold of employees. He purported that those who adhere to what he referred to as 'theory X' believe that workers are basically lazy, want to avoid responsibility, have selfish self-interests, do not care about the organization, avoid making decisions, and need to be given firm directions. Theory X managers believe that employees must be driven by threats and punishment. In our experience this type of person sees the audit as an entirely worthless exercise. As one manager put it to us: 'What is the point of carrying out an audit? All it would do is give them the opportunity to complain.' As with the authoritarian manager, this type of cynical individual is difficult to deal with.

6 Futility

People who hold this perspective see the entire exercise as misguided. Their view is that audits are pointless, as you are seeking advice from those with no real breadth or depth of knowledge base or insight. Thus, any information that is collected is misinformed, misguided, and inherently valueless. Only managers have the wider picture. As expressed by one such manager: 'What we would get would be unrealistic suggestions. Employees operate in a narrow world and don't understand the constraints we face.' This viewpoint is becoming increasingly untenable. It is now widely accepted that employees build up an invaluable bank of insightful, and often individually unique, job-related information. This knowledge must be shared if the organization is to function at its optimum level (see Chapter 6, for a full discussion of knowledge management).

7 Paranoia

Some senior managers believe that information is a precious commodity to be protected by being locked away and shared with only a very select few. The perception here is that audits might endanger commercially sensitive information, by compelling managers to disclose more of it than they would wish. It is believed that if the audit leads to demands from employees for greater openness and more communication, this may have concomitant risks and inherent dangers. One manager told us: 'Staff should only be informed on a 'need to know basis'. If you ask, of course they will say they want more information. But we can't afford to give it to them.' However, research has shown that this is in fact not the case. In a follow-up audit study of a major organization, Hargie *et al.* (2002) showed that when management increased their information flow on topics desired by employees as identified in an initial audit, the desire for more information decreased. In addition, the second audit also showed that employees then demonstrated realistic objectives as to how much information they could expect to receive from various managerial sources.

8 Defeatism

Managers who suffer from this condition believe that communication is inherently problematic in large corporations, and there is very little that can be done to alter it. Any change that can be implemented is viewed as likely to be miniscule and so not worth the effort. As one departmental manager put it: 'Isn't communication like the weather? We'd all like it to be better but there's not much that we can do about it.' Our answer to this was that an organization is like a house that you have to protect from the weather. The audit allows you to identify where repairs are required to be made so that the edifice is safe from the operational rain and storms that may arrive at any time.

9 Exhaustion

Even those who might in principle favour the audit rationale can believe that in practice it could be the final straw that will break their back. When people are under pressure and feel stretched the notion of engaging in any additional task can seem like a bridge too far. As one stressed senior executive put it: 'I couldn't cope with an audit right now. It is all we can do just to do our jobs.' This is often related to a feeling of 'paralysis by analysis' if the organization has been carrying out a series of surveys or quality investigations. Paradoxically, managers are often stressed by the consequences of poor communication – for example, fractured relationships with their staff, low morale, absenteeism. The effort of managing the mess can prevent them addressing its causes, like a sailor too busy bailing out the vessel to ever plug a leak. But bail-outs that ignore the primary problem simply prepare the 'boat' for even greater catastrophes in the future.

10 Frugality

Some managers treat finance as a god to be worshipped – for them the only true goal is profit. As such, monetary concerns take primacy and are valued well above employee relations. Consequently, communication audits are viewed simply as a non-productive drain on the fiscal purse. The following is a comment we have witnessed, in varying forms, in a number of organizations: 'We have more important things to spend our money on than wasting it on this.' The notion that improvements in communication can actually lead to higher profits, and so an audit should be seen as an investment rather than a cost, can be difficult to sell to this type of manager.

In their analysis of how to overcome objections in the sales process, Hargie *et al.* (1999) recommended the strategy of recognizing objections openly (even if these are not expressed by the sales target) and then dealing with them. This is a strategy we personally use, as a matter of course, when discussing the possibility of an audit with SMTs. As part of our presentation we list the above obstacles, and highlight the fact that some of the managers present may harbour one or more of these thoughts. We then try to overcome these objections with persuasive counter-arguments, and have an open debate on the issues involved. We also highlight the fact that audit opponents usually respond by attacking the methodology, trying to sabotage the implementation, disputing the analysis of data, or contesting the conclusions. In a majority of cases this acts as a preemptive strike, allowing the audit process to flow smoothly. However, in other instances the auditor may have to complete the exercise knowing that certain people are opposed to it.

What do audits tend to tell us?

There is no substitute for completing an individual audit. Every organization is different and will have specific needs. These can only be identified through a specific, tailored assessment. However, in general terms, we have identified five main recurring themes across a wide number of audits in a variety of different organizations.

1   Immediate line managers are crucial for effectiveness

The most prominent finding from our research has been that the key to organizational success is to have first line supervisors who are effective communicators. This was confirmed by Clampitt *et al.* (2000: 43), who found that in surveys: 'Employees routinely report that they prefer to receive information from their immediate supervisor.' The importance of conducive leader–member exchange (LMX) for effective organizational functioning has been well documented (J. Lee, 2001). The LMX is the linchpin of corporate communication, and particularly in relation to the role of first-level supervisor. It is hardly surprising that employees relate most closely to the person to whom they are immediately responsible on a day-to-day basis. If this relationship is positive, then there is a halo effect for the organization as a whole, whereas if it is negative there tends to be a horn effect. In one of our audits, in response to an open question, one respondent noted rather enigmatically: 'My line manager always does his best to keep me informed, even when he doesn't know what's going on himself.' Clearly, the honesty of this person's immediate manager was a significant feature. Good supervisors also serve as 'crap umbrellas', in that they protect their staff from unnecessary and unwarranted flak from above. In essence, people want supervisors who:

- take a personal interest in their lives
- seem to care for them as individuals
- listen to their concerns and respond to these quickly and appropriately
- give regular feedback on performance in a sensitive manner
- hold efficient regular meetings at which information is freely exchanged
- explain what is happening within the company.

It is therefore important for organizations to disseminate information swiftly to first line supervisors. They should also provide them with comprehensive communication training so that they can optimize the impact they have upon the workforce. Unfortunately, we have often found that many organizations are reluctant to do this, assuming that their managers should be innately capable of sustaining a world-class communication environment. Mutual frustration ensues.

2   The views of employees should be regularly and systematically obtained

The results of our audits confirm the review of research presented in Chapter 12, that employees appreciate a climate in which bottom-up communication is encouraged. They want to feel that they play an active part in driving the operating system, rather than being mere functional parts of the corporate engine. Thus, in their study of the best UK companies to work for, Moskowitz and Levering (2001: 3) found that 'The winners are providing an environment in which their workers are treated as important contributors rather than as hired hands'. The quality of communication is one of the most important determinants of overall corporate reputation (Schreiber, 2001). This means that systems must be put in place to allow vertical transmission of information and opinions up the hierarchy. Such data must also be acted upon and feedback given on its worth. This does not always happen. For example, Coles (1998) described one company in which a total of £10m. was spent on internal communications, yet only £50,000 was devoted to listening to and understanding the views of employees; this latter sum also compared very unfavourably to the £800,000 spent on recruitment. This is far from atypical, but it is also dysfunctional. Thus, Kassing (2000) showed that employees in workplaces where feedback is encouraged have a high level of identification with the organization and openly articulate dissenting views, knowing that these will be welcomed. By contrast, where feedback is discouraged employees have a low level of identification with the organization and are less likely to openly express their views. Repressed dissent leads to resentment and a desire for revenge. Employees are then more likely to try to sabotage management initiatives.

3 Information should be widely shared

Staff want to be 'in the know' rather than being ill-informed. West (2000: 462) illustrated how effective team functioning occurs when it is the case that: 'team members are clear about and committed to their objectives, that they have high levels of participation (information sharing, shared influence over decision making and interaction) and that there is an emphasis on equality and support'. Likewise, in their study of over 2,000 employees across twenty-one organizations in seven different countries, Shockley-Zalabak and Ellis (2000: 384) found that: 'information reception has a stronger relationship to effectiveness and job satisfaction than other measured communication activities. This supports the importance of planning and monitoring the frequency of messages about organizational performance, practices, policies, and a variety of job-related issues'. In other words, audits are essential tools for measuring and monitoring this pivotal aspect of information flow. There is clear research evidence to show that being 'kept in the dark' leads to feelings of exclusion, rejection or betrayal (Finkenauer and Rimme, 1998). The more 'secrets' that a company keeps from its employees the lower will be their level of trust in what managers tell them. The norm of social exchange will also operate in that staff are likely to reciprocate by keeping vital information from management. This is bad practice, as businesses need to ensure a smooth flow of knowledge across the organization. The traditional pyramid management structure is rapidly being replaced and knowledge sharing is now essential for effective corporate functioning. Furthermore, information seeking is a natural human need (Morrison, 2002), and if formal organizational channels do not satisfy this, then the grapevine will fill the vacuum. It is therefore imperative that systems are in place for staff to disseminate and exchange information rapidly. In organizations with disparate geographical locations, e-communications play a central role in this regard (see Chapter 5).

4 Maximum use should be made of face-to-face channels

It is perhaps a reassuring finding that in our ever-increasing technological world, humans still prefer to interact with one another in person. Employees especially want to meet and talk with senior managers. Interestingly, our findings show that their expectations tend to be very realistic (Hargie et al., 2002). They know that senior managers are busy people and do not expect huge amounts of interpersonal contact with them. However, they do want to see them from time to time. In all walks of life, individuals value being with powerful or famous people (Hargie and Dickson, 2004). The work setting is no different. Thus, managers who hide permanently in their bunkers, and run their operation by firing out salvos of e-mail directives, are missing out on a potent influencing opportunity. Management by talking with staff is eminently preferable. A related finding here is that staff also value video communication from senior managers. We live in a televisual era, and so employees readily assimilate information via this channel.

5   Staff value communication training

This finding has two sides. First, employees report that they personally wish to receive systematic training in the communication skills that are central to their work. Second, they want their managers to be trained in the appropriate skills to enable them to manage effectively. Communication skills training has been shown to be effective across a range of professional contexts (Hargie, 1997), yet many organizations fail to realize the full potential of their staff owing to a lack of investment in such training.

Can the audit be used as a teaching tool?

In their analyses of the pedagogical value of having students carry out audits as part of their organizational communication course, Scott *et al.* (1999: 67) answered the above question in the affirmative, arguing that 'the communication audit provides a unique educational tool that few other activities can equal'. A number of positive aspects of the audit as a teaching tool have been highlighted by various scholars (Conaway, 1994; Shelby and Reinsch, 1996; Tourish and Hargie, 2000c), namely that it requires students to:

- consider different theoretical models of 'organization' and understand how these carry with them differing assumptions about evaluation approaches
- link theory directly to practice; the audit can be a great motivator as it brings the related textbook and classroom material to life
- review research findings into how effective organizations communicate, in order to be able to assess how well the corporation being audited is performing
- experience a 'real world' communication investigation with all its inherent complications (this is almost impossible to teach in a classroom)
- understand the different audit tools that can be employed, and realize which are likely to be best suited to particular contexts
- negotiate with the organization the exact methodology to be implemented, sample to be studied, data collection technicalities, etc.
- develop and refine their own interpersonal skills when dealing with employees and management at all levels
- write a tailored report based on their analyses (and present this orally either to the organization or to the rest of the class)
- play the role of neophyte communication consultant.

Thus, the audit offers many benefits for both the student and the college lecturer. Indeed, Shelby and Reinsch (1996: 107), in recommending this as a vehicle for teaching students about the full gambit of organizational communication, asserted that the use of audits 'represents some of the best teaching we have ever done'. We would concur with these sentiments. In our experience the process of audit not only provides a platform for the discussion of a wide range of aspects of theory and practice in organizational communication, but it is popular with and stimulating for students allowing them to appreciate the import of what they are studying.

Conclusion

It is now widely accepted that organizations are changing radically and at a pace hitherto unforeseen. As illustrated in Chapter 5, the speed of developments has been accentuated by technology. The Internet, intranet and e-mail have created a new shape to organizational geography. They have also led to an information revolution. One outcome from this, as noted by Axelrod (1999: 116), is that 'There is more information to manage just to keep up'. As a result, the functions of management have been dramatically altered. We are moving from an era of *manager-as-role* to one of *manager-of-project*. Management is a function increasingly carried out by a range of people. A key implication of this is that communications must flow smoothly in all directions. But this will not just happen – it has to be facilitated. Many managers have assumed, wrongly, that the role of communication is to duplicate the thoughts of leaders to ensure that everyone follows a set script – what has been dubbed the photocopier school of communication (Smythe, 2002). Audits can help move organizations away from such conceptions, by rigorously evaluating communication in all its multi-dimensional facets.

Thus, it is essential for organizations to monitor, or audit, the effectiveness of their communications. One problem with many organizational mission statements is that they lack mission control. As mentioned at the start of this chapter, this is also true with many communication initiatives. Feedback is essential for effective performance. This means that organizations must regularly assess how well they are communicating with their publics. The main method whereby this is achieved is through some form of audit. In this chapter we have discussed the nature, functions and benefits of auditing, outlined different conceptualizations thereof, and highlighted the main obstacles presented by those opposed to this approach. We have also briefly noted the potency of the audit as a pedagogical tool. In conclusion, it is therefore abundantly clear that the measurement and monitoring of communication is a key issue for all organizations.

References

Abrahamson, E. (1996) Management fashion. *Academy of Management Review* 21: 254–85.

Abrahamson, E. and Fairchild, G. (1999) Management fashion: Lifecycles, triggers, and collective learning processes. *Administrative Science Quarterly* 44: 708–40.

Abrahamson, E. and Park, C. (1994) Concealment of negative organizational outcomes: An agency theory perspective. *Academy of Management Journal* 37: 1302–34.

Abramson, L.Y., Metalsky, G.I., and Alloy, L.B. (1989) Hopelessness depression: A theory-based subtype of depression. *Psychological Review* 96: 358–72.

Abramson, L.Y., Seligman, M.E.P., and Teasdale, J.D. (1978) Learned helplessness in humans: Critique and reformulation. *Journal of Abnormal Psychology* 87: 49–74.

Adler, N.J. (1991) *International Dimensions of Organizational Behaviour*. Kent: PWS.

Adler, P. (2002) Critical in the name of whom and what? *Organization* 9: 387–95.

Adorno, T. and Horkheimer, M. (1989 [1944]) *Dialectic of Enlightenment*. New York: Verso.

Adorno, T.W., Frenkel-Brunswik, E., Levinson, D.J., and Sanford, R.N. (1950) *The Authoritarian Personality*. New York: Harper.

Albrecht, L., Chadwick, B.A., and Jacobson, C.K. (1987) *Social Psychology*. 2nd Edition. Englewood Cliffs, NJ: Prentice Hall.

Aldag, R. and Stearns, T. (1991) *Management*. Cincinnati: South-Western.

Allan, C. (1995) The process and politics of change at Vicbank. In P. Dawson and G. Palmer (eds), *Quality Management*. Melbourne: Longman.

Allport, G.W. (1935) Attitudes. In C. Murchison (ed.) *A Handbook of Social Psychology*. San Diego, CA: Academic Press.

Allport, G.W. (1954) *The Nature of Prejudice*. Cambridge, MA: Addison-Wesley.

Alston, W. (1964) *Philosophy of Language*. Englewood Cliffs, NJ: Prentice-Hall.

Alvesson, M. (1993) *Cultural Perspectives on Organizations*. Cambridge: Cambridge University Press.

Alvesson, M. (1995) *Management of Knowledge-intensive Companies*. New York: de Gruyter.

Alvesson, M. (2001) Knowledge work: Ambiguity, image and identity. *Human Relations* 54: 863–86.

Alvesson, M. (2002) *Understanding Organizational Culture*. London: Sage.

Alvesson, M. and Willmott, H. (1996) *Making Sense of Management: A Critical Introduction*. London: Sage.

Andersen, T.J. (2001) Information technology, strategic decision making approaches and organizational performance in different industrial settings. *Journal of Strategic Information Systems* 10: 101–19.

Anderson, R., Manoogian, S.T., and Reznick, J.S. (1976) The undermining and enhancing of intrinsic motivation in preschool children. *Journal of Personality and Social Psychology* 34: 915–22.

Anderson, S. (1998) Enhance communication with e-mail. *Rough Notes* 141: 98–9.

Annett, J. (1969) *Feedback and Human Behaviour*. Harmondsworth: Penguin.

Appelbaum, S., Bethune, M., and Tannenbaum, R. (1999) Downsizing and the emergence of self-managed teams. *Participation and Empowerment: An International Journal* 7: 109–30.

Argyle, M. (1987) *The Psychology of Happiness*. London: Routledge.

Argyris, C. (1994) Good communication that blocks learning. *Harvard Business Review* 72: 77–87.

Argyris, C. (2001) Foreword. In B. Jackson, *Management Gurus and Management Fashions*. London: Routledge.

Argyris, C. and Schön, D. (1978) *Organizational Learning: A Theory of Action Perspective*. Cambridge, MA: Addison-Wesley.

Arnold, M. (1978 [1869]) *Culture and Anarchy*. Cambridge: Cambridge University Press.

Aronson, E. (1990) *The Return of the Repressed: Dissonance Theory Makes a Comeback*. Santa Cruz, CA: University of California. (Printed 1992 in *Psychological Inquiry*, 3, 303–11).

Aronson, E., Wilson, T.D., and Akert, R.M. (2002) *Social Psychology*. 4th Edition. Upper Saddle River, NJ: Prentice Hall.

Asante, M.K. (1980) Intercultural communication: Inquiry and research directions. In D. Nimmo (ed.) *Communication Yearbook 4*. New Brunswick, NJ: Transaction Books, pp. 401–10.

Ashby, W.R. (1952) *Design for a Brain*. New York: John Wiley.

Ashford, S. and Northcraft, G. (1992) Conveying more (or less) than we realize: The role of impression-management in feedback seeking. *Organizational Behavior and Human Decision Processes* 53. 310–34.

Ashford, S. and Tsui, A. (1991) Self-regulation for managerial effectiveness: The role of active feedback seeking. *Academy of Management Journal* 34: 251–80.

Ashforth, B. and Gibbs, B. (1990) The double-edge of organizational legitimation. *Organizational Science* 1: 177–94.

Ashforth, B.E. and Humphrey, R.H. (1995) Emotion in the workplace: A reappraisal. *Human Relations* 48, 97–125.

Ashforth, B.E. and Mael, F. (1989) Social identity theory and the organization. *Academy of Management Review* 141: 20–39.

Ashkanasy, N.M., Härtel, C.E.J., and Daus, C.S. (2002a) Diversity and emotion: The new frontiers in organizational behavior research. *Journal of Management* 28: 307–38.

Ashkanasy, N.M., Härtel, C.E.J., and Zerbe, W.J. (eds) (2000) *Emotions in the Workplace: Research, Theory, and Practice*. Westport, Conn.: Quorum Books.

Ashkanasy, N.M., Härtel, C.E.J., and Zerbe, W.J. (eds) (2002b) *Managing Emotions in the Workplace*. Armonk, NY: M.E. Sharpe.

Ashkanasy, N.M., Wilderom, C.P.M., and Peterson, M.F. (eds) (2000) *Handbook of Organizational Culture and Climate*. Thousand Oaks, CA: Sage.

Ashmos, D. and Duchon, D. (2000) Spirituality at work: A conceptualisation and measure, *Journal of Management Inquiry* 9: 134–45.

Atkin, D.J., Jeffres, L.W., and Neuendorf, K.A. (1998) Understanding internet adoption as telecommunications behaviour. *Journal of Broadcasting and Electronic Media* 42: 475–90.

Atkins, P.W. (1984) *The Second Law*. New York: Scientific American Books.

Atkinson, J.W. (1964) *An Introduction to Motivation*. Princeton, NJ: Van Nostrand.

Atwater, L., Roush, P., and Fischthal, A. (1995) The influence of upward feedback on self- and follower ratings of leadership. *Personnel Psychology* 48: 35–9.

Atwater, L., Waldman, D., Atwater, D., and Cartier, P. (2000) An upward feedback field experiment: Supervisors' cynicism, reactions, and commitment to subordinates. *Personnel Psychology* 53: 275–97.

Austin, J.L. (1962) *How to Do Things With Words*. Oxford, UK: Clarendon Press.

Axelrod, S. (1999) *Work and the Evolving Self: Theoretical and Clinical Considerations*. Hillsdale, NJ: The Analytic Press.

Ayoko, O.B. and Härtel, C.E.J. (2000) Cultural differences at work: How managers deepen or lessen the cross-racial divide in their workgroups. *Queensland Review* 7: 77–87

Ayoko, O.B. and Härtel, C.E.J. (2002) The role of emotion and emotion management in destructive and productive conflict in culturally heterogeneous workgroups. In N.M. Ashkanasy, C.E.J. Härtel and W.J. Zerbe (eds), *Managing Emotions in the Workplace*. Armonk, NY: M.E. Sharpe.

Ayoko, O.B. and Härtel, C.E.J. (2003) The role of space as both a conflict trigger and a conflict control mechanism in culturally heterogeneous workgroups. *Applied Psychology: An International Review* (Special Issue on Workforce Diversity in the International Context) 52: 383–412.

Ayoko, O., Härtel, C.E.J., and Callan, V.J. (in press) Disentangling the Complexity of Productive and Destructive Conflict in Culturally Heterogeneous workgroups: A communication accommodation theory approach. *International Journal of Conflict Management*.

Babcock, R.D. and Babcock, B.D. (2001) Language-based communication zones in international business communication. *The Journal of Business Communication* 38: 372–41.

Bachrach, P. and Botwinick, A. (1992) *Power and Empowerment: A Radical Theory of Participation*. Philadelphia: Temple University Press.

Bandura, A. (1977) *Social Learning Theory*. Englewood Cliffs, NJ: Prentice Hall.

Barber, B. (1984) *Strong Democracy*. Berkeley, CA: University of California Press.

Barker, J. (1997) *The Team Makes the Rules: Culture and Control in Self-Managed Teams*. Thousand Oaks, CA: Sage.

Barker, S. and Härtel, C.E.J. (1999) The interface of front line employees and demographically diverse customers. *Paper presented at the International Conference on Immigrants and Immigration*, Toronto, Canada, 13 August.

Barker, S. and Härtel, C.E.J. (2002) Culturally diverse customers and equitable service encounters. *Paper presented at the International Services Marketing Conference*, Brisbane, Australia, July.

Barley, S.R. and Kunda, G. (1992) Design and devotion: Surges of rational and normative ideologies of control in managerial discourse. *Administrative Science Quarterly* 37: 363–99.

Baron, R. (1996) 'La vie en rose' revisited: Contrasting perceptions of informal upward feedback among managers and subordinates. *Management Communication Quarterly* 9: 338–48.

Barrett, M. (1999) An introduction to the nature of language and to the central themes in the study of language development. In M. Barrett (ed.) *The Development of Language*. East Sussex: Psychology Press.

Bartlett, C. (1989) Procter and Gamble, Europe. In W.H. Davidson and J. de la Torre (eds) *Managing the Global Corporation: Case Studies in Strategy and Management*. New York: McGraw-Hill.

Baxter, L. (1984) An investigation into compliance-gaining as politeness. *Human Communication Research* 10: 427–56.

Beach, W. and Metzger, T. (1997) Claiming insufficient knowledge. *Human Communication Research* 23: 562–88.

Beckhard, R. (1969) *Organizational Development: Strategies and Models*. Reading, Mass.: Addison-Wesley.

Beebe, L. and Giles, H. (1984) Speech accommodation theories: A discussion in terms of second language acquisition. *International Journal of the Sociology of Language* 46: 5–32.

Beer, M. and Eisenstat, R. (2000) The silent killers of strategy implementation and learning, *Sloan Management Review* (Summer): 29–40.

Belasen, A. (2001) *Leading the Learning Organization*. New York: State University of New York Press.

Bell, D. (1973) *The Coming of Post-Industrial Society: A Venture in Social Forecasting*. New York: Basic Books.

Benders, J. and van Bijsterveld, M. (2000) Leaning on lean: The reception of a management fashion in Germany. *New Technology, Work and Employment* 15(1): 50–64

Benders, J. and van Veen, K. (2001) What is a fashion? Interpretative viability and management fashions. *Organization* 8: 33–53.

Benders, J., van den Berg, R.J., and van Bijsterveld, M. (1998) Hitch-hiking on a hype: Dutch consultants engineering re-engineering *Journal of Organizational Change Management* 11: 201–15.

Bennis, W. (1984) The 4 competencies of leadership. *Training and Development Journal* 38: 15.

Benoit, W.L. (1995) *Accounts, Excuses and Apologies: A Theory of Image Restoration Strategies*. Albany, NY: SUNY Press.

Berger, C.R. and Calabrese, R.J. (1975) Some explorations in initial interaction and beyond. Toward a developmental theory of interpersonal communication. *Human Communication Research* 1: 99–112.

Berger, P. and Luckmann, T. (1966) *The Social Construction of Reality*. Garden City, NY: Doubleday.

Berkowitz, L. (1986) *A Survey of Social Psychology*. 3rd Edition. New York: CBS College Publishing.

Berlo, D.K. (1960) *The Process of Communication: An Introduction to Theory and Practice*. New York: Holt, Rinehart and Winston.

Berry, L.L. and Parasuraman, A. (1991) *Marketing Services: Competing Through Quality*. New York: Free Press.

Bevan, J. (2001) *The Rise and Fall of Marks and Spencer*. London: Profile Books.

Beyer, J. and Lutze, S. (1993) The ethical nexus: Organizations, values, and decision-making. In C. Conrad (ed.) *The Ethical Nexus*. Norwood, NJ: Ablex.

Beyer, J.M. and Niño, D. (2001) Culture as a source, expression, and reinforcer of emotions in organizations. In R. Payne and C.L. Cooper (eds) *Emotions at Work: Theory, Research and Applications in Management*. New York: Wiley.

Bicheno, J. (2000) *The Lean Toolbox*. Buckingham: PICSIE Books.

Biggart, N.W. (1977) The creative-destructive process of organizational change: The case of the post office. *Administrative Science Quarterly* 22: 410–26.

Bird, F. and Waters, J. (1987) The nature of managerial moral standards. *Journal of Business Ethics* 6: 1–13.

Byrne, D. (1971) *The Attraction Paradigm*. New York: Academic Press.

Birdwhistell, R. (1970) *Kinesics and Context*. New York: Ballantine.

Bjorkegren, D. (1996) *The Culture Business: Management Strategies for the Arts-Related Business*. London: Routledge.

Björkman, T. (1998) The American challenge once again: Are the American management fads unbeatable? *Lecture at the conference Human Resources Management*, Elisnore, Denmark, 17–19 December.

Blais, M.R. and Briere, N.M. (1992) On the mediational role of feelings of self-determination in the workplace: Further evidence and generalization. Unpublished manuscript: University of Quebec.

Blanchard, K. and Johnson, S. (1983) *The One Minute Manager*. London: HarperCollins Business.

Blanchard-Fields, F. (1996) Emotion and everyday problem solving in adult life. In C. Magai and S.H. McFadden (eds), *Handbook of Emotion, Adult Development and Aging*. San Diego: Academic Press.

Blanck, P.D., Reis, H.T., and Jackson, L. (1984) The effects of verbal reinforcement on intrinsic motivation for sex-linked tasks. *Sex Roles* 10: 369–87.

Bloom-Mirski, D. (2000) E-mail epiphany: Technology is not enough. *C@ll Center CRM Solutions* 18: 50–2.

Bochner, S. (1965) Defining intolerance of ambiguity. *Psychological Record* 15, 393–400.

Bochner, S. (1973) The mediating man and cultural diversity. *Topics in Culture Learning* 1: 23–37.

Boehle, S. (2000) They're watching you. *Training* 37: 68–72.

Bourdieu, P. (1988 [1984]) *Homo Academicus*. Cambridge, UK: Polity Press.

Bourdieu, P. (1991) *Language and Symbolic Power*. Cambridge, Mass.: Harvard University Press.

Bowen, David E. (1996) Market-focused HRM in service organizations: Satisfying internal and external customers. *Journal of Market-Focused Management* 1: 31–47.

Bowen, S.A. (2002) The breakdown of communication in action: A critical analysis of the Enron code of ethics, *Paper presented at the Meeting of the National Communication Association*, New Orleans, 24 November.

Boyett, J.H. and Boyett, J.T. (1995) *Beyond Workplace 2000: Essential Strategies for the New American Corporation*. New York: Penguin Books.

Boyle, D. (2000) *The Tyranny of Numbers: Why Counting Can't Make us Happy*. London: HarperCollins.

Brashers, D. (2001) Communication and uncertainty reduction. *Journal of Communication* 51: 477–97.

Bray, P. (2001) The future of work: Our survey results, *Sunday Times*, 29 April, B2E section.

Brehm, J.W. (1966) *A Theory of Psychological Reactance*, New York: Academic Press.

Brehm, S. and Brehm, J.W. (1981) *Psychological Reactance: A Theory of Freedom and Control*. New York: Academic Press.

Brewer, A. (1996) Developing commitment between managers and employees. *Journal of Managerial Psychology* 11: 24–34.

Brief, A.P. (1998) *Attitudes in and Around Organizations*. Thousand Oaks, CA: Sage Publications.

Brock, D., Powell, M., and Hinings, C.R. (Bob) (eds) (1999) *Restructuring the Professional Organization: Accounting, Health Care and Law*. London: Routledge.

Brockner, J., Wiesenfeld, B., and Martin, C. (1995) Decision frame, procedural justice, and survivors' reactions to job layoffs. *Organizational Behavior and Human Decision Processes* 63: 59–68.

Brown, A. (1997) Narcissism, identity, and legitimacy. *Academy of Management Review* 22: 643–86.

Brown, G.I. (1976) Human is as confluent does. In G.I. Brown, T. Yeomans and L. Grizzard (eds) *The Live Classroom: Innovation Through Confluent Education and Gestalt.* Harmondsworth: Penguin.

Brown, J.S. and Duguid, P. (2000) *The Social Life of Information.* Boston: Harvard Business School Press.

Brown, M.T. (1990) *Working Ethics.* San Francisco, CA: Jossey-Bass.

Brown, R. (2000) *Group Processes.* 2nd Edition. Oxford: Blackwell.

Brown, R.J. and Smith, A. (1989) Perception of and by minority groups: The case of women in academia. *European Journal of Social Psychology* 19: 61–75.

Buchanan, D. and Badham, R. (1999) *Power, Politics, and Organizational Change: Winning the Turf Game.* London: Sage.

Buchanan, D. and Boddy, D. (1992) *The Expertise of the Change Agent: Public Performance and Backstage Activity.* London: Prentice-Hall International.

Buck, R. (1984) *The Communication of Emotion.* New York: Guildford Press.

Budner, S. (1962) Intolerance of ambiguity as a personality variable. *Journal of Personality* 30: 29–59.

Buller, P.F. and McEvoy, G.M. (1999) Creating and sustaining ethical capability in the multi-national corporation. *Journal of World Business* 34: 326–43.

Buono, A.F. and Nichols, L. (1995) *Corporate Policy, Values, and Social Responsibility.* New York: Praeger.

Burke, R. and Cooper, C. (2000) The new organizational reality: Transition and renewal. In R. Burke and C. Cooper (eds) *The Organization in Crisis: Downsizing, Restructuring and Privatisation.* Oxford: Blackwell.

Burke, R. and Greenglass, E. (2000) Organizational restructuring: Identifying effective hospital downsizing processes. In R. Burke and C. Cooper (eds) *The Organization in Crisis: Downsizing, Restructuring and Privatization.* Oxford: Blackwell.

Burke, W. (1994) *Organization Development: A Process of Learning and Changing.* Reading, Mass.: Addison-Wesley.

Burnes, B. (2000) *Managing Change: A Strategic Approach to Organizational Dynamics.* 3rd Edition. London: Pitman.

Burns, J.M. (1978) *Leadership.* New York: Harper and Row.

Burns, T. and Stalker, G.M. (1961) *The Management of Innovation.* London: Tavistock.

Burrell, G. (1997) *Pandemonium: Towards a Retro-organization Theory.* London: Sage.

Burrell, G. and Morgan, G. (2000) Two dimensions: Four paradigms. In P. Frost, A. Lewin and R. Daft (eds) *Talking About Organization Science: Debates and Dialogue from Crossroads.* London: Sage.

Burton, M. and O'Reilly, C. (2000) The impact of high commitment values and practises on technology start-ups. Unpublished manuscript: Sloan School of Management, MIT.

Byrne, D.E. (1971) *The Attraction Paradigm.* New York: Academic Press.

Byrne, J.A. (1986) Business fads: What's in – and out. *Business Week* 7 August: 30–3.

Byrne, J.A. (1992) Management's new gurus. *Business Week* 31 August: 42–50.

Calás, M. and Smircich, L. (1991) Voicing seduction to silence leadership. *Organization Studies* 12: 567–602.

Cameron, K. (1994) Strategies for successful organizational downsizing. *Human Resource Management* 33: 189–211.

Cameron, K., Freeman, S., and Mishra, A. (1991) Best practices in white-collar downsizing: Managing contradictions. *Academy of Management Executive* 5: 57–73.

Carlson, J.R. and Zmud, R.W. (1999) Channel expansion theory and the experiential nature of media richness. *Academy of Management Journal* 42: 153–70.

Carlyle, T. (1941 [1843]) *Past and Present*. London: J.M. Dent and Sons Ltd.

Carnall, C. (2003) *Managing Change in Organizations*. 4th Edition. London: Prentice Hall.

Carroll, J.B. (1967) Words, meaning, and concepts: Part One. In J.P. De Cecco (ed.) *The Psychology of Language, Thought, and Instruction*. Reading: Holt, Rinehart and Winston.

Carruthers, P. (1997) *Language, Thought and Consciousness: An Essay in Philosophical Psychology*. Cambridge, UK: Cambridge University Press.

Casey, C. (1999) Come, join our family: Discipline and integration in corporate organizational culture. *Human Relation* 52: 155–78.

Cassidy, D.C. (1992) *Uncertainty: The Life and Science of Werner Heisenberg*. New York: W.H. Freeman.

Cassidy, J. (2002) *Dot.con: The Greatest Story Ever Told*. London: Allen Lane.

Caulkin, S. (1997) Collective bargaining makes better managers. *Observer*, 8 September, Business Supplement, 6.

Caulkin, S. (1998) How that pat on the back can mean money in the bank. *Observer*, 19 April, Work section, 1.

Caulkin, S. (2003) The scary world of Mr Mintzberg. *Observer*, 26 January, Business Supplement, 10.

Cavanagh, G.F. and Bandsuch, M.R. (2002) Virtue as a benchmark for spirituality in business. *Journal of Business Ethics* 38: 109–20.

Cavanaugh, M. and Noe, R. (1999) Antecedents and consequences of relational components of the new psychological contract. *Journal of Organizational Behavior* 20: 323–40.

Chatman, J.A., Polzer, J.T., Barsade, S.G., and Neale, M.A. (1998) Being different yet feeling similar: The influence of demographic composition an organizational culture on work processes and outcomes. *Administrative Science Quarterly* 43(4): 749.

Cheney, G. (1991) *Rhetoric in an Organizational Society*, Columbia, SC: University of South Carolina Press.

Cheney, G. (1995) Democracy in the workplace: Theory and practice from the perspective of communication. *Journal of Applied Communication Research* 23: 167–200.

Cheney, G. (1999) *Values at Work*. Ithaca, NY: Cornell University Press.

Cheney, G. and Christensen, L.T. (2001) Organizational identity: Linkages between internal and external communication. In F.M. Jablin and L.L. Putnam (eds) *New Handbook of Organizational Communication*. Thousand Oaks, CA: Sage.

Cheney, G., Mumby, D., Stohl, C., and Harrison, T. (1997) Communication and organizational democracy. *Communication Studies* 48: 277–8.

Cheney, G., Straub, J., Speirs-Glebe, L., Stohl, C., DeGooyer, D., Whalen, S., Garvin-Doxas, K., and Carlone, D. (1998) Democracy, participation and communication at work: A multidisciplinary review. In M.E. Roloff (ed.) *Communication Yearbook 21*. Thousand Oaks, CA: Sage.

Child, J. (1972) Organization structure, environment and performance: The role of strategic choice. *Sociology* 6: 1–22.

Chow, C., Hwang, R., and Liao, W. (2000) Motivating truthful upward communication of private information: An experimental study of mechanisms from theory and practice. *Abacus* 36: 160–79.

Chrislip, D. and Larson, C. (1995) *Collaborative Leadership: How Citizens and Civil Leaders can Make a Difference*. San Francisco: Jossey-Bass.

Church, J. (1961) *Language and the Discovery of Reality: A developmental Psychology of Cognition*. New York: Random House.

Cialdini, R. (2001) *Influence: Science and Practice*. Boston: Allyn and Bacon.

Clair, R. (1993) The use of framing devices to sequester organizational narratives: Hegemony and harassment. *Communication Monographs* 60: 113–36.

Clampitt, P. (2000) 'The questionnaire approach'. In Hargie, O. and Tourish, D. (eds) *Handbook of Communication Audits for Organizations*. London: Routledge.

Clampitt, P. (2001) *Communicating for Managerial Effectiveness*. 2nd Edition. London: Sage.

Clampitt, P. and Berk, L. (1996) Strategically communicating organizational change. *Journal of Communication Management* 1: 15–28.

Clampitt, P. and DeKoch, B. (2001) *Embracing Uncertainty: The Essence of Leadership*. New York: M.E. Sharpe.

Clampitt, P. and Downs, C. (1993) Employee perceptions of the relationship between communication and productivity: A field study. *Journal of Business Communication* 30: 5–28.

Clampitt, P., DeKoch, B., and Cashman, T. (2000) A strategy for communicating about uncertainty. *The Academy of Management Executive* 14: 41–57.

Clampitt, P., Williams, M.L., and Korenak, A. (2000) Managing organizational uncertainty: Conceptualization and measurement, *Paper presented at the International Communication Association*, Acapulco, Mexico, May.

Clark, T. and Salaman, G. (1998) Telling tales: Management gurus' narratives and the construction of managerial identity. *Journal of Management Studies* 35(2): 137–61.

Clegg, S. (2000) The vicissitudes of power/knowledge, *Keynote address*, ANZAM Conference, Sydney, Australia, 3–6 December.

Clegg, S. (2003) Managing organization futures in a changing world of power/knowledge. In H. Tsoukas and C. Knudsen (eds) *The Oxford Handbook of Organization Theory*. Oxford: Oxford University Press.

Clutterbuck, D. and Crainer, S. (1990) *Makers of Management: Men and Women Who Changed the Business World*. London: Macmillan.

Cohen, A.N. (2000) Web revolutionizing benefits communication. *Business Insurance* 34: 12–13.

Cole, R. (1993) Learning from learning theory: Implications for quality improvement of turnover, use of contingent workers and job rotation policies. *Quality Management Journal* 1: 9–25.

Coleman, J. (1988) Social capital in the creation of human capital. *American Journal of Sociology* 94: S95–S120.

Coles, M. (1998) Companies find it's good to talk. *Sunday Times*, 13 September, Appointments section, 32.

Collier, M.J. (1989) Cultural and intercultural communication competence: Current approaches and directions for future research. *International Journal of Intercultural Relations* 13: 287–302.

Collins, B. (2001) Net gains. *Sunday Times*, 4 February, Doors section.

Collins, D. (1998) *Organizational Change: Sociological Perspectives*. London: Routledge.

Collins, D. (2000) *Management Fads and Buzzwords*. London: Routledge.

Collins, J. (2001) *Good to Great*. London: Random House.

Collins, J. and Porras, J. (2000) *Built to Last: Successful Habits of Visionary Companies*. 3rd Edition. London: Random House.

Collinson, D. (1988) 'Engineering humor': Masculinity, joking and conflict in shop-floor relations. *Organization Studies* 9: 191–9.

Conaway, R. (1994) The communication audit as a class project. *The Bulletin of Association for Business Communication* 57: 39–43.

Conger, J. (1990) The dark side of leadership. *Organizational Dynamics* (Autumn) 44–55.

Conner, D.R. (1993) *Managing at the Speed of Change*. New York: Villard Books.

Connon, H. (2003) Three years that shook the world. *Observer*, 9 March, Business supplement, 6–7.

Conrad, C. (1985) Review of A Passion for Excellence: The leadership difference. *Administrative Science Quarterly* 30: 426–9.

Conrad, C. (1993) *The Ethical Nexus*. Norwood, NJ: Ablex.

Conrad, C. and Haynes, J. (2001) Development of key constructs. In F. Jablin and L. Putnam (eds) *The New Handbook of Organizational Communication: Advances in Theory, Research and Methods*. London: Sage.

Conrad, C. and Poole, M. (1998) *Strategic Organizational Communication: Into the Twenty-First Century*. 4th Edition. Fort Worth, TX: Harcourt Brace College Publishers.

Contractor, N.S. and Monge, P.R. (2002) Managing knowledge networks. *Management Communication Quarterly* 16, 249–58.

Cooley, R.C. and Roach, D.A. (1984) Theoretical approaches to communication competence: A conceptual framework. In R.N. Bostrom (ed.) *Competence in communication*. Beverly Hills, CA: Sage: 11–32.

Coombs, R. and Hull, R. (1996) The politics of IT strategy and development in organizations. In W. Dutton (ed.) *Information and Communication Technologies: Visions and Realities*. New York: Oxford University Press.

Cooper, C. and Burke, R. (eds) (2000) *The Organization in Crisis*. Oxford: Blackwell.

Cooper, D., Greenwood, R., Hinings, C.R. (Bob), and Brown, J.L. (1996) Sedimentation and transformation in organizational change: The case of Canadian law firms. *Organization Studies* 17: 623–47.

Cooren, F. and Fairhurst, G. (2002) Globalizing and dislocating: Scaling up organizational interactions. *National Communication Association Conference*, New Orleans.

Corman, S. and Poole, M. (eds) (2000) *Perspectives on Organizational Communication*. New York: Guilford Press.

Cotton, J., Vollrath, D., Froggatt, K., Lengnick-Hall, M., and Jennings, K. (1988) Employee participation: Diverse forms and different outcomes. *Academy of Management Review* 13: 8–22.

Coupland, N., Coupland, J., Giles, H., and Henwood, K. (1988) Accommodating the elderly: Invoking and extending a theory. *Language in Society* 17: 1–41.

Courtney, H., Kirkland, J., and Viguerie, P. (1997) Strategy under uncertainty. *Harvard Business Review* 75(6): 66–81.

Covey, S. (1989) *The Seven Habits of Highly Effective People*. New York: Simon & Schuster.

Covey, S., Merrill, A.R., and Merrill, R.R. (1994) *First Things First: To Live, to Love, to Learn, to Leave a Legacy*. New York: Simon and Schuster.

Cox, J. and Dale, B.G. (2002) Key quality factors in web site design and use: An examination. *International Journal of Quality and Reliability Management* 19: 862–88.

Cox, T.H. and Blake, S. (1991) Managing cultural diversity: Implications for organizational competitiveness. *Academy of Management Executive* 5: 45–56.

Craig, R. (1999) Communication theory as a field. *Communication Theory* 9: 116–61.

Cravens, D., Piercy, N., and Shipp, S. (1996) New organisational forms for competing in highly dynamic environments: The network paradigm. *British Journal of Management* 7: 203–18.

Crystal, D. (2001) *Language and the Internet.* Cambridge, UK: Cambridge University Press.

Culley, S. (1992) Counselling skills : An integrative framework. In W. Dryden (ed.) *Integrative and Eclectic Therapy: A Handbook.* Berkshire, UK: Open University Press.

Currie, G. (1999) The influence of middle managers in the business planning process: A case study in the UK NHS. *British Journal of Management* 10: 141–55.

Cyert, R. and March, J. (1963) *A Behavioral Theory of the Firm.* New York: Prentice-Hall.

Czarniawska, B. (1999) *Writing Management: Organization Theory as a Literary Genre.* Oxford: Oxford University Press.

Daft, R.L. and Lengel, R.H. (1984) Information richness: A new approach to managerial behavior and organization design. *Research in Organizational Behavior* 6: 191–233.

Daft, R.L. and Lengel, R.H. (1986) Organizational information requirements, media richness and structural design. *Management Science* 32: 554–71.

Damsgaard, J. and Scheepers, R. (2000) Managing the crises in intranet implementation: A stage model. *Information Systems Journal* 10: 131–49.

Darwin, C. (1985 [1872]) *The Expression of the Emotions in Man and Animals.* London: John Murray.

Daugherty, E.L. (2001) Public relations and social responsibility. In R.L. Heath (ed.) *Handbook of Public Relations.* Thousand Oaks, CA: Sage.

Dawes, R. (1994) *House of Cards: Psychology and Psychotherapy Built on Myth.* New York: Free Press.

Dawes, R. (2001) *Everyday Irrationality: How Pseudo-Scientists, Lunatics and The Rest of Us Fail To Think Rationally.* Colorado: Westview.

Dawson, J.W. (1999) Godel and the limits of logic. *Scientific American* (June) 76–81.

Dawson, P. (1994) *Organizational Change: A Processual Approach.* London: Paul Chapman Publishing.

Dawson, P. (2003) *Understanding Organizational Change: The Contemporary Experience of People at Work.* London: Paul Chapman Publishing.

Dawson, P. and Palmer, G. (1995) *Quality Management: The Theory and Practice of Implementing Change.* Melbourne: Longman Cheshire.

Daymon, C. and Holloway, I. (2002) *Qualitative Research Methods in Public Relations and Marketing Communications.* London: Routledge.

De Board, R. (1978) *The Psychoanlysis of Organizations: A Psychoanalytic Approach to Behaviour in Groups and Organizations.* London: Tavistock.

De Dreu, C., West, M., Fischer, A., and MacCurtain, S. (2001) Origins and consequences of emotions in organizational teams. In R. Payne and C.L. Cooper (eds) *Emotions at Work.* New York: Wiley.

De Guy, P. (1990) Enterprise culture and the ideology of excellence. *New Formations* 13: 45–61.

De Nisi, A. (1996) *A Cognitive Approach to Performance Appraisal.* London: Routledge.

De Rivera, J. (1977) *A Structural Theory of the Emotions.* New York: International Universities Press.

De Vries, M. (2001) *The Leadership Mystique.* London: Financial Times/Prentice-Hall.

Deal, T. and Kennedy, A. (1982) *Corporate Culture: The Rites and Rituals of Corporate Life*. Reading, MA: Addison-Wesley.

Deal, T. and Kennedy, A. (1999) *The New Corporate Culture: Revitalizing the Workplace after Downsizing, Mergers and Reengineering*. London: Orion.

Dean, O. and Popp, G.E. (1990) Intercultural communication effectiveness as perceived by American managers in Saudi Arabia and French managers in the US. *International Journal of Intercultural Relations* 14(4): 405–24.

Deci, E.L. and Ryan, R.M. (1985) *Intrinsic Motivation and Self-determination in Human Behavior*. New York: Plenum.

Deci, E.L. and Ryan, R.M. (1992) The initiation and regulation of intrinsically motivated learning and achievement. In A.K. Boggiano and T.S. Pitman (eds) *Achievement and Motivation: A Social Development Perspective*. Cambridge Studies in Social and Emotional Development. New York: Cambridge University Press, 9–36.

Deci, E.L. and Ryan, R.M. (1994) Promoting self-determined education. *Scandinavian Journal of Educational Research* 38: 3–14.

Deci, E.L. and Ryan, R.M. (2000) The 'what' and 'why' of goal pursuits: Human needs and the self-determination of behavior. *Psychological Inquiry* 11: 227–68.

Deci, E.L., Nezlek, J., and Sheinman, L. (1981) Characteristics of the rewarder and intrinsic motivation of the rewardee. *Journal of Personality and Social Psychology* 40: 1–10.

Deetz, S. (1990) Reclaiming the subject matter as a guide to mutual understanding: Effectiveness and ethics in interpersonal interaction. *Communication Quarterly* 38: 226–43.

Deetz, S. (1992) *Democracy in the Age of Corporate Colonization: Developments in Communication and the Politics of Everyday Life*. Albany: State University of New York Press.

Deetz, S. (1995a) Character, corporate responsibility and the dialogic in the postmodern context. *Organization: The Interdisciplinary Journal of Organization, Theory, and Society* 3: 217–25.

Deetz, S. (1995b) *Transforming Communication, Transforming Business: Building Responsive and Responsible Workplaces*. Cresskill, NJ: Hampton Press, Inc.

Deetz, S. (1995c) Transforming communication, transforming business: Stimulating value negotiation for more responsive and responsible workplaces. *International Journal of Value-Based Management* 8: 255–78.

Deetz, S. (1998) Discursive formations, strategized subordination, and self-surveillance: An empirical case. In A. McKinlay and K. Starkey (eds) *Managing Foucault: A Reader*. London: Sage.

Deetz, S. (2001) Conceptual foundations. In F. Jablin and L. Putnam (eds) *The New Handbook of Organizational Communication*. London: Sage.

Deetz, S.A., Tracey, S.J., and Simpson, J.L. (2000) *Leading Organizations Through Change*. London: Sage.

Deetz, S. and Mumby, D. (1990) Power, discourse, and the workplace: Reclaiming the critical tradition in communication studies in organizations. In J. Anderson (ed.) *Communication Yearbook 13*. Thousand Oaks, CA: Sage.

Deetz, S. and Simpson, J. (2003) Critical organizational dialogue: Open formation and the demand of 'otherness'. In R. Anderson, L. Baxter, and K. Cissna (eds) *Dialogic Approaches to Communication*. New York: Lawrence Erlbaum.

Dekker, S. and Schaufeli, W. (1995) The effects of job insecurity on psychological health and withdrawal: A longitudinal study. *Australian Psychologist* 30: 57–63.

Demoulin, S., Leyens, J. Ph., Paladino, M.P., Rodriguez, R., Rodriguez, A., and Dovidio,

J.F. (in press) Dimensions of 'uniquely' and 'non uniquely' human emotions. *Cognition and Emotion*.

Denis, J., Langley, A., and Pineault, M. (2000) Becoming a leader in a complex organization. *Journal of Management Studies* 37: 1063–99.

Dess, G. and Picken, J. (2000) Changing roles: Leadership in the 21st century. *Organizational Dynamics* (Winter): 18–33.

Diamond, A. (1989) Differences between adult and infant cognition: Is the crucial variable presence or absence of language? In L. Weiskrantz (ed.) *Thought Without Language*. New York: Oxford University Press.

Dickson, D. (1999) Barriers to communication. In A. Long (ed.) *Interaction for Practice in Community Nursing*. Houndmills, Hampshire: MacMillan.

Dickson, D., Hargie, O., and Morrow, N. (1997) *Communication Skills Training for Health Professionals*. London: Chapman and Hall.

Dickson, D., Rainey, S., and Hargie, O. (2003) Communicating sensitive business issues: Part 1. *Corporate Communications: An International Journal* 8: 35–43.

DiSalvo, V.S. (1980). A summary of current research identifying communication skills in various organizational contexts. *Communication Education* 29: 269–75.

DiSalvo, V.S. and Larsen, J.K. (1987) A contingency approach to communication skill importance: The impact of occupation, direction, and position. *The Journal of Business Communication* 24: 3–22.

DMNews (2002) E-mail marketing contributes to increased sales. *NUA Internet Surveys*. Online. Available HTTP: <www.nua.ie/surveys/index.cgi?f=VS&art_id=905357820&rel=true>. Accessed 19 April 2002.

Dobrzynski, J. (1993) Rethinking IBM: An exclusive account of Lou Gerstner's first six months. *Business Week* 4 October: 86–97.

Doubleclick (2001) Dartmail study. Online. Available HTTP: <http://www.doubleclick.com/us/corporate/presskit/pressreleases.asp?asp_object_1=&press%5Frelease%5Fid-2554>. Accessed 5 November 2001.

Dowling, J. and Pfeffer, J. (1975) Organizational legitimacy: Social values and organizational behavior. *Pacific Sociological Review* 18: 122–30.

Downs, A. (1995) *Corporate Executions: The Ugly Truth About Layoffs – How Corporate Greed is Shattering Lives, Companies and Communities*. New York: AMACOM.

Downs, C. (1988) *Communication Audits*. Glenview, Ill.: Scott, Foresman.

Downs, C. and Adrian, A. (1997) *Communication Audits*. Lawrence, KS: Communication Management.

Downs, C. and Hazen, M. (1977) A factor analytic study of communication satisfaction. *Journal of Business Communication* 14: 63–73.

Drost, E.A. and Von Glinow, M.A. (1998) Leadership behaviour in Mexico: Etic philosophies – emic practices. In T.A. Scandura and M.G. Serapio (eds) *Research in International Business and International Relations: Leadership and Innovation in Emerging Markets*. Stamford, USA: Jai Press, 7: 3–28.

Drucker, P. (1995) The information executives truly need. *Harvard Business Review* (Jan–Feb): 54–62.

Drury, J. and Van Doren, D. (1999) Realistic choices for web-based call centers. *Business Communication Review* 29: 56–61.

Dryden, W. (1991) *A Dialogue with Albert Ellis Against Dogma*. Open University Press.

Dunford, R., Bramble, T., and Littler, C. (1998) Gain and pain: The effects of Australian public sector restructuring. *Public Productivity and Management Review* 21: 386–402.

Dunford, R., Steane, P., and Guthrie, J. (2001) Introduction: Overviewing intellectual capital, the management of knowledge and organizational learning. *Journal of Intellectual Capita* 2: 339–44.

Dunlop, F. (1984) *Education of Feeling and Emotion.* Boston: George Allen and Unwin.

Dunphy, D. and Stace, D. (1990) *Under New Management: Australian Organizations in Transition.* Sydney: McGraw-Hill.

Earley, P.C. and Francis, C.A. (2002) International perspectives on emotion and work. In R.G. Lord, R.J. Kimoski, and R. Kanfer (eds) *Emotions in the Workplace: Understanding the Structure and Role of Emotions in Organizational Behavior.* San Francisco: Jossey-Bass.

Edmunds, A. and Morris, A. (2000) The problem of information overload in business organizations: a review of the literature. *International Journal of Information Management* 20: 17–28.

Ehrlich, D. (1965) Intolerance of ambiguity, Walk's A scale: Historical comment. *Psychological Reports* 17: 591–4.

Eisenberg, E.M. and Riley, P. (1988) Organizational symbols and sense-making. In G.M. Goldhaber and G.A. Barnett (eds) *Handbook of Organizational Communication* Norwood, NJ: Ablex.

Eisenberg, E.M. and Riley, P. (2001) Organizational culture. In F.M. Jablin and L.L. Putnam (eds) *New Handbook of Organizational Communication.* Thousand Oaks, CA: Sage.

Elden, M. and Levin, M. (1991) Co-generative learning: Bringing participants into action research. In W.F. Whyte (ed.) *Participatory Action Research.* Newbury Park, CA: Sage.

Elias, N. (1978a [1939]) *The Civilizing Process, Vol. 1: The History of Manners.* Oxford: Basil Blackwell.

Elias, N. (1978b [1939]) *The Civilizing Process, Vol. 2: State Formation and Civilization.* Oxford: Basil Blackwell.

Ellis, A. (1977) *Reason and Emotion in Psychotherapy.* Sacramento, CA: The Citadel Press.

Ellis, A. (1996) *Better, Deeper, and More Enduring Brief Therapy: The Rational Emotive Behavior Therapy Approach.* New York: Brunner/Mazel Inc.

Elwood, W.N. (1995) *Public Relations Inquiry as Rhetorical Criticism: Case Studies of Corporate Discourse and Social Influence.* Westport, CT: Praeger.

Emmanuel, M. (1985) Auditing communication practices. In C. Reuss and R. DiSilvas (eds) *Inside Organizational Communication.* 2nd edition. New York: Longman.

Ethics Resource Center (1997) National Business Ethics Survey 1997. Online. Available HTTP: <http://www.ethics/org/nbes>. Accessed 22 August 2002.

Ethics Resource Center (2000) National Business Ethics Survey 2000. Online. Available HTTP: <http://www.ethics/org/nbes>. Assessed 22 August 2002.

Evans, A. (1993) Working at home: A new career dimension. *International Journal of Career Management* 5: 16–23.

Fairhurst, G. (2000) Paradigm skirmishes in the review process. In S. Corman and M. Poole (eds) *Perspectives on Organizational Communication.* New York: Guilford Press.

Fayol, H. (1949) *General and Industrial Management.* London: Pitman.

Fedor, D., Davis, W., Maslyn, J., and Mathieson, K. (2002) Performance improvement efforts in response to negative feedback: The roles of source power and recipient self-esteem. *Journal of Management* 27: 79–97.

Feldheim, M. and Liou, K.L. (1999) Downsizing trust. M@n@gement 2: 55–67.

Feldman, D. and Leana, C. (1994) Better practices in managing layoffs. *Human Resource Management* 33: 239–60.

Feldman, L. (1989) Duracell's first-aid for downsizing survivors. *Personnel Journal* 69: 40–9.

Festinger, L. (1962) A *Theory of Cognitive Dissonance*. Stanford, CA: Stanford University Press.

Filby, I. and Willmott, H. (1988) Ideologies and contradictions in a public relations department: The seduction and impotency of a living myth. *Organization Studies* 9: 335–49.

Filipczak, B. (1996) Training on intranets: The hope and the hype. *Training* 33: 24–32.

Fineman, S. (1996) Emotion and organizing. In S.R. Clegg, C. Hardy, and W.R. Nord (eds) *Handbook of Organisation Studies*. London: Sage.

Fineman, S. (2001) Emotions and organizational control. In R. Payne and C.L. Cooper (eds) *Emotions at work*. New York: Wiley.

Finkenauer, C. and Rime, B. (1998) Socially shared emotional experiences vs. emotional experiences kept secret: Differential characteristics and consequences. *Journal of Social and Clinical Psychology* 17: 295–318.

Finnegan, R. (1989) Communication and technology. *Language & Communication* 9: 107–27.

First Union Corporation (2002) *First Union Corporation*. Online. Available HTTP: <http://www.adobe.com/epaper/spotlights/firstunion/pdfs/firstunioncorp.pdf>. Accessed 30 March.

Fishbein, M. (1963) Attitude and the prediction of behavior. In M. Fishbein (ed.) *Readings in Attitude Theory and Measurement*. New York: Wiley.

Fisher, C.D. (1978) The effects of personal control, competence, and extrinsic reward systems on intrinsic motivation. *Organizational Behavior and Human Decision Processes* 21: 273–88.

Fisher, C., Ashkanasy, N., and Härtel, C.E.J. (2001a) *Affective Events in the Workplace: Extensions, Empirical Tests and Interventions*. Large ARC Grant Application, unpublished.

Fisher, G. and Härtel, C.E.J. (2002) *The Impact of Socio-biographical Characteristics on Perceptions of Effectiveness of the Western Expatriate Working in Thailand*. Proceedings of the Australian and New Zealand Academy of Management Conference (ANZAM).

Fisher, G., Bibo, M., and Youngsamart, D. (2001b) Virtual teams and entrepreneurship: A proposed research agenda. *Proceedings of the Technological Entrepreneurship in the Emerging Regions of the New Millennium Conference*, Singapore, 13–15 June 2001.

Fisher, G., Härtel, C.E.J., and Bibo, M. (2000) Two rhetorics and two realities: Similarities and differences in how Thai and Western colleagues perceive the performance of Western managers working in Thailand. *Refereed Proceedings of the Asian Academy of Management*, December, Singapore.

Fisher, R. and Ury, W. (1991) *Getting to Yes: Negotiating Agreement without Giving In*. New York: Penguin Books.

Flanagin, A.J. (2000) Social pressures on organizational website adoption. *Human Communication Research* 26: 618–46.

Flanagin, A.J. (2002) The elusive benefits of the technological support of knowledge management. *Management Communication Quarterly* 16: 242–8.

Flauto, F. (1999) Walking the talk: The relationship between leadership and communication competence. *The Journal of Leadership Studies* 6: 86–97.

Foreman, S. (1997) IC and the healthy organization. In E. Scholes (ed.) *Gower Handbook of Internal Communication*. Aldershot: Gower.

Forester, J. (1999) *The Deliberative Practitioner: Encouraging Participatory Planning Processes*. Cambridge, MA: MIT Press.

Forgas, J. (1995) Mood and judgement: The affect infusion model (AIM). *Psychological Bulletin* 117(1): 39–66.

Foster, H. (ed.) (1985 [1983]) *Postmodern Culture*. London: Pluto Press.

Fraisse, P. (1968) *Experimental Psychology and its Scope*. New York: University Press.

Frankel, M. (1989) Professional codes: Why, how and with what input? *Journal of Business Ethics* 8: 109–15.

Frankl, V., Crumbaugh, J.C., Gerz, H.O., and Maholick, L. (1967) *Psychotherapy and Existentialism*. New York: Washington Square Press.

Freeman, F.H. (1985) Books that mean business: The management best seller. *Academy of Management Review* 10: 345–50.

Freeman, R.E. (1984) *Strategic Management: A Stakeholder Approach*. Marshfield, MA: Pitman Publishing.

Freeman, R.E. and Gilbert, D.R. (1987) Managing stakeholder interests. In S.P. Sethi and C.M. Fable (eds) *Business and Society: Dimensions of Conflict and Cooperation*. Lexington, MA: Lexington Books.

Freeman, S. (1999) The gestalt of organizational downsizing: Downsizing strategies as packages of change. *Human Relations* 52: 1505–41.

French, K. (1995) Men and locations of power: Why move over? In C. Itzin and J. Newman (eds) *Gender, Culture and Organizational Change: Putting Theory into Practice*. London: Routledge.

French, W. (1969) Organization development: Objectives, assumptions and strategies. *California Management Review* 12: 23–46.

French, W. and Bell, C. (1983) *Organization Development: Behavioural Science Interventions for Organization Improvement*. Englewood Cliffs: Prentice-Hall.

Frenkel-Brunswik, E. (1949) Intolerance of ambiguity as an emotional perceptual personality variable. *Journal of Personality* 18: 108–43.

Frick, W. (1971) *Humanistic Psychology: Interviews with Maslow, Murphy, and Rogers*. Ohio: Charles E. Merrill Publishing Company.

Fridja, N. (1993) Moods, emotion episodes and emotions. In M. Lewis and J. Haviland (eds) *Handbook of Emotions*, New York: The Guilford Press.

Fridja, N. and Mesquita, B. (1994) The social roles and functions of emotions. In S. Kitayama and H. Markus (eds) *Emotion and Culture: Empirical Studies of Mutual Influence*. Washington, DC: American Psychological Association.

Friedrichs. D.O. (1980) The legitimacy crisis in the United States: A conceptual analysis. *Social Problems* 27: 540–53.

Friere, P. (1985) *The Politics of Education: Culture, Power, and Liberation*. Bergen and Garvey Publishers Inc.

Frijda, N. (1996) Passions, emotions and socially consequential behavior. In R.D. Kavanaugh, B. Zimmerberg and S. Fein (eds) *Emotion: Interdisciplinary Perspectives*. Mahwah, NJ: Lawrence Erlbaum Associates.

Frost, P.J., Moore, L.F., Louis, M.R., Lundberg, C.C., and Martin, J. (eds) (1991) *Reframing Organizational Culture*. London: Sage Publications.

Fujimoto, Y. and Härtel, C.E.J. (in press) Emotional experience of individualist-collectivist workgroups: Findings from a study of 14 multinationals located in Australia. In C.E.J. Härtel, W.J. Zerbe., and N.M. Ashkanasy (eds) *Understanding organizations through emotions*. New York: M.E. Sharpe, Inc.

Fujimoto, Y., Härtel, C.E.J., Härtel, G.F., and Baker, N.J. (2000). Openness to dissimilarity moderates the consequences of diversity in well-established groups. *Asia Pacific Journal of Human Resources* 38: 46–61.

Fukuyama, F. (1995) *Trust: The Social Virtues and the Creation of Prosperity*. New York: Free Press.

Fulk, J. and Collins-Jarvis, L. (2001) Wired meetings: Technological mediation of organizational gatherings. In F. Jablin and L. Putnam (eds) *The New Handbook of Organizational Communication: Advances in Theory, Research and Methods*. London: Sage.

Furnham, A. (1987) The adjustment of sojourners. Cross-cultural adaptation: Current approaches. In Y.Y. Kim and W.B. Gudykunst (eds) *International and Intercultural Communication Annual, Vol. XI*. New York: Sage, 43–61.

Furnham, A. (1992) *Personality at Work*. London: Routledge

Furnham, A. (1994) A content, correlational and factor analytic study of four tolerance of ambiguity questionnaires. *Personality and Individual Differences* 16: 403–10.

Furnham, A. (1995) Tolerance of ambiguity: A review of the concept, its measurement and applications. *Current Psychology* 14: 179–200.

Furnham, A. and Gunter, B. (1993) *Corporate Assessment: Auditing a Company's Personality*. London: Routledge.

Gabriel, Y. (1995) The unmanaged organization: Stories, fantasies, subjectivity. *Organization Studies* 16: 477–501.

Gabriel, Y. (2000) *Storytelling in Organizations: Facts, Fictions, and Fantasies*. Oxford: Oxford University Press.

Gagne, M., Senecal, C.B., and Koestner, R. (1997) Proximal job characteristics, feelings of empowerment, and intrinsic motivation: A multidimensional model. *Journal of Applied Social Psychology* 27: 1222–40.

Gainey, T.W., Kelley, D.E. and Hill, J.A. (1999) Telecommuting's impact on corporate culture and individual workers: Examining the effect of employee isolation. *S.A.M. Advanced Management Journal* 64: 4–10.

Gallois, C. and Giles, H. (1998) Accommodating mutual influence in intergroup encounters. In M. Palmer and G.A. Barnett (eds) *Mutual Influence in Interpersonal Communication: Theory and Research in Cognition, Affect, and Behavior* (Progress in Communication Sciences, Vol. 14). Stamford, Conn.: Ablex, 135–62.

Gallois, C., Franklyn-Stokes, A., Giles, H. and Coupland, N. (1988) Communication accommodation in intercultural encounters. In Y. Kim and W. Gudykunst (eds) *Theories in Intercultural Communication*. Newbury Park, CA: Sage.

Garcia, D. (2002) E-Mail Savings Threaten a $196.8 Billion Direct Mail Market. *Gartner G2 Research*, Stamford.

Gardner, J. and Oswald, A. (2001) *What has been Happening to the Quality of Workers' Lives in Britain?* Warwick: Department of Economics, University of Warwick.

Gattiker, U. (2001) *The Internet as a Diverse Community: Cultural, Organizational, and Political Issues*. Mahwah, NJ: Erlbaum.

Geertz, C. (1973) *The Interpretation of Cultures: Selected Essay*. New York: Basic Books.

Geneen, H. with Moscow, A. (1986) *Managing*. London: Grafton Books.

George, J.M. (2002) Affect regulation in groups and teams. In R.G. Lord, R.J. Kimoski and R. Kanfer (eds) *Emotions in the Workplace: Understanding the Structure and Role of Emotions in Organizational Behavior*. San Francisco: Jossey-Bass.

Gibson, C.B. (1999) Do they do what they believe they can? Group efficacy and group effectiveness across cultures. *Academy of Management Journal* 42: 138–52.

Giles, H. (1973) Communication effectiveness as a function of accented speech. *Speech Monographs* 40: 330–1.

Giles, H. and Coupland, N. (1991) *Language: Contexts and Consequences*. Milton Keynes: Open University Press.

Giles, H. and Powesland, P. (1975) *Speech Style and Social Evaluation*. London: Academic Press.

Giles, H., Coupland, J., and Coupland, N. (1991) Accommodation theory: Communication contexts and consequences. In H. Giles, N. Coupland and J. Coupland (eds) *Contexts of Accommodation: Developments in Applied Sociolinguistics*. Cambridge, UK: Cambridge University Press.

Giles, H., Mulac, A., Bradac, J., and Johnson, P. (1987) Speech accommodation theory: The first decade and beyond. In M. McLaughlin (ed.) *Communication Yearbook 10*. Newbury Park, CA: Sage.

Gini, A. (1996) *Moral Leadership and Business Ethics*. Online. Available HTTP: <http://www.academy.umd.edu/scholarship/casl/klspdocs/agini-p1.htm>. Accessed 12 August 2002.

Giroux, H. and Taylor, J.R. (2002) The justification of knowledge: Tracking the translations of quality. *Management Learning* 33(4): 497–517.

Glomb, T.M, Steel, P.D.G., and Arvey, R.D. (2002) Office sneers, snipes, and stab wounds: Antecedents, consequences, and implications of workplace violence and aggression. In R.G. Lord, R.J. Kimoski and R. Kanfer (eds) *Emotions in the Workplace: Understanding the Structure and Role of Emotions in Organizational Behavior*. San Francisco: Jossey-Bass.

Goldhaber, G. (2002) Communication audits in the age of the internet. *Management Communication Quarterly* 15: 451–7.

Goldhaber, G. and Rogers, D. (1979) *Auditing Organizational Communication Systems: The ICA Communication Audit*, Dubuque, Ia.: Kendall/ Hunt.

Goldratt, E. and Cox, J. (1986) *The Goal: A Process of Ongoing Improvement*. New York: North River Press.

Goleman, D. (1997) *Emotional Intelligence*. London: Bloomsbury.

Goodley, S. (2002) Say what you like, but who overhears? *Daily Telegraph*, 22 January, 22.

Goodwin, C. and Goodwin, M.H. (1996) Seeing as situated activity: Formulating planes. In Y.E.D. Middleton (ed.) *Cognition and Communication at Work*. Cambridge, UK: Cambridge University Press, 61–95.

Gopinath, C. and Becker, T. (2000) Communication, procedural justice, and employee attitudes: Relationships under conditions of divestiture. *Journal of Management* 26: 63–83.

Gopnik, A. and Meltzoff, A.N. (1997) *Words, Thoughts, and Theories*. Cambridge, Mass.: MIT Press.

Gorden, W.I. and Mermer, D. (1989) A conceptualization of workplace citizenship: A critique of freedom. Unpublished manuscript.

Gordon, H.R.D. (1993) Analysis of the computer anxiety levels of secondary technical education teachers in West Virigina. *ERIC: ED* 357: 218. Online. Available HTTP: <http://www.ericfacility.net/servlet/com.artesiatech.servlet.search.SearchServlet?action=9>.

Gottleib, J.Z. and Sanzgiri, J. (1996) Towards an ethical dimension of decision making in organizations. *Journal of Business Ethics* 15: 1275–85.

Graetz, F., Rimmer, M., Lawrence, A. and Smith, A. (2002) *Managing Organizational Change*. Queensland: John Wiley & Sons.

Grandey, A.A and Brauburger, A.L. (2002) The emotion regulation behind the customer service smile. In R.G. Lord, R.J. Kimoski and R. Kanfer (eds) *Emotions in the Workplace: Understanding the Structure and Role of Emotions in Organizational Behavior.* San Francisco: Jossey-Bass.

Gratton, L., Hope Hailey, V., Stiles, P., and Truss, C. (1999) *Strategic Human Resource Management.* Oxford: Oxford University Press.

Gray, B. (1989) *Collaborating: Finding Common Ground for Multi-Party Problems.* San Francisco: Jossey-Bass.

Gray, B. and Wood, D. (1991) Collaborative alliances: Moving from practice to theory. *Journal of Applied Behavioral Science* 27: 3–22.

Gray, J.L. and Starke, F.A. (1988) *Organizational Behavior: Concepts and Applications.* Columbus: Merrill.

Greenberg, J. and Baron, R.A. (1997) *Behavior in Organizations.* 6th Edition. Upper Saddle River, NJ: Prentice Hall.

Greenberg, I.S. (1996) Allowing and accepting of emotional experience. In R.D. Kavanaugh, B. Zimmerberg and S. Fein (eds) *Emotion: Interdisciplinary Perspectives.* Mahwah, NJ: Lawrence Erlbaum Associates.

Greenhalgh, L. (1993) Managing the job insecurity crisis. *Human Resource Management* 22: 431–44.

Greenwood, D. and Levin, M. (1998) *Introduction to Action Research.* Newbury Park, CA: Sage.

Greenwood, R. and Hinings, C.R. (1993) Understanding strategic change: The contribution of archetypes. *Academy of Management Journal* 36: 1052–81.

Greenwood, R. and Hinings, C.R. (1996) Understanding radical organizational change: Bringing together the old and new institutionalism. *Academy of Management Review* 21: 1022–54.

Greiner, L.E. (1972) Evolution and revolution as organizations grow. *Harvard Business Review* (July–August) 72407: 37–46.

Grey, C. and Willmott, H. (2002) Contexts of CMS. *Organization* 9: 411–18.

Grey, M. and MacDonald, N. (2001) How to rescue e-mail systems from occupational spammers. *Gartner First Take*, 23 April.

Grint, K. (2000) *The Arts of Leadership.* Oxford: Oxford University Press.

Grint, K. and Woolgar, S. (1997) *The Machine at Work.* Cambridge: Polity Press.

Gudykunst, W.B. (1997) *Bridging Differences: Effective Intergroup Communication.* 3rd Edition. Thousand Oaks, CA: Sage.

Gudykunst, W. and Kim, Y.Y. (1984) *Communicating with Strangers.* New York: Random House.

Gudykunst, W.B. and Hammer, M.R. (1984) Dimensions of intercultural effectiveness: Culture specific or culture general? *International Journal of Intercultural Relations* 8: 1–10.

Guest, D. (1990) Human resource management and the American dream. *Journal of Management Studies* 27: 377–97.

Habermas, J. (1974) The public sphere. *New German Critique* 3: 49–55.

Hall, E. (1959) *The Silent Language.* New York: Fawcett.

Hall, R.J., Workman, J.W., and Marchioro, C.A. (1998) Sex, task and behavioural flexibility effects on leadership perceptions. *Organizational Behaviour and Human Decision Processes* 74: 1–32.

Hall, S. (1985) Signification, representation, ideology: Althusser and the post-structuralist debates. *Critical Studies in Mass Communication* 2: 91–114.

Hall, S. and du Gay, P. (1996) *Questions of Cultural Identity*. London: Sage.

Hambrick, D. (1995) Fragmentation and the other problems CEOs have with their top management teams. *California Management Review* 37: 110–27.

Hambrick, D.C. (1994) Top management groups: A conceptual integration and reconsideration of the 'team' label. In B.M. Shaw and L.L Cummings (eds), *Research in Organizational Behavior*. Greenwich, CT: JAI Press.

Hamilton, H.E. (1991) Accommodation and mental disability. In H. Giles, J. Coupland and N. Coupland (eds) *Contexts of Accommodation*. Cambridge, UK: Cambridge University Press.

Hamilton, V. (1957) Perceptual and personality dynamics in reactions to ambiguity. *British Journal of Psychology* 4: 200–15.

Hammer, M. (1987) Behavioral dimensions of intercultural effectiveness: A replication and extension. *International Journal of Intercultural Relation* 11: 65–88.

Hammer, M. and Champy, J. (1993) *Reengineering the Corporation: A Manifesto for Business Revolution*. London: Nicolas Brealey.

Handy, C. (2001) *The Elephant and the Flea: Looking Backwards to the Future*. London: Hutchinson.

Hannan, M., Baron, J., Hsu, O., and Kocak, O. (2000) Staying the course: Early organization building and the success of high–technology firms. Unpublished MS: Graduate School of Business, Stanford University.

Harding, S. (1991) *Whose Science? Whose Knowledge?* Ithaca, NY: Cornell University Press.

Hargie, C. and Tourish, D. (1997) Relational communication. In O. Hargie (ed.), *The Handbook of Communication Skills*. 2nd Edition. London: Routledge.

Hargie, O. (1997) Training in communication skills: research, theory and practice. In O. Hargie (ed.) *The Handbook of Communication Skills*. 2nd Edition. London: Routledge.

Hargie, O. and Dickson, D. (2004) *Skilled Interpersonal Communication: Research, Theory and Practice*. London: Routledge.

Hargie, O. and Lount, M. (2000) Auditing communication practices in the Catholic church. In O. Hargie and D. Tourish (eds) *Handbook of Communication Audits for Organisations*. London: Routledge.

Hargie, O. and Tourish, D. (1999) The psychology of interpersonal skill. In A. Memon and R. Bull (eds) *Handbook of the Psychology of Interviewing*. Chichester: Wiley.

Hargie, O. and Tourish, D. (eds) (2000) *Handbook of Communication Audits for Organisations*, London: Routledge.

Hargie, O., Dickson, D., and Tourish, D. (1999) *Communication in Management*, Aldershot: Gower.

Hargie, O., Dickson, D., and Tourish, D. (2004) *Communication Skills for Effective Management*. Basingstoke: Palgrave.

Hargie, O., Tourish, D., and Wilson, N. (2002) Communication audits and the effects of increased information: A follow-up study. *Journal of Business Communication* 39: 414–36.

Harlow, E., Hearn, J., and Parkin, W. (1995) 'Gendered noise: Organizations and the silence and din of domination. In C. Itzin and J. Newman (eds) *Gender, Culture and Organizational Change: Putting Theory into Practice*. London: Routledge.

Harrington, S.J. and Ruppel, C.P. (1999) Telecommuting: A test of trust, competing values, and relative advantage. *IEEE Transactions on Professional Communication* 42: 223–39.

Harris, L. and Cronen, V.E. (1979) A rules-based model for the analysis and evaluation of organizational communication. *Communication Quarterly* 27: 12–28.

Harrison, A. (1995) Business prosesses: Their nature and properties. In G. Burke and J. Peppard (eds) *Examining Business Process Re-engineering: Current Perspectives and Research Directions*. London: The Cranfield Management Series.

Harrison-Walker, L.J. (1995) The relative effects of national stereotypes and advertising information on the selection of a service provider: An empirical study. *Journal of Services Marketing* 9: 47–59.

Härtel, C.E.J. (2001) *Affective Events in the Workplace: Extensions Empirical Tests and Interventions*. Unpublished Large ARC Grant Application.

Härtel, C.E.J. and Fujimoto, Y. (1999) Explaining why diversity sometimes has positive effects in organisations and sometimes has negative effects in organisations: The perceived dissimilarity openness moderator model. *Academy of Management Best Papers Proceedings*, August.

Härtel, C.E.J. and Fujimoto, Y. (2000) Diversity is not a problem to be managed by organisations but openness to perceived dissimilarity is. *Journal of Australian and New Zealand Academy of Management* 6: 14–27.

Härtel, C.E.J., Barker, S., and Baker, N. (1999) A model for predicting the effects of employee-customer interactions on consumer attitudes, intentions, and behaviours: The role of emotional intelligence in service encounters. *Australian Journal of Communication* 26: 77–87.

Härtel, C.E.J., Douthitt, S., Härtel, G.F., and Douthitt, S. (1999) Equally qualified but unequally perceived: General cultural openness as a predictor of discriminatory performance ratings. *Human Resource Development Quarterly* 10: 79–89.

Härtel, C.E.J., Hsu, A.C.F., and Boyle, M. (2002) A conceptual examination of the causal sequences of emotional labor, emotional dissonance and emotional exhaustion: The argument for the role of contextual and provider characteristics. In N.M. Ashkanasy, C.E.J. Hartel, and W.J. Zerbe (eds) *Managing Emotions in the Workplace*. Armonk, NY: M.E. Sharpe.

Härtel, C.E.J., Gough, H., and Härtel, G.F. (in press) Work group emotional climate, emotion management skills and service attitudes and performance. *Asia Pacific Journal of Human Resources*.

Harvey, M. and Buckley, M. (2002) Assessing the 'conventional wisdoms' of management for the 21st century organization. *Organizational Dynamics* 30: 368–78.

Hatch, M. and Yanow, D. (2003) Organization theory as interpretive science. In H. Tsoukas and C. Knudsen (eds), *The Oxford Handbook of Organization Theory*. Oxford: Oxford University Press.

Hatfield, E., Cacioppo, J., and Rapson, R.L. (1994) *Emotional Contagion*. New York: Cambridge University Press.

Haworth, D.A. and Savage, G.T. (1989) A channel-ratio model of intercultural communication: The trains won't sell, fix them please. *The Journal of Business Communication* 26: 231–54.

Hayes, J. (2002) *The Theory and Practice of Change Management*. Basingstoke: Palgrave.

Head, A.J. (2000) Demystifying intranet design. *Online* 24: 36–42.

Hearit, K.M. (1995) From 'We didn't do it' to 'It's not our fault': The use of apologia in public relations crises. In W.N. Elwood (ed.) *Public Relations Inquiry as Rhetorical Criticism: Case Studies of Corporate Discourse and Social Influence*. Westport, CT: Praeger.

Heath, C. and Luff, P. (1996) Convergent activities: Line control and passenger information on the London Underground. In Y. Engeström and D. Middleton (eds) *Cognition and Communication at Work*. Cambridge, UK: Cambridge University Press.

Heath, R.L. (1997) *Strategic Issues Management*. Newbury Park, CA: Sage.

Heaton, L. and Taylor, J.R. (2002) Knowledge management and professional work. *Management Communication Quarterly* 16: 210–36.

Hecht, M. (1978) Measures of communication satisfaction. *Human Communication Research* 4: 351–68.

Heckscher, C. (1997) The failure of participatory management. *Management Development Review* 10: 148.

Heenan, D. (1991) The right way to downsize. *The Journal of Business Strategy* 12: 4–6.

Hegarty, W. (1974) Using subordinate ratings to elicit behavioural changes in supervisors. *Journal of Applied Psychology* 59: 764–6.

Heller, F. (1998) Influence at work: A 25–year program of research. *Human Relations* 51: 1425–44.

Hemby, K.V. (1998) Predicting computer anxiety in the business communication classroom: Facts, figures and teaching strategies. *Journal of Business and Technical Communication* 12: 89–108.

Henkoff, R. (1994) Getting beyond downsizing. *Fortune*, 10 January, 58–74.

Henriques, J., Hollway, W., Urwin, C., Venn, C., and Walkerdine, V. (eds) (1984) *Changing the Subject*. New York: Methuen.

Henry, N. (1975) Bureaucracy, technology, and knowledge management. *Public Administration Review* 35: 572–8.

Heracleous, L. and Barrett, M. (2001) 'Organizational change as discourse: Communicative actions and deep structures in the context of information technology implementation. *Academy of Management Journal* 44: 755–78.

Hersey, P. and Blanchard, K. (1988) *Organizational Behaviour*. New York: Prentice Hall.

Herson, M. (2000) Why today shared knowledge is power. *Daily Telegraph Business File* August: A3.

Hildebrandt, E. and Seltz, R. (1989) *Wandel betrieblicher Sozialverfassung durch systemische Kontrolle?* Berlin: Sigma.

Hill, T., Smith, N., and Lewicki, P. (1989) The development of self-image bias: A real-world demonstration. *Personality and Social Psychology Bulletin* 15: 205–11.

Hinings, C.R., Brown, J., and Greenwood, R. (1991) Change in an autonomous professional organization. *Journal of Management Studies* 28: 375–93.

Hitt, M. (2000) The new frontier: Transformation of management for the new millennium. *Sloan Management Review* (Winter) 7–16.

Hochschild, A.R. (1983) *The Managed Heart*. Berkeley: University of California Press.

Hofstede, G. (1980) *Cultures' Consequences: International Differences in Work-Related Values*. Beverly Hills, CA: Sage.

Hofstede, G. (1991) *Cultures and Organization: Software of the Mind – Intercultural Cooperation and its Importance for Survival*. Berkshire, UK: McGraw-Hill.

Hofstede, G. (1995) The business of international business is culture. *International Business Review* 3(1): 1–14.

Hoggart, R. (1977 [1957]) *The Uses of Literacy*. Harmondsworth: Penguin Books.

Hollingshead, A.B. (1996a) The rank-order effect in group decision making. *Organizational Behaviour and Human Decision Processes* 68: 181–93.

Hollingshead, A.B. (1996b) Information suppression and status persistence in group decision making: The effects of communication media. *Human Communication Research* 23: 193–219.

Holmer-Nadesan, M. (1997) Constructing paper dolls: The discourse of personality testing in organizational practice. *Communication Theory* 7: 189–218.

Hoover, J.D. (1997) *Corporate Advocacy in the 20th Century*. Westport, CT: Quorum Press.

Hubbard, N. (2000) *Acquisition: Strategy and Implementation*. Houndmills: Macmillan.

Huczynski, A. (1993) *Management Gurus: What Makes Them and How to Become One*. London: Routledge.

Huczynski, A. and Buchanan, D. (2001) *Organizational Behaviour: An Introductory Text*. 4th Edition. Harlow: FT, Pearson Education.

Hughes, M. (1992) Decluding organization. In M. Reed and M. Hughes, *Rethinking Organization: New Directions in Organization Theory and Analysis*. London: Sage.

Hurst, B. (1991) *The Handbook of Communication Skills*. London: Kogan Page.

Huse, E. (1982) *Management*. New York: West.

Hutchins, E. (1995) *Cognition in the Wild*, Cambridge, MA.: MIT Press.

Hutchins, E. and Klausen, T. (1996) Distributed cognition in an airline cockpit. In Y. Engeström and D. Middleton (eds) *Cognition and Communication at Work*. Cambridge, UK: Cambridge University Press, 15–34.

Huy, Q. (1999) Emotional capability, emotional intelligence, and radical change. *Academy of Management Review* 24: 325–45.

Huy, Q. (2001) In praise of middle managers. *Harvard Business Review* 79: 72–9.

Huy, Q. (2002) Emotional balancing: The role of middle managers in radical change. *Administrative Science Quarterly* 47: 31–63.

Iacocca, L. with Novak, B. (1985) *Iacocca: An Autobiography*. London: Sidgwick & Jackson.

Ihator, A.S. (2001) Communication style in the information age. *Corporate Communications: An International Journal* 6: 199–204.

Internal Communication – News Item (2000) *Internal Communication* (April): 7.

Itzin, C. and Newman, J. (eds) (1995) *Gender, Culture and Organizational Change: Putting Theory into Practice*. London: Routledge.

Izard, C.E. (1977) *Human Emotions*. New York: Plenum.

Izard, C.E. (1993) Four systems for emotion activation: Cognitive and noncognitive processes. *Psychological Review* 100: 68–90.

Jablin, F.M., Cude, R.L., House, A., Lee, J., and Roth, N.L. (1994) Communication competence in organizations: Conceptualization and comparison across multiple levels of analysis. In L. Thayer and G. Barnett (eds) *Organization Communication: Emerging Perspectives* Vol. 4. Norwood, NJ: Ablex.

Jackall, R. (1988) *Moral Mazes: The World of Corporate Managers*. London: Oxford University Press.

Jackson, B. (1996) Re-engineering the sense of self: The manager and the management guru. *Journal of Management Studies* 33: 571–90.

Jackson, B. (2001) *Management Gurus and Management Fashions: A Dramatistic Inquiry*. Routledge: London.

Jackson, R. and Callan, V. (2001) Managing and leading organizational change. In K. Parry (ed.), *Leadership in the Antipodes: Findings, Implications and a Leader Profile*. Wellington: Institute of Policy Studies and Centre for the Study of Leadership.

Jackson, S.E., Stone, V.K., and Alvarez, E.B. (1993) Socialisation amidst diversity: The impact of demographics on work team oldtimers and newcomers. In L. Cummings and B. Staw (eds) *Research in Organizational Behaviour* Vol. 15. Greenwich, CT: JAI Press: 45–109.

Jacques, R. (1996) *Manufacturing the employee: Management Knowledge from the 19th to 21st Centuries*. Thousand Oaks, CA: Sage.

Janis, I. (1982) Groupthink. 2nd Edition. Boston: Houghton Mifflin.

Jehn, K.A. (1995) A multimethod examination of the benefits and detriments of intragroup conflict. Administrative Science Quarterly 40: 256–84.

Jehn, K.A. (1997) Qualitative analysis of conflict types and dimensions in organizational groups. Administrative Science Quarterly 42: 538–66.

Jehn, K.A., Northcraft, G.B., and Neale, M.A. (1999) Why differences make a difference: A study of diversity, conflict and performance in workgroups. Administrative Science Quarterly 44: 741.

Jick, T. and Peiperl, M. (eds) (2003) Managing Change: Cases and Concepts. 2nd Edition. Boston: McGraw-Hill.

Johannesen, R.L. (2002) Ethics in Human Communication. 5th Edition. Prospect Heights, Ill.: Waveland Press.

Johnson, C. (2002) Enron's ethical collapse: Lessons from the top. Paper presented at the National Communication Association Convention, New Orleans.

Johnson, C.E. (2001) Meeting the ethical challenges of leadership: Casting Light or Shadow. Thousand Oaks, CA: Sage.

Johnson, J., Bernhagen, M., Miller, V., and Allen, M. (1996) The role of communication in managing reductions in work force. Journal of Applied Communication Research 24: 139–64.

Jones, D. (1997) Employees as stakeholders. Business Strategy Review 8: 21–4.

Jones, D. (2002) The interpretive auditor: Reframing the communication audit. Management Communication Quarterly 15: 466–71.

Jones, E. (1964) Ingratiation. New York: Appleton-Century-Crofts.

Jones, E. (1990) Interpersonal Perception. New York: Freeman.

Jones, M. (2000) Convergence platforms. Telecommunications 34: 81–4.

Jones, M.O., Moore, M.D., and Snyder, R.C. (eds) (1988) Inside Organizations: Understanding the Human Dimension. Beverly Hills, CA: Sage.

Jones, R.G. and Rittman, A. (2002) Interpersonal interactions in organisations. In N.M. Ashkanasy, C.E.J. Härtel, and W.J. Zerbe (eds) Managing Emotions in the Workplace. Armonk, NY: M.E. Sharpe.

Jordan, P.J., Ashkanasy, N.M., and Härtel, C.E.J. (2002) Emotional intelligence as a moderator of emotional and behavioural reactions to job insecurity. Academy of Management Review 27: 361–72.

Jung, D.I. and Avolio, B.J. (1999) Effects of leadership style and followers' cultural orientation on performance in group and individual task conditions. Academy of Management Journal 42: 208–19.

Kabanoff, B., Palmer, I., and Brown, S. (2000) Financial consequences of downsizing and the role of managerial attention. Paper presented at the US Academy of Management Conference, Toronto, Canada, 7–9 August.

Kagan, J. (1972) Motives and development. Journal of Personality and Social Psychology 22: 51–66.

Kahn, W.A. (1992) To be fully there: Psychological presence at work. Human Relations 45: 321–50.

Kahn, W.A. (1995) Organizational change and the provision of a secure base: Lessons from the field. Human Relations 48: 489–515.

Kahn, W.A. (1998) Relational systems at work. Research in Organizational Behavior 20: 39–76.

Kahneman, D., Slovic, P., and Tversky, A. (1982) Judgment Under Uncertainty: Heuristics and Biases. Cambridge, UK: Cambridge University Press.

Kallifatides, M. (2001) The tough ones. In S.-E. Sjostrand, J. Sandberg and M. Tyrstrup (eds) *Invisible Management: The Social Construction of Leadership*. London: Thomson Learning.

Kamp, A. (2000) Breaking up old marriages: The political process of change and continuity at work. *Technology Analysis and Strategic Management* 12: 75–90.

Kanter, R.M. (1990) *When Giants Learn to Dance: Mastering the Challenges of Strategy, Management, and Careers in the 1990s*. London: Unwin Hyman.

Kanter, R.M., Stein, B.A. and Jick, T.D. (1992) *The Challenge of Organizational Change: How Companies Experience It and Leaders Guide It*. New York: Free Press.

Kaplan, R. and Norton, D. (1996) *The Balanced Scorecard: Translating Strategy into Action*. Boston: Harvard Business School Press.

Kapoor, I. (2002) The devil's in the theory. *Third World Quarterly* 23: 101–17.

Kassing, J. (2000) Exploring the relationship between workplace freedom of speech, organizational identification, and employee dissent. *Communication Research Reports* 17: 387–96.

Kassing, J. (2001) From the look of things: Assessing perceptions of organizational dissenters. *Management Communication Quarterly* 14: 442–70.

Keesing, R.M. (1974) Theories of culture. *Annual Review of Anthropology* 3: 73–97.

Kegan, R. (1994) *In Over Our Heads: The Mental Demands of Modern Life*. Cambridge, MA: Harvard University Press.

Kelemen, M., Forrester, P., and Hassard, J. (2000) BPR and TQM: Divergence or convergence? In D. Knights and H. Willmott (eds) *The Reengineering Revolution: Critical Studies of Corporate Change*. London: Sage.

Kellerman, K. and Reynolds, R. (1990) When ignorance is bliss: The role of motivation to reduce uncertainty in Uncertainty Reduction Theory. *Human Communication Research* 17: 5–75.

Kelly, J.R. and Barsade, S.G. (2001) Mood and emotions in small groups and work teams. *Organizational Behavior and Human Decision Processes* 86: 99–130.

Kibby, L. and Hartel, C.E.J. (2002) Intelligent emotions management: Insights and strategies for managers and leaders. *Paper presented at the 3rd Bi-Annual Meeting of the Emotions in Organizational Life Conference*, July 14–16, Gold Coast, Australia.

Kieser, A. (1997) Rhetoric and myth in management fashion. *Organization* 4: 49–74

Kiesler, S. and Sproull, L. (1992) Group decision making and communication technology. *Organizational Behavior and Human Decision Processes* 52: 96–123.

Kilpatrick, A. (1999) When in doubt, don't: Alternatives to downsizing. *M@nagement* 2: 209–19.

Kimble, C. and McLoughlin, K. (1995) Computer based information systems and managers' work. *New Technology, Work and Employment* 10: 56–67.

Kirkman, B. and Rosen, B. (2000) Powering up teams. *Organizational Dynamics* (Winter) 48–65.

Kirshenberg, S. (1997) No joking matter (monitoring of e-mail communication). *Training and Development* 51: 49–50.

Kirton, M. (1981) A reanalysis of two scales of tolerance of ambiguity. *Journal of Personality Assessment* 45: 407–15.

Knights, D. and Murray, F. (1994) *Managers Divided: Organization Politics and Information Technology Management*. Chichester: John Wiley & Sons.

Knights, D. and Willmott, H. (eds) (2000) *The Reengineering Revolution: Critical Studies of Corporate Change*. London: Sage.

Komin, S. (1995) Cross-cultural management communication in Thailand. *Paper presented at the SEAMEO's RELC Regional Seminar on Exploring Language, Culture and Literature in Language Learning*, SEAMEO Regional Language Centre, Singapore.

Kotter, J. (1996) *Leading Change*. Harvard: Harvard Business School Press.

Kotter, J.P. and Schlesinger, L.A. (1979) Choosing strategies for change. *Harvard Business Review* 57: 106–14.

Kozan, M.K. and Ergin, C. (1998) Preference for the third party help in conflict management in the United States and Turkey: An experimental study. *Journal of Cross-Cultural Psychology* 29: 525–39.

Krackhardt, D. (1994) Constraints on the interactive organization as an ideal type. In C. Heckscher and A. Donnellon (eds), *The Post-Bureaucratic Organization: New Perspectives on Organizational Change*. Thousand Oaks, CA: Sage.

Kreitler, S., Maguen, T., and Kreitler, H. (1975) The three faces of intolerance for ambiguity. *Archiv fur Psychologie* 127: 238–50.

Kreitner, R. and Kinicki, A. (1992) *Organizational Behaviour*. 2nd Edition. Homewood: Irwin.

Krone, K. (1992) A comparison of organizational, structural, and relationship effects on subordinates' upward influence choices. *Communication Quarterly* 40: 1–15.

Kropotkin, P. (1974 [1899]) *Fields, Factories and Workshops Tomorrow*. London: George Allen & Unwin Ltd.

Kucaj II, S.A. (1999) The world of words: Thoughts on the development of Lexicon. In M. Barrett (ed.) *The Development of Language*. East Sussex: Psychology Press.

Kunda, G. (1992) *Engineering Culture: Control and Commitment in a High Tech Corporation*. Philadelphia: Temple University Press.

Kuntonbutr, C. (1999) A comparative study between Thai and American subordinates' perception of managerial values in the banking industry. Unpublished dissertation: University of Sarasota.

LaBarre, P. (2001) Marcus Buckingham thinks your boss has an attitude problem. *Fast Company* (August) 49: 88.

Laclau, E. and Mouffe, C. (1985) *Hegemony and Socialist Strategy*. Trans. W. Moore and P. Cammack. London: Verso.

Lam, A. (2000) Tacit knowledge, organizational learning and societal institutions: An integrated framework. *Organization Studies* 21: 487–513.

Lange, J. (2002) Environmental collaboration and constituency communication. In L. Frey (ed.) *Group Communication in Context*. Hillsdale, NJ: Erlbaum.

Langnau, L. (2000) Are management jobs on the line? *Material Handling Management* 55: 26.

Laughlin, H. (1970) *The Ego and its Defenses*. New York: Appleton-Century-Crofts.

Lave, J. (1988) *Cognition in Practice: Mind, Mathematics and Culture in Everyday Life*. Cambridge, UK: Cambridge University Press.

Lave, J. and Wenger, E. (1991) *Situated Learning: Legitimate Peripheral Participation*. Cambridge, UK: Cambridge University Press.

Lawler, E. (1999) Employee involvement makes a difference. *Journal for Quality and Participation* 22: 18–20.

Lawrence, P. and Lorsch, J. (1967) *Organization and Environment: Managing Differentiation and Integration*. Boston: Harvard Business School.

Lazarus, R. (1989) Cognition and emotion from the R.E.T. viewpoint. In M.E. Bernard and R. DiGuiseppe (eds) *Inside Rational Emotive Therapy: A critical Appraisal of the Theory and Therapy of Albert Ellis*. San Diego: Academic Press.

Lazarus, R.S. (1991) *Emotion and Adaptation*. New York: Oxford University Press.

Leana, C. and Van Buren, H. (2000) Eroding organizational social capital among US firms: The price of job instability. In R. Burke and C. Cooper (eds) *The Organization in Crisis: Downsizing, Restructuring and Privatization*. Oxford: Blackwell.

Ledford, G.E., Mohram, S.A., Mohrman, A.M., and Lawler, E.E. (1990) The phenomenon of large-scale organizational change. In A.M. Mohrman, S.A. Mohram, G.E. Ledford, T.G. Cummings, and E.E. Lawler (eds) *Large-Scale Organizational Change*. San Francisco: Jossey-Bass.

Lee, C.S. (2001) An analytical framework for evaluating e-commerce business models and strategies. *Internet Research: Electronic Networking Applications and Policy* 11: 349–59.

Lee, J. (2001) Leader-member exchange, perceived organizational justice, and cooperative communication. *Management Communication Quarterly* 14: 574–89.

Leichty, G. and Esrock, S. (2001) Change and response on the corporate web site. *American Communication Journal* 5 (1). Online. Available HTTP: <http://acjournal.org/holdings/vol5/iss1/articles/leichtyesrock.htm>. Accessed 27 November 2002.

Levering, R. and Moskowitz, M. (2000) The 100 best companies to work for. *Fortune*, 10 January, 82–110.

Lewin, K. (1947) Frontiers in group dynamics. *Human Relations* 1: 5–42.

Lewin, K. (1951) *Field Theory in Social Science*. New York: Harper.

Lewis, D. (1992) Communicating organizational culture. *Australian Journal of Communication* 19: 47–57.

Lewis, L. and Seibold, D. (1998) Reconceptualizing organizational change implementation as a communication problem: A review of literature and research agenda. In M. Roloff and G. Paulson (eds) *Communication Yearbook Vol. 21*, Newbury Park, CA: Sage.

Liebgig, J.F. (1990) *Business Ethics Profiles in Civic Virtue*. Golden, CO: Fulcrum Publishing.

Limaye, M.R. and Victor, D.A. (1995) Cross-cultural business communication research: State of the art and hypotheses for the 1990s. In T. Jackson (ed.) *Cross-Cultural Management*. Oxford: Butterworth-Heinemann.

Littler, C., Dunford, R., Bramble, T., and Hale, A. (1997) The dynamics of downsizing in Australia and New Zealand. *Asia Pacific Journal of Human Resources* 35: 65–79.

Liu, Y. and Perrewe, P. (forthcoming) The role of emotion in employee counterproductive work behavior: Integrating the psychoevolutionary and constructivist perspective. In C.E.J. Härtel, W.J. Zerbe and N.M. Ashkanasy (eds) *Organizational Behavior: An Emotions Perspective*. Armonk, NY: M.E. Sharpe.

Lloyd, S. and Härtel, C.E.J. (2003) The intercultural competencies required for inclusive and effective culturally diverse work teams. *Paper presented at the Third International Conference on Diversity in Organizations*, Honolulu: University of Hawaii.

London, M. and Wohlers, A. (1991) Agreement between subordinate and self-ratings on upward feedback. *Personnel Psychology* 44: 375–90.

Lord, R., Klimoski, R., and Kanfer, R. (eds) (2002) *Emotions in the Workplace: Understanding the Structure and Role of Emotions in Organizational Behavior*. San Francisco: Jossey-Bass.

Luthans, F. and Larsen, J. (1986) How managers really communicate. *Human Relations* 39: 161–78.

Lynch, T. and Cruise, P. (1999) Can the public sector leviathan be reformed? Right sizing possibility for the twenty-first century. *M@n@gement* 2: 149–61.

Mabey, C. (2001) Closing the circle: Participant views of a 360 degree feedback programme. *Human Resource Management Journal* 11: 41–53.

McAdam, R. and McCreedy, S.A. (1999) A critical review of knowledge management models. *The Learning Organization* 6: 91–101.

McCarthy, E. (2000) From toys to tools: Technology's effect on client communications. *Journal of Financial Planning* 13: 62–70.

Maccoby, M. (2000) Narcissistic leaders: The incredible pros, the inevitable cons. *Harvard Business Review* 78: 69–77.

McCormick, A.E. and Kinloch, G.C. (1986) Interracial contact in the customer-clerk situation. *The Journal of Social Psychology* 126: 551–3.

MacCrimmon, K. and Wehrung, D. (1986) *Taking Risks: The Management of Uncertainty*. New York: Free Press.

MacDonald, A. (1970). Revised scale for ambiguity tolerance: Reliability and validity. *Psychological Reports* 26: 791–8.

McDonald, L.M. and Härtel, C.E.J. (2002). Consumer emotions may run high during organizational crises. *Paper presented at the 3rd Bi-Annual Meeting of the Emotions in Organizational Life Conference*, Gold Coast, Australia, July.

McGregor, D. (1960) *The Human Side of Enterprise*. New York: McGraw-Hill.

McKinley, W., Zhao, J., and Rust, K. (2000) A sociocognitive interpretation of organizational downsizing. *The Academy of Management Review* 25: 227–43.

McLagan, P. and Nel, C. (1995) *The Age of Participation: New Governance for the Workplace and the World*. San Francisco: Berrett-Koehler Publishers.

McLoughlin, I. and Clark, J. (1994) *Technological Change at Work*. 2nd Edition. Buckingham: Open University Press.

McPhee, R.D., Corman, S.R., and Dooley, K. (2002) Organizational knowledge expression and management. *Management Communication Quarterly* 16: 274–81.

McPherson, K. (1983) Opinion-related information seeking: Personal and situational variables. *Personality and Social Psychology Bulletin* 9: 116–24.

Mandler, G. (1984) *Mind and Body*. New York: Norton.

Manning, P.K. (1997) *The Social Organization of Policing*. 2nd Edition. Prospect Heights, Ill.: Waveland Press.

March, J. and Simon, H. (1958) *Organizations*. New York: Wiley.

Marshall, G. (1999) The opportunities of electronic commerce. *Agency Sales Magazine* 29: 4–7.

Marsick, V. and Watkins, K. (1996) A framework for the learning organization. In K. Watkins and V. Marsick (eds) *In Action: Creating the Learning Organization*. Alexandria, VA: American Society for Training and Development.

Martensson, M. (2000) A critical view of knowledge management as a management tool. *Journal of Knowledge Management* 4: 204–16.

Martin, J. (1990) Deconstructing organizational taboos: The suppression of gender conflict in organizations. *Organization Science* 11: 339–59.

Martin, J. (1992) *Cultures in Organizations: Three Perspectives*. Oxford: Oxford University Press.

Martin, J. and Meyerson, D. (1988) Organizational culture and the denial, channeling, and acknowledgement of ambiguity. In L.R. Pondy, R.J. Boland Jr., and H. Thomas (eds) *Managing Ambiguity and Change*. New York: John Wiley.

Martin, J. and Siehl, C. (1983) Organizational culture and counterculture: An uneasy symbiosis. *Organizational Dynamics* 12: 52–64.

Martin, J., Knopoff, K., and Beckman, C. (1998) An alternative to bureaucratic impersonality and emotional labor: Bounded emotionality at The Body Shop. *Administrative Science Quarterly* 43: 429–69.

Martin, T.N. and Hafer, J.C. (2002) Internet procurement by corporate purchasing agents: Is it all hype? *S.A.M. Advanced Management Journal* 67: 41–8.

Maslow, A.H. (1970) *Motivation and Personality*. 2nd Edition. New York: Harper.

Mastenbroek, W. (2000) Emotion management, a hype? In N.M. Ashkanasy, C.E.J. Härtel, and W.J. Zerbe (eds) *Emotions in the Workplace: Research, Theory, and Practice*. Westport, Conn.: Quorum Books.

Mehrabian, A. (1981) *Silent Messages: Implicit Communication of Emotions and Attitudes*. 2nd Edition. Belmont: Wadsworth.

Meindl, F., Erlich, S., and Dukerich, J. (1985) The romance of leadership. *Administrative Science Quarterly* 30: 78–102.

Metzler, M.B. (2001) The centrality of organizational legitimacy to public relations practice. In R.L. Heath (ed.) *Handbook of Public Relations*. Thousand Oaks, CA: Sage.

Meyer, J. (2002) Organizational communication assessment: Fuzzy methods and the accessibility of symbols. *Management Communication Quarterly* 15: 472–9.

Michener, H., Plazewski, J., and Vaske, J. (1979) Ingratiation tactics channelled by target values and threat capability. *Journal of Personality* 47: 35–56.

Micklethwait, J. and Wooldridge, A. (1997) *The Witch Doctors: What Management Gurus are Saying, Why it Matters and How to Make Sense of It*. London: Mandarin Paperbacks.

Micklethwait, J. and Wooldridge, A. (2000) *A Future Perfect: The Challenge and Hidden Promise of Globalization*. London: Heinemann.

Miles, R. (2001) Beyond the age of Dilbert: Accelerating corporate transformations by rapidly engaging all employees. *Organizational Dynamics* (Spring): 313–21.

Millar, R. and Gallagher, M. (2000) The interview approach. In O. Hargie and D. Tourish (eds) *Handbook of Communication Audits for Organisations*. London: Routledge.

Miller, P. and Rose, N. (1990) Governing economic life. *Economy and Society* 19: 1–31.

Miller, V., Johnson, J., and Grau, J. (1994) Antecedents to willingness to participate in a planned organisational change. *Journal of Applied Communication Research* 22: 59–80.

Milliken, F.J. and Martins, L.L. (1996) Searching for common threads: Understanding the multiple effects of diversity in organizational groups. *Academy of Management Review* 21: 402–33.

Mills, T.L., Boylstein, C.A., and Lorean, S. (2001) 'Doing' organizational culture in the Saturn corporation. *Organization Studies* 22: 117–43.

Millward, N., Bryson, A., and Forth, J. (2000) *All Change at Work?* London: Routledge.

Mintzberg, H. (1989) *Mintzberg on Management*. New York: The Free Press.

Mintzberg, H. (1996) Musings on management. *Harvard Business Review* 74: 61–7.

Mirvis, P. (1997) 'Soul work' in organizations. *Organization Science* 8: 193–206.

Mishra, A. and Spreitzer, G. (1998) Explaining how survivors respond to downsizing: The roles of trust, empowerment, justice, and work redesign. *Academy of Management Review* 23: 567–88.

Mishra, K., Spreitzer, G., and Mishra, A. (1998) Preserving employee morale during downsizing. *Sloan Management Review* (Winter): 83–95.

Mitroff, I. and Denton, E. (1999) *A Spiritual Audit of Corporate America: A Hard Look at Spirituality, Religion, and Values in the Workplace*. New York: McGraw-Hill.

Mohr, L.A. and Henson, S.W. (1996) Impact of employee gender and job congruency on customer satisfaction. *Journal of Consumer Psychology* 5: 161–87.

Monge, P. and Contractor, N. (2001) Emergence of communication networks. In F. Jablin and L. Putnam (eds) *The New Handbook of Organizational Communication: Advances in Theory, Research and Methods*. London: Sage.

Montgomery, D.J., Heald, G.R., MacNamara, S.R., and Pincus, L.B. (1995) Malpractice and the communication consultant: A proactive approach. *Management Communication Quarterly* 8: 368–84.

Montgomery, D.J., Pincus, L.B., and Heald, G.R. (1994) Privacy: Legal and ethical considerations for consultants. *Organizational Development Journal* 12: 95–103.

Moravec, M., Gyr, H., and Friedman, L. (1993) A 21st century communication tool. *HR Magazine* (July): 77–81.

Morgan, G. (1997) *Images of Organization*. 2nd Edition. London: Sage.

Morgan, O. (2001a) A Corus of disapproval, *Observer*, 4 February, Business supplement, 5.

Morgan, O. (2001b) No job safe as Corus bans UK investment. *Observer*, 4 February, Business supplement, 1.

Morley, D., Shockley-Zalabak, P., and Cesaria, R. (2002) Organizational influence processes: Perceptions of values, communication and effectiveness. *Studies in Communication Sciences* 2: 69–104.

Morrill, C. (1991) Conflict management, honor, and organizational change. *American Journal of Sociology* 97: 585–621.

Morris, J., Cascio, W., and Young, C. (1999) Downsizing after all these years: Questions and answers about who did it, how many did it, and who benefited from it. *Organizational Dynamics* (Winter) 78–87.

Morrison, E. (2002) Information seeking within organizations. *Human Communication Research* 28: 229–42.

Moskowitz, M. and Levering, R. (2001) Voted the best by their own workforces. *Sunday Times*, 4 February, '50 Best Companies to Work For' supplement: 2–3.

Mullaney, A. (1989) Downsizing: How one hospital responded to decreasing demand. *Health Care Management Review* 14: 41–8.

Mumby, D. (1988) *Communication and Power in Organizations: Discourse, Ideology and Domination*. Norwood, NJ: Ablex.

Mumby, D. (1996) Feminism, postmodernism, and organizational communication: A critical reading. *Management Communication Quarterly* 9: 259–95.

Mumby, D. and Stohl, C. (1996) Disciplining organizational communication studies. *Communication Quarterly* 10: 50–72.

Murgolo-Poore, M.E., Pitt, L.F., and Ewing, M.T. (2002) Intranet effectiveness: A public relations paper-and-pencil checklist. *Public Relations Review* 28: 113–23.

Murphy, E. (1994) *Strategies for Health Care Excellence*. Washington, DC: American Society for Work Redesign.

Myers, D.G. (1996) *Social Psychology*. 5th Edition. New York: McGraw-Hill.

Nadesan, M. (2001) Fortune on globalization and the new economy. *Management Communication Quarterly* 14: 498–506.

Narasimha, S. (2000) Organizational knowledge, human resource management, and sustained competitive advantage: Toward a framework. *Competitiveness Review* 10: 123–35.

NCA (National Communication Association) (1999) Credo for ethical communication. Online. Available HTTP: <http://www.rollins.edu/communication/wschmidt/nca_credo.htm>. Accessed 19 September 2002.

Neef, D. (1999) Making the case for knowledge management: The bigger picture. *Management Decision* 37: 72–8.

Nelsen, B.J. and Barley, S.R. (1997) For love or money? Commodification and the construction of an occupational mandate. *Administrative Science Quarterly* 42: 619–53.

Newell, S., Robertson, M. and Swan, J. (2001) Management Fads and Fashions. *Organization* 8: 5–15.

Newman, J. (1995) Gender and cultural change. In C. Itzin and J. Newman (eds) *Gender, Culture and Organizational Change: Putting Theory into Practice*. London: Routledge.

Nicholls, J. (1979) Quality and equality in intellectual development: The role of motivation in education. *American Psychologist* 34: 1071–83.

Nicholls, J. (1983) Conceptions of ability and achievement motivation: A theory and its implications for education. In S. Paris, G. Olson, and H. Stevenson (eds) *Learning and Motivation in the Classroom*. Hillsdale, HJ: Erlbaum.

Nilakant, V. and Ramnarayan, S. (1998) *Managing Organizational Change*, New Delhi: Response Books.

Nonaka, I. and Takeuchi, H. (1995) *The Knowledge Creating Company: How Japanese Companies Create the Dynamics of Innovation*. New York: Oxford University Press.

Norton, R.W. (1975) Measurement of ambiguity tolerance. *Journal of Personality Assessment* 39: 607–19.

Nutt, P. (1999) Surprising but true: Half the decisions in organizations fail. *Academy of Management Executive* 13: 75–90.

Nutt, P. (2002) *Why Decisions Fail: Avoiding the Blunders and Traps that Lead to Debacles*. San Francisco, CA: Berret-Koehler.

Nye, R. (1975) *Three Views of Man Perspectives from Sigmund Freud, B.F. Skinner and Carl Rogers*. Monterey, CA: Brooks/Cole Publishing Company.

Oatley, K. (1993) Social construction in emotions. In M. Lewis and J. Haviland (eds) *Handbook of Emotions*. New York: The Guilford Press.

Ober, S. (1998) *Contemporary Business Communication*. 3rd Edition. Boston: Houghton Mifflin.

O'Brien, R. (2001) *Trust: Releasing the Energy to Succeed*. Chichester: John Wiley.

Ocasio, W. (2001) How do organizations think? In T. Lant and Z. Shapira (eds) *Organizational Cognition: Computation and Interpretation*. Mahwah, NJ: Lawrence Erlbaum.

Ochs, E. (1986) From feelings to grammar: A Samoan case study. In B.B. Schieffelin and E. Ochs (eds) *Language Socialization Across Cultures*. New York: Cambridge University Press.

O'Creevy, M. (2001) Employee involvement and the middle manager: Saboteur or scapegoat? *Human Resource Management Journal* 11: 24–40.

Odom, M. (1993) Kissing up really works on boss. *San Diego Union-Tribune*, 12 August, E12.

O'Hair, D., Friedrich, G., and Dixon, L. (2002) *Strategic Communication in Business and the Professions*. 4th Edition. Boston: Houghton Mifflin.

Oliver, N. (1999) Rational choice or leap of faith? The creation and defence of a management orthodoxy. *Iconoclastic Papers* 1: 1–18.

Olson, D.R. (1980) Some social aspects of meaning in oral and written language. *The Social Foundations of Language and Thought: Essays in Honor of Jerome S. Bruner*. New York: Norton and Co.

Oppenheim, B. (1982) An exercise in attitude measurement. In G.M. Breakwell, H. Foot, and R. Gilmour (eds) *Social Psychology: A Practical Manual*. London: Macmillan, 38–52.

O'Reilly, C.A., Caldwell, D.F., and Barnett, W.P. (1989) Workgroup demography, social integration, and turnover. *Administrative Science Quarterly* 34: 21–37.

O'Reilly, C., Chatman, J., and Anderson, J. (1987) Message flow and decision making.

In F. Jablin, L. Putnam, K. Roberts, and L. Porter (eds) *Handbook of Organizational Communication*. Newbury Park, CA: Sage.

O'Reilly, C. and Pfeffer, J. (2000) *Hidden Value: How Great Companies Achieve Extraordinary Results with Ordinary People*. Boston, MA: Harvard Business School Press.

Organ, D. (1988) *Organizational Citizenship Behavior: The Good Soldier Syndrome*. Lexington, MA: Lexington Books.

Orr, J.E. (1996) *Talking about Machines: An Ethnography of a Modern Job*. Ithaca, NY: Cornell University Press.

Øyum, L. (1999) *Changing as enrolment*. Doctoral Thesis, Trondheim: Norwegian University of Science and Technology (NTNU).

Øyum, L. (2000): Like barn leker best? (Equal children play best?). In M. Rolfsen, *Trendenes tyranni* (The Tyranny of trends). Bergen, Norway: Fagbokforlaget.

Pace, R.W. (2002) The organizational learning audit. *Management Communication Quarterly* 15: 458–65.

Pajak, E. and Glickman, C.D. (1989) Informational and controlling language in simulated supervisory conferences. *American Educational Research Journal* 26: 93–106.

Parker, M. (2000) *Organizational Culture and Identity: Unity and Division at Work*. London: Sage.

Pascale, R. (1990) *Managing on the Edge*. Harmondsworth: Penguin.

Paterson, J. and Härtel, C.E.J. (2002) Integrating cognition and emotion in a model of change. In N.M. Ashkanasy, C.E.J. Härtel, and W.J. Zerbe (eds) *Managing Emotions in a Changing Workplace*. Armonk, NY: M.E. Sharpe.

Paton, R. and McCalman, J. (2000) *Change Management: A Guide to Effective Implementation*. 2nd Edition. London: Sage.

Pattison, S. (1997) *The Faith of the Managers: When Management Becomes Religion*. London: Cassel.

Pelled, L.H., Eisenhardt, K.M. and Xin, K.R. (1999) Exploring the black box: An analysis of work group diversity, conflict and performance. *Administrative Science Quarterly* 44: 1–3.

Peters, T. (1988) *Thriving on Chaos: Handbook for a Management Revolution*. London: Pan Books.

Peters, T. (2000) *Forbered deg på hvitsnipp-revolusjonen* (translated from 'Re-inventing Work'). Norway: Egmont Hjemmets Bokforlag.

Peters, T. (1993) *Liberation Management: Necessary Disorganisation for Nanosecond Nineties*. London: Pan Books.

Peters, T. (1997) *The Circle of Innovation*. New York: Alfred A. Knopf.

Peters, T. and Waterman, R. (1982) *In search of excellence*. New York: Harper & Row.

Peters, T.J. (1978) Symbols, patterns and settings: An optimistic case for getting things done. *Organizational Dynamics* 9: 3–23.

Pettigrew, A.M. (1973) *The Politics of Organizational Decision-Making*. London: Tavistock.

Pettigrew, A.M. (1985) *The Awakening Giant: Continuity and Change in Imperial Chemical Industries*. Oxford: Basil Blackwell.

Pettigrew, A.W. (1979) On studying organizational cultures. *Administrative Science Quarterly* 24: 570–81.

Pfeffer, J. (1981) *Power in Organizations*. Boston: Pitman.

Pfeffer, J. (1993) Understanding power in organizations. In C. Mabey and B. Mayon-White (eds) *Managing Change*. London: Paul Chapman Publishing.

Pfeffer, J. (1994) *Competitive Advantage Through People: Unleashing the Power of the Work-force*. Boston: Harvard Business School Press.

Pfeffer, J. (1998) *The Human Equation*. Boston: Harvard Business School Press.

Pfeffer, J. (2000) Barriers to the advance of organisational science: Paradigm development as a dependent variable. In P. Frost, A. Lewin and R. Daft (eds) *Talking About Organization Science: Debates and Dialogue from Crossroads*. London: Sage.

Pfeffer, J. (2001) Business and the spirit: Management practices that sustain values. *Research Paper Series: No. 1713*. Stanford: Graduate School of Business, Stanford University.

Phaneuf, R. (2000) Plug employees in with online benefits. *Risk Management* (July) 47: 47–9.

Pil, F. and MacDuffie, J. (1996) The adoption of high-performance workplace practices. *Industrial Relations* 25: 423–55.

Pillai, R. and Meindl, J.R. (1998) Context and charisma: A meso level approach to the relationship of organic structure, collectivism and crisis to charismatic leadership. *Journal of Management* 24(5): 643–71.

Pizer, M. and Härtel, C.E.J. (2002) For better or worse: Organizational culture and emotions. *Paper presented at the 3rd Bi-Annual Meeting of the Emotions in Organizational Life Conference*, Gold Coast, July.

Pizer, M. and Härtel, C.E.J. (forthcoming, 2004). For better or worse: organizational culture and emotions. In C.E.J. Härtel, W.J. Zerbe and N.M. Ashkanasy (eds) *Organizational Behavior: An Emotions Perspective*. Armonk, NY: M.E. Sharpe.

Plutchik, R. (1980) A general psychoevolutionary theory of emotion. In R. Plutchick and H. Kellerman (eds) *Emotion: Theory, Research, and Experience*. New York: Academic Press.

Poe, A.C. (2001) Don't touch that 'send' button! *HR Magazine* 46, July: 74–80.

Polanyi, M. (1966) *The Tacit Dimension*. London: Routledge & Kegan Paul.

Polanyi, M. (1969) *Knowing and Being*. London: Routledge & Kegan Paul.

Porter, M. (1985) *Competitive Advantage*. New York: Free Press.

Postma, O.J. and Brokke, M. (2002) Personalisation in practice: The proven effects of personalisation. *Journal of Database Marketing* 9: 137–42.

Pratkanis, A. and Aronson, E. (1991) *Age of Propaganda: The Everyday Use and Abuse of Persuasion*. New York: Freeman.

Pratto, F. and John, O. (1991) Automatic vigilance: The attention grabbing power of negative social information. *Journal of Personality and Social Psychology* 51: 380–91.

Pribble, P.T. (1990) Making an ethical commitment: A rhetorical case study of organizational socialization. *Communication Quarterly* 38: 255–67.

Prince, C.P. (2001) U.S. lags on globalization. *Chief Executives* 165: 12.

Pruter, R. (1998) Web communications are different from paper. *Employee Benefit Plan Review* 53: 14–16.

Putnam, L. (1982) Paradigms for organizational communication research. *Western Journal of Speech Communication* 46: 192–206.

Putnam, L. and Fairhurst, G.T. (2001) Discourse analysis in organizations: Issues and concerns. In F.M. Jablin and L.L. Putnam (eds) *New Handbook of Organizational Communication*. Thousand Oaks, CA: Sage.

Putnam, R. (2001) *Bowling Alone*. New York: Simon and Schuster.

Rajecki, D.W. (1982) *Attitudes, Themes and Advances*. Sunderland, Ma.: Sinauer.

Ramirez, A., Walther, J., Burgoon, J., and Sunnafrank, M. (2002) Information seeking strategies, uncertainty, and computer-mediated communication. *Human Communication Research* 28: 213–28.

Redding, C. (1996) Communication ethics: A case of culpable neglect. In J. Jaksa and M. Pritchard (eds) *Ethics of Technological Transfer*. Cresskill, NJ: Hampton Press.

Reed Employment Services (2002) *Motivating People at Work: What is to be Done?* London: Reed Employment Services.

Reed, M.I. (2001) Organization trust and control: A realist analysis. *Organization Studies* 22: 201–28.

Reich, R. (2001) *The Future of Success: Work and Life in the New Economy*. London: Heinemann.

Reichfield, F. (2001) *Loyalty Rules! How Today's Leaders Build Lasting Relationships*. Boston: Harvard Business School Press.

Reilly, R., Smither, J., and Vasilopoulous, N. (1996) A longitudinal study of upward feedback. *Personnel Psychology* 49: 599–612.

Reis, H.T. and Patrick, B.C. (1996) Attachment and intimacy: Component processes. In E.T. Higgins and A. Kruglanski (eds) *Social Psychology: Handbook of Basic Principles*. New York: Guilford, 523–63.

Rice, R. and Gattiker, U. (2001) New media and organizational structuring. In F. Jablin and L. Putnam (eds) *The New Handbook of Organizational Communication: Advances in Theory, Research and Methods*. London: Sage.

Rigby, D.J. (2001) *Disseminating E-business Globally and Locally: A Rhetorical Inquiry into the Role of the 'Big Five' Management Consulting Firms*. Wellington: Department of Management, Victoria University of Wellington.

Robbins, S. (1996) *Organizational Behaviour: Concepts, Controversies, Applications*. 7th Edition. Englewood Cliffs, NJ: Prentice-Hall International.

Robertson, R. (1992) *Globalization: Social Theory and Global Culture*. London: Sage Publications.

Robichaud, D., Giroux, H., and Taylor, J.R. (in press) The meta-conversation: The recursive property of language as the key to organizing. *Academy of Management Review*.

Rodwell, J., Kienzle, R., and Shadur, M. (1998) The relationships among work-related perceptions, employee attitudes, and employee performance: The integral role of communication. *Human Resource Management* 37: 277–93.

Rogers, A. (1996) Inside knowledge. *Marketing*, 16th May: 35–6.

Rogers, C. (1966) A theory of therapy as developed in client-centered frameworks. In B. Ard (ed.) *Counseling and Psychotherapy Classics on Theories and Issues*. California: Science and Behavior Books Inc.

Rolfsen, M. (1994) *Japanisme i norske bedrifter* (Japanism in Norwegian companies). Bergen, Norway: Fagbokforlaget.

Rolfsen, M. (2000) *Trendenes tyranni* (The Tyranny of trends). Bergen, Norway: Fagbokforlaget.

Rose, H.R. and Rose, S. (eds) (2000) *Alas, Poor Darwin: Arguments Against Evolutionary Psychology*. London: Jonathan Cape.

Rose, M.R. (1998) *Darwin's Spectre: Evolutionary Biology in the Modern World*. New Jersey: Princeton University Press.

Rose, N. (1990) *Governing the Soul: The Shaping of the Private Self*. London: Routledge.

Rose, N. (1996) Identity, genealogy, history. In S. Hall and P. du Gay (eds) *Questions of Cultural Identity*. London: Sage.

Rosenblatt, Z. and Schaeffer, Z. (2000) Ethical problems in downsizing. In R. Burke and C. Cooper (eds) *The Organization in Crisis: Downsizing, Restructuring and Privatization*. Oxford: Blackwell.

Rosenfeld, P., Giacalone, R., and Riordan, C. (1995) *Impression Management in Organizations*. London: Routledge.

Rosenthal, D.M. and Shehadi, F. (1988) *Applied Ethics and Ethical Theory*. Salt Lake City, UT: University of Utah Press.

Ross, J. and Staw, B. (1993) Organizational escalation and exit: Lessons from the Shoreham Nuclear Power Plant. *Academy of Management Journal* 36: 701–32.

Rossini, F.D. (1950) *Chemical Thermodynamics*. New York: John Wiley.

Rothschild-Whitt, J. and Lindenfeld, F. (1982) Reshaping work: Prospects and problems of workplace democracy. In F. Lindenfeld and J. Rothschild-Whitt (eds) *Workplace Democracy and Social Change*. Boston: Porter Sargent Publishers.

Røvik, K.A. (1998) *Moderne organisasjoner* (Modern Organisations). Bergen, Norway: Fagbokforlaget.

Rubin, R. (1990) Communication competence. In G.M. Phillips and J.T. Woods (eds), *Speech Communication: Essays to Commemorate the 75th Anniversary of the Speech Communication Association*, Carbondale: Southern Illinois University Press.

Rubinstein, S., Bennett, M., and Kochan, T. (1993) The Saturn partnership: Co-management and the reinvention of the local union. In B. Kaufman and M. Kleiner (eds), *Employee Representation: Alternatives and Future Directions*. Madison, WI: The Industrial Relations Research Association.

Russell, R. (1997) Workplace democracy and organizational communication. *Communication Studies* 48: 279–84.

Ryan, R.M. and Deci, E.L. (2000a) Self-determination theory and the facilitation of intrinsic motivation, social development, and well-being. *American Psychologist* 55: 68–78.

Ryan, R.M. and Deci, E.L. (2000b) Intrinsic and extrinsic motivations: Classic definitions and new directions. *Contemporary Educational Psychology* 25: 54–67.

Sako, M. (1998) Does trust improve business performance? In C. Lane and R. Bachmann (eds) *Trust Within and Between Organizations. Conceptual Issues and Empirical Applications*. Oxford: Oxford University Press.

Salem, P. (2002) Assessment, change and complexity. *Management Communication Quarterly* 15: 442–50.

Salovey, P. and Mayer, J.D. (1990) Emotional intelligence. *Imagination, Cognition, and Personality* 9: 185–211.

Samuels, P. (1997) The impact of computer-based communications networks. In E. Scholes (ed.) *Gower Handbook of Internal Communication*. Aldershot: Gower.

Sands, D.R. (2001) Getting global. *Insight on the News* 17(8): 33.

Sapp, G. (2000) Alas, poor Darwin: Arguments against evolutionary psychology/are we hardwired? The role of genes in human behavior. *Library Journal* 125: 98.

Scandura, T.A., Von Glinow, M.A., and Lowe, K.B. (1999) When East meets West: Leadership 'best practices' in the United States and Middle East. In W.H. Mobley (ed.) *Advances in Global Leadership, Vol. 1.*, Stamford, Conn.: JAI Press.

Schachter, S. (1971) *Emotion, Obesity and Crime*. London: Academic Press.

Schachter, S. and Singer, J.E. (1962) Cognitive, social and physiological determinants of emotional state. *Psychological Review* 69: 379–99.

Schein, E. with Schneier, I., and Barker, C. (1961) *Coercive Persuasion*. New York: Norton.

Schein, E.H. (1992) *Organizational Culture and Leadership*. 2nd Edition. San Francisco, CA: Jossey-Bass.

Schein, E.H. (2000) Sense and nonsense about culture and climate. In N.M. Ashkanasy,

C. Wilderom, and M.F. Peterson (eds) *Handbook of Organizational Culture and Climate*. Thousand Oaks: Sage Publications.

Schermerhorn, J.R. (1996) *Management and Organizational Behavior*. New York: Wiley.

Schneider, B. (1987) The people make the place. *Personnel Psychology* 40: 437–53.

Schneider, B. and Bowen, D.E. (1985) Employee and customer perceptions of service in banks: Replication and extension. *Journal of Applied Psychology* 70: 423–33.

Schneider, B. and Bowen, D.E. (1995) *Winning the Service Game*. Boston: Harvard Business School Press.

Schooler, J. (2001) Putting 'e-delivery' to work. *Credit Union Management* 24: 46–9.

Schreiber, E. (2001) Why do many otherwise smart CEOs mismanage the reputation asset of their company? *Journal of Communication Management* 6: 209–19.

Schuler, R.S. (1996) Market-focused management: Human resource management implications. *Journal of Market-focused Management* 1: 13–29.

Schultze, C. (2000) Has job security eroded for American workers? In M. Blair and T. Kochan (eds) *The New Relationship: Human Capital in the American Corporation*. Washington, DC: Brookings Institution Press.

Schutz, A. (1998) Assertive, offensive, protective, and defensive styles of self-presentation: A taxonomy. *The Journal of Psychology* 132: 611–28.

Schwartz, M. (2001) The nature and relationship between corporate codes of ethics and behaviour. *Journal of Business Ethics* 31: 247–62.

Schweiger, D. and DeNisi, A. (1991) Communication with employees following a merger: A longitudinal field experiment. *Academy of Management Journal* 34: 110–35.

Scott, C., Shaw, S., Timmerman, C., Volker, F., and Quinn, L. (1999) Using communication audits to teach organizational communication to students and employees. *Business Communication Quarterly* 62: 53–70.

Searle, J.R. (1969) *Speech Acts: An Essay in the Philosophy of Language*. Cambridge, UK: Cambridge University Press.

Secord, P.F. and Backman, C.W. (1964) *Social Psychology*. New York: McGraw-Hill.

Seeger, M. (2001) Ethics and communication in organizational contexts: Moving from the fringe to the center. *American Communication Journal* 51. Online. Available HTTP: <http://www.acjournal.org/holdings/vol5/iss1/special/seeger.htm>. Accessed 13 August 2002.

Seeger, M. and Ulmer, R.R. (2001) Virtuous responses to organizational crisis: Aaron Feuerstein and Milt Cole. *Journal of Business Ethics* 31: 369–76.

Seeger, M.W. (1997) *Organizational Communication Ethics: Decisions and Dilemmas*, Cresskill, NJ: Hampton Press.

Seibold, D. and Shea, B.C. (2001) Participation and decision making. In F. Jablin and L. Putnam (eds) *The New Handbook of Organizational Communication*. Thousand Oaks, CA: Sage: 664–703.

Seligman, M.E.P. (1974) Depression and helplessness. In R.J. Friedman and M.M. Katz (eds) *The Psychology of Depression: Contemporary Theory and Research*. New York: Wiley.

Seligman, M.E.P. (1975) *Helplessness: On Depression, Development, and Death*. San Francisco: Freedman.

Selmer, J. (1997) Differences in leadership behaviour between expatriate and local bosses as perceived by their host country national subordinates. *Leadership and Organisational Development Journal* 18: 13–23.

Senge, P. (1990) *The Fifth Discipline*. London: Century Business.

Senge, P. (1991) The learning organization made plain (Interview with Peter Senge). *Training and Development* (October): 37–44.

Senge, P. (1994) *The Fifth Discipline: The Art and Practice of the Learning Organization*. New York: Doubleday.

Senior, B. (1997) *Organizational Change*. London: Pitman Publishing.

Sergeant, A. and Frenkel, S. (2000) When do customer contact employees satisfy customers? *Journal of Service Research* 3: 18–34.

Sethi, S.P. (1987) A conceptual framework for environmental analysis of social issues and evaluation of business response patterns. In S.P. Sethi and C.M. Fable, *Business and Society*. Lexington, MA: Lexington Books.

Shannon, C.E. and Weaver, W. (1949) *The Mathematical Theory of Communication*. Urbana: University of Illinois Press.

Shapiro, E. (1995) *Fad Surfing in the Boardroom*. London: HarperCollins.

Shaughnessy, C. (1986) Attitudes of senior personnel officials and employees towards RIF policies. *Public Administration Quarterly* 10: 23–35.

Shaver, P., Schwartz, J., Kirson, D., and O'Connor, C. (1987) Emotion knowledge: Further exploration of a Prototype Approach. *Journal of Personality and Social Psychology* 52: 1061–86.

Shelby, A. and Reinsch, N. (1996) The communication audit: A framework for teaching management communication. *Business Communication Quarterly* 59: 95–108.

Shenhar, A. (1990) Improving upward communication through open-door policies. *Human Systems Management* 9: 77–88.

Sherblom, J. (1998) Transforming business communication by building on Forman's translation metaphor. *The Journal of Business Communication* 35: 74–86.

Shiller, R. (2001) *Irrational Exuberance*. New Jersey: Princeton University Press.

Shockley-Zalabak, P. and Ellis, K. (2000) Perceived organizational effectiveness, job satisfaction, culture, and communication: Challenging the traditional view. *Communication Research Reports* 17: 375–86.

Short, J., Williams, E., and Christie, B. (1976) *The Social Psychology of Telecommunications*. London: John Wiley.

Sidanuis, J. (1978) Intolerance of ambiguity and socio-politico ideology: A multidimensional analysis. *European Journal of Social Psychology* 8: 215–35.

Silverman, E.B. (1999) *NYPD Battles Crime: Innovative Strategies in Policing*. Northeastern University Press, Boston.

Simms, R.R. and Brinkman, J. (2002) Leaders as moral role models: The case of John Gutfreund at Salomon Brothers. *Journal of Business Ethics* 35: 327–39.

Simon, H. (1957) *Administrative Behavior*. New York: Free Press.

Singer, P. (1986) *Applied Ethics*. London: Oxford University Press.

Sipior, J.C. and Ward, B.T. (1998) Recommendations for managing employee e-mail. *Journal of Computer Information Systems* 39: 34–9.

Sipior, J.C., Ward, B.T., and Rainone, S.M. (1998) Ethical management of employee e-mail privacy. *Information Systems Management* 15: 41–7.

Smith, A. (1991) *Innovative Employee Communication: New Approaches to Improving Trust, Teamwork and Performance*. Englewood Cliffs, NJ: Prentice-Hall.

Smith, J.A. (1946) *The Nicomachean Ethics of Aristotle*. New York: E.P. Dutton & Co. Introduction.

Smith, P.B., Misumi, J., Tayeb, M., Peterson, M., and Bond, M. (1995) On the generality of leadership style measures across cultures. In T. Jackson (ed.) *Cross-Cultural Management*. Oxford: Butterworth-Heinemann.

Smythe, J. (2002) The rise and fall of the internal communicator. *Profile* (May): 1.

Snyder, R. and Morris, J. (1984) Organisational communication and performance. *Journal of Applied Psychology* 69: 461–5.

Sorod, Bung-on (1991) The influence of national and organizational cultures on managerial values, attitudes, and performance. Unpublished doctoral dissertation: University of Utah, Salt Lake City.

Spiegel, D. (1999) Healing words, emotional expression and disease outcomes. *Journal of the American Medical Association* 281: 1328–9.

Spiker, B. and Daniels, T. (1981) Information adequacy and communication relationships: An empirical investigation of 18 organizations. *Western Journal of Speech Communication* 45: 342–54.

Starbuck, W. (2003) The origins of organization theory. In H. Tsoukas and C. Knudsen (eds) *The Oxford Handbook of Organization Theory*. Oxford: Oxford University Press.

Starbuck, W., Greve, A., and Hedberg, B. (1978) Responding to crisis. *Journal of Business Administration* 9: 111–37.

Starbuck, W.H. (1992) Learning by Knowledge-Intensive Firms. *Journal of Management Studies* 29: 713–40.

Starkweather, R. and Steinbacher, C. (1998) Job satisfaction affects the bottom line. *HR Magazine* (September) 1–2.

Staw, B. and Epstein, L. (2000) What bandwagons bring: Effects of popular management techniques on corporate performance, reputation and CEO pay. *Administrative Science Quarterly* 45: 523–56.

Stein, N.L. and Devine, L.J. (1991) Making sense out of emotion: The representation and use of goal-structured knowledge. *Memories, Thoughts, and Emotions: Essays in Honor of George Mandler*. Mahwah, NJ: Lawrence Erlbaum and Associates.

Stensaasen, S. and Sletta, O. (1996) *Gruppeprossesser. Læring og samarbeid i grupper*. 3rd Edition. Oslo: Universitetsforlaget.

Stephan, W.G. and Stephan, C. (1996) Predicting prejudice. *International Journal of Intercultural Relations* 20: 1–12.

Stephan, W.G., Ybarra, O., Martínez, C.M., Schwarzwald, J., and Tur-Kaspa, M. (1998) Prejudice toward immigrants to Spain and Israel: An integrated threat theory analysis. *Journal of Cross-cultural Psychology* 29: 559–76.

Sterne, J. and Priore, A. (2000) *Email Marketing: Using Email to Reach your Target Audience and Build Customer Relationships*. Wiley: New York.

Stevens, B. (1994) An analysis of corporate ethical code studies: Where do we go from here? *Journal of Business Ethics* 13: 63–72.

Stewart, J. and Logan, C. (1998) *Together: Communicating Interpersonally*. 5th edition. Boston, Mass.: McGraw-Hill.

Stiles, P. (1999) Performance management in fast-changing environments. In L. Gratton, V. Hope Hailey, P. Stiles, and C. Truss (eds) *Strategic Human Resource Management*. Oxford: Oxford University Press.

Stipek, D. (1998) Differences between Americans and Chinese in the circumstances evoking pride, shame, and guilt. *Journal of Cross-Cultural Psychology* 29: 616–29.

Stohl, C. and Cheney, G. (2001) Participatory processes/paradoxical practices: Communication and the dilemmas of organizational democracy. *Management Communication Quarterly* 14: 349–407.

Strauss, B. and Mang, P. (1999) 'Culture shocks' in inter-cultural, service encounters? *Journal of Services Marketing* 13: 329–46.

Street, R.L. (1991) Accommodation in medical consultations. In H. Giles, J. Coupland

and N. Coupland (eds) *Contexts of Accommodation*. Cambridge, UK: Cambridge University Press.

Strongman, K.T. (1977) *The Psychology of Emotion*. 2nd Edition. Chichester: Wiley.

Suchman, L.A. (1987) *Plans and Situated Actions: The Problem of Human/Machine Communication*. Cambridge, UK: Cambridge University Press.

Suchman, L.A. (1996) Constituting shared workspaces. In Y. Engeström and D. Middleton (eds) *Cognition and Communication at Work*. Cambridge, UK: Cambridge University Press.

Suh, K. (1999) Impact of communication medium on task performance and satisfaction: An examination of media-richness theory. *Information and Management* 35: 295–312.

Sullivan, J. (1999) What are the functions of corporate homepages? *Journal of World Business* 34: 193–210.

Sunday Times (2003) 100 best companies to work for, *Sunday Times*, 2 March. Online. Available HTTP: <http://www.timesonline.co.uk/section/0,,2096,00.html>. Accessed 10 March 2003.

Sunnafrank, M. (1990) Predicted outcome value and uncertainty reduction theories: A test of competing perspectives. *Human Communication Research* 17: 76–103.

Sutcliffe, K.M. (2001) Organizational environments and organizational information processing. In F.M. Jablin and L.L. Putnam (eds) *New Handbook of Organizational Communication*. Thousand Oaks, CA: Sage.

Sutherland, S. (1992) *Irrationality*. London: Constable.

Sutton, R. and Callahan, A. (1987) The stigma of bankruptcy: Spoiled organizational image and its management. *Academy of Management Journal* 30: 405–36.

Sweeney, M. and Szwejczewski, M. (2002) *Strategic Global Manufacturing Management: A Study of the Process and Current Practice*. Bedford: Cranfield University School of Management.

Sydow, J. (1998) Understanding the constitution of interorganizational trust. In C. Lane and R. Bachmann (eds) *Trust Within and Between Organizations: Conceptual Issues and Empirical Applications*. Oxford: Oxford University Press.

Sypher, B.D. (1984) The importance of social cognitive abilities in organizations. In R.N. Bostrom (ed.) *Competence in Communication*. Beverly Hills, CA.: Sage.

Sypher, B.D. and Zorn, T. (1986) Communication-related abilities and upward mobility: A longitudinal investigation. *Human Communication Research* 12: 420–31.

Tajfel, H. and Turner, J.C. (1986) The social identity theory of intergroup behaviour. In S. Worchel and W.G. Austain (eds) *Psychology of Intergroup Relations*. Chicago: Nelson.

Tannenbaum, S.I., Salas, E., and Cannon-Bowers, J.A. (1996) Promoting team effectiveness. In M.A. West (ed.) *Handbook of Work Group Psychology*. Chichester: Wiley.

Taylor, F. (1911) *The Principles of Scientific Management*. NY: Harper.

Taylor, J.R. and Van Every, E.J. (2000) *The Emergent Organization: Communication as its Site and Surface*. Mahwah, NJ: Lawrence Erlbaum.

Teboul, J. (1994) Facing and coping with uncertainty during Organizational encounter. *Management Communication Quarterly* 8: 190–224.

Teich J., Wallenius, H., and Wallenius, J. (1999) World-Wide-Web technology in support of negotiation and communication. *International Journal of Management* 17: 223–9.

Thayer, L. (1967) *Communication Theory and Research*. Springfield, IL: Charles C. Thomas.

Thibodeau, R. and Aronson, E. (1992) Taking a closer look: Reasserting the role of the self-concept in dissonance theory. *Personality and Social Psychology Bulletin* 18: 591–602.

Thomas, A. (2003) *Controversies in Management: Issues, Debates and Answers*. 2nd Edition. London: Routledge.

Thompson, M. (2002) *The SPAC Human Capital Audit*. Oxford: Templeton College, University of Oxford.

Thompson, P., Warhurst, C., and Callaghan, G. (2001) Ignorant theory and knowledgeable workers: Interrogating the connections between knowledge, skills and services. *Journal of Management Studies* 38: 923–1036.

Tinsulanonda, T. (1998) A study of the relationship between leadership style and motivation of the Royal Thai Army Officers. Unpublished dissertation: Nova Southeastern University, USA.

Tjosvold, D. (1991) *Team Organization: An Enduring Competitive Advantage*. New York: Wiley.

Toffler, B.E. (1986) *Tough Choices*. New York: John Wiley & Sons.

Tompkins, P. (1993) *Organizational Communication Imperatives: Lessons of the Space Program*. Los Angeles: Roxbury.

Tompkins, P. and Wanca-Thibault, M. (2001) Organizational communication: Prelude and prospects. In F. Jablin and L. Putnam (eds) *The New Handbook of Organisational Communication*, London: Sage.

Tourish, D. (1998) 'The God that failed': Replacing false messiahs with open communication. *Australian Journal of Communication* 25: 99–114.

Tourish, D. (2000) Management and managerialism: Mis/managing Australian Universities? *New Horizons in Education* 103: 20–42.

Tourish, D. and Hargie, O. (1993) Don't you wish sometimes you were better informed? *Health Service Journal* 103: 28–9.

Tourish, D. and Hargie, O. (1998) Communication between managers and staff in the NHS: Trends and prospects. *British Journal of Management* 9: 53–71.

Tourish, D. and Hargie, O. (2000a) Communication and organisational success. In O. Hargie and D. Tourish (eds) *Handbook of Communication Audits for Organisations*. London: Routledge.

Tourish, D. and Hargie, O. (2000b) Auditing the communications revolution. In O. Hargie and D. Tourish (eds) *Handbook of Communication Audits for Organisations*. London: Routledge.

Tourish, D. and Hargie, O. (2000c) Strategy, research and pedagogy: The role of audits. In O. Hargie and D. Tourish (eds) *Handbook of Communication Audits for Organisations*. London: Routledge.

Tourish, D. and Pinnington, A. (2002) Transformational leadership, corporate cultism and the spirituality paradigm: An unholy trinity in the workplace? *Human Relations* 55: 147–72.

Tourish, D. and Robson, P. (2001) The status we're in. *Health Service Journal* 6 December: 30

Tourish, D. and Robson, P. (in press) Critical upward feedback in organizations: processes, problems and implications for communication management. *Journal of Communication Managment*.

Tourish, D. and Vatcha, N. (2003) Critical upward communication: The dynamics of proxemic/ ultimate causality. *Paper presented at Annual Conference of European Communication Association*, Munich, 25 March.

Tourish, D. and Wohlforth, T. (2000) *On the Edge: Political Cults Right and Left*. New York: Sharpe.

Tourish, D., Paulsen, N., and Bordia, P. (unpublished manuscript) The downsides of downsizing: Communication processes and information needs in the aftermath of a workforce reduction strategy. Aberdeen Business School, Robert Gordon University, Aberdeen.

Towers-Perrin (1993) *Improving Business Performance Through Your People*. San Francisco: Towers-Perrin.

Townley, B. (1993) Foucault, power/knowledge, and its relevance for human resource management. *Academy of Management Review* 18: 518–45.

Trethewey, A. and Corman, S. (2001) Anticipating K-commerce: E-commerce, knowledge management and organizational communication. *Management Communication Quarterly* 14: 619–28.

Triandis, H.C. (1990) Cross-cultural studies of individualism and collectivism. In J.J. Berman (ed.) *Nebraska Symposium on Motivation: Cross-cultural Perspective. Current Theory and Research in Motivation (Vol. 37)*. Lincoln, NE: University of Nebraska Press: 41–133.

Triandis, H.C. (1994) *Culture and Social Behaviour*. New York: McGraw-Hill.

Trice, H.M. and Beyer, J.M. (1993) *The Cultures of Work Organizations*. Englewood Cliffs, NJ: Prentice Hall.

Tsang, E. (2002) Self-serving attributions in corporate annual reports: A replicated study. *Journal of Management Studies* 39: 51–65.

Tsui, A.S., Egan, T.D., and O'Reilly, C.A. (1992) Being different: Relational demography and organizational attachment. *Administrative Science Quarterly* 37: 549–79.

Turner, J.C., Hogg, M., Oakes, P.J. and Reicher, S.D. (1987) *Rediscovering the Social Group: A Self Categorization Theory*. New York: Basil Blackwell.

Ulizin, J. (2001) Martin Parker: Organizational culture and identity. *Organization Studies* 22: 885–92.

Ulrich, T.J., Allen, M., Mabry, E.A., and Sahlstein, E. (2001) A meta-analysis of decision quality in computer-mediated and face-to-face groups. *Paper presented at Top Four Panel, Group Communication Division, National Communication Association Convention*, Atlanta, GA, November.

Vaes, J., Paladino, M., and Leyens, J. (2002) The lost e-mail: Prosocial reactions induced by uniquely human emotions. *The British Journal of Social Psychology* 41: 521–34.

Valås, H. and Søvik, N. (1993) Variables affecting students' intrinsic motivation for school mathematics: Two empirical studies based on Deci and Ryan's theory on motivation. *Learning and Instruction* 3: 281–98.

Valesquez, M., Moberg, D., and Cavanaugh, C. (1983) Organizational statesmanship and dirty politics: Ethical guidelines for the organizational politician, *Organizational Dynamics* 12: 65–80.

Van Buskirk, W. and McGrath, D. (1999) Organizational cultures as holding environments: A psychodynamic look at organizational symbolism. *Human Relations* 52: 805–32.

Van Mannen, J. (1988) *Tales of the Field: On Writing Ethnography*. Chicago: University of Chicago Press.

Van Maanen, J. (2000) Style as theory. In P. Frost, A. Lewin, and R. Daft (eds) *Talking About Organization Science: Debates and Dialogue from Crossroads*. London: Sage.

Van Maanen, J. and Kunda, G. (1989) 'Real feelings': Emotional expression and organizational culture. *Organizational Behavior* 11: 43–103.

Victor, B. and Cullen, J.B. (1988) The organizational basis of ethical work climates. *Administrative Science Quarterly* 33: 101–25.

Violino, B. (2001) The search for e-business returns: As the economy sputters, companies must assess how internet technology will improve the bottom line. *Internet Week* 882: 9–13.

Vygotsky, L.S. (1971) *Thought and Language*. Ed. and trans. E. Hanfmann and G. Vakar. Cambridge, MA: Massachusetts Institute of Technology.

Wachman, R. (2003) Is Ford going to go bust? *Observer*, 16 March, Business supplement, 5.

Wagar, T. and Rondeau, K. (2000) Reducing the workforce: Examining its consequences in health care organisations. *Leadership in Health Services* 13: i–viii.

Wagner, J. (1994) Participation's effects on performance and satisfaction. *Academy of Management Review* 19: 312–30.

Wah, L. (1999) Diversity at Allstate: A competitive weapon. *Management Review* 88: 24–30.

Waldman, D. and Atwater, L. (2001) Attitudinal and behavioural outcomes of an upward feedback process. *Group and Organization Management* 26: 189–205.

Waldron, V. and Krone, K. (1991) The experience and expression of emotion in the workplace: A study of a corrections organization. *Management Communication Quarterly* 4: 287–309.

Walsham, G. (2002) What can knowledge management systems deliver? *Management Communication Quarterly* 16: 267–73.

Walther, J.B. (1992) Interpersonal effects in computer-mediated interaction: A relational perspective. *Communication Research* 19: 52–90.

Walther, J.B. (1993) Impression development in computer-mediated interaction. *Western Journal of Communication* 57: 381–98.

Walther, J.B. (1994) Anticipated ongoing interaction versus channel effects on relational communication in computer-mediated interaction. *Human Communication Research* 20: 473–501.

Wanous, J. (1980) *Organizational Entry: Recruitment, Selection, and Socialization of Newcomers*. Reading, MA: Addison-Wesley.

Waterman, R. (1990) *Adhocracy: The Power to Change*. Memphis, TN: Whittle Direct Books.

Waters, J.A. and Bird, F. (1987) The moral dimensions of organizational culture. *Journal of Business Ethics* 6: 15–22.

Watkins, K.E. and Marsick, V. (1997) *Dimensions of the Learning Organization Questionnaire*. Warwick, RI: Partners for the Learning Organization.

Watson, B. and Gallois, C. (1998) Nurturing communication by health professionals toward patients: A communication accommodation approach. *Health Communication* 10: 343–55.

Watson, T. (1994a) *In Search of Management*. London: Routledge.

Watson, T. (1994b) Management 'flavours of the month': Their role in managers' lives. *International Journal of Human Resource Management* 5: 893–909.

Watson, T. and Harris, P. (1999) *The Emergent Manager*. London: Sage.

Watson, W.E., Kumar, K., and Michaelsen, L.K. (1993) Cultural diversity's impact on interaction process and performance: Comparing homogeneous and diverse task groups. *Academy of Management Journal* 36: 590–602.

Weaver, William G. (1998) Corporations as Intentional Systems. *Journal of Business Ethics* 17: 87–97.

Weedon, C. (1997) *Feminist Practice and Poststructuralist Theory*. Oxford: Basil Blackwell.

Weick, K. (1979) *The Social Psychology of Organizing*. 2nd Edition. New York: Random House.

Weick, K.E. (1985) Sources of order in under-organized systems: Themes in recent organizational theory. In Y.S Lincoln (ed.) *Organizational Theory and Inquiry*. Beverly Hills, CA: Sage.

Weick, K. (1988) Enacted sensemaking in a crisis situation. *Journal of Management Studies* 25: 305–17.

Weick, K. (1995) *Sensemaking in Organisations*. London: Sage.

Weick, K. and Ashford, S. (2001) Learning in organizations. In F. Jablin and L. Putnam (eds) *The New Handbook of Organizational Communication: Advances in Theory, Research and Methods*. London: Sage.

Weil, M.M. (1997) *TechnoStress: Coping with Technology @ Work, @ Play*. New York: John Wiley & Sons, Inc.

Weisband, S.P., Schneider, S.K. and Connolly, T. (1995) Computer-mediated communication and social information: Status salience and status differences. *Academy of Management Journal* 38: 1124–51.

Weisbord, M.R. (1988) *Productive Workplaces: Organizing and Managing for Dignity, Meaning and Community*. San Francisco: Jossey-Bass.

Weiss, H. and Cropanzano, R. (1996) Affective events theory: A theoretical discussion of the structure, causes and consequences of affective experiences at work. *Research in Organizational Behavior* 18: 1–74.

Wenger, E. (1998) *Communities of Practice: Learning, Meaning and Identity*. Oxford: Oxford University Press.

Wenger, E.C. and Snyder, W.M. (2000) Communities of practice: The organizational frontier. *Harvard Business Review* 78(1): 139–45.

West, M. (2000) State of the art: Creativity and innovation at work. *The Psychologist* 13: 460–4.

Westmyer, S.A., DiCioccio, R.L., and Rubin, R.B. (1998) Appropriateness and effectiveness of communication channels in competent interpersonal communication. *Journal of Communication* 48: 27–48.

Whetton, D. (1980) Organizational decline: A neglected topic in organizational science. *Academy of Management Review* 5: 577–88.

White, R.W. (1959) Motivation reconsidered: The concept of competence. *Psychological Review* 66: 297–333.

Whittington, R., McNulty, T., and Whipp, R. (1994) Market-driven change in professional services: Problems and processes. *Journal of Management Studies* 31: 829–45.

Whitty, M. (1996) Co-management for workplace democracy. *Journal of Organizational Change* 9: 7–11.

Wicks, D. (2001) Institutionalized mindsets of invulnerability. Differentiated institutional fields and the antecedents of organizational crisis. *Organization Studies* 22: 659–92.

Wierzbicka, A. (1992) *Semantics, Culture, and Cognition: Universal Human Concepts in Culture-Specific Configurations*. New York: Oxford University Press.

Wilkinson, A. and Marchington, M. (1994) TQM: Instant Pudding for the Personnel Function? *Human Resource Management Journal* 5: 33–49.

Williams, G. and Macalpine, M. (1995) The gender lens: Management development for women in 'developing countries'. In C. Itzin and J. Newman (eds) *Gender, Culture and Organizational Change: Putting Theory into Practice*. London: Routledge.

Williams, K.Y. and O'Reilly, C.A. (1998) Demography and diversity in organizations: A review of 40 years of research. *Research in Organizational Behaviour* 20: 77–140.

Williams, M.L. and Goss, B. (1975) Equivocation: Character insurance. *Human Communication Theory* 1: 265–70.

Williams, R. (1961 [1958]) *Culture and Society, 1780–1950*. Harmondsworth: Penguin Books.

Willmott, H. (2003) Organization theory as a critical science? Forms of analysis and 'new organizational forms'. In H. Tsoukas and C. Knudsen (eds) *The Oxford Handbook of Organization Theory*. Oxford: Oxford University Press.

Wilson, D.C. (1992) *A Strategy of Change: Concepts and Controversies in the Management of Change*. London: Routledge.

Wisman, J. (1997) The ignored question of workplace democracy in political discourse. *International Journal of Social Economics* 24: 1388–403.

Womack, J.P., Jones, D. and Roos, D. (1990) *The Machine that Changed the World*. New York: Rawson Associates.

Womack, J.P., Jones, D. and Roos, D. (1991) *Princippet der ændrede verden. Trimmet Produktion* (Danish translation). Centrum.

Wong, E. (2001) A stinging office memo boomerangs: Chief executive is criticized after upbraiding workers by e-mail, *New York Times*, 5 April, Section C, 1.

Wood, D. and Gray, B. (1991) Toward a comprehensive theory of collaboration. *Journal of Applied Behavioral Science* 27: 139–62.

Worrall, L., Cooper, C., and Campbell, F. (2000) The impact of organizational change on UK managers' perceptions of their working lives. In R. Burke and C. Cooper (eds) *The Organization in Crisis: Downsizing, Restructuring and Privatisation*. Oxford: Blackwell.

Young, M. and Post, J. (1993) Managing to communicate, communicating to manage: How leading companies communicate with employees. *Organizational Dynamics* 22: 31–3.

Yukl, G. (1999a) An evaluative essay on current perceptions of effective leadership. *Journal of Work and Organizational Psychology* 8: 33–48.

Yukl, G. (1999b) An evaluation of conceptual weaknesses in transformational and charismatic leadership theories. *Leadership Quarterly* 10: 285–305.

Yukl, G.A. (1981) *Leadership in Organizations*. London: Prentice-Hall.

Zebrowitz, L. (1990) *Social Perception*. Milton Keynes: Open University/Sage.

Zenger, T.R. and Lawrence, B.S. (1989) Organizational demography: The differential effects of age and tenure distributions on technical communication. *Academy of Management Journal* 32: 353–76.

Zibergeld, B.A. (1984) A one-minute essay, more or less, on the one-minute books. *Psychology Today* (August): 6–7.

Zoller, H. (2000) A place you haven't visited before: Creating the conditions of community dialogue. *Southern Communication Journal* 65: 191–207.

Zorn, T.E. (2002a) Forum introduction: Current uses, critical appraisals and future prospects. *Management Communication Quarterly* 15: 439–41.

Zorn, T.E. and May, S.K. (2002b) Forum introduction: Knowledge management and/as organizational communication. *Management Communication Quarterly* 16: 237–41.

Zorn, T.E. (2002c) The emotionality of information and communication technology implementation. *Journal of Communication Management* 7: 160–71.

Zorn, T.E. and Violanti, M.T. (1996) Communication abilities and individual achievement in organizations. *Management Communication Quarterly* 10: 139–67.

Zorn, T.E., Christensen, L.T., and Cheney, G. (1999) *Do We Really Want Constant Change? Beyond the Bottom Line, No. 2 booklet*. San Francisco, CA: Berrett-Koehler Communications.

Index